Effective Prosecution

Effective Prosecution

Working in Partnership with the CPS

Yvonne Moreno OBE and
Paul Hughes

OXFORD

UNIVERSITY PRESS

Great Clarendon Street, Oxford OX2 6DP

Oxford University Press is a department of the University of Oxford.
It furthers the University's objective of excellence in research, scholarship,
and education by publishing worldwide in

Oxford New York

Auckland Cape Town Dar es Salaam Hong Kong Karachi
Kuala Lumpur Madrid Melbourne Mexico City Nairobi
New Delhi Shanghai Taipei Toronto

With offices in

Argentina Austria Brazil Chile Czech Republic France Greece
Guatemala Hungary Italy Japan Poland Portugal Singapore
South Korea Switzerland Thailand Turkey Ukraine Vietnam

Oxford is a registered trade mark of Oxford University Press
in the UK and in certain other countries

Published in the United States
by Oxford University Press Inc., New York

British Library Cataloguing in Publication Data

Data available

Library of Congress Cataloging-in-Publication Data

Data available

Typeset by Laserwords Private Ltd, Chennai, India
Printed in Great Britain
on acid-free paper by
CPI Antony Rowe, Chippenham

ISBN 978–0–19–923774–6

10 9 8 7 6 5 4 3 2 1

Foreword

This book signals a very important development in criminal justice in England and Wales. It has been quite a long journey for those of us who were there at the beginning in early meetings between the emergent Crown Prosecution Service and a police service that was bruised by the recommendations of the Phillips Royal Commission and still trying to cope with the revolution wrought by the Police and Criminal Evidence Act. Since then, with leadership and imagination on both sides and a growing sense of joint purpose, police and prosecutors have become a 'prosecution team'. From the early days when 'independence' and separation were the main features of the relationship, the 21st century team of police and prosecutor are increasingly supported by shared office teams and shared IT.

This book highlights the next stage in that move towards interdependence—the emergence of joint doctrine and practice and joint training. This is the first comprehensive treatment of the subject and it is a real sign of the new world that it is co-written by two experienced practitioners from police and prosecution. As my friend and colleague Sir Ken Macdonald QC says in his foreword, this is a really important development and we both welcome it, as I am sure will the many practitioners who will benefit.

Peter Neyroud
Chief Constable and Chief Executive, National Policing Improvement Agency

Foreword

I should like to congratulate Yvonne Moreno, OBE from the Crown Prosecution Service and Paul Hughes, Detective Sergeant at Hendon Crime Academy, for providing police officers and Crown Prosecutors alike with the first book to deal comprehensively with the joint prosecution team approach to criminal justice.

At a time of major change and in the light of a raft of new initiatives, this book attempts to identify all the implications of these changes for police and CPS alike. It reflects the importance and benefits of working closely together to produce well investigated, effectively prepared and prosecuted cases, while preserving professional independence on both sides.

Both of the authors have some 30 years' practical experience in their respective fields, and it clearly shows. In a readable and user-friendly format, the book provides a practical guide covering all aspects from arrest to conviction with best practice highlighted throughout.

It will certainly provide readers with a deeper understanding of their respective roles as police officer and public prosecutor, and in that way help to build the joint prosecution team.

Sir Ken Macdonald QC
Director of Public Prosecutions

Acknowledgements

Paul would like to say a big thank you to the very many people within the Metropolitan Police Service, the Crown Prosecution Service and other organisations who have freely given their assistance and without whom the book would never have materialised. The staff of the Criminal Justice Faculty of the Crime Academy deserve a special mention for their help and support.

In particular Paul would like to express his gratitude to Kevin Davis of Operation Trident for his encouragement in the early stages, and to mention those people who provided extremely helpful comments and contributions to early drafts of chapters including Ian Tremble, Layton Williams and Kelvin Retallick. Also Sean Crotty and Malcolm Davies for arranging for operational police officers to provide invaluable observations and criticisms.

Lindsey Davis and Peter Daniell of Oxford University Press both deserve medals for their enthusiasm for the project and forbearance of the highest degree in their dealings with the authors. Paul would also like to thank Yvonne Moreno for her courage in involving him in the project in the first place.

Finally thank you Helen without whom nothing would have been possible.

Paul Hughes

Acknowledgements

Yvonne wishes to express particular thanks to the typist, Kathy Martinez, for her patience and dedication in typing the entire book, without whom the book would never have materialised, also to Paul Hughes her co-author, without whose support it would never have been finished.

Throughout the book she has utilised material from the Crown Prosecution Service, from the website, legal guidance and other sources, especially the policy unit and from excellent training packages and case studies devised by the CPS (eg proactive prosecutors course, statutory charging course, CJSSS and SP). Comments from CCP Paul Whittaker have proved invaluable. Additionally within the CPS, Dan Jones, Suraj Minocha and John Grealis and all her Harrow CPS colleagues are to be thanked for continually answering questions. From the Metropolitan Police Service she should like to thank DC Peter Smith (FIU Harrow) and Patrick Griffin (BFM). Yvonne would like to also thank Alastair Dicker from the Department of Business, Enterprise & Regulatory Reform.

Additionally thanks to Adam Pacifico (formerly of BPP) for the experience of working with such a talented trainer at Hendon Crime Academy, training the Met on witness familiarisation techniques and for allowing her to try and put some of his course into words in Chapters 2 and 8 (probably not doing it justice).

Any views expressed are her own and not attributable to the CPS and all errors are totally her responsibility.

One final big thank you to her boss, Nazir Afzal, and husband Ian Moran. Writing a book is very time consuming and requires considerable tolerance and consideration at work and at home.

Yvonne Moreno OBE

Summary Table of Contents

Contents

Contents

List of Figures

Table of Cases

Table of Legislation

The reference to article 5 of European Convention on Human Rights has been tabled under Schedule 1 of the Human Rights Act 1998

Special Features

This book contains several specific special features intended to assist the reader.

Checklist/Key considerations/Point to Note

Information requiring particular emphasis or material that will amplify and elaborate the content of this book has been highlighted.

Definitions

Where appropriate definitions of concepts are provided.

Figures

Some information core concepts have been illustrated in diagrammatic form for ease of presentation.

Scenarios

To provide illustrative examples of certain points and issues, both real and hypothetical scenarios have been used.

Glossary Including Useful Websites

All website url details correct at August 2008

ABE Achieving Best Evidence.
<http://www.homeoffice.gov.uk/documents/achieving-best-evidence/>

ACPO Association of Chief Police Officers.

AJF Adverse judicial finding.

AP Associate Prosecutor.

ARA Asset Recovery Agency.

ASBOs Anti-social Behaviour Orders.

A/S No Arrest/summons number.

Attorney General's guidelines on disclosure
<http://www.cps.gov.uk/legal/section20/chapter_c.html>

BCU Borough Crime Unit.

BFM Borough Forensic Managers.

CAD Computer assisted despatch (or log of messages).

CCPs Chief Crown Prosecutors.

CICA Criminal Injuries Compensation Scheme.

CHIS Covert Human Intelligence Source.

CJS criminal justice system.

CJSSS Simple, Speedy, Summary Justice.
<http://www.cjsonline.gov.uk/the_cjs/whats_new/news-3512.html>

CJU Criminal justice unit.

Code for Crown Prosecutors <http://www.cps.gov.uk/publications/docs/
code2004english.pdf>

CPS Crown Prosecution Service.
<http://www.cps.gov.uk/>

CPS Direct CPS Direct is a national out-of-hours telephone service
(0800 692 0999).
<http://www.cps.gov.uk/direct/about/>

Criminal Justice Act 1991 <http://www.opsi.gov.uk/Acts/acts1991/
ukpga_19910053_en_1>

Criminal Justice Act 2003 <http://www.opsi.gov.uk/acts/acts2003/
ukpga_20030044_en_1>

Criminal Justice and Immigration Act 2008
<http://www.opsi.gov.uk/acts2008/ukpga_20080004_en_1>

CPIA 1996 Criminal Procedure and Investigations Act 1996.
<http://www.opsi.gov.uk/acts/acts1996/ukpga_19960025_en_1>

CYPA 1969 Children and Young Person's Act 1969.

DCI Detective chief inspector.

Director's Guidance on Charging *Director of Public Prosecution's Guidance on Charging.*
<http://www.cps.gov.uk/publications/docs/dpp_guidance.pdf>

Director's Guidance on the Streamlined Process <http://lcjb.cjsonline.gov.uk/area23/library/Programme/Streamlined%20DPP%20Guidance%20Test%20Area%20version%20Jan%2008.doc>

Disclosure manual <http://www.cps.gov.uk/legal/section20/chapter_a.html>

DPP Director of Public Prosecution.

EAB Evidence and arrest book.

ESMs Early special measures meetings.

FIO Financial investigation officer.

FIU Financial investigation unit.

Flanagan Report <http://police.homeoffice.gov.uk/publications/police-reform/Review_of_policing_final_report/>

FPN Fixed penalty notice.

FSP Forensic Science Provider.

Going to Court—a step by step guide to being a witness, **HMCS** <http://video.direct.gov.uk/goingtocourtvideo/>

HOLMES Home Office Large Major Enquiry System.

HOPO Home Office Production Order.

HSG Handling stolen goods.

IDVA Independent domestic violence assessor.

IPT Integrated Prosecution Teams.

JARD Joint Asset Recovery Database.

LCJBs Local Criminal Justice Boards.

MIRSAP Major Incident Room Standard Administration Procedures.

NFA No further action.

NIIS National Investigative Interviewing Strategy.

NPIA National Policing Improvement Agency.
<http://www.npia.police.uk/>

NWNJ No witness no justice.

OBTJ Offences brought to justice.

OCJR Office of Criminal Justice Reform.
<http://www.cjsonline.gov.uk/the_cjs/departments_of_the_cjs/ocjr/>

OIC Officer in the case.

OP Observation point.

PACE Police and Criminal Evidence Act 1984.
<http://police.homeoffice.gov.uk/operational-policing/powers-pace-codes/>

PCMH Plea and case management hearing.

PCSOs Police Community Support Officers.

PII Public Interest Immunity.

PND penalty notice for disorder.

PNC Police national computer.

PNLD Police National Legal Database.
<http://www.pnld.co.uk/docportal/content/commercial3.htm>

POCA Proceeds of Crime Act 2002.
<http://www.opsi.gov.uk/acts/acts2002/ukpga_20020029_en_1>

PPO Priority prolific offender.

Prosecutors' Pledge <http://www.cps.gov.uk/publications/prosecution/
prosecutor_pledge.html>

PYOs Persistent Young/Youth Offenders.

ROTI Record of taped interview.

ROVI Record of visual interview.

Review of the Criminal Courts of England and Wales <http://www.
criminal-courts-review.org.uk/auldconts.htm>

RTA Road traffic accident.

SDN Short descriptive note.

Seven Principles of Investigative Interviewing To be found in *MPS
Investigative Interviewing*.
<http://www.met.police.uk/foi/pdfs/policies/investigative_interviewing_
policy.pdf>

SOCA Serious Organised Crime Agency governed by SOCPA 2005.

SOCPA 2005 Serious Organised Crime and Police Act 2005.
<http://www.opsi.gov.uk/acts/acts2005/ukpga_20050015_en_1>

SIO Senior Investigating Officer.

SP Streamlined process.

Speaking up for Justice Report <http://www.crimereduction.homeoffice.gov.
uk/victims/victims30.htm>

TIC Offence taken into consideration.

URN Unique reference number.

VANS Violence, abduction, neglect, or sex.

Victims' Charter The Victims' Charter—Standards of Service for Victims of Crime 1996.
<http://www.homeoffice.gov.uk/documents/victims-charter>

Victim Code <http://www.homeoffice.gov.uk/documents/victims-code-of-practice>

VFS Victim Focus Scheme.

VPS Victim's personal statement.

WAVES Witness and victim experience survey.

WCUs Witness care units.

YO Youth offender.

YOT Youth offender team.

Youth Justice and Criminal Evidence Act 1999 <http://www.opsi.gov.uk/Acts/acts1999/ukpga_19990023_en_1>

Introduction

1.1 **Introduction**

The criminal justice system (CJS) is a dynamic entity that is constantly changing. Some of those changes are dramatic, for example the introduction of statutory charging or the use of video testimony for certain types of interview. Others—such as the disclosure protocols—though less dramatic, are no less significant for the prosecution of the case.

It has certainly been an exciting challenge, and one far more difficult than we originally anticipated, to write a 'one-stop-shop' book aimed at helping the police and Crown Prosecution Service (CPS) to come together as a team rather than seeing themselves responsible for two distinct procedures of investigating and prosecuting.

The fundamental purpose of the book is to encourage the elimination of that distinction. We—the police and the CPS—must together raise our game and become far more proactive, professional and responsive than ever before if we are going to be effective and bring more criminals to justice. We hope that this book, written from the joint standpoint of an experienced Crown Prosecutor and police officer, will increase the knowledge and awareness of the partnership approach and lead to better understanding and communication between the police and the CPS. By pooling our joint skills if you like, we hope to contribute to better decision making—bringing the right cases, on the right charges and evidence at the right time, to court thereby ensuring more effective outcomes. This book is unique in that it is, we believe, the first practical guide on the market dedicated to how police officers can work with the CPS throughout the entire criminal justice process.

The police and the CPS must operate in a close partnership as a criminal justice 'service'. The CPS will, in the beginning, provide advice and assistance at the investigation stage. The procedures that follow—the marshalling of the evidence and the case building, the preparation and submission of the papers, right through to their subsequent presentation in court—are the all-important stages where we can either stand or fall.

Investigation needs to be objective and all reasonable lines of enquiry must be carried out. Investigators must approach the interviewing of witnesses mindful of how the evidence can be best obtained and presented in the courts. Suspect interviews need to be concluded with an open mind, but must be founded on the offence and possible defences open to those charged.

Police officers and prosecutors together must therefore be of one mindset of 'thinking trial': knowing what it takes successfully to present a case in court; being able to spot potential defence challenges; and making the case as watertight as possible. The investigative talents of the police and the trial advocacy and legal experience of the prosecutor need to be combined into one single focus for a successful prosecution. By pooling our resources and learning from and feeding off each other, the police and the CPS will come together to act as one single joint prosecution team in a symbiotic independent relationship.

1.2 **Putting you in the Picture**

Change within the CJS is unfortunately driven by a number of factors outside the control of police officers and prosecutors alike. New legislation, policy initiatives and organizational changes, to name but a few, also play their part, as does the government's own criminal justice agenda.

All of the changes have been designed to give greater clarity to the roles and responsibilities of all players within the CJS and encourage far closer liaison amongst them. The emphasis throughout is on improved efficiency and effectiveness in the delivery of criminal justice. By bringing more offenders to justice, this in turn should meet the needs of the public it serves. All such initiatives are interlinked and interdependent.

1.2.1 **New legislation**

The Criminal Justice Act 2003, an important piece of legislation, sought to re-balance the criminal justice system in favour of victims and witnesses. It strengthens the prosecution process, providing a number of new evidential opportunities for prosecutors to use in their prosecution tool kit (ie bad character and hearsay provisions), but only if investigators find and provide such material in evidential form for the CPS.

Similarly, the Serious Organised Crime and Police Act 2005 involved major changes aimed at strengthening the prosecution of organized crime. For the first time we have seen the introduction of specialist trained units within the CPS to deal with terrorism, organized crime and complex casework as well as a separate fraud provision. Additionally, numerous other pieces of legislation have increased police powers and/or provided victims with more redress.

1.2.2 **Statutory charging**

Statutory charging passed responsibility from the police to the CPS for the decision to bring criminal charges. This generated a fundamental change in the relationship between the two. However, instead of being seen as the police losing or CPS gaining, it should be viewed within the context of the prosecution team approach: the police and the CPS involved as a single unit with different but complementary skills working towards a joint purpose.

The inception of CPS Direct, a round-the-clock telephone advice service provided by Crown Prosecutors, has not been without its teething problems. However, the underlying principle of providing a 24/7 CPS service to the police is a sound and useful one.

1.2.3 **CPS advocacy strategy**

Statutory charging may have been the most radical reform within the CPS to date, but it is supported and stands shoulder to shoulder with the internal advocacy strategy of the CPS. This basically involved vastly increasing the numbers of Crown Prosecutors doing their own advocacy in the Crown Courts, handling the case from start to finish and being far less reliant on the external bar than ever before. The growing presence of the CPS in the Crown Court has driven up their profile at the same time as ensuring that their increased trial experience assists them in case building and making a case prosecutable.

1.2.4 **Increased powers**

The last few years have also seen additional powers given to the police and prosecutors to tackle offending (eg Anti-social Behaviour Orders (ASBOs) and the Proceeds of Crime Act 2002 (POCA), which ensures that the prosecution team are provided with new powers to recover cash from criminals and sends a clear message that crime does not pay). Additionally, we have fixed penalty notices and conditional cautioning, which for the first time involves prosecutors in the sentencing process but also provides out-of-court alternatives for low level crime.

All of these changes are just the tip of the iceberg; the beginning not the end of a major change in the responsibilities and power of the prosecution team. Joint police and CPS initiatives relating to disclosure, hate crime, rape and domestic violence are public statements endorsing the commitment of the prosecution team to the investigation and the handling of all such issues in a far more professional and sensitive manner.

1.2.5 **Court reforms**

Simultaneously, the courts, under the auspices of the effective trial management programme and a new consolidation and codification of the Criminal Procedure Rules (April 2005), have been given very wide-ranging powers to manage cases from beginning to end. The emphasis is on case progression by all parties including the defence, who are also under an obligation to assist the court in fulfilling its duty to manage cases. The anticipated active, robust and well-informed case management by magistrates and the judiciary will reduce the number of ineffective hearings and delays within the court process.

Such improvement in the court's case management has had enormous implications for the CPS and the police in terms of case preparation in conjunction with the statutory charging initiative. It has meant files need to be 'trial ready', in many cases, from the moment of charges being brought. This has been emphasized more recently with the government's review of 'Simple, Speedy, Summary Justice' (July 2006)—or CJSSS, as it is more informally called—aimed at taking practical measures to deal more effectively and speedily with low level crime (ie fast tracking simple cases in the magistrates' courts).

By 'front loading' and ensuring all paperwork is correct for the first hearing, and providing advance information to both the defence and the court prior to that hearing, the pilots have already shown an increase in guilty pleas and a reduction in the number of hearings between plea and trial.

1.2.6 Framework for change

Further pilots and initiatives throughout the country aim to bring in a streamlined process so that files are in fact proportionate to the type of charges and anticipated plea. The outcome here will be that although 'not guilty' and Crown Court cases are 'front loaded' from the start, far less paperwork will be required from the police in any case in the future. This will therefore target resources where they are most needed—on the street rather than on form filling. It will also leave the road clear for the investigation and handling of more complex serious criminal cases, which the Crown Court initiatives are concentrating upon, thereby removing unnecessary procedures and improving timeliness and effectiveness of delivery.

Further developments within both the police and the CPS are specifically designed to create a framework for change and this continues to improve linked processes and initiatives.

1.2.7 Technology

Many initiatives are to be supported throughout by the greater use of technology so that all relevant agencies can access the right information at the right time. Over the last few years, we have seen the strategic implementation of information systems through the collaboration of all the criminal justice partners. They have developed case management tools and improved management information, thereby ensuring a solid foundation for a modern, effective and joined up CJS. Moreover, the electronic exchange of documents is now well advanced in some police services and national roll-out has commenced. This demonstrates the importance of the CPS and the police improving their communications and working together as a team and should improve the quality and management of case files generally.

Virtual courts

'Virtual courts' are being piloted as we write, again making better use of technology so that prisoners will stay where they are in the cells and be dealt with shortly after they are charged. This will save time and money in moving prisoners or bailing prisoners to a later date from the police station. Again, modern working practices should reduce administrative burdens and allow the police to focus on tackling real crime.

1.2.8 **Reforms for witnesses**

Since the coming into force of the Youth Justice and Criminal Evidence Act 1999, there have been ongoing reforms aimed at ensuring victims and witnesses are better informed, protected and supported than ever before and ensuring that they receive a high standard of service. The 'No Witness No Justice' campaign, as it has been called, was aimed at increasing witness attendance at trials and preventing the drop out rate.

The joint agency response of the development of witness care units as a single point of contact has provided a needs assessment of victims and witnesses right from the start. Legislative change in relation to special measures has also ensured improved services.

The Prosecutors' Pledge from the Attorney General ensured that prosecutors considered victim's needs from the outset and stood up for their rights in court. In one document, the Victim Code now puts in the public domain the minimum standards of service which victims and witness can expect from those within the CJS at every stage of the process.

Pre-trial witness interviews, now rolled out nationally, allow prosecutors to conduct interviews with witnesses prior to trial in more serious and complicated cases. This initiative assists prosecutors in making the correct charging decisions.

1.2.9 **Collaborative and community justice**

The Office of Criminal Justice Reform (OCJR) is a cross-departmental organization which supports all criminal justice agencies in working together to provide an improved service to the public.

In the form of the three ministers jointly responsible for criminal justice (Home Secretary, Secretary of State for Justice, Attorney General), the government published a strategic plan (2008–2011) aimed at delivering 'a fair and effective criminal justice service that puts the victims of crime and law abiding citizens first'.

All agencies involved in criminal justice are therefore working together to respond more effectively to crime, bring more offenders to justice, and help to tackle crime by reducing reoffending. By placing the victim at the heart of the CJS, it is anticipated that it will improve public confidence in that very system. Moreover, Local Criminal Justice Boards (LCJBs) based on police service areas bring together the heads of all the criminal justice agencies in a leadership role on a regular basis, to drive through reform and deliver services to meet the needs of the local area. Basically they empower the front line to respond to the needs of local communities. Crime and Disorder Reduction Partnerships and Community

Safety Partnerships work with the LCJBs to address community needs, to provide methods for tackling crime, and to reduce reoffending.

Dedicated neighbourhood policing teams in every community provide visible, accessible, and responsive policing and are supported by the creation of the role of the Police Community Support Officers (PCSOs).

To regain public confidence we must ensure that all sections of the community are engaged. The further recent development of community courts is an extension also of the community justice approach.

1.2.10 Police reform

The police service, like all other parts of the CJS, has had to undergo considerable change to meet the challenges which policing faces today. In February 2008 the Flanagan Report, an independent review into policing in England and Wales, was published. The report highlighted the complexities of modern policing and how best to integrate local accountability and involvement with the demands of serious crime whilst making best use of resources. Some of the suggested reforms—mainstreaming neighbourhood policing and reducing bureaucracy for police officers—have already been taken forward.

Finally, within the police service itself we have seen the creation of a National Policing Improvement Agency (NPIA), which represents the most significant reform of policing in recent years and the development of a fundamentally different approach to achieving business change within the police service. This new organization will support the implementation of national standards in policing and be a forward-looking strategic body responsible for the identification of and planning for future challenges to policing. It will form a culture of continuous transformational change within the police service.

1.3 The Way Forward

It is essential that police officers and prosecutors alike fulfil their obligations under all these new exciting initiatives. We must all be flexible and responsive towards the changes taking place and challenges ahead.

Each chapter of this book takes the reader through the various stages of the criminal justice process including: the gathering of evidence (taking statements and interviewing witnesses); the statutory charging process; the submission of cases papers and manual of guidance forms; and presentation of that evidence in court. Many frequently asked questions and problems that arise are included in a user-friendly format. The reader should be able to access key information quickly since the layout of each chapter adopts a clear synopsis in the Introduction with a summary of clear messages at the end. This enables the reader to grasp the essentials, have clear direction in their development, and also reinforces key learning points throughout.

We hope that this book supplements existing materials on the market and steers you on the path to best practice through those muddy waters of change so that you do your job better—lock up villains, reduce crime and make our community a safer place.

Joint Investigation

2.1 **Introduction—Why Joint Investigation and Proactive Prosecuting?**

Police officers and prosecutors working together more intelligently as a joint prosecution team need to be able to analyse a case from the same standpoint. In this chapter, the focus is on the prosecutors' mindset: thinking 'trial' from the outset—'proactive prosecuting' as it is called in the CPS. Basic case analysis techniques are considered, demonstrating how a strong case can be built up to maximize effectiveness with emphasis at the inception on what final outcome is required. The importance of full information about a case from the police is stressed so that both they and the prosecutor together are looking behind and beyond the case papers. By combining police investigative talents with the CPS prosecutor's trial experience, it will make a significant contribution to the development of cases and their final outcome.

2.2 **Statutory Charging**

Statutory charging by the CPS has been the most major development in the CJS. It has brought the CPS into the picture at a much earlier stage than before and as a result there has been a total change of focus by prosecutors. Investigation and prosecution are no longer distinct processes. The police and CPS should work as partners to ensure that the ongoing investigation is focused on gathering all the necessary evidence to build the case up, so that it has a maximum prospect of success when it gets to trial. This requires both police and prosecutors to raise their game, with far more communication and interaction between them than ever before.

2.3 **The Criminal Justice System—A Continuing Process**

Experience has taught all trial lawyers that it is the development of effective case analysis skills that underpins every prosecution action in any case. This is particularly important within the CJS, which can be seen as one continuous decision-making process. The police and the CPS are involved at the outset in the charging centre. However it does not just stop at the charge, because they are both involved at every stage of the process thereafter. Any action taken in any one part always affects another. The basic case analysis techniques we shall be discussing therefore also continue throughout the whole case. They can be seen as part of the review process, which itself is continuous and goes on into the trial court itself.

By applying a detailed forensic eye from the very beginning of the case and focusing on the trial from the outset (it is hoped) that by the time of the trial there is a strong case with a fully realistic prospect of conviction in court.

2.4 **The Crown Prosecutor's Role**

2.4.1 **Providing advice and assistance**

Paragraph 2.4 of the Code for Crown Prosecutors, a public document, clearly spells out the Crown Prosecutor's role:

> Crown Prosecutors should provide guidance and advice to investigators throughout the investigative and prosecuting process. This may include lines of inquiry, evidential requirements and assistance in any pre-charge procedures. Crown Prosecutors will be proactive in identifying, and where possible, rectifying evidential deficiencies and in bringing to an early conclusion those cases that cannot be strengthened by further investigation.

So by providing advice and guidance at the investigative stage, the prosecutor is not trying to tell the police how to do their job, but rather assisting in directing the police as to exactly what evidence is required to make a case stand up in court. If there has been an arrest for an offence of theft, for example, the CPS will be able to advise on the defences available and the elements of the offence. It is vital to prove dishonesty—but what exactly needs to be proved and how may that be done? In the case of a robbery, it must be proved that any force used was in order to steal the property. Some cases that appear at first sight to be a robbery may only be an assault and a theft. These are matters on which the CPS will be in a position to advise officers at an early stage in the investigation to ensure that the correct evidence is sought.

For this to work, police and prosecutors alike need to understand where the other is coming from so that there is a true combination of police investigative skills and the prosecutors' legal and trial experience. Prosecutors therefore will be able to give specific investigative advice where appropriate, and counteract defences and suggest further positive lines of enquiry. They can continuously focus on what needs to be done to build an effective prosecution, on how the CPS can assist and support the police in their investigations and enable them to concentrate on the actual evidence required.

2.4.2 **Proactive prosecuting**

The term 'proactive prosecuting' was introduced within the CPS to support the charging initiative. It requires the prosecutor to adopt a proactive, as opposed to a reactive, stance in all aspects of case review: to provide a comprehensive holistic analysis of the case, followed up by a case-specific, detailed, realistic and time bound action plan, to police officers, resulting in qualitative investigative advice.

The application of a detailed forensic eye from the beginning of the case, on the receipt of the key evidence from the police, allows the prosecutor to get down to brass tacks:

11

- **Evidentially: Is there a realistic prospect of conviction?**
  Are the witnesses credible and reliable?
  Is the evidence admissible?
  Are the correct questions being asked about forensics?
  Have all reasonable enquiries been followed up?
- **Holistically: Is it in the public interest to proceed?**
  What is the case really about?
  What outcome is required for justice to be done?
  Does the case justify the resources necessary to build it into a strong enough case for court?

As gatekeepers of the CJS at the charging centre the CPS needs to ensure that they control the casework rather than the casework controlling them. Moreover, prosecutors need to ensure that all decisions taken in the case in the exercise of their prosecutional discretion are formed wisely and in accordance with the Code for Crown Prosecutors.

2.4.3 **The options**

When a the case is submitted to the CPS by the police, the prosecutor in the charging centre will have a number of options available dependent on the stage at which it is submitted and the type of case.

Investigative advice

To provide early **investigative advice** to the police in a consultative capacity from the very beginning of a case.

Here the police officer will not be looking for a charging decision but rather, at the very early stages of the investigation, even within the 'golden hour' immediately after the alleged crime, he will seek guidance from the CPS; the time can be used to best advantage by the officer receiving advice from the CPS on the direction a case should take evidentially.

> ## Examples
>
> - Sensitive sexual offence with vulnerable witness—how to handle/special measures
> - Complex conspiracy with a number of strands—which way to go for the most cogent evidence
> - Forensic evidence—how much work is required?
> - New legislation—how should it be interpreted?
> - Points of law within an offence—what are the implications?
> - Covert operations—how to deal with sensitive material

Run with case

To **run** with the case as it stands. In this instance the task will be to strengthen a runable case into an unbeatable one at court.

It may be a potential straightforward guilty plea—for example, there is a full admission in interview, clear CCTV evidence or multiple police witnesses or a guilty plea may be obtained with some planning or further advice. Where the defendant is pleading not guilty it is likely that, however competent and full the police investigations, the CPS will still be able to offer advice on evidence or, for example, the handling of unused material in the light of a defence statement in the course of continuing review.

Build the case up

To **build** up a case which needs work doing on it in order to have a realistic prospect of conviction at court.

It could be that the prosecutor has authorized charge in a custody case but further significant evidence (eg forensics) is still outstanding. Alternatively the prosecutor may have advised bailing the suspect for further enquiries and evidence to be obtained prior to charge. In either of these situations, after discussion with the officer in the case, a detailed timebound action plan from the prosecutor must spell out to the officer exactly what further action is required to strengthen the case so that it is effective in court.

However a prosecutor cannot ignore the implications of his decision to proceed. The potential cost in terms of deployment of the police resources to make it a 'runner' must be weighed against the other factors in the case: its potential seriousness and what is actually achievable by such deployment. Does the cost justify the action proposed? Sometimes the answer will be no and both the police and the CPS will agree it is simply not viable in the context of the likely outcome at court to use valuable resources to build the case up any further.

Moreover, going through the criminal court process is no longer the only route available. A number of alternative courses of action exist such as diversion, fixed penalty notices and civil remedies which may be the most appropriate answer in all the circumstances.

Bin the case

To **bin** the case either immediately or after relatively brief further enquiries.

It is the responsibility of the prosecutor to weed out from the beginning cases that are simply not going to stand up in court. They cannot be strengthened by any further investigation and police resources will not be wasted in further pointless enquiries. If the CPS prosecutor is effective there should be little need to discontinue a case after charge (unless the position actually changes with regard to the existing evidence).

In this regard it obviously assists the prosecutor if the police officer does not ask for a charging decision in the first place in a case where they know it is not well founded and it is not likely to go anywhere contrary to the Director's Statutory Charging Guidance discussed in detail in Chapter 3. Where the evidence is just simply not there, it is an ineffective use of the prosecutors' time to submit such a case primarily with a view to passing responsibility for dropping the case onto the charging lawyer, as has happened in the past.

2.4.4 What is the Crown Prosecutor's role?

A CPS prosecutor is, in effect, the custodian of the public interest (and arguably their purse), acting as a 'minister of justice' to ensure that the rights of all those involved in the criminal justice process (including the victim, the defendant and the wider community) are safeguarded.

The legal training of the prosecutor and their independence from the police enables a second objective eye to be cast over every case. Always acting in the interests of justice and never solely for the purpose of obtaining a conviction, they will provide advice and guidance to the police, reviewing the case in accordance with the Code for Crown Prosecutors. Subsequently, as advocates, they will present the case in court on behalf of the prosecution. These greater responsibilities for the CPS prosecutors contrast with the narrower responsibilities of the defence lawyer focusing on what is best for their client.

By working together, the CPS and the police can formulate strong cases and weed out the weak ones. Teamwork will ensure, by better understanding of the facts of the case submitted by the police officer, that the prosecutor can do justice in accordance with those facts.

So where do we begin when we want to understand the facts?

2.5 Effective Case Analysis

This term may belong to lawyers but the process it explains is one that is familiar to police officers as well.

2.5.1 Preparation by anticipation

At the start of an investigation police officers will pursue reasonable lines of enquiry, exploring the surrounding circumstances of the incident in order to build up a picture of what has occurred. At this early stage it is a simple objective process of finding out what happened. At a certain point the officers will take stock and ask themselves 'what have I got?'. If their investigation has progressed to identifying a suspect they will have developed a 'case theory'—this is simply what they think happened. At this stage they may well look to plug any gaps in their case, in anticipation of what the defence may say.

What is being proposed here is that a combined effort of police officers and prosecutors—a collaborative focus rather than merely an 'investigators one'—is more likely to obtain the required outcome. Such a joint measured and formalised focus on what is effectively continuous case review with emphasis throughout on the facts and how best to use them, will help achieve the desired outcome.

Preparation by anticipation is the key; 'frontloading' from the beginning of the investigation, not just when the file hits the lawyer's desk. The police officer understands what he has done, why he has done it, and precisely how he fits into the case as a whole.

2.5.2 **Thinking trial, not charge**

This involves both police officers and prosecutors analysing the case with the final trial in the forefront of their minds and picturing exactly how the case will be presented in court to a jury. The key issues in the case need to be identified and dealt with individually, be they legal or factual issues. Good investigators and prosecutors can and must view their own cases dispassionately through the eyes of all players, including the defence. By identifying the strengths and weaknesses of a case and anticipating what may be coming, it will enable the prosecution team to fill gaps in the evidence and utilize evidential opportunities and new legislative tools to full advantage. This will enable the prosecution team to close the doors to the defendant being acquitted.

This is a fluid and flexible approach which has to adapt and respond to changing circumstances in the course of an investigation, or even in the course of a trial itself. Strengths may become weaknesses and vice versa since unforeseen events may occur.

2.5.3 **Fact analysis and investigation**

It necessary to understand exactly what a fact is before, if you like, we can do justice according to the facts and appreciate exactly what facts are in existence at any given moment in time and what facts are missing.

Definition—Fact

A fact is information and matters which require proof.

For example, the car was being driven at 25 mph. The car was a black Volvo. A fact can be agreed or in dispute and is therefore open to proof or disproof.

Compare a fact with the evidence.

Definition—Proof

Evidence is the means of proof—the means by which facts are proved or disproved.

For example, the passenger in the car may say that the car was being driven at 29 mph. The GATSO officer may say the reading was 25 mph. The driver may say the car was green not black.

Each of these people may come to the trial and give evidence on the facts, which can then be believed or disbelieved.

It is vitally important that we concentrate only on the facts of the case. Inferences can be drawn from the facts but we do not want to add two and two together and make five by jumping to conclusions ourselves. For example:

1 Car was driven at 35 mph
2 Speed limit is 30 mph
3 Car was speeding

1 and 2 are facts that are provable by evidence and 3 is not a fact proved by evidence but a conclusion from the facts.

Unfortunately, it is very easy to jump to conclusions and make assumptions and many witness statements are littered with them.

For example:

1 Suspect shouted '**** off'

2 Suspect raised right hand and formed a 'v' sign

3 Suspect clenched left hand into fist and waved it in the air

4 Suspect was aggressive and rude

1, 2, and 3 are facts provable by evidence and 4 is a conclusion. The statement and the evidence of the witness should only be about the facts.

The facts will allow any jury to draw their own conclusion that the suspect was being aggressive and rude and will be far more persuasive than any subjective conclusion drawn in the statement itself.

Supportive and negative facts

So we stick to the facts but we must also analyse those facts in terms of the facts that help our case and the facts that hinder it:

- Supportive facts support the prosecution case and damage the defendant's case
- Negative facts damage the prosecution case and support the defendant's case
- Supportive facts can turn into negative facts and vice versa

It is a bit of a balancing act weighing up the facts on each side of the scales as it were: the strengths and weaknesses of the case. When examining a case in these terms if there are too many negative facts it may be necessary to think hard about how, if at all, they can be changed into supportive ones. At the end of the day if they cannot, the case may not be able to proceed at all. It will be seen that some facts are neither supportive nor negative or rather can be used by both sides to assist their cause.

Scenario—Road traffic

It is 10 December at 6 pm. X meets a friend Y from work for a drink in a pub. In the pub X has four pints and Y has two gin and tonics. They stay in the pub talking for two hours.

The road outside the pub is a 20 mph speed limit and a one-way street travelling north towards Y's place of work. The pub which they are drinking in is on the corner and X's car is parked outside. The scene looks like this:

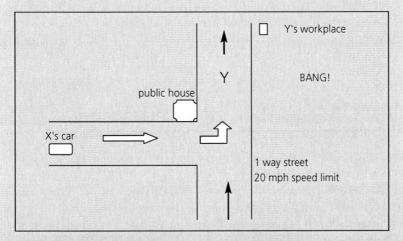

Y leaves the pub to go back to work at 8 pm but stops in the middle of the road because he thinks he has left his wallet in the pub. X leaves the pub a few minutes later, gets into his car and drives along the road towards their work place travelling at 25 mph. He leans over to pick up his jacket which has fallen to the floor from the passenger seat, as he does so—bang—he drives straight into Y in the middle of the road, seeing him too late to brake. Y falls over hurting his leg and calls the police.

X is now a suspect for the charge of driving without due care and attention, contrary to section 3 of the Road Traffic Act 1988.

So what has the prosecution team got to do?

The lawyer will certainly be analysing the components of the criminal offence which can be broken down into a number of elements, each of which has to be proved, for example:

- that X was driving—this is likely to be an undisputed fact;

- that X exercised care below that expected of a reasonable, prudent, and competent driver when he hit Y—the legal test.

This is where the facts relied on are crucial.

What were your first thoughts on the scenario?

Did you stick to the facts, or jump straight to conclusions, ie X was drunk, X was speeding, X was not concentrating, it was dark outside. These are assumptions or conclusions.

It is necessary to be more forensic here and stick to the facts:

- X was drunk—he drunk four pints. Four pints of what? It could be lemonade;

- X was speeding—be precise—he was doing 25 mph in a 20 mph speed limit;

- X was not concentrating—look at the facts which make you come to this inevitable conclusion, ie 'he leaned over to retrieve his jacket;

- it was dark—assumption, the fact was it was 8 pm on 10 December. But what were the lighting arrangements on that street on that particular evening in question? This needs to be investigated.

Are they supportive or negative facts?

- If X had four pints of beer and then drove this would be a good fact assisting the prosecution case. If he was drinking lemonade, then the defence could turn this into a negative fact by stressing he was totally sober at the time of the accident.

- If X is doing 25 mph in a 20 mph speed limit this is a supportive fact from which one can infer he was speeding.

- If X was reaching for his jacket while driving this is also a supportive fact from which a jury could infer that he was not concentrating.

- We do not know until it has been investigated whether the time of the incident, 8 pm on 10 December is a relevant supportive or negative fact. This would depend on the outcome of enquiries into the lighting arrangements on the road at that time.

Note that there are also other facts. For example 'Y' in the middle of the road—is this a supportive or negative fact? Arguably it could be either.

The prosecution will say that Y was standing in the middle of the road so that X should have seen him. But the defence may argue that Y shouldn't have been dithering in the middle of the road and thus was partly responsible for the subsequent accident.

So here you have facts which are not disputed but are open to different interpretation by the prosecution and the defence. We need to be aware of this and deal with it accordingly, making it work for the prosecution case if possible.

Hopefully this lengthy example of facts analysis demonstrates that it is not merely essential at the investigation and decision-making stage, but that it should pervade all other aspects as well: the taking of statements, the officer's own statements, interviewing techniques and the subsequent giving of evidence in court.

POINT TO NOTE

- Always ensure you are being factual
- Determine what facts exist
- What facts are required to achieve the desired outcome?
- What further investigation is needed if you do not have the right facts?
- What evidence will be used to prove or disprove those facts?
- What inferences may be drawn from those facts?
- Remove all extraneous materials: rumours, assumptions, and conclusions
- First establish the facts and then draw conclusions

2.6 Practical Example—Attention to Detail

When a prosecutor first receives a statement from the police officer, if it has been 'poorly' taken it may require a considerable amount of investigation to fill the gaps. Paying attention to the detail in any statement is another key aspect of case analysis.

This applies equally to the officer in the taking or making of the statement and in the subsequent review by the prosecutor. Further advice follows on best practice in statement taking in Chapter 4. The example that follows has been chosen to demonstrate and provide insight into the case analysis techniques of the lawyer in relation to any statement in any type of case.

Scenario—Assault

This is an assault scenario (a real case). This relates to an apparently unprovoked assault in a nightclub where the complainant has part of her ear bitten off. Such an injury merits a thorough investigation.

The prosecution were provided with only two key witness statements in this case. Swift (the suspect) was arrested for assault as a result of information received by the police. There was no other evidence submitted. In interview Swift admitted being on the premises in question and being aware of an incident occurring. She stated that although she was ejected from the premises at the time she was not involved. She answered 'no comment' to all other questions put to her.

This example has been deliberately chosen because of the poor quality of the statements taken and the many questions they leave unanswered. It is merely a vehicle to illustrate a point albeit it may also remind officers of the importance of paying attention to detail and to obtain all necessary facts and evidence first time around.

The following statements only were submitted by the police in this case:

A statement from Lucy Flirt (the complainant).

A statement from Barry Brown (the manager of the club).

Statement of Lucy Flirt

I am Lucy Flirt and I live at the address overleaf. On Friday 8 April 2005 I attended the Mustard Bar near Covent Garden to celebrate my birthday. Before arriving at the Mustard Bar we had visited a number of pubs in the Covent Garden area. We arrived at the Mustard Bar at about 11.20 pm. At about 12.45 am I was on the dance floor with many other people when I suddenly felt a severe push and experienced pain to my left ear. I realized that another girl was attacking me and biting my ear. Very quickly someone was pulling this girl away from me and I think it was one of the club bouncers. That girl was then ejected from the club and I did not see her again. I realized then that my ear was badly injured and bleeding. I went outside with one of my friends and summoned a taxi which took us to the nearest hospital. During the journey I was advised that part of my ear had been bitten off. At the hospital my injuries were treated and I was allowed to go home. The next day I was told that the girl who had attacked me was Freda Swift. I had not seen her in that club earlier that evening. I passed that information on to the police.

What is missing here?

The complainant's statement lacks any detail and is inadequate. The case would not stand up as it is without further enquiries taking place and a much more thorough investigation:

- Who was she with?
- How much had she been drinking?
- Had anything happened earlier in the evening?

Lucy was celebrating her birthday with others: 'we had visited a number of pubs … I was on the dance floor with many other people'.

Obviously this incident happened in a very public place and there must have been other witnesses, in particular her own friends including the one who took her to hospital after she had been injured. Additionally the bouncers saw something since they decided whom they thought should be ejected from the club. So what about statements from them?

There is presently no admissible evidence of the identification of the subject:

- How is Swift identified?
- Who supplied the name of Swift to Lucy?
- How did they say they knew? (Were they eye-witnesses?)
- Who was talking to her about the incident?

The facts are that Lucy apparently does not see the person who attacked her: 'I realized that another girl was attacking me … the next day I was told the girl who attacked me was Freda Swift':

- Why did she not go to the police when it happened rather than after she was told who attacked her?

The penultimate sentence of Lucy's statement is also very telling—suggesting she knew the suspect: 'I had not seen her in that club earlier in the evening':

- Was this incident a stranger attack out of the blue, or is there in fact more to it?

Not only were there no other witnesses other evidential opportunities appear to have been ignored:

- What about possible blood forensics from the suspect's clothes (seized and preserved at the house of the suspect)?
- What about preserving any CCTV from the club?
- What about medical evidence relating to injuries?

Statement of Barry Brown

I am Barry Brown and I live at the address overleaf. I am the manager of the Mustard Bar in Covent Garden and I was working behind the bar serving customers on the evening of Friday 8 April 2005. My wife Betty and my daughter often assist me and on that evening my wife was also serving customers at the bar. It was a busy evening and the premises were packed. I employ security staff to patrol the premises and prevent disorder. At about 12.45 am I noticed a disturbance taking place on the dance floor which one of my security staff swiftly responded to. I saw a person subsequently being ejected from the premises. I did not know who that person was. Immediately afterwards I realized that a customer had been injured and also saw her leaving the premises. I did not know that person. Order was quickly restored and there were no further disturbances that evening.

Again the statement is vague and Barry Brown appears concerned to demonstrate that he immediately restored order to the premises after the incident:

- What about other bar staff, especially his wife?
- Was Swift the only person ejected that night?
- Can he provide all details of bouncers working that evening?
- Which bouncer was involved in the ejection?
  'I noticed a disturbance taking place on the dance floor which one of my security staff swiftly responded to. I saw a person subsequently being ejected from the premises.'
- Does he know either of the parties concerned?
- Was this the only incident?
- What made the bouncer eject only Swift?
- How does he know the incident related to Swift?
- Is there any CCTV on the exit?

Let us now consider possible lines of defence. We only know Swift denies being involved in the incident although she accepts she was ejected.

As indicated there is an identification issue which needs to be dealt with. Moreover in any assault case self-defence arguments must be considered. We personally know nothing about Swift or her friends and whether or not there is any history between her and the complainant.

We need to investigate both sides of the picture here: the complainants and the suspect. This is the only way we will get a clear idea of what the case is really about. In any assault case the investigation should aim to exclude the possibility of self defence being put forward.

> **POINT TO NOTE**
>
> This was in fact a real case and at Crown Court Swift came along with two friends to back her up saying the complainant attacked her first. She was acquitted by the jury.

The above provides an exaggerated example of case analysis techniques, looking at the facts which are needed to prove a conviction. This involves: identifying the level of seriousness; critically examining the statements provided in a case in detail; plugging the gaps in the evidence necessary to prove those facts (by means of an action plan); and getting to the heart of the matter. Preparation by anticipation of how others might see the case and what the defence may say is crucial. Thinking what will happen at trial if in fact the prosecution team just relies on the case papers submitted is essential.

Good investigation will, therefore, build good cases.

2.7 **Admissibility, Credibility, and Reliability**

> **POINT TO NOTE**
>
> Paragraph 5.4 of the Code for Crown Prosecutors tells prosecutors:
>
> When deciding whether there is enough evidence to prosecute CPS must consider whether the evidence can be used and is reliable ... are there any concerns over the accuracy or credibility of a witness ... is it likely that the evidence will be excluded by the court because of the way in which it was gathered.

In assessing whether there is a realistic prospect of conviction in a case, prosecutors always take into account an assessment of the reliability and credibility of victims and witnesses and the admissibility of evidence. This is also an important part of effective case analysis. Again, it is suggested that this is a technique which police officers utilize intuitively every time they interview a defendant or take a witness statement; they are trying to assess the reliability and credibility of a witness to know what the facts of the case are.

2.7.1 **Admissibility and the police officer's actions**

Similarly, for example, before a police officer enters premises to search them or conducts a street identification or interview, he should be fully mindful of the PACE Codes and his professional obligations. As long as he has acted in accordance with them there will be no subsequent problems at trial with regard to the admissibility of evidence obtained by his actions. Apart from that, admissibility or otherwise of evidence is essentially a legal issue for the lawyer to consider.

2.7.2 **Reliability and credibility**

However, with regards to credibility and reliability it is, of course, the police officer who has seen the witnesses and the defendant and has had a first-hand opportunity to assess them. The officer's views of the witnesses are an important factor for the prosecutor to take into consideration at the outset of the case. Such opinions should, it is suggested, be included on the MG6 case file information form.

Is there a difference between credibility and reliability? **There is a slight difference, but they are closely interconnected.**

Credibility

Credibility is about whether or not the witness or the defendant will be believed by the fact finders—ie the magistrates or the jury. Here the nature and agenda of the parties concerned in the case is important. It may be, for example, that a witness's background may weaken the prosecution case. The witness in the case may have a motive which may affect their attitude to it; perhaps the witness has a previous conviction for telling lies which will affect the jury's view of their truthfulness.

The defendant may have provided an explanation for the offence in interview which may be found credible as an innocent explanation in the light of the evidence as a whole (see Swift previously—self defence).

Reliability

Reliability is more about whether or not the witness is dependable, accurate and consistent throughout the giving of evidence process. It is about the witness being able to 'sell' themselves to the jury and being able to withstand cross-examination at trial. A witness who is very young, a drug addict, an alcoholic or suffers from mental health problems may prove to be more unreliable than one who does not have those characteristics. The reliability of a defendant's confession may be affected by factors such as youth, intelligence, level of understanding, etc.

In assessing reliability and credibility therefore the prosecutor will go behind and beyond the papers in their detailed analysis of the case. He will look for corroboration of witness testimony and other supporting evidence and consistency of their account with the main facts of the case. He will also ensure that the police officer has fully investigated the background and personal characteristics of all parties in the case. This is particularly important in domestic violence and sexual offence allegations, for example, where the prosecutor will rely on the police officer to keep them informed of the state of play and the willingness or otherwise of the complainant to give evidence at trial.

Obviously, for both the CPS and the police, intuition and experience may inform the facts of the case. However, we all need to be aware of any personal baggage (or stereotyping) that is brought to our case investigation and review, always keeping an open mind and not allowing it to distort objectivity.

All such issues need to be considered at the outset of the case, not at the door of court before trial. It is interesting to note that one of the latest developments within the CJS is the prosecutor holding a pre-trial interview with the complainant to assess their credibility and/or clarify their evidence in a complex case. Additionally, there are numerous recommendations for use of expert evidence to assist the court in appropriate cases. In domestic violence and rape cases expert evidence can be used to explain why victims have reacted in a way which the fact finders might consider unusual, for example by complying with the aggressor or failing to report the offence immediately.

2.8 **Forensic Awareness**

Neither police officers nor prosecutors are forensic scientists but it is imperative that both have an understanding of the potential forensic evidence present at the scene and the cost and impact of forensics generally. It is essential to maintain continuous liaison and involvement between the prosecution team and the forensic department from the outset in line with case analysis skills.

Different types of forensic evidence can be conclusive in a case (eg fingerprints, tool marks, footprints). It is important therefore that in the investigative process officers pay close attention to issues of integrity of exhibits, their identification, packaging, preservation, etc, and are forensically aware of continuity and contamination issues. Forensic evidence must also stand up to scrutiny by the defence and must deal with any defence explanations and rebut them (eg negative forensics—fingerprints of another discovered—'therefore it wasn't me').

The success of the service which forensic scientists can provide is largely dependent on the standard of evidence submitted to them in the first place and on the development of close dialogue at an early stage with them. This involves the prosecution team providing the forensic scientist with all essential information in the case from the outset, keeping them continuously updated and asking them the right questions to progress the case and get the best results. There must always be a total commitment to maximizing the potential of forensic intervention and a robust prosecution.

2.9 **Conclusion**

Through such a combination of police investigative skills and CPS knowledge and experience of the trial process and case analysis techniques, it is hoped that this will lead to improved investigation and improved decision making which will ultimately assist the final outcome: doing justice according to the facts of the case.

Building better cases from the outset may well require more groundwork from the police in the initial stages and also Crown Prosecutors in the charging centres. However, one result of this is more guilty pleas. This saves much remedial work later in the day and is also a more effective use of resources.

Key considerations

- Joint partnership working from the outset

- Prosecutors giving advice and guidance to the police at the investigative stage

- Think trial, not charge

- Build up cases or weed out weak ones

- Analyse the facts, paying attention to detail

- First establish the facts and then draw conclusions

- Identify strengths and weaknesses in the evidence

- Plug evidential deficiencies

- Anticipate and deal with the defence case

- Understand where the witness is coming from

- Be forensically aware

- Do justice according to the facts of the case

3

Statutory Charging and its Implications

3.1 **Introduction**

In this chapter, the reasoning behind the new statutory charging regime is explained—as is the whole charging process framework under the Director's Guidance on Charging. Getting the charge right 'first time' involves the police providing the necessary information and evidence from the outset. This chapter highlights good practice in relation to the decision-making process for the submission of case files and the completion of the MG3 (the actual joint case analysis of files is dealt with in Chapter 2). The tests applied by the police and CPS are discussed in detail, as are the charging standards and other relevant protocols. The importance of joint case building by the CPS and the police is stressed throughout, as is efficient utilization of pre-charge conditional bail and CPS action plans.

The key message in this chapter is that both the CPS and the police need to be committed and professional in their approach to the charging regime and have confidence in each other's decision making. Increased knowledge and understanding of their respective roles will assist this process.

3.2 **The Fundamental Change**

3.2.1 **The need for change**

In 2002, Lord Justice Auld was tasked by the government with improving efficiency and effectiveness within the CJS. He identified that one of the biggest problems was the large number of cases incorrectly often overcharged by the police. These were subsequently altered or discontinued at court after CPS review of the charge at a very late stage. He pointed out that this led to late guilty pleas and ineffective trials, with consequential disappointment for victims and costs to the CJS.

The existing system placed the CPS in an essentially reactive role with heavy reliance on the investigative and charging decisions of the police. This made little sense when police officers had sparse contact with the court trial system and difficulties in knowing exactly what offence should be charged or what evidence was required to prove a case at court.

It was thought that the charging decision was in effect a legal one which must be evidence based, with the trial lawyer adding huge value at the early stages of a case but at the same time allowing the police to concentrate on their investigative role. By working closely together, investigators and prosecutors could ensure they built more robust prosecutions from the start, securing the right evidence for the prosecution and saving valuable resources by weeding out hopeless cases and removing unnecessary lines of enquiry. Thus evolved the statutory charging scheme which followed the recommendations in the *Review of the Criminal Courts of England and Wales* by Lord Justice Auld in 2002.

3.2.2 **The fundamental change**

Part 4 of the Criminal Justice Act 2003 introduced the biggest changes in the CJS since the inception of the CPS. Statutory charging, specifically designed to improve case handling and prosecutions, was initiated in a staged process as a joint initiative between the police and the CPS and was finally completed throughout the 42 CPS areas in England and Wales by April 2006.

From that date there was a brand new method of charging suspects, replacing the existing system of police charging and representing a fundamental change in the allocation of charging responsibilities between the police and the CPS. It would be the prosecutor, not the police officer who in the future had responsibility for determining the charge to be brought against the suspect in the more serious and contested cases. It would be the prosecutor therefore who from now on would in effect control entry into the CJS. Prosecutors were to be based in police stations and would work with the police on cases from start to finish, bringing police and prosecutors together as never before. It is noteworthy that this brought England and Wales into line with the majority of prosecution processes in other 'fair trial' jurisdictions. This, however, did not diminish within England and Wales the shock to all at the coalface, police officers and prosecutors alike, at such an enormous change in their working practices.

The Criminal Justice Act 2003 (section 28 of, and Schedule 2 to, that Act) amended key provisions in PACE (Code C). The DPP also issued guidance under section 37A of PACE, outlining how cases would be referred to the CPS from then onwards for charging decisions and guidance to custody officers on how to deal with the changes in the new charging procedures.

The Director's Guidance is a very important and comprehensive document. The last version is the third edition published in February 2007 and is available on police and CPS websites.

Although it is referred to as guidance it is issued under a statutory power and is binding for police officers and prosecutors.

Director of Public Prosecutions message to CPS staff (2004)

- Charging represents the greatest transformation in the Service's history since its formation in 1986 and will have the biggest impact of any single reform in terms of raising the performance of the criminal justice system.
- It will strengthen the prosecution process by ensuring that charges are right from the start and ensure that we work effectively with the police to obtain safe convictions against guilty defendants.
- It also marks our coming of age as a Service that is confident and mature in our ability to provide quality independent advice to our partners in the prosecution team.

> **POINT TO NOTE**
>
> **The Director's Guidance is mandatory and has the force of law**
>
> Section 37(A)(3) of PACE: custody officers are to have regard to Guidance under this section in deciding how persons are dealt with under section 37(7).
> Section 37(B)(2) of PACE: the DPP shall decide whether there is sufficient evidence to charge a person with an offence.
>
> **The decision to change or caution is final**
>
> Section 37B(6) of PACE: if the decision of the DPP is that the person should be charged with an offence, or be given a caution in respect of an offence, the person shall be charged or cautioned accordingly.

3.2.3 The context of change

It is evident that the change within the CJS of statutory charging is only one part—albeit one of the biggest—of a vast number of changes occurring within the system at this time. All the changes are designed to rebalance the CJS in favour of victims and witnesses and are all interrelated and complement each other with the common aim of 'narrowing the justice gap' (ie the difference between the number of crimes recorded by the police and the number of defendants convicted at the end of the day) and of making the CJS more efficient. Such new charging arrangements recognize the independence of the CPS and the police service whilst at the same time developing opportunities to work seamlessly as a team and deliver more offenders to justice:

> The charging scheme is the engine that will power the criminal prosecution process of the future.
>
> Richard Foster (then Chief Executive of the CPS)

3.2.4 The benefits of change

> Getting the right charge from the start means a good deal for the public as more criminals plead guilty; a good deal for victims and witnesses, as their cases are dealt with speedily; and a good deal for the criminal justice system, as police, prosecutors and the courts make the best use of their time.
>
> Sir Ken MacDonald (DPP)

The fundamental change at the coalface of the CJS leads to a closer working partnership between the CPS and police and cements the prosecution team approach. By making decisions from the very beginning of cases and deciding on the appropriate charge, the CPS influence the 'front end' of the criminal justice process, whilst at the same time supporting the police in their investigative process. Legal advice enables the police to become more focused in their investigations and a file of evidence is assembled to a mutually agreed standard.

Appropriate use of deferred bail arrangements also allows contested cases to be built before a charging decision is made enabling the prosecution to disclose the evidence in the case at the point of charge. This increases guilty pleas at an early stage and reduces ineffective trials. Cases are better prepared from the outset allowing more time to be spent on difficult cases. At the same time cases that should not proceed can be removed early on, before additional resources are expended on building a complete case file only to be discontinued at a later stage. More robust cases are built that lead to an increase in successful prosecutions, thus helping to narrow the justice gap by reducing the attrition rate and at the same time providing a better service to the public, particularly victims and witnesses. In turn it is anticipated that this will help to rebuild public confidence in the CJS.

As Chief Inspector Julian Moss from the CJS Department pointed out prior to statutory charging: 'for years we have been playing a cat and mouse game of us and the CPS chasing each other for evidence, court cases being put back and cracked or ineffective trials resulting'.

Based on findings from the charging pilots anticipated benefits were thought to be:

- an increase in the guilty plea rate by 30%;
- a reduction in the rate of discontinuance by the early identification of non-viable cases by 69%; and
- a reduction of the rate of attrition by 23% (the difference between the numbers charged and the numbers convicted).

These are in fact the three key performance indicators: the discontinuance rate, the guilty plea rate, and the attrition rate. They are covered in 'pre-charge benefit data' published every month and provide targets, which the CPS had officially undertaken to meet when money was provided by the government to roll out statutory charging.

To date, the results are very positive. Targets have now been achieved for the first time in all indicators. Thus there has been a definite increase in guilty pleas and a decrease in attrition and discontinuance rates. New national targets have been introduced since April 2008. All CPS areas and police services are assessed on their performance against these targets.

The April 2008 targets are as follows:

Magistrates' Court	Discontinuance rate	13%
	Guilty plea rate	70%
	Attrition rate	23%
Crown Court	Discontinuance rate	11%
	Guilty plea rate	70%
	Attrition rate	23%

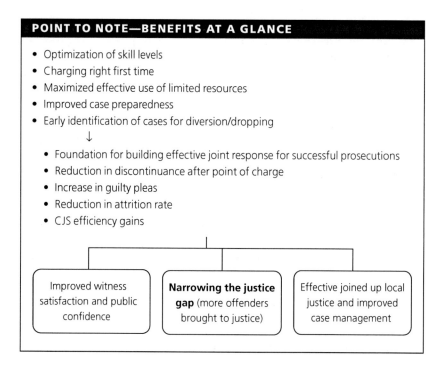

POINT TO NOTE—BENEFITS AT A GLANCE

- Optimization of skill levels
- Charging right first time
- Maximized effective use of limited resources
- Improved case preparedness
- Early identification of cases for diversion/dropping

↓

- Foundation for building effective joint response for successful prosecutions
- Reduction in discontinuance after point of charge
- Increase in guilty pleas
- Reduction in attrition rate
- CJS efficiency gains

| Improved witness satisfaction and public confidence | **Narrowing the justice gap** (more offenders brought to justice) | Effective joined up local justice and improved case management |

3.2.5 Closing the justice gap and targets

Targets are set by central government and are owned by the CPS and the police jointly by area. Chief Crown Prosecutors (CCPs) and Chief Constables are jointly accountable to ministers for meeting these targets. Unfortunately, there is a tension within the prosecution team since police are also judged on 'clear up rates'; that is the percentage of cases where the culprit is identified as well as final conviction rates. This has led police officers to concentrate on clear up rates only, which has also had a detrimental effect within the police—especially on the resources being allocated to a case after charge.

Imagine crime and performance as a tiered cake with the biggest tier at the bottom:

- The largest and first tier is **all crime**—its size is a matter of some conjecture but the public perception is certainly that crime is rising at a time that official statistics show it to be falling.
- The next tier is **reported crime**—not all crime is reported and in some categories such as rape there is evidence to suggest quite severe under-reporting. Again there is a public perception that much low level crime is simply not investigated by the police in any meaningful sense encouraging under-reporting.
- The third tier is **recorded crime**—these are reported crimes which must be notified to the Home Office.

- The fourth tier is **detected crime**—smaller numbers still are detected. Where the police have a known offender but do not prosecute because of public interest reasons this is called a **'non-sanction detection'**. It is inappropriate to obtain a non-sanctioned detection on these grounds such that it remains a detected crime when, in truth, there is insufficient evidence.
- The fifth tier is called a **'sanction detection'**, because they are proceedings that have the sanction of the law. This tier relates to a charge, an offence taken into consideration (TIC), a caution, a fixed penalty notice (FPN), a reprimand or final warning.
- The final tier of **'offences brought to justice'** includes any TIC, caution, FPN, reprimand and final warning and 'a conviction'. The so-called 'justice gap', which the government wants to 'narrow', is the difference between the number of offences recorded and the number of offenders brought to justice. Detected crimes are clear-ups, and as we have seen this is where police performance is judged. However, although this criteria for judging police performance is unlikely to change dramatically the prosecution team need to focus on securing a conviction as it is this that will lead to narrowing the justice gap. **Charges do not narrow the justice gap—convictions do!**

Therefore what the prosecution team need to be looking at, as indeed does the whole CJS, is the final tier of offences brought to justice (OBTJ).

Figure 3.1 Targets in crime

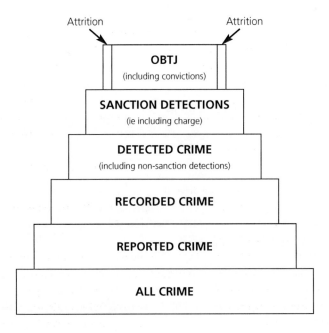

33

It is noteworthy that the Flanagan Report recognized that performance targets for the police and the National Crime Reporting Standards did not always operate to encourage efficient policing. The fixation on 'sanction and detection rates' with targets as ends in themselves in the past has meant that every incident which occurs, however minor, is recorded in detail leaving police officers with no discretion in the bulk of low level crime. This in turn has led to a decrease in public confidence and dissatisfaction amongst a number of officers:

> Officers are struggling to bring some common sense to the increased demands of a target driven culture which is all too often resulting in arrests to boost the statistics which are judged upon rather than to do what is right for the public.

> Paul McKeever (Chairman of the Police Federation)

A key recommendation of Flanagan, therefore, was for proportionate crime recording with a reduction of the information required for many crimes, but with comprehensive recording for the small percentage of serious ones. He hoped that this would achieve the 'goal of public confidence and trust in crime statistics'.

There is no simple resolution of the tension in the performance indicators, however the aim of the prosecution team is to think trial and conviction from the outset. Bringing a charge cannot be an end in itself but merely a step towards a conviction. It is anticipated that in the very near future developments focusing on new joint efficiency and effectiveness targets will ease this tension.

3.3 The Charging Process Framework

3.3.1 Deployment of duty prosecutors

Like the police service, the CPS has limited resources and must try to deploy Crown Prosecutors to achieve the most efficient service. The CPS is presently required to provide Crown Prosecutor coverage under statutory charging from Monday to Friday, 9 am to 5 pm. Wherever possible this is on a face-to-face basis with duty prosecutors based at the police stations. At the very least a duty prosecutor will be available on the end of a telephone within those times.

It is conceded that individual areas experienced teething problems where insufficient duty prosecutors were available. The response has been extended coverage dependent on work volumes and the needs of the police in some areas. This may ultimately include evening or Saturday coverage also.

It is the responsibility of the Chief Crown Prosecutor and the Chief Constable to agree appropriate arrangements locally to deploy CPS at local custody charging centres, so as effectively to discharge their charging function. Local arrangements should also be identified for dealing with complex and sensitive cases where early consultation is required and it is not appropriate for this to take place in the charging centre.

3.3.2 **CPS Direct**

Presently CPS Direct complement the daytime service described above by operating from 5 pm to 9 am Monday to Friday and 24 hours a day at weekends and public holidays, thereby providing the police with a 24/7 service. CPS Direct is a national out of hours telephone service. By calling a single number police officers around the country can contact experienced prosecutors for charging decisions outside of office hours. Lawyers working from home will provide charging advice via fax and secure IT links.

The primary purpose of CPS Direct is to provide a charging decision expeditiously in those cases where an immediate decision is required because a remand in custody is sought. It is not an alternative to local duty prosecutor schemes and wherever possible best practice dictates that police officers should use the 9–5 face-to-face service wherever possible. CPS Direct will only exceptionally deal with those cases that could have been referred to a CPS area during the bail period.

Where a subject is suitable for bail, CPS Direct may decline to deal with the case where it takes the view that it is too sensitive and complex a case to advise by phone or there is significant recorded media material as part of the evidence which needs to be viewed in order for a proper decision to be made. Additionally CPS Direct will make a conditional cautioning decision in those cases where a person has been detained out of hours. Exceptionally they can also be contacted for early legal advice where the custody officer is satisfied that advice is required immediately and delay may prejudice the investigation.

It is to be noted that the speed of response and availability of CPS Direct is dependent on referral of appropriate cases by the police in the first instance.

As will be seen, all cases must go through the custody officer first and the threshold test must have been passed. The custody officer must also give an indication of whether the suspect is to be bailed or remanded in custody post-charge. The police officer who wishes to obtain the charging decision should have to hand all the necessary evidence to support the charge together with a completed MG3 (report to CPS for a charging decision—see 6.4). Officers should ensure that they are close to telephones and fax machines when making the call.

The prosecutor will generally provide an immediate decision over the phone with calls generally lasting 35–40 minutes. Priority is given to custody cases especially at the end of the PACE clock where this is specified since, occasionally, for other cases, queuing is unavoidable. In more complex cases the prosecutor may need to research law and phone back the police officer. Written confirmation of the prosecutor's decision is sent out by email within 15 minutes.

It is useful for the police to remember that presently CPS Direct is comprised of prosecutors from all over the country, so prosecutors need to be advised of any relevant local protocols problems or issues which may effect a charging decision and similarly police officers need to avoid any local jargon.

Any police officer who does not agree with the charging decision or advice of CPS Direct may refer the case to a manager of at least inspector rank. In the event of the latter's agreement with the police officer the decision will be escalated in accordance with the Director's guidance. He will contact the CPS Direct manager, one of whom is always on duty, and the latter will review the decision after liaison with both parties.

Figure 3.2 CPS Direct process—charging decision

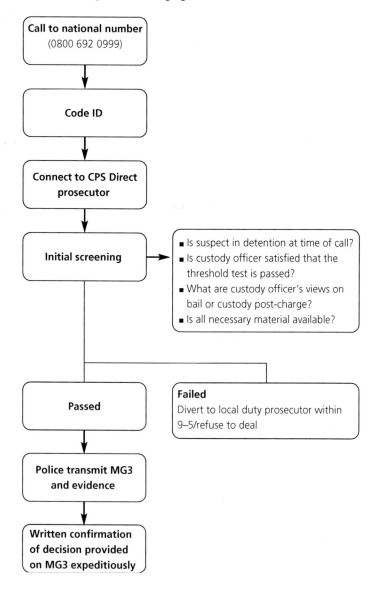

3.3.3 **Responsibility for charging decisions—what can the police charge?**

Generally speaking, the CPS must authorize charge in all serious and complex cases and in nearly all contested matters. This leaves the police with certain either-way and summary offences which they can charge without reference to a Crown Prosecutor. This is usually only when there is an anticipated guilty plea or where a sentence of imprisonment is not likely to be more than six months' imprisonment or £5000 compensation—ie within the magistrates' jurisdiction.

However, the police continue to charge approximately 60% of all cases appearing before the court. It is imperative that all police officers are fully aware of the Director's Guidance on Charging where it sets out what the police alone are authorized to charge. **Annex A** of the Director's Guidance—which is replicated for ease of reference—sets out a number of offences which are excluded from the police charge remit.

The Director's Guidance on Charging

Annex A

Offences or circumstances, which must Always be referred to a Crown Prosecutor for early consultation and charging decision—whether admitted or not

- Offences requiring the Attorney General's or Director of Public Prosecution's consent.
- Any indictable only offence.
- Any either way offence triable only on indictment due to the surrounding circumstances of the commission of the offence or the previous convictions of the person.

In so far as not covered by the above:

- Offences under the Terrorism Act 2000, the Prevention of Terrorism Act 2005 or any other offence linked with terrorist activity.
- Offences under the Anti-Terrorism, Crime and Security Act 2001.
- Offences under the Explosive Substances Act 1883.
- Offences under any of the Official Secrets Acts.
- Offences involving any racial, religious or homophobic aggravation.
- Offences classified as Domestic Violence.
- Offences under the Sexual Offences Act 2003 committed by or upon persons under the age of 18 years.
- Offences involving Persistent Young Offenders, unless chargeable by the police under Paragraph 3.3.
- Offences arising directly or indirectly out of activities associated with hunting wild mammals with dogs under the Hunting Act 2004.

The following specific offences (File requirements for these cases will be in accordance with the Manual of Guidance expedited file, to include key witness statements or other compelling evidence and a short descriptive note of any interview conducted):

- Wounding or inflicting grievous bodily harm, contrary to Section 20 of the Offences Against the Person Act 1861
- Assault occasioning actual bodily harm, contrary to Section 47 of the Offences Against the Person Act 1861
- Violent Disorder contrary to Section 2 of the Public Order Act 1986.
- Affray, contrary to Section 3 of the Public Order Act 1986
- Offences involving deception, contrary to the Theft Acts 1968 & 1978 (If the offence was committed before 15 January 2007)
- Handling stolen goods, contrary to Section 22 of the Theft Act 1968
- Offences under the Fraud Act 2006

All police officers should be aware of the following:

- Any case, even when police are authorized to charge may be referred to a prosecutor for an out of court disposal.
- Any summary only offence punishable with less than three months' imprisonment can be charged by the police (subject to Annex A).
- Police officers require some experience to assess whether an 'anticipated guilty plea is likely'. This is often a source of confusion and controversy when in the past police officers have noted that the defendant made 'a full and frank admission to the offence' (and the custody officer has authorized charge themselves). In fact, in interview, the suspect had raised an excuse or a defence for his behaviour which therefore implied that it would be a contested case which the police are not authorized to charge, eg 'I hit him first because I thought he was going to hit me'. The custody officer may have to justify his decision to charge in such cases and should specifically record his reasoning behind his belief on the MG3.

  A guilty plea could also arise where the suspect is not interviewed and he or his representative may have indicated outside of PACE that he is going to admit the offence. This would suffice, or where there is strong evidence of the offence being committed (eg CCTV, police officers as witnesses, etc).
- Police officers are also required to have knowledge of mode of trial and sentencing guidelines. All indictable offences must be referred to a Crown Prosecutor as must any either-way and summary offence where it is likely that the offender will receive a sentence greater than the magistrates' powers of punishment (ie more than six months' imprisonment or more than £5000 compensation).
- There are also a number of common offences where the police officer must refer to a prosecutor for a charging decision. For example, all 'hate crimes' including domestic violence, dangerous driving, all either-way assaults and public order offences, deception offences and handling. Notable summary offences for referral include disqualified driving where the offender does not make an

admission, driving with excess alcohol where the statutory defence may be raised and unlawful motor vehicle taking in certain cases. These examples are not exhaustive.

- Where there is a combination of offences some of which could be charged by the police the custody officer must refer all cases to a Crown Prosecutor for determination.
- A case should not be referred to a Crown Prosecutor in any event where it is incapable of ever reaching a realistic prospect of conviction—a 'no hoper'. They must be dealt with by the police themselves.
- Even when the police do authorize a charge correctly the case will always be subsequently subject to a review by a Crown Prosecutor in accordance with the Code for Crown Prosecutors.
- Police officers can refer any case to a Crown Prosecutor at any stage where they consider that investigative advice and assistance would be helpful to them, indeed this is to be encouraged.
- Whenever there is a case in which the police are authorized to charge the only test that can be applied is that of a realistic prospect of conviction and that it is in the public interest in accordance with the Code for Crown Prosecutors. The assessment of the case will be made on the available evidence at the time together with any admissions made during interview. The evidential test comes first and where a custody officer considers that there is a realistic prospect of conviction he will then consider the public interest element and specifically consider the appropriateness of any out of court disposal for the offence instead of charge.
- If the police wrongly charge a case where they are not authorized to do so such a charge is not per se unlawful. If such a situation arises the Crown Prosecutor should immediately review the case in accordance with the DPP Guidance and the Code for Crown Prosecutors to cure the procedural error or discontinue the case prior to any court appearance and notify the defence accordingly. The Crown Prosecutor's decision will be final and line management on both sides would be informed.
- Where the police charge contrary to a CPS decision not to charge the position is slightly different. It is uncertain whether such a charge would be illegal but the police will also have breached PACE and not complied with the statutory requirement of written notice to the suspect. A prosecutor could only cure such a charge by further review if it could be shown that the prosecutor's original decision was fundamentally wrong and could not stand.

However, in both situations, the decision could be subject to judicial review or give rise to civil liability for malicious prosecution or misfeasance in public office. The responsibility for ensuring the procedure is followed is a joint one and failure to do so will result in undermining of the prosecution team and loss of public confidence in the system.

3.3.4 **Early investigative advice pre-charge**

The statutory charging process is not just about charging decisions. Police officers may seek early consultation with the Crown Prosecutor whatever the case, even those where the police can charge themselves. Moreover, in some types of more complex and sensitive cases early consultation is to be regarded as standard best practice. Indeed the Director's Guidance positively encourages it, since it will provide an opportunity for investigators and prosecutors to undertake joint provisional assessment of the case. Advice and guidance by the prosecutor may include lines of enquiry, evidential requirements and pre-charge procedures. The earlier the consultation the better, so that the 'golden hour rule' is used to best advantage. Even if there is no identifiable suspect, early involvement by the prosecutor may assist, for example, in the questions to be asked of a suspect subsequently or the strategy for a likely prosecution.

In exercising this function, Crown Prosecutors will be proactive in identifying and, where possible, rectifying evidential deficiencies, pinpointing those cases that can proceed to court as an early guilty plea or terminating weak cases which cannot be rectified by any further investigation. The prosecutor's role here is a directional and advisory one—advising on evidential issues, screening cases and guiding officers as to case investigation and enquiry.

Such early consultation has many advantages:

- The early identification and elimination of evidentially weak cases prevents unnecessary work by the investigator and saves resources.
- Actions may be identified which can turn apparently weak cases into viable investigations.
- The correct charges can be identified early and appropriate lines of enquiry identified to obtain the evidence to support them.
- File requirements can be identified thus ensuring that the preparation of full files by the police is kept to a minimum.
- There is an early opportunity to consider whether an out of court disposal is more appropriate and take the necessary action.
- Specific needs of witnesses can be addressed and an early assessment of their reliability and credibility made.

It is particularly important therefore that in complex and sensitive cases (indictable only) such consultations allow for the early development of a joint strategy for the prosecution where the case is going to be contested.

In particular types of cases (eg homicide, rape, and fatal road collisions), once there is an identifiable suspect and the threshold test has been passed (see 3.4.1.3) it is to be standard best practice to make prompt contact with the local Crown Prosecutor who is going to have responsibility for the case (rather than the duty prosecutor).

POINT TO NOTE—STEPS FOR THE INVESTIGATING OFFICER PRIOR TO CHARGING DECISION PHASE WHERE SUSPECT IS IN CUSTODY

1 Investigative strategy

- What evidence is available and readily obtainable?
- What can be achieved during initial period in custody?
- What outcome is sought?
- Any specific victim or witness issues?

2 Ensure initial 'golden hour' investigation completed

- Obtain statements of key witnesses (and details of all other witnesses)
- Identify any witness care issues
- Carry out house-to-house enquiries
- Gather evidence: forensic—CCTV—photos—scene preservation—house search—mobile phones

3 Liaise with your supervisor

- Ensure you have obtained initial evidence
- Identify and write-off obvious 'no further action' (NFA) cases
- In police charge cases agree an action plan with supervisor

4 Do you need to seek advice from a duty prosecutor?

- Can you identify lines of enquiry, likely charges and defences?
- Identify NFAs—write-off or identify ways of turning them into viable cases

5 Go back to your supervisor if there has been consultation with the CPS

- Consider how lines of enquiry identified during consultation are to be pursued
- Identify resources to assist (eg statement taking)

6 Continue with custody procedure

- Interview suspect—identify defences raised and likely plea
- If further evidence required attempt to do so whilst suspect in custody
- Consider further consultation with duty prosecutor

↓

Over to custody officer

3.3.5 **Custody officer as gatekeeper**

It has been seen that in most cases Crown Prosecutors have the ultimate charging decision now within the CJS. However, following a suspect's arrest it is the custody officer who effectively becomes the gatekeeper of the statutory charging scheme. The custody officer will have a number of different options at his disposal, including: out of court disposals such as penalty notice for disorder (PND); simple caution or referral for a conditional caution; decisions to charge where the police are authorized to do so; or referrals to a Crown Prosecutor for either an early consultation or a charging decision in other cases. Most importantly, the custody officer must decide whether the suspect should be bailed prior to charge where all the evidence is not available or be remanded in custody for a charging decision by the Crown Prosecutor. In relation to the exercise of all these responsibilities it is necessary for the custody officer to follow certain tests laid down in the Director's Guidance and in PACE (section 37(7)(a)–(d) as amended) which are mandatory.

The custody officer therefore acts as the first sift of cases prior to them reaching the CPS. Inappropriate handling of suspects involving unauthorized charging, weak decision making by referral of 'no hoper' cases, remands in custody where a suspect should have been bailed, or referral to prosecutors without sufficient evidence will all clog up an already overstretched system. It is imperative therefore that the custody officer fully appreciates his role and complies with his responsibilities.

It is important that custody officers liaise with duty Crown Prosecutors at the earliest opportunity at the charging centre to assess the workload and type of cases for the day ahead. The custody officer should be identifying those cases that may require early consultation with a duty prosecutor and cases which are sensitive and complex and unsuitable to be dealt with at the charging centre and arrangements should be made where appropriate for these to be referred to a specialist prosecutor within a CPS office.

The custody officer's main priority, however, will be those suspects who are in custody where the permitted period of detention will expire during the day. Where these are to be referred to a prosecutor for a charging decision, the expiry time should be anticipated and referral for a decision must not be left until the last minute.

3.4 **The Decision-making Process**

3.4.1 **Custody officer's assessment**

1. **Full code test**

   In relation to any cases where the police are authorized to charge it has already been noted that the custody officer must apply the Code for Crown

Prosecutors' test, ie is there a realistic prospect of conviction and is it in the public interest to proceed?

2. **The initial evidential assessment**

   Where the police are not so authorized to charge and the case is therefore referable to a Crown Prosecutor for charging it is in fact the same evidential test that the custody officer must first apply to the case before him.

   The custody officer, however, must try to make best use of any available custody time to direct the investigating officer to obtain more evidence so as to reach that standard where it is practical and appropriate to do so within that time limit.

3. **Threshold test**

   Where, however, the custody officer concludes that the realistic prospect of conviction test cannot be met on the available evidence the custody officer will proceed to apply the threshold test. Following a suspect's arrest the custody officer must decide 'whether there is sufficient evidence to charge a detained person' (section 37(1)08 PACE). The custody officer must also conclude that there is a reasonable likelihood of further evidence being gathered to provide a realistic prospect of conviction. Additionally he must consider that it is in the public interest to proceed (based) on the available information at the time.

4. **Threshold test not met**

   If the threshold test is not met the suspect must be released. Exceptionally the custody officer is allowed by section 37(2) and (3) of PACE to continue to keep the suspect in custody without charge where he reasonably believes that the suspect's continued detention is necessary to secure or preserve evidence relating to the offence (eg identification parades, locating physical evidence) or obtain such evidence by questioning the suspect.

   However, if the above does not apply, the threshold test is not met and the custody officer considers further investigation is appropriate the suspect must be released on unconditional bail under section 34(5) of PACE.

   If the custody officer decides further enquiries will not produce any additional evidence he must then release the suspect without reference to a duty prosecutor. In the past there have been problems where the custody officer has referred cases in such circumstances merely for endorsement by the prosecutor of a police NFA decision.

POINT TO NOTE—THE OPTIONS FOR THE CUSTODY OFFICER

Section 37(7) of PACE as amended now provides:

> . . . if the Custody Officer determines that he has before him sufficient evidence to charge the person arrested with the offence for which he was arrested, the person arrested:

> a) shall be
>   i) released without charge and on bail, or
>   ii) kept in police detention for the purpose of enabling the Director of Public Prosecutions to make a decision under section 37B below,
> (b shall be released without charge and on bail but not for that purpose,
> (c) shall be released without charge and without bail, or
> (d) shall be charged.

3.4.2 Bail or custody? The decision of the custody officer

Only where the custody officer has decided that the threshold test is met and that it is not practicable to obtain further evidence within the detention period can he then refer the case to a duty prosecutor for a charging decision. It is at this stage that the custody officer must then decide whether the referral should be on bail or whether he should detain the suspect in custody for such a charging decision. The decision to bail remains that of the custody officer at this time.

Pre-charge bail

Section 37(7) of PACE (as amended) provides the custody officer with the power to bail detained persons for the specific purpose of referring the case to a Crown Prosecutor for a charging (or alternative disposal) decision, ie the point at which the suspect would have previously been charged by the police.

The added option of bail with **conditions** under section 37(7)(a) for the custody officer widens the range of cases that may benefit these arrangements by providing at least a limited control on the suspect. However, any conditions must always be proportionate to the offence charged, necessary, and reasonable.

This power was introduced to facilitate the making of charging decisions by prosecutors and for police to ensure that they complete their investigations prior to charge so that the file is built up at an early stage into a realistic prospect of conviction.

Section 37(7)(b) allows a custody officer, where he considers it premature, to ask for a charging decision because the police need to make further investigation to bail the suspect himself where the threshold test has been met. However, in this situation he can only bail the suspect unconditionally. This is to be distinguished from the use of section 34(5) bail where the threshold test has not been met.

It is good practice in any situation where a custody office is unsure to refer the case to a duty prosecutor in any event so that he can advise the officer in relation to lines of enquiry. However, it is to be noted specifically that the power to bail under section 37(7)(a) conditionally or unconditionally can be taken prior to referral to a duty prosecutor or following a consultation with a duty prosecutor in order to complete the investigation and assemble the case papers.

In the early stages of statutory charging there appeared to be some confusion or reluctance amongst custody officers to use pre-charge conditional bail as a tool. It was thought that there was a duty on the police to provide all the evidence to the duty prosecutor at the time the suspect was bailed rather than at the time the suspect was referred to a duty prosecutor, this was simply not the case. As can be seen the police are allowed to impose conditions of bail on the suspect once the custody officer is satisfied that the threshold test is passed where they are intending to make a charging decision in due course and require further evidence and still wish to obtain all key evidence in a case to satisfy the Director's Guidance.

The importance of pre-charge bail and particularly conditional bail to the efficient operation of statutory charging schemes cannot be over emphasized. The days of charging when there is only sufficient evidence have now well and truly disappeared. This new regime has changed the rules of the game and the goal posts. It is vital that prosecutors and police remember that at all times.

POINT TO NOTE

An even more fundamental challenge perhaps is to change the culture among police officers away from one in which the early charging of suspects is seen as a mark of completion and even success, towards an acceptance that suspects may remain on pre-charge bail longer while evidence is amassed and case files built.

Ian D Brownlee, *Criminal Law Review,* 906 (November 2004)

This is indeed a culture change for both police officers and prosecutors but only a joint wholehearted approach to the implementation of the new regime will work.

A person released under section 37(7)(a) may apply to **vary those conditions** at the police station where they were imposed. The custody officer has no power to vary them unless requested to do so. If the custody officer refuses to vary them the suspect can apply to a magistrates' court in which case a prosecutor should be consulted.

Where a person is released on pre-charge conditional bail and he **breaches his bail** the position is different from post-charge breaches. The suspect may only be arrested where the police officer has reasonable grounds for believing that a bail condition has actually been breached (as opposed to a suspicion that a breach is likely). There is no power of arrest for such a breach and no requirement to put the suspect immediately before the court. The suspect must be returned to the police station where they were due to surrender.

The custody officer then has two choices:

- to release on bail on the same conditions as before. He cannot extend those conditions, however a suspect could request a variation of the original conditions which may be at the custody officer's suggestion where they are no longer appropriate due to change of circumstances; or

- to refuse bail and refer the case directly to a duty prosecutor for a charging decision. The duty prosecutor will then make the final decision with regard to the detained person.

Pre-charge custody

The custody officer is authorized to detain and arrest the person in custody for a reasonable time to obtain a charging decision once the threshold test has been passed (section 37(7)(a)(ii)). The custody officer will determine whether there are reasonable grounds for not releasing the arrested person on bail post-charge under section 38 of PACE. It is to be noted that the test under PACE is a lower, ie easier, test to fulfil than that under the Bail Act 1976 which prosecutors must comply with, albeit the grounds for consideration are virtually identical. Under the Bail Act 1976 the test for the court is one of 'substantial grounds'.

The **grounds** he must consider are as follows:

- name and address cannot be ascertained;
- risk of absconding;
- interference with administration of justice/investigation of offences;
- commission of further (imprisonable) offences;
- own protection; and
- welfare of juvenile.

If the custody officer decides it is effectively a custody case ready for immediate referral while the suspect remains in the cells he is acting under section 37(7)(d) and proceeding to deal with the charge. The suspect can be detained for as long as necessary for the charge to take place (subject to the overall PACE clock). However, guidance suggested in Parliament that a reasonable detention period for this purpose was that it should not ordinarily exceed three hours to deal with a suspect and the aim should be considerably less in most cases. This is not a hard and fast rule, time limits will obviously depend on the overall circumstances of the offender, the case and any problems in the custody centre.

The need for proactive liaison and prioritization of such custody cases between the custody officer and the duty prosecutor has already been highlighted.

Unfortunately problems may occur where a custody officer cannot obtain a charging decision within the overall time limit on detention in accordance with PACE. In such exceptional circumstances **emergency provisions** exist whereby a custody officer may go to a duty inspector. The latter may then authorize charge where all practical steps have been taken to refer to a duty prosecutor. The case must then be referred to a Crown Prosecutor as soon as is practical thereafter and certainly prior to any court appearance to obtain authority to continue with the prosecution.

3.4.3 **Over to the Crown Prosecutor—the staged approach**

Once the custody officer has referred the case to a Crown Prosecutor with the suspect either already on bail or in custody, it is now down to the Crown Prosecutor to decide whether or not to authorize a charge (or an out of court disposal) and whether or not to make an application to the court to remand a detained suspect in custody or whether to bail him for the police to do further work.

In fulfilling their responsibilities, Crown Prosecutors are guided by the Code for Crown Prosecutors and the Director's Guidance. Any decision made will be dependent upon the available evidence put before them by the police and their assessment of whether or not the suspect is a potential bail risk where he is in custody.

POINT TO NOTE—INITIAL CHARGING STANDARDS

However, it should be stressed at the outset that the same initial charging standards apply to both the police and the CPS. Police charges must not reflect a lower evidential standard. Police and prosecutors alike when determining charges will therefore always apply the principles contained in the Code for Crown Prosecutors as well as the Director's Guidance. This is a higher evidential standard than the test for charging under PACE previously used by custody officers prior to statutory charging.

Initial review—the full code test

The full code test which must be applied on initial review by the prosecutor has two stages. The first stage is the consideration of the evidence and if the case does not pass the evidential test it must not go ahead no matter how serious it may be. The evidential test for prosecutors is that they must be satisfied that there is sufficient evidence to provide 'a realistic prospect of conviction' against each suspect on each charge.

This is an objective test and means that a court hearing a case properly directed in accordance with the law is more likely than not to convict the defendant of the charge alleged. In considering this, prosecutors will assess what the defence case may be and how it is likely to affect the prosecution case as well as the admissibility and reliability of the evidence submitted. Chapter 2 considers in detail how a prosecutor and police officer should analyse cases in depth when applying these tests.

Only where the evidential test is passed will prosecutors then decide whether a prosecution is required in the public interest.

> A prosecution will usually take place unless there are public interest factors tending against prosecution which clearly outweigh those tending in favour or it appears more appropriate in all circumstances of the case to divert the person from prosecution.
>
> The Code for Crown Prosecutors (2004), para 5.7

The Code lists a number of factors in favour and against prosecution but it is not exhaustive. Such public interest factors that can affect the decision to prosecute usually depend on the seriousness of the offence or the circumstances of the suspect. The more serious the offence, the more likely it is that a prosecution will be required in the public interest.

It is the custody officer's duty to notify the person in writing wherever a prosecutor has decided not to proceed on either evidential or public interest grounds.

That, however, is not the end of the matter. Where there is insufficient evidence to meet the full code test and the suspect has already been bailed or is deemed suitable for bail the person may be released on conditional or unconditional bail for a specified period. During that bail time the police will be advised by the prosecutor in writing as to the best course of action to gather sufficient evidence so that there is a realistic prospect of conviction by the time the suspect answers his bail. This will happen in advance of any charging decision being made.

This process enables the prosecution team to build a file of evidence, considering all evidential issues and lines of enquiry from the outset of the case, to a high standard so that they are case ready at the point of charge for the first hearing. It is important that bail time periods are managed proactively.

The threshold test

Where the suspect has been referred by the custody officer to a duty prosecutor in detention (after the custody officer has applied the threshold test) and where there is insufficient available evidence for the full code test to be passed a different test will exceptionally apply.

This test is only an interim measure to be used by prosecutors in exceptional circumstances in order to manage high risk offenders whilst significant outstanding evidence is obtained by the police within a reasonable time.

The prosecutor must decide that on the evidence that does exist there is a reasonable suspicion that the suspect has committed the offence. Article 5 of the European Convention on Human Rights requires there to be a reasonable suspicion of having committed an offence before a suspect can be detained.

> **POINT TO NOTE—APPLYING THE THRESHOLD TEST**
>
> - The seriousness or circumstances of the case justify the making of an immediate charging decision
> - There are continuing substantial grounds to object to bail in accordance with the Bail Act 1976 and in all the circumstances of the case a remand in custody is justified
> - The investigation is continuing and, though it is likely that further evidence will be obtained, it will not be practicable to gather sufficient evidence to provide a realistic prospect of conviction during any permitted initial or extended period of detention
> - There are reasonable grounds for believing that further admissible evidence capable of providing a realistic prospect of conviction can be obtained

The prosecutor must then make two decisions based on:

1. **his assessment of the risk to the public if the suspect is freed prior to a charging decision**

   It is to be noted that in assessing the level of risk of the suspect being granted bail the prosecutor applies the Bail Act 1976. Within that Act the test laid down is whether there are 'substantial grounds' for believing that one of the exceptions to the right to bail in the Bail Act 1976 are met (a higher test than within section 38 of PACE albeit covering nearly identical exceptions). The prosecutor must be confident that he can properly make an application to withhold bail in the case before him. If the prosecutor does not so believe that there are substantial grounds he must advise to bail the suspect in order for further evidence to be obtained.

2. **the available evidence and his assessment of whether within a reasonable time evidence can be obtained to turn the case into a realistic prospect of conviction**

   A suspect should only be charged and remanded in custody and put before the court where the outstanding evidence is not available at the time, action is underway to obtain that evidence, and there is a likelihood of it becoming available within a reasonable time and that outstanding evidence will be so significant that on an objective test it will provide a realistic prospect of conviction in the case. Even where this test is met the prosecutor must still consider whether the public interest requires the person to be charged on the available information at that time.

Only at that stage when the prosecutor has considered all of the above factors will he authorize a charge and put the defendant before the court in custody.

The DP's application of the 'threshold test' is not to be regarded by police officers as a short cut for a charging decision. It is about managing substantial bail risks where all of the evidence is not available at the time and the need to manage the risks is the justification for charging on the lower evidential standard.

It is usually inadvisable to accept an early guilty plea to a case charged under the lower test because the case will still be incomplete and further evidence obtained may reveal other offences or even aggravating or mitigating factors that should have been taken into account by the court when sentencing.

Any suspect charged and refused bail must go before the court as soon as practicable and in any event at the court sitting after charge. It will then be for the court to decide whether pre-trial custody is appropriate.

Continuous review and the full code test

The case will be kept under continuous review to ensure that the further evidence is gathered to meet the full code test. Indeed the Crown Prosecutor will complete an action plan specifically identifying the outstanding evidence to be obtained and also the date for a further review of the file on the full code test on all the available evidence.

Obviously any case going before the court on the interim test, however serious, would have to be discontinued if it did not subsequently meet that full code test. Such a course of action would be considered a failure for both the police and the prosecutor. Alternatively if further significant evidence could not be obtained within a reasonable time the suspect could be released on bail for this to take place.

Example—Threshold test correctly applied

The police attend the duty prosecutor with a case where an elderly lady disturbed a burglar at her warden controlled flat. She was pushed to the ground and suffered cuts. She is able to give a moderately detailed description of the intruder, including his clothing and a distinctive coin ring he was wearing. She is now briefly detained in hospital. The warden saw a small blue car in the car park which was unknown to her and saw a male driving out of the premises shortly after the attack. Some hours later D is stopped while driving a blue hatchback. In the foot-well is a pension book belonging to the victim. There is a small trace of blood on the sleeve of his jacket. His appearance and clothing match the type and colour described by the victim. He is wearing a sovereign ring. He is arrested. In interview he denies the offence and says the car is his brother's and he has borrowed it. He adds that he is of universal appearance and the jacket and ring are common items of apparel. The police have yet to take a statement from the warden, conduct ID, seize CCTV from the flat and conduct any DNA testing on the blood. The suspect has previous convictions for aggravated burglary and an MO for targeting vulnerable pensioners. The MG7 reveals he is on bail for common assault.

In determining whether the threshold test is appropriate the prosecutor must assess the level of risk. The allegation is serious with a substantial bail risk and potential for harm to the public. There is a reasonable suspicion that the person arrested committed the offence. There is likely to be significant evidence which can be expected in a reasonable time, viz statements from victim and warden; enquiries with the brother; CCTV; ID parade; DNA; and bad character issues. The public interest is satisfied due to the seriousness of the allegation, vulnerability of the victim and likely sentence. The bail risk justifies ongoing detention and the suspect could either be sentenced for the outstanding common assault or further bailed in respect of it. The potential for risk to the public is therefore considerable. This is an appropriate case where the interim test can be applied.

Escalation procedures

Where a custody officer is of the opinion that the suspect should be remanded in custody but the prosecutor does not consider the suspect a substantial bail risk, or alternatively the prosecutor is of the opinion that further evidence to make the case viable is unlikely to be forthcoming, then he will apply the full code test. The case submitted as it stands will fail the charging test and the defendant should then be released.

In any case where an investigating or custody officer is not in agreement with the decision of the duty prosecutor there are formalised escalation procedures incorporated into the Director's Guidance. It is important they are followed in all cases and that a senior police officer does not try to exercise influence over a duty prosecutor at the charging centre.

The police will approach the Borough Crime Unit (BCU) crime manager (usually of DCI rank) and the case should then be referred to the Borough Crown Prosecutor for discussion. Local arrangements should be in place for such referrals to be conducted speedily.

The escalation process should be regarded as part of the review process rather than a confrontational exercise and should be managed appropriately by the police and the CPS.

Figure 3.3 Referral in custody for a charging decision

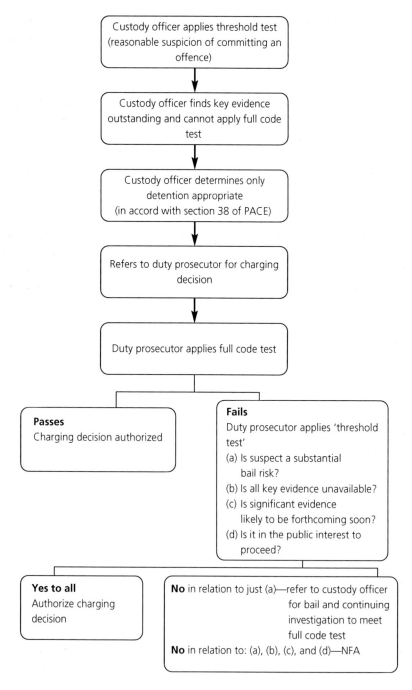

3.5 **Necessary Information for a Charging Decision**

It is vitally important that police officers appreciate that the quality of the decision about charging which the CPS makes is totally dependent upon the quality of information they receive from the police at the charging centre. The CPS is completely reliant on the police in this regard.

The *Prosecution Team Manual of Guidance—2004 Edition* (Manual of Guidance) lays down minimum requirements for file submission to the CPS as does the Director's Guidance. The content of the file will be dependent on the reason for the referral to a Crown Prosecutor, whether or not the suspect intends to plead guilty, and whether or not a remand in custody is sought. Local arrangements around simple speedy summary justice (CJSSS) and the streamlined process (SP) may introduce some variation between areas (see Chapter 9). An investigating officer should seek clarification from a duty prosecutor if he is unclear about what information is required in a particular instance.

In many areas it has been found, on inspection of statutory charging centres, that removing file supervision from the custody officers and placing that task in the hands of dedicated gatekeepers, often retired police officers, leads to better supervision and more guidance for the investigating officer prior to consultation with a duty prosecutor.

3.5.1 **Police and the MG3**

In all cases the key document is the MG3 form: 'Report to Crown Prosecutor for a Charging Decision'. This is considered briefly here but it is also dealt with in detail in the Manual of Guidance at 6.4. All police officers must be fully aware of all guidance relating to contents of file submission and must also ensure that the MG3 is comprehensively completed to assist the prosecutor or custody officer in coming to a correct decision. This important form is intended to provide an audit trail of the information provided by the investigating officer and the subsequent charging decision and any follow up action agreed in the case.

The form is divided into two parts. Part A (the front page) is completed by the police officer and part B is completed by the duty prosecutor. The form is to be completed and submitted in every case, even where a charging decision remains a police responsibility.

Since the MG3, when completed, is likely to contain information which is confidential, it is subject to legal professional privilege and public interest immunity and is not disclosable to the defence.

As a minimum the MG3 will contain brief details of the charges being pursued (eg burglary/assault) to give a clear indication of the type of case being presented. It will further contain a summary of the facts of the case—specifically including key points which the investigating officer considers relevant to the case and a summary of interview with the defendant. Other matters that could be included are evidential points, strengths and weaknesses of the case, possible lines of defence, witness reliability and credibility, or whether there are any financial or asset recovery issues or any public interest issues. This is not an exhaustive list but it is important that the investigator has a full understanding of his case prior to the completion and submission of the MG3. This ensures that all relevant details are provided and that an informed decision can subsequently be made.

3.5.2 **File content accompanying MG3**

The MG3 should also be accompanied by sufficient information, material, or evidence capable of establishing a case. This available information will obviously vary according to the type of enquiry being pursued and the stage that the investigation has reached and as previously stated subject to ongoing national pilots (SP) (see Chapter 9). Investigators are required to fill out a checklist of evidence and information provided on form A.

(a) Early consultations

In the early stages it is unlikely that all the evidence obtained is necessarily in an evidentially admissible format. As long as it is capable of becoming so, that is sufficient for the duty prosecutor to advise. All relevant statements and any other compelling evidence should accompany the MG3. In such cases an oral briefing to supplement the written MG3 may also assist the duty prosecutor.

(b) Referral for a charging decision to the duty prosecutor where a remand in custody is sought

This applies where the case has passed the threshold test and the custody officer has decided that the person is not to be released on bail following the charge.

Again it is unlikely that all evidence is at this stage in an evidentially admissible format for court. This may be sufficient as long as it can be provided in an admissible format within a reasonable time (the duty prosecutor and investigating officer should agree steps to be taken to obtain it if the case is to proceed).

The investigating officer must complete an MG3 and submit sufficient information, evidence or material capable of establishing a case with details of what outstanding evidence is likely to be forthcoming within a reasonable period of time.

Since the investigating officer is asking the duty prosecutor to remand the suspect in custody it is important that the MG3 is accompanied by an MG7 outlining in detail the officer's reasons for opposing bail. Hearsay evidence is admissible in a bail application, however, the prosecutor in court will be given short shrift by a judge if allegations made are not backed up by detailed evidence, eg as to those offences for which the defendant is on bail and other details. (A detailed analysis of the MG7 takes place at 6.18.)

Additionally the officer will provide a copy of the suspect's antecedent history and evidence (eg compensation claims) in relation to any anticipated ancillary orders.

(c) Referral for a charging decision on the full code test where there is an admission

In this situation, the report must contain the victim and other witness statements together with a record of admission in interview.

This is designed to save resources where it is likely that the suspect will appear in court and be dealt with on his first appearance. However, there must still be sufficient evidence provided for a full code test decision to be made in accordance with the Code for Crown Prosecutors. This will be in addition to the submission of a fully completed MG3, antecedent history, and MG7 where appropriate. Local protocols may require, by agreement, submission of unused material as well.

(d) Full code test where no admission—evidential report

These will be primarily bail cases where the custody officer has passed the case on the threshold test. The test that has to be passed on submission of the report of evidence when the suspect returns from bail is the full code test—a realistic prospect of conviction and it is in the public interest to proceed. Such cases will be indictable only either way, going to the Crown Court, or likely to be contested.

In this situation the file requirements are more onerous. They must be complied with since if they are not files will fail the full code test and the suspect will not be charged at that stage. The duty prosecutor is entitled to request any other material in order to make a decision. There must be sufficiently admissible material (including the victim's statement) capable of proving each element of each offence to be charged and also copies of any material or evidence that undermines the prosecution case or is capable of assisting the defence.

Thus the officer will provide a completed MG3 (with case outline and suggested charges), all key witness statements in an admissible format and copies of key documentary exhibits including a summary of interview. The submission will include evidence to prove every limb of the proposed charge as well as key evidence disproving any defence the suspect may have raised.

For example: take the case of an assault witnessed by the friend of a victim. The defence are saying it was self defence or perhaps the defence of alibi, ie saying 'it was not me' in interview. The friend would need to be spoken to and a statement taken or the alibi investigated prior to submission for the full code test to be applied.

It is noteworthy that here all evidence submitted must itself at that stage be admissible save for certain exceptions which will be mentioned below shortly.

Additionally an MG6: 'Case File Information form' should be submitted with information relevant to the case (for detailed analysis see 6.12) and an MG10 (witness non-availability form, see 6.21). Furthermore an MG16 (relating to a suspect's bad character, see 6.27) and an MG2 (in relation to witness care issues, see 6.3) respectively may also be submitted where appropriate.

In relation to an MG16, investigators must always consider the potential relevance of bad character to an issue in the case (eg previous shoplifting convictions where the suspect's current defence is forgetfulness on a theft charge). Where it is deemed relevant completion of an MG16 outlining not only the fact of conviction but also the circumstances of the offence leading to it are required, or any other relevant reprehensible behaviour (eg a crime incident report of previous call outs to the same victim of domestic violence). A prosecutor will rarely hold up a charging decision where additional information on bad character of a suspect is unavailable but best practice is the earlier the prosecution has that information the better.

In relation to the MG2, unless witness issues are addressed at a very early stage the charging process may be a waste of time if the witness subsequently disappears, does not attend, or fails to give best evidence. Police officers and prosecutors have a vital role to play in the provision of improved services to victims and witnesses. The officer must make an initial early assessment of the needs of the witness when taking a statement. The details on the back of the MG11 (see 6.22 together with the early submission of an MG2 (for vulnerable and intimidated witnesses)) will trigger the relevant support, alerting CPS and assisting in the review process.

Although disclosure schedules are not usually required at this stage an evidential report must also be accompanied by any unused material that may undermine the prosecution case or assist the defence. This would also include previous convictions of any prosecution witnesses, if relevant, or negative forensic evidence.

However, even for an evidential report, corroborative and other supporting evidence is not required at the charging decision stage.

(e) Advice files (complex/sensitive cases)—full evidential report

Unless an MG3 is submitted for an early consultation outlining issues upon which advice is sought in any other case a full evidential report as at (d) above will be required with the full code test applied.

3.5.3 DNA and fingerprint protocols

Where material evidence in the case consists of DNA or fingerprint analysis, the charge can be authorized on preliminary documentation prior to obtaining an evidentially admissible report. This staged reporting system is designed to free up the forensic service and ensure results are obtained in a timely fashion. Full evidential statements in both cases detailing the analysis will only be required if the case proceeds to trial and the veracity of the report is challenged by the defence.

3.5.4 Visual or audio recorded material

It is essential when a duty prosecutor is applying the full code test that he watches or listens to any significant evidence in the case which is in that format. Hence a copy of the material in a playable format must be provided on referral.

In some cases CPS Direct may decline a case where it is thought essential for the reviewing lawyer to view a video prior to a charging decision being made.

However, an officer (or other witness) who has viewed or listened to the recording may provide a summary of the material contents and report on its quality where the 'threshold test' is applied. A copy of the recording in playable format must be provided by the first hearing to facilitate further review.

Similarly, where a suspect in the course of a PACE interview has been shown the recording and the person confirms it is him committing the acts alleged—the record of interview will suffice.

3.5.5 Medical evidence in assault cases

In the early stages of statutory charging, duty prosecutors often requested evidence of a medical practitioner in all cases of assault causing unnecessary delay in the charging process. Medical evidence, generally, is often only relevant to the seriousness and extent of any injuries and therefore the level of charge. It will be rarely required in the case of an assault occasioning actual bodily harm, contrary to section 47 of the Offences Against the Person Act 1861 even on the full code test. It should be obtained only where any injuries can be proved with the interpretation of medical records or X-rays by medical practitioners. It will also not be required where during interview the suspect accepts the nature and extent of the injuries in a case.

It must be remembered that evidence of injury can often come from police officers or photographs or other reliable eye witnesses, and this suffices for most common assaults and other minor assault cases. Where the victim of an assault does receive medical attention it is important that the CPS is informed of that fact so that it can be disclosed to the defence.

Evidence of a medical practitioner on the application of the full code test for a charging decision will, however, be required where the proposed charges are section 20 or section 18 of the Offences Against the Person Act 1861. In such a case the medical notes should always be obtained where a statement is submitted.

3.5.6 Priority offenders

Cases involving persistent youth offenders (PYOs) and other persistent priority offenders have always presented practical problems to the statutory charging process. This is particularly so where the defendant is charged with another who is bailed and that case is not necessarily expedited. Officers should be mindful of the problems posed in such cases and try to ensure that short bail dates for the co-defendant to tie up quickly with the priority offender are sought.

Persistent youth offenders

PYOs are youth offenders aged between 10 and 17 who have been sentenced on three or more separate occasions for one or more recordable offences and within the last three years of the last sentencing occasion have been subsequently arrested for a further recordable offence. The government has set targets in these cases to ensure effective and timely finalization. The current target is 71 days. This means that police officers (especially the custody officer) must make an early identification of such youth offenders. The charging procedure should always be used (other than for routine road traffic offences).

Charging responsibilities for PYOs are the same as for adult offenders. However, because of the need for speed, where a custody officer bails a PYO (after the threshold test has been passed) the case must be referred to a prosecutor within three days of arrest to confirm likely charges and evidential requirements in the case. Thereafter these cases must be proactively managed.

Priority and prolific offenders

Again, cases involving priority and prolific offenders (PPOs, as defined locally by local criminal justice boards) who are basically persistent offenders, need to be prioritized to ensure timely case progression. Early consultations are advised as above as are short pre-charge bail dates.

3.6 The Case Building Process

3.6.1 Dialogue of the prosecution team

By working together the prosecution team, including the custody officer, the investigating officer, and the duty prosecutor, will be able to deliver a better performance drawing on each other's skills to the shared goal of bringing offenders to justice. By effective joint use of the early consultation process the police and the CPS will be able to identify weak cases and bring them to an early conclusion. It will also enable the identification of cases which can in fact be strengthened to provide a realistic prospect of conviction, providing advice to the police on necessary steps to be taken to do this or simply provide further guidance to the police on any lines of enquiry, evidential requirements, or legal points.

Example—Practical and realistic joint common sense at the charging centre

Allegation by the complainant of blackmail and kidnapping, lasting an hour in total, in an attempt to obtain monies from her. The suspect in interview said that he was in fact in a relationship with the complainant. He had lent her money and she had sent him numerous texts alleging she was with another male spending that money. The next day, therefore, he decided to confront the complainant about this and ask for the money back. He alleged that she agreed to go to a cashpoint and get the money which she did and then gave it to him.

The prosecution team did not know who to believe. There were obviously other aspects of 'real evidence' in this case but it was felt important to analyse the phone records to see if the texts alleged by the suspect were there. The results of the phone analysis appeared shortly prior to trial, at a cost of £6000, confirming the suspect's story in interview. Furthermore, CCTV footage was eventually watched by the prosecution team which confirmed that no violence or force was used at the cashpoint and the parties appeared amicable.

This is a real case—what does it tell us?

This defendant spent a considerable period of time in custody for what was essentially a case of domestic violence with one partner alleging against another a spurious allegation of blackmail. **The mobile phone and CCTV footage should have been checked at the outset, either on the police officer's own initiative or after advice from the prosecutor.**

Early action, collaboration, and pragmatic thinking cut corners enabling all parties to reach a decision about a case bringing it to an early and less costly conclusion.

It is essential therefore, that duty prosecutors and police officers develop opportunities for close liaison and regular dialogue throughout the investigative and prosecution process ensuring at all times that there is common understanding of the responsibilities of each and where each is coming from.

3.6.2 **CPS and the MG3**

Part A of the MG3 is completed by the police officer. Part B is completed by the duty prosecutor.

After reviewing all the evidence provided against the Code for Crown Prosecutors, the duty prosecutor will decide whether a charging decision can be taken. The charging decision and advice section of the MG3 for the duty prosecutor is not just to give a decision to the police but also to explain that decision. A fully completed MG3 should provide a proper and appropriate record of the charging decision and the thought process behind that decision. This is important so that police officers are able to understand essential, legal, and public interest factors that may impact on a case and are therefore in a better position to carry out any outstanding necessary action where it is required.

The duty prosecutor will always provide a copy of a completed MG3 to the investigating officer. A fully endorsed MG3 is also extremely useful to the prosecutors themselves, since it negates the necessity for further initial review and by identifying the key issues in a case saves subsequent time, unnecessary effort and resources.

3.6.3 **The charges (and charging standards)**

Where a charging decision can be made there and then, it is the duty of the prosecutor to specify the charges and draft them where necessary.

At the beginning of the chapter, reference is made to the problem of police over-charging prior to statutory charging. Police officers tended to choose the most serious of optional charges available rather than a lesser offence. The Code for Crown Prosecutors at paragraph 7 provides guidance for prosecutors on the choice of charge and specifically says that prosecutors may not always choose or continue with the most serious charge where there is a choice.

What is important is: that the charge reflects the seriousness and extent of the offending; that the charge gives the court adequate sentencing powers; and that it enables the case to be presented in a clear and simple way. Getting the charge right from the beginning is the priority. Since 2004 there have been very useful **charging standards** written jointly by the police and the CPS. Presently there are six standards relating to assaults, public order, driving offences, theft, drugs, and public justice offences. Each charging standard is in a similar format beginning with general charging guidance before the specific considerations of each offence and ending with public interest considerations.

Familiarity with these charging standards will enable police officers to understand whatever evidence is required to prove particular charges including some of the regular pitfalls. These charging standards do not override the Code for Crown Prosecutors, but are complementary to them and provide further guidance on factors to be taken into account in the most usual charging situations.

3.6.4 **Action plans**

In most cases, however strong, there will be some advice and assistance that the prosecutor can give to the police officer. This will certainly be the situation when the police have referred the case for an early consultation or where the prosecutor forms the opinion (on either test) that there is insufficient evidence to proceed at that time.

What the duty prosecutor is expected to provide here is case specific action plans for the police, listing precisely outstanding evidence or information that is required before a charging decision can be taken. Such action plans must clearly identify all necessary steps to be taken and what evidence is to be gathered. They should be detailed and focus on the trial.

The emphasis for the prosecutor apart from analysis of the case itself will be to get the best out of the police officer at the charging centre rather than sending him on his way with a list of more or less useful tasks to complete or merely requesting from him a 'full file'. A successful action plan is an integral part of case analysis.

Action plans must be action dated specifying a time for completion of the work and with a further review date in the case. The prosecutor's duty is of continuous review and, particularly where a charging decision is made on the 'threshold test', it is imperative that a review date is agreed between the police and the CPS for a time of submission of all the evidence such that the full code test can be applied and that the return bail date allows such time for full review.

Prosecutors need to be pragmatic and realistic about timetables set for police officers to complete necessary actions. They should not send the police on a mission impossible but consider seriously what can be achieved within the timescale to build the prosecution to a realistic prospect of conviction. Account will be taken of the following factors: the nature and circumstances of the case; the further evidence required; the time obtaining the further evidence will take (especially if in the hands of a third party); and the steps being taken to gather it. It is essential; for both police officers and prosecutors alike; that the case file does not merely fall into a void once an action plan has been submitted to the police. Both the action plan and the action date will be recorded on the MG3. There is a further one page form, the MG3A, which can be used to update the duty prosecutor on the progress of an enquiry in cases where further evidence is sought.

It is to be noted, however, that persons will not be charged until all agreed actions are completed. Moreover in any case referred to the duty prosecutor for advice on charging decision, and the decision of the prosecutor is to charge, caution, obtain additional evidence, or take no further action, the police should not proceed in any other way without referring the matter back to the Crown Prosecutor. The normal escalation procedures for discussion at a higher level would then follow.

3.6.5 **Alternatives to prosecution**

Both the custody officer and the Crown Prosecutor may decide that an out of court disposal is appropriate. The Code for Crown Prosecutors at paragraph 8 directs the CPS always to consider in appropriate cases the 'availability of suitable rehabilitative, reparative or restorative justice processes'.

Such alternatives will only apply where it is considered that the public interest does not require the suspect to go through the criminal courts. Other criteria also need to be met dependent on the alternative course of action.

Once the threshold test is passed the custody officer may decide to issue a fixed penalty notice for disorder or provide a simple caution. With the exception of indictable offences where the custody officer must refer the case to a duty prosecutor for a decision on a simple caution the custody officer will finalize the case accordingly. Where police have charged and the duty prosecutor considered it an appropriate case to be dealt with by way of caution, the suspect will be cautioned by the police.

Where it is an indictable case or one which must be referred to a prosecutor for a charging decision the Crown Prosecutor has a duty to consider out of court disposals and also now has the conditional caution as an option. The introduction of conditional cautioning for adults has added significantly to the range of available disposals. Cases which previously may have been charged by a custody officer alone will now require referral to a duty prosecutor before such disposal by conditional caution. There are conditional cautioning codes of practice which must be followed in reaching any decision. The duty prosecutor will advise the police on the administering of such caution in appropriate circumstances.

3.7 **Police Dos and Don'ts of Statutory Charging**

	DOs	DON'Ts
1	Do be fully aware of the Director's Guidance; s 37A–37D of PACE; the Code for Crown Prosecutors; the Charging Standards and the Manual of Guidance	Don't ignore useful guidance which is mandatory for all police officers to follow
2	Do keep up with all initiatives in your Borough—CJSSS and SP	Don't fall by the wayside in file submission
3	Do make effective use of early consultations with the CPS	Don't try to go it alone—use the trial expertise of the lawyers to assist in the investigative process
4	Do ensure all cases go through the custody officer and the threshold test is passed and that there is proper supervision of the file at the outset	Don't bypass the custody officer or try and get round the Director's Guidance by your choice of charge
5	Do make good use of pre-charge conditional bail in appropriate cases to ensure that the trial file is ready prior to charge	Don't hark back to the old days of charging on reasonable suspicion
6	Do ensure there is always a properly completed MG3 providing a clear audit trail and that the evidence appropriate to the type of case is attached	Don't hold back from informing the prosecutor of all key issues in a case and any reservations you may have about it and don't forget the relevant protocols regarding submission of evidence
7	Do ensure charging decisions are made on the full code test unless the suspect is detained in custody for a prosecutor to authorize charging	Don't refer cases in custody unnecessarily to the CPS for a lower test to be applied or promise evidence that may not be forthcoming at a later date
8	Do ensure you come away from the prosecutor with case-specific advice on evidence and an action plan	Don't be afraid to ask the prosecutor to explain, clarify, and prioritize requests for action
9	Do adhere to all completion dates on the action plan	Don't leave the action advised to take care of itself
10	Do go through the proper escalation procedures if you disagree with the duty prosecutor	Don't put pressure on the duty prosecutor at the charging centre to agree with you
11	Do begin a dialogue between yourself and duty prosecutor and continue it throughout the life of the case	Don't forget a case once it is charged or fail to notify the CPS of any changes on key issues in a case

Checklist—Key features of the statutory charging scheme

- Close working relationship between the police and CPS required—the joint prosecution team approach

- CPS, not police, authorize charge in all but routine cases—getting the charge right first time

- Police compliance with statutory charging provisions and Director's Guidance is mandatory

- Custody officers as initial gatekeepers to the duty prosecutors

- Early advice and guidance for the police on the exercise of their investigatory powers and evidential issues from the outset of a case

- Proactive duty prosecutors frontloading and focusing on the outcome from the beginning, making pragmatic and robust decisions

- Determination of charge based on a review of all the evidence submitted by the police in the appropriate format together with a full detailed MG3 report

- Charging decisions for both the police and the CPS made on the full code test, save in exceptional circumstances

- No conditional authorization of charges even where there is a substantial bail risk in anticipation of evidence being supplied

- Case-specific detailed realistic and time-bound action plans to be provided as good practice in nearly all cases

- Importance of continuous review and monitoring of all work to be done

- Improved performance and 'narrowing of the justice gap' through the benefits of statutory charging

4

Dealing with Victims and Witnesses

4.1 **Introduction**

Witnesses are central to the criminal justice process, both in relation to the initial investigation, leading to the identification of the suspect, and to the subsequent prosecution of the defendant up to trial. For the purposes of this chapter, dealing with witnesses will be examined from these two separate but linked perspectives. The first half will address issues more pertinent to the investigator in obtaining an account from the witness, while the second will look at the developments regarding witness support and testimony leading up to and during the trial, where the involvement of the CPS and the partnership approach is of greater significance.

4.1.1 **The witness and the investigation**

In all but very few proactive investigations it is information from private witnesses that leads to the identification of the suspect(s). At this—the investigative stage—the key issue with any witness is fundamentally straightforward: to obtain an untainted, truthful, and comprehensive account of what they know and is relevant to the enquiry. The apparent simplicity of this requirement does not, however, adequately reflect the numerous difficulties facing the investigative interviewer in dealing with an individual. Some witnesses are articulate and methodical with good memory retrieval skills, most however are not and will require varying degrees of assistance from the interviewer to bring out their 'best evidence'. For the purposes of this discussion a witness to an event has been assumed that requires a witness to recall details, rather than a witness who provides simple factual evidence such as a loser, or someone who produces an exhibit.

This chapter will look briefly at how the memory functions and how the interviewer can impact on the witness's ability to accurately recall events. Good interviewing technique will both assist the witness to remember more detail of the incident and limit the dangers of tainting their account. The basic structure of the interview—PEACE—will be addressed and note taking and writing the witness statement itself, including the five-part structure, will be explained. After looking at the more general witness interview the chapter will move onto looking at special considerations such as identifying and interviewing vulnerable and intimidated witnesses including children, as well as significant/key witnesses and reluctant and/or hostile witnesses. The use of videotapes at witness interviews will be discussed, both where the tape is unused material in support of a written witness statement and where the recording can be used as the witness's testimony—commonly referred to as an Achieving Best Evidence (ABE) interview.

4.1.2 **The witness and the prosecution**

In the past, after the witness had made a statement, often there would be little or no contact with the police until a court date was set for trial. There was little support beyond the initiative of the officer in the case and often witnesses were bewildered and worried about giving evidence. Prosecuting counsel were precluded from speaking to witnesses and their anxieties and convenience were often a long way down the list of priorities for the court. Considering the importance of witness testimony to the trial process little concern was given to helping the witness to provide their evidence.

Today the CJS is much more committed to finding ways to make the process more witness-friendly in order to ensure that the testimony the court hears is the most accurate and reliable available. In the second part of this chapter the special measures available to assist the witness in giving evidence and the use of live-link testimony will be considered as will the problems encountered with witnesses. Here the CPS takes a more proactive role, together with the police, in witness assessment and care and in ensuring the witness gets to court to give their best evidence.

4.2 **Witness Interviewing**

4.2.1 **Free recall**

Historically training for investigators on how to deal with witnesses was limited to writing a witness's statement and was focused on creating a succinct account of what admissible evidence that individual would be able to provide. The court was concerned simply with the quality of the testimony that was given and little reference was made to the interview of the witness. Over the last 25 years there has been much more focus at trials on how the witness interview that led to their statement was conducted, with the defence moving from attacking the testimony of the witness itself to attacking the process by which the statement was obtained. In addition a great deal of academic work showed that the interviewing style of the statement taker is capable of inadvertently tainting the account of the witness, while at the same time not necessarily helping the witness to provide the best account of the event that they could.

Today the whole process by which a witness account came into existence is subject to examination by the court, especially how did the witness's important pieces of evidence emerge? Was it as a result of the witness freely remembering the event? Or was it after the interviewer asked a particular question? If so, what question? Consider a witness who at trial, having refreshed his/her memory by reading their statement, says the following in evidence:

Then I heard him say to the other man—I shot him.

The witness statement records the same evidence. However, let us ask how this piece of information—that the witness heard this comment—became known.

Consider if it was said by the witness during the interview, but in response to each of the following three different questions:

> Can you tell me what happened?
> Did you hear what he said?
> Did you hear him say 'I shot him'?

In each case the witness statements would read much the same, however, in the first example the witness has recalled the evidence without any particular input by the interviewer. In the second the witness recalled the evidence but only after prompting by the interviewer. Here the interviewer is effectively telling the witness, that the man did speak. In the third example the witness only mentions the evidence when the interviewer specifically puts the question as something that occurred and which the witness either did or did not hear.

This is not to suggest that in any example the witness is lying or mistaken, but it is clearly the case that the quality of the witness evidence in the first instance is much better because it is the witness's free recall, while the third example taints the account because the information came first from the interviewer. Clearly, therefore, evidence obtained through free recall is the best evidence available and the efforts of the interviewer should be directed towards securing as much of this type of information as possible.

4.2.2 **Witnesses and memory**

The investigator wants to obtain a comprehensive, untainted and truthful account of an event, or series of events, from a witness. But the investigator and the lawyer(s) want that account in an organized, coherent, and ideally chronological form. This opens up a tension between what the interviewer wants and what the witness is able to provide for memory does not work in this way. If we were to ask an acquaintance to tell us about their holiday, they might say:

> We went to Spain, had a great time, the kids loved it, really nice resort, food was good, not too busy. We really like it, we've been there before.

What happens is that asking about their holiday triggers some key memories—the place, the generality of how the holiday went, some highlights—or perhaps particular low points—some information of significance to the witness. All of the information the witness has about the holiday is not stored together in the memory, there is no category of 'Foreign Holiday 2007' that the witness can access and will open up all the information in the order needed to write a chronological statement. The most abiding memory might be something that happened at the end of the holiday:

> Q   Tell me about your holiday last year.
> A   It was awful, Michael ended up in hospital, we were on our way to the
>   airport to come home and the coach crashed.

If the purpose of asking the question was to elicit an account in order to write a statement the interviewer would want to start perhaps with the booking of the holiday and then move onto the travel arrangements, before asking for a day-by-day account, leaving the accident until the end. This tension explains why interviewers frequently interrupt witnesses. In the example, the resort is at the forefront of the witness memory but the interviewer wants to start with the booking.

Consider this interview of a robbery victim:

Q   Can you tell me what happened yesterday?
A   Well I went to the post office and when I came out this horrible man pushed me down and took my purse.
Q   OK I know it's upsetting, but can we please start with when you left home.

The interviewer here is forcing the witness to recollect the event in a way that makes it easier to produce a chronological account. Most witnesses will allow this to happen and if it is done with kindness and consideration the witness will feel happy with the outcome. However, it will make the process of remembering much more difficult for the witness and will result in less relevant information being recalled.

Interviewers must be aware that information about an event is stored in the memory in a variety of places and what comes out first tends to be that which is most important to the witness. Equally, the memory has a tendency to dismiss and filter that which is considered unimportant. The witness needs the freedom to move about the event, in order to bring out the detail.

The witness's free account provides the best evidence and that evidence is likely to be most detailed if the witness is encouraged to access their memory of the event in a way that suits that individual, with the minimal influence from the interviewer. Cognitive interviewing techniques—which will be examined later—may be used by the interviewer to help this process without tainting the resulting information.

4.2.3 **PEACE**

While there is a bewildering array of instructions, techniques, and advice on how best to interview particular types of witnesses, the core skill for an interviewer is a good understanding of the PEACE model and how to apply it in particular circumstances. PEACE forms the structured basis of any investigative interview—whether with a suspect or a witness. It is sufficiently adaptable for approaching any witness interview from the most mature and articulate to children or vulnerable adults, and should be the starting point for considering in advance how the interview should be conducted in order to elicit a comprehensive, truthful, and accurate account.

P Planning and preparation
E Engage and explain
A Account, clarify, and challenge
C Closure
E Evaluate

The model, developed from academic research, is now internationally recognized.

Planning and preparation

This involves thinking in advance about the interview that is to be conducted and covers the following broad areas:

- the investigation;
- the witness;
- the law; and
- practicalities.

The investigation will cover the circumstances of the offence, why this person is being interviewed, and what evidence may they be able to provide. Each interview will have aims and objectives and these should be identified. The nature of the offence under investigation—such as violence or sexual offences—may have an impact on the practical arrangements. Some commentators feel that the less an interviewer knows about the circumstances of the offence the better, as it reduces the chances of contamination or of confirmatory bias—where the interviewer looks only for that information which supports an existing hypothesis. In reality, however, an interviewer needs to know about the offence in order to conduct a properly focused interview and an awareness of the potential problems of bias should be enough to reduce the risk.

The witness is the most important factor because the nature of the person will often dictate the nature of the interview. It is vital to identify whether the witness is a child or a vulnerable adult, a key or significant witness, or whether they are intimidated—although this is something that may not become apparent until the interview is actually being conducted. Definitions of these special witnesses and guidance regarding interviews with them will be discussed later. Interviewers should in every case focus on the needs and convenience of the individual witness during their preparation and planning in order to allow the best possible chance of obtaining their best evidence.

The law involves ensuring that the witness account is compiled in accordance with section 9 of the Magistrates' Court Act 1980 so that it is admissible in evidence. This is the case regardless of whether the statement is written or visually recorded. Any exhibits referred to will need to be introduced in accordance with instructions.

Practicalities will cover such issues as plans, documents, or photographs that would assist in obtaining the account, whether sufficient time has been set aside to complete the interview, or where and when the interview should be conducted.

Checklist—Planning and preparation

- Aim and objective(s) of interview
- Type/severity of offence
- Circumstances of offence
- How offence came to police notice
- Age of witness
- Mental capacity of witness
- Nature of any disorder or disability
- Effect of disorder on witness behaviour
- Reading and writing abilities
- Gender and sexuality
- Race, culture, and ethnicity
- Language
- Effects of any drugs or drink
- Is witness frightened/concerned?
- Use of intermediary
- Videotape
- Time of day for interview
- Location of interview
- Anticipated length of interview
- Effects of traumatic recall
- Presence of guardian/friend
- Previous experience of police
- Experience and training of interviewer
- Note taking
- Passing urgent information back to investigation
- CPS early involvement

Engage and explain

This may be seen in terms of rapport building: explaining to the witnesses the formal aspects of the process; whether the interviewer will be videotaping the interview or just producing a written record; how the interview will proceed, how long it will take, and that the witness is free to ask for a break. The interviewer should ensure that the process is personalized and an acceptable form of address is used. Every effort needs to be made to reduce anxiety in the witness as this is a barrier to effective recollection; the interviewer needs to listen actively and not interrupt unless absolutely necessary. The witness should be told to concentrate on the event and to take their time to provide as much detail as possible. They should be encouraged to ask questions about anything that is not clear to them and they must be prepared to go over the event more than once. It will always be useful to ensure that it is made clear to the witness that they should report everything.

Account, clarify, and challenge

This would generally amount to encouraging the witness to produce a free recall of the event before clarifying that recall through questioning. A free recall involves the witness giving their account, in their own words, at their own pace, and in their own chronological order. The more comprehensive this account can be the better the quality of the evidence. The opening question should be considered carefully prior to the interview, taking account of what it is intended to generate in the witness. Allowing the witness time for free recall does not mean that the interviewer should be silent. It would be a rare witness who was able to provide a full account without any assistance or encouragement from an interviewer, such as nodding or reminding the witness to take their time. Questions at this stage should be limited to such things as 'What happened then?' or 'How?'.

After the witness has provided a free recall the interviewer should divide up the account into manageable parts or topics, such as the journey to the scene, the suspect, the attack, the property, the weapon, injuries, or whatever is appropriate for the event. These topics should then be covered in turn by the witness focusing on each topic area one by one. This allows the witness to go through the whole event a second time but with more specific focus. Once each topic area has been covered by the witness some details may need to be clarified by the interviewer and this will involve specific questioning. Open questions based around 'What happened next?' or 'How did that happen?' are still more productive in terms of the quality and quantity of information they reveal. However, it may be necessary to ask much more focused questions such as 'What colour was the car?' or 'Did he say anything?'. It is vitally important that no information is given away in the question, as in the earlier example of 'Did you hear him say "I shot him"?', rather ask the witness to go over that part of the event again.

Challenging is an important phase in the witness interview. This is where the interviewer needs to confront the witness with any inconsistencies in their account, and/or any conflicting material from elsewhere in the investigation. There is, however, much debate about whether this is appropriate in cases of sexual assault. In the past challenging has been focused on the interviewer making moral judgements about a victim's sexual behaviour, their alcohol or drug use, or just a perceived implausibility of their account. Challenging in such cases must have a factual basis, there should be a clear factual conflict either between something the witness said earlier or on another occasion—such as at the first time a victim told somebody what had happened—or where what the witness says is in direct contrast to other information. Where there is any doubt in such cases, challenging the witness should be postponed until advice from either a tier 5 interview adviser or the CPS has been sought.

Closure

Attention to closure is important because it can create a favourable attitude in the witness towards future dealings with police. Considering whether the interview has covered the aims and objectives identified in the planning stage is part of closure and may lead back to the account phase. A core aim is always to ensure that the witness has provided all the information that they are able—and are willing—to provide. Further interviews and statements covering more detail of matters already discussed do not help the credibility of the witness. Every effort should be made to obtain a full account at the first opportunity. The witness should be clear about what has happened and what is likely to happen next, in particular that they have provided a witness statement which may require them to attend court and give evidence. Support services such as Victim Support or if appropriate Family Liaison should be made available. Leave the witness feeling happy to discuss matters in the future.

Evaluate

This involves assessing the investigation in the light of the new material provided by the witness, however it also provides an opportunity for reflection on interviewing performance. It is generally the case in interviewing that we underestimate the extent to which an interviewer can influence the interview. If the interview went well it would be due in no small part to the actions of the interviewer in the way they managed the witness and drew out their account. Equally, though, responsibility must be accepted for an interview that went badly.

4.2.4 **Phased interviewing**

Phased interviewing is a particular structure that is compatible with PEACE but focuses fully on the actual interaction with the witness. The main phases are:

- Establish rapport
- Obtain free recall
- Question
- Closure

Establishing rapport involves the interviewer working to ensure that there is mutually successful communication with the witness. It involves building trust with the witness and treating them with respect and consideration. This is generated by openness and personalizing the interaction, and by the overt display of attentiveness. Empathy in terms of understanding the witness's predicament, their difficulty in remembering the detail, their anxiety about making a statement, and their concerns about attending court, will help immensely. Too many interviewers see rapport as simply chatting about a non-relevant issue like football or TV programmes. Rapport in truth is far more about the manner of interaction with someone than it is about what is being discussed.

The phased interview accents the importance of the witness's free recall and its independence from questioning by the interviewer. The evidence/information obtained in this free recall phase is—as we have seen—of significantly better quality than that which emerges from specific questioning.

The question phase involves the interviewer seeking more detail and greater clarification from the witness. As the evidence obtained here will be in response to the interviewers questioning its quality is weaker than that obtained through free recall.

Finally the closure phase is again important and the same as laid out above in the PEACE model.

Understanding this model should prevent the interviewers forcing the witness to try and provide a chronological account to the convenience of the interviewer but to the detriment of the witness's ability to recall the event. Phased interviewing is the base structure upon which cognitive interviewing and enhanced cognitive interviewing techniques are used to help witnesses in their recollection of events.

4.2.5 Cognitive and enhanced cognitive interviewing

On *Crimewatch* the presenter frequently asks whether viewers can remember anything unusual happening on a particular day, and when doing so s/he often holds up a copy of a newspaper from the day of interest and describes what was in the news headlines or talks about what was on TV. The purpose of this is to assist us in remembering detail if we are able to think back to what we were doing and experiencing at that particular time. If we lose something—like our door keys—we may retrace our steps at the time of the loss:

> Now what did I do? I let myself in the house with the keys and then put my bag down inside the door, took off my coat and went into the kitchen, etc.

In academic terms this is called 'mentally restating the context' and it is a very important cognitive interviewing technique.

All of these techniques come from research into what helps us to remember detail and conversely what hinders us from doing so. It is not necessary to use all the techniques all of the time, some will be more appropriate than others according to the circumstances of the investigation and the event(s) being recalled by the witness. However, each has been shown to assist a witness in memory retrieval to some extent.

Checklist—Cognitive interviewing techniques

- Focused concentration

- Report everything

- Transfer of control

- Mental restatement of context

- Extensive retrieval

- Varied recall

- Witness compatible questioning

Focused concentration is necessary for memory retrieval and the witness should be told that they have as much time as they need, without interruptions, to concentrate on remembering detail. The witness will search their own memory at a pace that suits them, interference by the interviewer will mitigate against detailed memory retrieval. The witness should be told to report everything that they can without editing and that no detail is insignificant. Witnesses might assume that the interviewer already knows something and does not need to be told again or they might think something is not important. The interviewer's role here is to help the witness remember an event, and although the witness might expect to be asked a long series of questions, they should instead be encouraged to feel a transfer of control from the interviewer to the witness. They dictate the flow of information they are supplying. The interviewer should make it clear that their job is to listen, it is for the witness to do the talking, uninterrupted. This is often very difficult for interviewers used to being in control.

Having set a series of ground rules for the witness, the interviewer needs to talk to the witness about mentally recreating the context in which the event originally occurred. It may sometimes be possible to do this by taking the witness to the actual location, although this is not always necessary. The witness could be asked to think about the sights and sounds or smells associated with the event—called multiple representations. Plans or photographs or objects may help to set the scene. There are some suggestions that this should be talked of in the present tense as if the witness were reliving the event, however interviewers need to be acutely aware of the stress and anxiety that this can generate in a witness who is being encouraged to recall a traumatic event.

The more often a witness thinks about an event the more detail will be remembered, so extensive retrieval should be encouraged. This may be as simple as asking the witness to go through their account once more, taking it more slowly and searching for greater detail. Alternatively the witness could be asked to vary their recall, to think about the event in a different order, perhaps starting at the end of the event and thinking about what happened immediately before.

Finally, any questioning following the witness's free recall must be witness compatible. This means that questions must arise from what the witness has said and not from any pre-prepared interviewer list. Clearly the interviewer's agenda will influence the interview in terms of areas of relevance, but particular questions must arise from what the witness says. This is not simply to prevent the interviewer introducing material in the hope that the witness will corroborate it, it is to ensure that it is the witness who is recalling the event in their own way and at their own pace and that the interviewer is actively listening and engaging with the witness who is in control.

4.2.6 Achieving Best Evidence (ABE)

The **Criminal Justice Act 1991** introduced provisions to enable child witnesses to be interviewed on videotape and have the recording used as testimony at court. To accompany the legislation the Home Office subsequently published the *Memorandum of Good Practice on Video Recorded Interviews with Child Witnesses for Criminal Proceedings*, and interviews conducted in accordance with these guidelines became known as Memorandum interviews. The **Youth Justice and Criminal Evidence Act 1999** extended these provisions to include vulnerable and/or intimidated adult witnesses—each defined by the act—as well as introducing a raft of additional special measures available from the investigation through to trial to help the witness to provide the best evidence that they could. The Home Office guidance that accompanied these changes became known as Achieving Best Evidence (ABE).

Initially the expression ABE was used to refer to those interviews that were videotaped in the expectation that the recording would be used in court as the testimony of the witness. However, over time ABE has come to be used more generally to refer to dealing with witnesses who require particular assistance in order to provide their evidence by reason of their physical or mental condition. The current ABE guidelines therefore deal both with the conduct of the interview and the support measures available thereafter and potentially cover interviews with child witnesses, vulnerable witnesses, intimidated witnesses, significant witnesses, reluctant witnesses, and hostile witnesses. Of course witnesses may well fall into more than one of those categories.

Child, vulnerable, and intimidated witnesses will be interviewed by ABE trained interviewers, and—with the consent of the witness—the interview will be videotaped in the expectation that the video can be played in court as the witness's evidence. Interviews with these different categories of special witnesses will be dealt with in more detail later.

4.2.7 **Making notes**

The **Criminal Procedure and Investigations Act 1996** requires that during a criminal investigation all relevant material is recorded and retained so that it is not difficult to see that what is said between an interviewer and a witness in preparation of a witness is relevant. We have seen how it is very unlikely that a witness will provide information to an interviewer in the order and detail in which it can be immediately turned into a witness statement. It is the case therefore that in all but the most simple of statements the interviewer will make notes of what the witness says before s/he begins to write the statement. Those notes will form the basis of the statement and will become unused material.

If we consider note taking within the phased interview model (rapport, free recall, questions, and closure), we can see that during the rapport phase the making of notes needs to be explained to the witness. The witness should be told of the need to record accurately and in detail what they say and that the interviewer will be writing in long hand and using the words of the witnesses. It is good practice to record the opening question to the witness designed to elicit the first recall and some thought needs to go into this opening question. The witness should also be told that that they will not be asked questions until they have finished saying what they can remember about the event. The interviewer needs to record this without interrupting the witness—it is useful to agree in advance a sign—like a raised hand—to slow the witness down if they are speaking too quickly. As we have seen this free recall is the best evidence that a witness can provide—a free and uninfluenced recollection of the event.

From these notes the interviewer is able to see topic areas that require further detail. This might be about how the witness came to be where they were, further information about the scene, a description of the suspect or words used during the event: anything that the interviewer needs the witness to elaborate on. The interviewer then conducts a series of mini interviews focusing the witness on each of these areas in turn. The topics might cover the whole of the witness's first recall divided into manageable parts and there is no reason why they may not run chronologically. Notes therefore would consist of a lengthy initial free recall, which will probably not be chronological and will have varied degrees of detail. Thereafter there should be a note of a particular topic raised by the interviewer— the journey to the scene for example—followed by more of what the witness says when asked to focus on this particular topic. By this means the witness is not taken repeatedly through the event as a whole, but is given more attempts at further recall of isolated or self-contained sections. Once the topics have been fully explored the interviewer may need to ask very specific questions to clarify particular details, and these may be open or closed questions. The responses to these should be noted separately.

At this stage the interviewer will have comprehensive notes which reveal not only what information was recalled by the witness but how, in what order, and in response to what input from the interviewer. The notes provide a detailed and accurate record of the progress of the interview that led to the witness's statement.

4.2.8 The five-part structured witness statement

The notes created should provide the interviewer with sufficient information to allow the creation of a comprehensive witness statement. The 'five-part structured statement' has its origins in the Major Incident Room Standard Administration Procedures (MIRSAP), and the Home Office Large Major Enquiry System (HOLMES). These are both organizational structures for managing large investigations, usually murder or terrorist cases, where the amount of material and information being generated by the investigation calls for a systematic approach to assessing it.

Indexing information lies at the core of the HOLMES system, this means pulling apart each piece of information and storing it on a retrievable index that can be searched as more information comes into the system. For example, if during house-to-house enquiries it emerges that a witness saw a motor cycle in the area immediately before a shooting and then again afterwards, making off at speed, a search could be made of indexes created from all the information received during the investigation to see whether a motor cycle has been referred to elsewhere. If not a new record will be made of the motor cycle that can be searched against future information. Indexes cover people, including descriptions, places, vehicle locations, telephone numbers, and various others. The information from a witness statement therefore needs to be easily identified for indexing and the five-part structure helps to do this.

Five-part statement structure

(1) Introduction
(2) People
(3) Places
(4) Evidence
(5) Legal

The statement should be written in accordance with this model therefore because it aids information retrieval for those reading it.

The introduction should state what the statement is about, for example:

> This statement refers to an incident that happened on Monday 1 January at about 2 pm when I was attacked and robbed.
>
> or
>
> This statement concerns a burglary that occurred at my workplace, Jenkins Electrics, 25 High Street.

This allows the statement to be clearly identified as relevant to the particular investigation.

The second part of the statement should introduce people—known to the witness—who will be referred to in the statement and their relationship with the witness:

> I shall refer to my brother Peter Smith, my personal friend, Colin Jones and the landlord of the pub, John Robertson.

The third part deals with places that the witness will talk about. It should cover full physical descriptions where relevant and if necessary include photographs and/or sketch plans referred to as exhibits:

> I shall refer to the Rose and Crown Public House, located at the junction of the High Street and Reynolds Avenue. This is a large detached building with a car park area in front and to the right-hand side and a large beer garden to the rear. The pub has two bars: a lounge to the left and a sports bar to the right side, with its own entrance from the car park.

The fourth part is the evidence itself and should consist of a chronological account of the event from the witness's perspective. It is important that the statement is, as much as possible, in the actual words of the witness in order to allow a reader to get a clear picture of what the witness is likely to say in giving evidence and how they are likely to say it. In the past witness accounts were often recorded in terms that the witness would not actually use. This was because many witnesses speak in a grammatical and incoherent way that does not lend itself to creating a concise and formal account of what they saw. Today this is considered bad practice.

The rules of admissibility have altered considerably over the past few years, in particular with regard to hearsay evidence. Hearsay is quite complicated but at the risk of over-simplification, it may be defined as something that the witness does not know for him/herself but has been told by someone else. In the past it was considered very important that the interviewing officer had a clear understanding of what constituted hearsay evidence and made sure that the witness statement did not contain anything inadmissible. Today hearsay may be admitted in evidence and so it should be included in the witness's statement where it is important.

The concluding part covers legal issues—where, for example, a description of the suspect would go—and the provisions of *R v Turnbull* [1977] QB 224. This is a case in which a suspect was seen by a witness and the defendant was subsequently identified at an identity parade as being the person involved. The defence argued that the witness had made a mistake in the identification. Clearly, it is possible for a witness to make an honest but wrong identification, so to help the jury decide whether the witness was accurate or not the court laid out a series of facts about the circumstances of the first sighting for the jury to consider. Including such things as: how long did the witness see the suspect; how far away were they; did they have clear visibility; had they seen the person before; and are there any mistakes in the witness's description given at the time compared with what the identified person looks like.

Since the case it has been good practice to deal with these factors at the time of taking the witness's interview and so they should be covered in all witness statements where a suspect description is given.

POINT TO NOTE—R v TURNBULL	
A	Amount of time observed
D	Distance witness was away from suspect
V	Visibility conditions
O	Obstructions to vision
K	Known to the witness before
A	Any particular reason to remember
T	Time since seeing the suspect
E	Errors in the witness account

The first witness statement—usually taken shortly after an incident but before any identification process—is not likely to have to deal with any errors. This is more likely to become an issue only once an identification has been made, when the witness will make a further statement, in which any discrepancy between their first description and the actual appearance of the suspect will have to be addressed.

The concluding part of the statement should also cover any consent issues relating to medical records, Data Protection Act material, or the release of documents from other agencies. It should include the values of property lost or damaged, compensation claims, or anything not already dealt with. It should not include a willingness or otherwise to attend court, but this should certainly be noted on the MG6 form as information to the CPS. The back of an MG11 (witness statement) also contains important information which the officer should complete. This is dealt with at 6.22 .

4.2.9 Victim personal statements

Part of a commitment to placing victims at the forefront of the CJS was the creation of the 'victim personal statement' (VPS), sometimes referred to as an impact statement. Its purpose is to give the victim an opportunity to make known to the various criminal justice agencies how they have been affected, emotionally, physically, financially, or psychologically by the offence. Also it allows the victim to make known their wishes regarding information about the case development, compensation, or other assistance. It is also a vehicle by which the victim may express concerns about intimidation from the offender.

It is not intended to provide a means for the victim to comment on any particular form of sentence, although the court is entitled to take account of all the evidence it has regarding the offence. It is entirely optional and no pressure should be placed on a victim to elicit a VPS.

The victim is entirely free to say whatever s/he wishes and the statement has the status of any other piece of evidence in the case. A victim should be provided with a leaflet explaining the VPS system at any early stage in the case. It is not necessary to wait until a prosecution is evident, indeed a VPS may be made shortly after the offence, to reflect the impact properly. Some victims may wish to make a VPS some time after the offence when the longer-term effects are more apparent, equally a victim may wish to make both an immediate VPS and a supplementary one at a later date. The statement itself should be separate from any evidential statement and should be in the actual words of the victim if at all possible.

4.2.10 **The problem of witness inconsistencies**

If all witnesses were able to give evidence the day after the event, the quality of the evidence would improve dramatically because the incident would be fresh in the mind of the witness. Usually when a witness makes a statement it is quite close to the event but when they give evidence it is often many months later. In most cases witnesses will read their statement to refresh their memory before going into the witness-box, but inevitably their recollection of the actual event is diminished.

Unfortunately, reliability of a witness is often judged by the consistency of a witness's evidence in the witness-box with their pre-trial statement. Although witnesses are allowed to refer to their statements as an aide memoire, advocates often prefer witness to give live evidence in court without reference to them. However, this does not stop the defence in cross-examination making the most of any inconsistency between the pre-trial statement and their live evidence, and in a significant number of cases the end result is an undeserved acquittal of the defendant.

Arguably, in at least a percentage of these cases, the written statement of the witness has been undermined by poor statement taking by the police officer. That is why it is so vitally important for the police officer to ensure that the written record is an accurate and undistorted account providing attention to detail.

POINT TO NOTE

Because the content of statements is controlled by what investigators who record them choose to include, attempts to use a statement to test consistency often degenerate into a farce with unresolved conflict over just exactly what the witness did or did not say to the police.

D Wolchover and A Heaton-Armstrong, *Counsel*, July 2007, 12

Wolchover and Heaton-Armstrong have stated that the traditional police practice of recording witness statements in writing is the reason why in fact many guilty defendants are acquitted. They suggest that interviews with all significant key witnesses in every either-way or indictable offence should be electronically recorded. In the meantime, however, police officers should take note of the tips given within the chapter on the best methods of interviewing witnesses and writing their statements correctly.

4.3 Special Witness Interviews

A solution to the problem of delay between witnessing an event and giving evidence about it is for the witness's statement actually to be their testimony. Instead of the statement merely being a written record of what the witness can say in evidence, the statement becomes their evidence. In order to safeguard the process the witness should give their statement on videotape, and so long as the interview which produced the account has been properly conducted the product should be the best evidence that that witness is capable of providing.

The law enabling the videotaped witness interview to be used as testimony has been in force for child witnesses/victims of sex or violence offences since 1988. So successful has this been that the facility has been extended by the Youth Justice and Criminal Evidence Act 1999 and the Criminal Justice Act 2003 to certain adult witnesses, although not all the provisions have yet been fully enacted. Currently this applies to any adult who is identified as vulnerable or who is the victim of a sex offence and witnesses who are identified as intimidated. It is anticipated that it will subsequently be extended to significant or key witnesses.

This section therefore will address those witnesses who are identified in the planning stage as needing special attention as a result of their age, their mental and/or physical condition or their closeness to the offence or offender. Such witnesses require greater skill on the part of the interviewers in order to assist them in bringing out their best evidence. The law recognizes too that such witnesses very often need extra help and has adopted the term 'special measures' to cover those arrangements that may be made to assist the witnesses to provide their best evidence. These will be addressed later in this chapter. (See further K Smith and S Tilney *Vulnerable and Adult Child Witnesses* (Oxford: Oxford University Press, 2007).)

4.3.1 Children

A child witness, ie a person under 17 years of age, is especially vulnerable to poor interviewing technique, and can be inadvertently led through the use of ill-considered questions. Most children will attempt to respond to authority figures in a way that they hope will meet with their approval. This leads to the danger of children saying what they think an interviewer wants to hear. So in all but the most simple cases, interviews of children should be carried out by experienced and trained interviewers. Interviews of child witnesses in cases of sex and/or violence should be video recorded unless the witness objects or videotaping is an element of the offence being investigated. In all other cases a decision needs to be made whether to video the interview or not, subject to the specific circumstances of the investigation. The over-riding considerations should be enabling the witness to provide their best possible evidence and the significance—or potential significance—of their evidence to the investigation.

There is now no need to prove a child's competence to give evidence. However, it is good practice to address the notion of truth and lies in the rapport phase at the start of the interview. An example of a child doing something and then denying it can be followed by the question:

Is (John) telling the truth or telling a lie or don't you know?

Assuming the child is able to identify the lie, s/he could then be asked what John should have said when he was asked. In addition during the rapport phase the interviewer must assure the child that s/he has done nothing wrong and ground rules should be set to reduce the risk of tainting the witness's account. This would include telling the witness they are free to say they don't know, or they don't understand, or correct any summary the interviewer might make if they get it wrong.

Interviewers need to be particularly careful about explaining the reason or purpose of the interview, as again there is a danger of leading the child witness. This concern needs to extend to the opening question, which must not be worded so as to pre-suppose an event happened or happened in a particular way. Equally, prompts during the free recall phase must be neutral such as: 'I see', rather than 'good' or 'oh right'. Children will vary in the amount of free recall they provide and patience is required to allow the child plenty of time to respond. Questions should be short and open where at all possible such as: 'What happened next?'. Closed questions should only be used when absolutely necessary because open questions are far more productive and less likely to lead to corrupting the account of the witness.

Closure of the interview should include a summary of the key evidential points, thanking the witness for their help and answering any questions that they may have about what has happened and what happens next.

4.3.2 **Vulnerable witnesses**

A vulnerable witness is defined by Chapter 1 of the Youth Justice and Criminal Evidence Act 1999 as:

- a witness with a mental disorder;
- a witness with a learning disability;
- a witness with a physical disability; and
- a witness aged under 17.

Child witnesses (under 17) are therefore all defined as vulnerable. Adult vulnerable witnesses, as we have seen may have the videotape recording of their interview used as their testimony, and need therefore to be identified at an early stage in the enquiry. In identifying adult vulnerable witnesses, interviewers should consider obtaining the assistance of a clinical psychologist, or a psychiatrist in some cases.

As with child witnesses, vulnerable witnesses are particularly susceptible to poor interviewing technique, especially in looking for approval from authority figures—such as police officers. The interviewer needs to be particularly careful to avoid inadvertently influencing the witness by implying, through their behaviour, that certain answers or responses are 'right' while others are not.

Mental disorder is defined under the Mental Health Act 1983 as mental illness, arrested or incomplete mental development, psychopathic disorder and any other disorder or disability of the mind. It may be very difficult to identify such individuals since mental disorders may fluctuate in severity.

Learning disability is a term used to describe a number of different conditions which do not amount to mental disorders but which impact negatively on a person's ability with regard to social functioning or learning. People suffering from learning disability may display the following signs:

- a slow or confused reaction to questioning;
- difficulty in understanding the questions being asked;
- inability and/or difficulty with reading and writing;
- speech problems;
- conceptual difficulties, eg sequences of events, times, and dates; and
- recall problems.

Some people with learning difficulties may be quite articulate and reluctant to reveal their condition.

Physical disabilities are generally easier to identify, however the essential principle with each of these types of witness remains the same: how may they be assisted to provide their best evidence?

Officers should be aware now of the availability of intermediaries at the interviewing stage to assist in assessing the needs of the witness and in communication.

4.3.3 **Intimidated witnesses**

An intimidated witness is any witness where the quality of their evidence is likely to be diminished because of fear or distress of testifying in court. Special measures are required to enable them to provide their best evidence. Subject to resource implications these witnesses may also have the opportunity to have their statement videotaped and then used as their testimony. Such a witness may otherwise have their interview video recorded but then a written statement produced, in these circumstances the witness will be required to give live evidence at court often via a TV link or behind screens.

Experience shows that intimidated witnesses are more likely to retract their statement or have apparent difficulty recalling events at court. Thus video recording their interview provides good evidence of the integrity of their account at the time of the interview.

Intimidated witnesses generally provide the interviewer with the opposite problems to a vulnerable witness, in that the interviewer is confronted with somebody who may not want to tell the interviewer anything or everything that they know. Patience and the ability of the interviewer to empathize with the situation in which the witness finds themselves will be decisive during the engaging/rapport phase. The skills of the interviewer to manage the conversation will be fully tested in these circumstances. Assurances as to the assistance that may be available will be necessary, and early consultation with the CPS will be essential.

In very serious cases there is a 'witness protection scheme' available for those under serious threat of harm including relocation and/or change of identity under the Serious Organised Crime and Police Act 2005. This should be viewed as an exceptional measure to be used sparingly.

4.3.4 Key/significant witnesses

This is a category of witness found only in major crime cases such as homicide. 'Key' or 'significant' witnesses' are defined in the Murder Manual as:

- those who may have been, or claim to have been, an eye-witness or a witness to the immediate event in some other way; and/or
- those who stand in a particular relationship to the victim or have a central position in the enquiry.

It is the responsibility of the senior investigating officer to designate such people.

These witnesses should generally be interviewed on video or if not then audio-taped, in order to improve the quality and quantity of their information. The video of their interview cannot be used as their testimony unless they are also vulnerable and/or intimidated, however the implementation of section 137 of the Criminal Justice Act 2003—see below—will change this.

4.3.5 Section 137 of the Criminal Justice Act 2003

This section will allow for the more extensive use of video-recorded interviews as testimony. Where the case is triable at Crown Court and the evidence is from a witness to:

(i) events alleged by the prosecution to include conduct constituting the offence or part of the offence; or
(ii) events closely connected with such events.

If so and the interview was video recorded, and at the time of the interview the events were fresh in the mind of the witness, then the court can allow the video recording to be played as the witness's testimony. The court would need to be satisfied that the witness's recollection was significantly better when videoed than it would be now. In other words finding the way to get the witness's best evidence.

Clearly there is a good deal of similarity between what might be called section 137 witnesses and key/significant witnesses, and there is no mention of vulnerability or intimidation. However, the resource implications of this section for both the police and the courts are so serious that it has not yet been enacted.

4.4 **Special Measures**

4.4.1 **Protection for witnesses**

Video-recorded testimony is just one of a raft of 'special measures' available to enable witnesses to give their best evidence at court. Under the Youth Justice and Criminal Evidence Act 1999 a court has the power to make a Special Measures Order where appropriate so that additional steps may be taken for those witnesses who need extra help. Those eligible for these special measures fall into two of the categories of witness already considered—vulnerable (section 16) and intimidated (section 17).

Additionally the courts have also had the discretion at common law to take appropriate steps to assist witnesses. These have included such things as witness anonymity and giving evidence under a pseudonym, and the use of screens and voice modifiers to hide the identity of the witness. Also, intermediaries have been used to facilitate communication with witnesses in the past under these common law provisions. Their use—or the use of intermediaries—has now been rolled out nationally.

The importance of the detailed completion of the MG2 form by the police officer at the earliest stage is dealt with in detail at 6.3. Ultimately it will be a decision for the judge based on all the circumstances of the case, the views of the victim, and the quality of information in the application made by the CPS as to the special measures allowed.

POINT TO NOTE—AVAILABLE SPECIAL MEASURES

- Screens to ensure the witness cannot see the defendant
- Live TV link to allow the witness to give evidence from outside the court
- Clearing the court so the evidence is given in private with no one in the public gallery
- Removal of lawyers' wigs and gowns in court
- Video-recorded evidence in chief
- Pre-recorded video cross-examination*
- Use of intermediaries—approved professionals to help a witness communicate
- Use of communication aids such as an alphabet board

*Not yet implemented

4.4.2 Special measures for vulnerable witnesses

All vulnerable witnesses, except children, must also show that unless a special measure is granted the quality of their evidence is likely to be diminished because of their disability and the court will take account of their views. In the case of children, there is a presumption that evidence in chief will be given by pre-recorded video and cross-examination by live TV link. The quality test is still applied unless the case is one of violence, abduction, neglect, or sex (VANS) in which case the quality test does not need to be met. However, the children's views should always be taken into consideration.

4.4.3 Special measures for intimidated witnesses

With intimidated witnesses the court needs to be satisfied that the quality of the evidence given by the witness is likely to be diminished by reasons of fear or distress in connection with testifying in the proceedings and in reaching that decision the court will take into account such factors as:

- nature and alleged circumstances of the offence (eg in particular the domestic violence cases);
- age of witness (young or old);
- social and cultural background and ethnic origins;
- domestic and employment circumstances;
- religious beliefs or political opinions; and
- any behaviour towards the witness on the part of: the accused or members of the family or associates of the accused or any other person who is likely to be an accused or a witness.

Again the court will consider the witness's views. There is automatic eligibility for the complainant in an alleged sexual offence unless they do not want special measures. The complainant in such offences is also entitled to have a video-recorded interview used as their evidence in chief. Screens and live TV links have been the usual special measures granted for intimidated witnesses.

However, a recent Court of Appeal case, *R v Rochester* [2008] EWCA Crim 678, has clarified that video evidence in chief has also, in theory, been available for all intimidated witnesses as well in the magistrates' court and Crown Court since 2002. This judgment was a surprise to all parties in the CJS since it has been assumed that, in fact, phased implementation of the relevant legislation was the government's intention. Therefore, video evidence in chief was not available to all types of vulnerable and intimidated witnesses.

It is anticipated that the prosecution team will employ a restrictive interpretation of this judgment in the first instance. Video recording the evidence in chief of all intimidated witnesses, which could include the elderly, frail, domestic violence victims, relatives of the defendant, etc would have major resource implications.

Obviously any decisions about whether or not any particular victim or witness is intimidated should be made on a case-by-case basis in line with the considerations indicated above followed by an in-depth analysis, together with the victim or witness, of the most appropriate special measures for them in each particular case.

Where the video-recorded evidence in chief takes place as a special measure (section 28) a record of visual interview (ROVI) must be completed by the police as standard practice. The ROVI assists informed decision making during the pre-charge stage by guiding the prosecutor through their viewing of the video interview. Full transcripts will only be available for contested hearings. The content of a ROVI is standard and is completed on a form MG15. Guidance on its completion has been published and agreed between the Association of Chief Police Officers (ACPO) and the CPS.

4.4.4 Early special measures meetings (ESMs)

The *Speaking up for Justice* report, which resulted in the provisions of the Youth Justice and Criminal Evidence Act 1999, provided a range of special measures to enable vulnerable and intimidated witnesses in a criminal trial to give the best possible evidence. Additionally, the report recommended that meetings should take place, ESMs, between the investigating officer and Crown Prosecutor in the first instance and then a subsequent meeting between the Crown Prosecutor and the witness in appropriate cases.

The police and the CPS issued joint guidance in 2002 comprising whether such an ESM should be held, on the conduct of such a meeting and of any subsequent meeting with a witness. Such a meeting initially allows the police and the CPS to discuss the eligibility of the witness and agree what special measures applications should be made to the court. Each case is obviously considered individually as is each witness in each case.

The police will initially be responsible for identifying the needs of the witness and indicating this to the CPS on the appropriate MG forms. If they require an ESM this should be indicated on the MG6. An MG2 special measures form should also be completed where appropriate to assist the prosecutor in their written application to the court for such special measures. This meeting should take place as soon as possible. These forms are discussed in detail in Chapter 6.

A face-to-face meeting with the witness him/herself where appropriate will allow the CPS to establish a link with that witness and provide them with re-assurance that their needs will be taken into account and assess which special measures are required. Thus, the ESM will ensure that applications are made in an efficient and timely manner consistent with the victim's views which the court must take into account as well as all the circumstances of the case. Additionally, if a witness asks, an explanation of the court procedure and the role of the various parties in court may be given. However, no discussion can be entered into with the victim about the evidence itself.

At the meeting with a witness, at which the CPS, investigating officer, and sometimes counsel may also be present, a full record must be kept of what has been said. Following that meeting the police have a responsibility of informing the witness of any decisions made (if not made within the meeting).

The ultimate decision of what if any special measures are allowed is a decision made by the court. This should be made clear to the witness. It is the court's job to balance the wishes of the witness against the right of the defendant to a fair trial. The prosecution may merely make an application to the court and put all relevant information before them. It will also be the duty of the prosecution team to monitor the witness closely prior to trial to ensure that their individual needs have not changed in the time between the commission of the offence and giving evidence in court.

POINT TO NOTE—EARLY SPECIAL MEASURES MEETINGS (ESMs)

- The basis of eligibility
- Completion of the relevant MG forms
- Is an expert witness required to show eligibility?
- Which special measure(s) are appropriate?
- The view of the witness
- All decisions to be fully documented
- The final decision will be made by the court

4.5 No Witness No Justice

It is essential that both the police and the CPS think about the care of their victims and witnesses from their first involvement with the case and continue to communicate with each other and them throughout the life of the case.

There has been a noticeable trend within the CJS itself away from defendant's rights and interests in favour of those of victims and witnesses and community interests. Indeed, championing the rights of victims has been at the forefront of the 'No Witness No Justice' campaign specifically aimed at improving the information, support, and protection given to victims. It is hoped witnesses will therefore be more likely to attend a trial of the defendant and that ultimately their more positive experiences will improve their satisfaction with the CJS generally.

Every individual has separate needs and it will be important to obtain a complete profile of the witness from the outset in order to support them in the most appropriate manner. The special needs of the victims (eg the vulnerable and intimidated) should be picked up at the earliest stage by the police officer by completing the back of the MG11 witness statement, mentioning it on the MG6, and completing an MG2 (special measures form) where appropriate at the pre-charge stage for the CPS. No victim should fall outside the scheme because of lack of awareness of the prosecution team.

As has been seen, tailored support to victims and witnesses can now be provided in a number of appropriate and innovative ways in order for them to be able to obtain the best possible information and treatment before, during, and after the conduct of the case.

4.5.1 Witness care units

Part of this ongoing programme has involved the introduction of 165 witness care units (WCUs) across England and Wales. This has been very much a joint agency prosecution team response. They provide a single point of contact and also a detailed needs assessment of every witness who is being called to court to identify any problems which would prevent the witness giving evidence (eg intimidation) or attending court (eg child care, transport, or language difficulties).

Witness care officers working in the units are now highly skilled in understanding the types of issues which may adversely affect people's ability to attend court and give their best evidence. They are also very useful in providing the witness with information on case progress. Moreover, at the end of the trial, they will make sure that the victims and witnesses are told the result and the sentence and thanked for their help and offered further support if they need it.

The WCUs manage the care of victims and witnesses from the point of charge through to the conclusion of the case. It is vitally important that the prosecution team ensure all procedures and practices are adhered to so that the WCUs can provide a much needed enhanced service of care and support to witnesses working closely with victim support and the witness service. As a result of all the efforts of the WCUs, the number of failed cases due to witnesses not attending has dropped considerably since the units were introduced.

POINT TO NOTE—WCUS

- Single point of contact for victims and witnesses
- Individual needs and risk assessment
- Tailored interventions
- Regular updating and contact with victims and witnesses
- Referral to support agencies
- Notification of results
- Legal obligations under the Victim Code

4.5.2 Code for Crown Prosecutors

Over the last decade there has been an increased importance attached to the role of the victim in the CJS as reflected in recent legislation and in the change of attitude and developments within the prosecution team. The Code for Crown Prosecutors, a public document, sets out the basic general principles which all Crown Prosecutors must follow when they make decisions about a case. Wherever the prosecutor feels that there is sufficient evidence to justify a prosecution they must then go on to consider whether it is in the public interest to bring the case to court.

It is important to note here that, although the interests of the victim are an important consideration when deciding where the public interest lies, the CPS prosecutes on behalf of the public at large and not just in the interests of a particular individual. Thus, although the interests of the victim are important they cannot be the final consideration when deciding whether or not to prosecute. For example, in relation to a domestic violence allegation, even if the victim wished to withdraw from the prosecution they may sometimes be witness summonsed to attend court to give evidence where there is a history of repeated violence and a risk of further reoffending or danger to children of the family.

> The Crown Prosecution Service does not act for victims or the families of victims in the same way as solicitors act for their clients. Crown Prosecutors act on behalf of the public and not just in the interests of any particular individual. However, when considering the public interest, Crown Prosecutors should always take into account the consequence for the victim of whether or not to prosecute, and any views expressed by the victim or the victim's family.
>
> Code for Crown Prosecutors 2004, para 5.12

In many situations some of the factors in favour of prosecution set out in the Code, including the seriousness of the offence, flow directly from the impact of the offence on the victim.

4.5.3 Direct communications with victims and witnesses

Since 2000 the CPS has assumed responsibility for communicating prosecuting decisions direct to victims rather than via the police. The CPS therefore writes to the victims about any decision to drop or substantially alter a charge giving as much detail as possible of the reasons for the decision and in some cases offer to meet with the victim to explain the decision further.

It is very important that the prosecution team present a unified front when explaining any such prosecution decision to the victim. The timeliness of the communication of these decisions is also important since, in relation to vulnerable victims, the Victim Code now lays down that the victim needs to be informed within one day (five days for all other victims).

4.5.4 Prosecutors' pledge

In addition to the WCUs, in 2005 the Attorney General introduced a ten-point pledge for prosecutors which articulated the level of service that victims could expect to receive from them. This Prosecutors' Pledge was the first time that there had been a public document endorsing the commitment of the CPS to enhance service to victims.

This document also underpinned the Attorney General's guidelines, which had been published on the 'acceptability of guilty pleas' (always seeking out the victim's view) and enhanced role of the prosecutor in the sentencing process (protecting the general public's interests and the specific interests of the victims).

The prosecutors pledge is generally reflective of best practice and of the numerous developments which have been taking place within the CPS in this regard.

POINT TO NOTE—PROSECUTORS' PLEDGE

Where there is an identifiable victim the prosecutor will:

- Take into account the impact on the victim or their family when making a charging decision
- Inform the victim where the charge is withdrawn, discontinued, or substantially altered
- Where practical seek a victim's view or that of the family when considering the acceptability of a plea
- Address the specific needs of a victim and where justified seek to protect their identity by making an appropriate application to the court
- Assist victims at court to refresh their memory from their written or video statement and answer their questions on court procedure and processes
- Promote and encourage two-way communication between victim and prosecutor at court
- Protect victims from unwarranted or irrelevant attacks on their character and seek the court's intervention where cross-examination is considered to be inappropriate or oppressive
- On conviction, robustly challenge defence mitigation which is derogatory to a victim's character
- On conviction, apply for an appropriate order for compensation, restitution, or future protection of the victim
- Keep victims informed of the progress of any appeal and explain the effect of the court's judgment

---

4.5.5 Victim Code

A number of the above guidelines are now of course also endorsed in the Code of Practice for Victims of Crime. This came into effect in April 2006, building on many of the original obligations laid down in the Victims' Charter in 1996.

For the first time ever the Code provided victims with a statutory right to minimum standards of service. Victims of crime now have a right to seek redress should they feel that the CJS providers have not delivered on their obligations in the Code and they can ultimately take their case to the parliamentary ombudsman. It is therefore vitally important that police officers and prosecutors are fully aware of all their obligations under the Code and adhere to them rigidly.

The joint police/CPS WCUs must conduct a full needs assessment with all victims when a not guilty plea is entered and keep the victim informed throughout the life of the case as has already been seen (section 6 of the Victim Code).

Obligations under the Victim Code include the early identification of vulnerable and intimidated victims of crime providing an enhanced service for them. Such enhanced obligations extend to child victims, victims of sexual offences or domestic abuse and criminal conduct resulting in death. Time limits for informing victims of significant changes in the state of the investigation have been set: one working day in the case of the enhanced service and five days for all other victims.

Significant changes include:

- the arrest of suspect;
- if the suspect is charged and any bail conditions imposed;
- if the suspect is released on police bail;
- if there is any alteration in the conditions of police bail or the date to return;
- if the investigation is taken no further or any other case disposal is decided;
- if any warrant is issued; and
- any other development which requires the victim to be notified.

Specific obligations of the CPS (section 7 of the Victim Code) include the following:

- Victims are always informed if the charges have substantially altered or dropped within set timescales.
- Prosecutors must consider whether or not to make an application for special measures where any victim is identified as vulnerable or intimidated.
- Victims are met at court and should have all their queries answered by the prosecution team.
- Victims should be advised of any delay, its reason and revised timetable in connection with any proceedings.
- At the end of a court hearing victims should be offered an explanation of what has happened including explanations of any decisions of the court, eg concerning bail or sentence.
- Prosecutors must ensure that the victim's voice is heard at court by drawing all aggravating features of the case to the judge's attention including the relevant sentencing provisions and by ensuring a VPS is known to the court.
- Victims should be given a big thank you for turning up and playing their part.

4.5.6 **Victim Focus Scheme (VFS)**

The VFS was rolled out across England and Wales in October 2007 and it may be seen as supplementing the VPS. The VPS has been seen to enable the court to gain a better understanding of the nature and impact of the crime on the victim when sentence is passed.

In the case of a homicide to which the VFS applies prosecutors will offer to meet bereaved families after charge to discuss processes, procedures, and progress in the case as well as the option of making a VPS:

> It is my belief that family impact statements have improved the public's perception of the CPS and increased community confidence.
>
> J Narwal, now Chief Crown Prosecutor Lincolnshire, former Head of Trial Unit at the Central Criminal Court

The end result, of course, is far greater consideration, by the entire prosecution team in their preparation and presentation of cases, of the victims and the views and feelings of the victims and in this case the bereaved families.

4.5.7 **Criminal Injuries Compensation Scheme (CICA)**

Given that it is the police officer who usually provides the interface between the victim of a crime and the CJS they now play an important part in referring victims to other agencies who can help them. One of these is the CICA. Indeed officers under the Victim Code are obliged to return completed form TB1 (enclosing more information on the incident) within 30 days. Such timeliness assists the processing of the claim.

In order for an applicant to claim they must be a blameless victim of a crime of violence, but there does not need to have been a conviction for such a claim to be made. Levels of compensation for personal or fatal injury including loss of earnings are published.

There has been heavy criticism of late of the CICA and the difficulties of form filling the 16-page claim form, of the time taken to process the claim, and the amount of compensation subsequently provided. Reforms are in the pipeline to make the process simpler, providing support to victims making a claim.

Police officers must play their part proactively by informing victims about the scheme, returning the TB1 form, and seeing the process right through to the end including, if necessary, attending hearings. They will be helping victims move on and also ensuring that they get the justice they deserve. It is to be noted that police officers themselves are also entitled to claim compensation under the scheme.

4.6 **Witness Difficulties**

4.6.1 **Pre-trial interviews with witnesses**

Historically the first opportunity the prosecutor had to speak to a witness was at the door of court prior to trial. Full reliance, therefore, had to be placed on the written statement submitted by the police to the CPS and any further comments by the officer on the witness's reliability or credibility. Such a situation was far from satisfactory especially in those cases, for example sexual and domestic violence allegations, which tended to revolve around one person's word against another at trial with very little additional evidence. It was thus a question of 'wait and see' whether or not the witness 'came up to proof' in the court scenario.

In 2004 the Attorney General published a report concluding that the prosecutors should be able to speak to witnesses in order to clarify their evidence or assess their reliability. Following the successful evaluation of a pilot scheme in the north west in 2006 and 2007 this scheme was rolled out nationally in 2008. Senior prosecutors have been specifically trained to interview witnesses about their evidence wherever they feel that it would enable them to reach a more informed decision about any aspect of the case.

Suitable cases where a pre-trial interview may be beneficial need to be identified at an early stage, ideally pre-charge, after discussion between investigator and prosecutor. The witness must have made a signed witness statement (or have provided a video-recorded statement) prior to any such interview taking place but it is best practice then to hold the interview as soon as possible after the police investigation is complete and the full file received.

The key purposes of a pre-trial interview are:

- to assess the reliability of witness evidence;
- to assist the prosecutor in understanding complex evidence and the strength of a case.

To avoid any allegation that prosecutors holding such interviews are in fact 'coaching' witnesses with a view to improving their evidence and performance in court, which is illegal, a stringent Code of Practice has been issued by the DPP in conjunction with the Bar, the Law Society, ACPO and Victim Support. The Code, for example, refers to how any questions must be framed and the requirement for the interview to be audio (or video) recorded. These measures, if adhered to, avoid disputes over witness evidence as well as protecting the prosecutor from any allegations of coaching.

The end result of these pre-trial interviews hold advantages for both prosecutors and witnesses alike. On the one hand it should lead to improved prosecutorial decision making enabling the prosecution to gain a clear understanding of the witness's evidence and how s/he might come across in the witness-box. On the other, witnesses will have the benefit of personal contact with the prosecutor prior to trial and will be able to air any concerns they have about giving evidence:

Victims will certainly feel better about a decision if we have actually seen them, met with them and know how effective they are likely to be in court.

Chief Crown Prosecutor Bob Marshall (Lancashire) speaking on *File on 4*, BBC Radio 4

4.6.2 **Reluctant/hostile witnesses**

Usually it is the responsibility of the police to ensure that the witness attends court and great care and attention will be paid to the more vulnerable and intimidated. However, there are situations where it is known in advance that the witness will simply not turn up at court voluntarily. The CPS needs to be kept fully informed by the police about such situations so that they can make an early decision as to whether or not to apply for a witness summons to secure the attendance of the witness at court.

It is often a difficult decision for the CPS to make and in the past prosecutors have not been robust enough in requesting them. In many domestic violence situations, for example, the mere issuing of a summons can be enough to take the pressure off the complainant in that it is no longer his/her fault or responsibility to come to court. In others, however, the danger of escalation of violence in a relationship or previous similar incidents may indicate to the CPS that it is in the public interest (ie the public at large) to apply for a witness summons.

Independent domestic violence assessors (IDVAs) who are trained specialists are available to work alongside the victim from the outset providing them with additional support and information. They also provide a coordinating role for other essential services to ensure that the victim is kept as safe as possible prior to, during and even after the court hearing.

Where an application is made and granted it is for the police personally then to serve the witness summons on the witness and also tender them the conduct money at the same time. It is helpful if a short statement to this effect covering both matters together with an endorsed copy of the summons when served is returned to the CPS so that proof that the summons was properly served and the witness correctly warned can be provided to the court in the event of the witness not appearing in answer to that summons.

Anyone disobeying such a summons is guilty of contempt of court and can potentially be arrested and imprisoned. There is often a dilemma for the prosecuting team who must consider all the circumstances of the case in deciding perhaps whether it is better to offer no evidence in a case where a crucial witness does not attend or go and arrest the witness bringing them to court for contempt and potentially having them punished. The prosecutor should only come to this decision once a detailed consideration of all the circumstances and the background history to a case and after discussion with the officer. Identifying and managing the risk to the victim in such circumstances is an important part of the prosecution team role and will be a key factor in their decision making.

Sometimes the witness will attend court but once there changes their mind in respect of the evidence they wish to give. This is a common occurrence again in domestic violence situations and also in situations where a witness has been intimidated. Thus the witness no longer wishes to give the evidence in their statement and retracts it or goes into the witness-box and puts a totally different spin on the evidence leaving out important details, for example.

When this occurs the Criminal Justice Act 2003 has some helpful provisions for the prosecution. In this situation the prosecution can apply for the witness's original statement (ie the previous inconsistent one) also to be admitted as evidence of the truth of its contents before the court. Thus the court itself can decide which 'version' it prefers. This prior statement is in effect 'hearsay' evidence since the witness is not repeating it again in open court but it may now be admissible under the specific provisions of the Criminal Justice Act. The idea is that the fact finders, ie the magistrates or jury, should be able to receive as full a picture as possible so that they can decide how much weight to attach to the original statement or the live evidence of the witness in the witness-box where it is given.

4.6.3 **Unavailable witnesses**

There are a number of situations where a witness is not in fact available to give evidence but may have an excuse for their absence. This could be because they are deceased, abroad and cannot attend, physically or mentally unfit or the police simply cannot find them.

Usually a police officer will need to give sufficient evidence to the court with regard to the specific reasons and then the court may allow the statement of that witness to be read.

The most common reason for non-attendance however, is one of fear, ie the witness is basically too frightened to come to court to give evidence and without that evidence the prosecution do not have a case. In the latter situation the leave of the court has to be applied for but it is possible in any of the circumstances outlined above that the court may allow that evidence to be read without the presence of the witness.

Where the reason is one of fear a more detailed consideration has to take place in order for the court to grant leave in the interests of justice. The court will look at the details and content of the statement itself and its importance to the case and the strength of the other evidence. This will be balanced against the unfairness to the defendant and his/her difficulty in challenging a statement where the witness is unavailable for cross-examination. However, case law has indicated that where it can be shown a defendant is responsible for keeping the witness away and the defendant then argues that he cannot get a fair trial without the witness it may not be readily open to him to argue that his right to a fair trial has been infringed by the witness's absence.

4.6.4 **Memory refreshing**

It was a common misconception that any witness that came to court often months or even years after the original allegation had to rely on their memory. In fact witnesses have always been allowed to see their statement prior to trial so as to refresh their memory before they came into the witness-box.

Since April 2004, by virtue of section 139 of the Criminal Justice Act 2003, in any trial either civilians or police officers are entitled (on application) to refresh their memory at any stage of the proceedings. This can be done from an early document made by him/her if the witness can say first that the document records his/her recollection of the matter at the earlier time and secondly that his/her recollection of the matter is likely to have been significantly better at that time than it is at the time of his or her oral evidence.

In practice police officers giving evidence routinely produce their notebooks and ask to use them as soon as they have taken the oath and told the court their name. Any witness, however, should be reminded that although this may be permissible it is only to refresh the memory. Anyone reading verbatim from a prior statement may fall foul of the court and is not likely to be thought of as a credible witness who speaks potentially from memory.

4.7 **Conclusion**

Recent developments within the CJS have focused on the plight of witnesses and victims in an unprecedented way. Experience and research has shown that we have not always been effective in obtaining the best evidence that a witness is capable of producing, and this has been especially evident in cases involving the most vulnerable in society.

It must always be remembered that the experience of victims attending court heavily influences their overall impression of the CJS and the likelihood of their coming forward in the future as witnesses of crime. The prosecution team cannot do justice unless witnesses are willing to report crime and come forward to give evidence in the first place.

New resources in the form of booklets and, for example, a DVD entitled *Going to Court—a step by step guide to being a witness* should assist in increasing a witness's confidence, allaying their fears and generally reassuring them about the support available to them.

A recent survey known as WAVES (witness and victim experience survey) has asked victims and witnesses of crime about their experiences within the CJS. The results will be used to target any gaps in service provision.

Additionally, the CPS has recently launched a four-year Victim and Witness Strategy 2008–2011 which will provide a framework for existing initiatives and future policy development. This should ensure that victims and witnesses become an integral part of the day-to-day work of the prosecution.

More effective support for victims and witnesses from first contact with police through to giving evidence at court, together with more effective interviewing techniques, will enable all witnesses to provide better evidence.

Interviewing Suspects

5.1 **Introduction**

This chapter pre-supposes a basic knowledge of police suspect interviewing and is intended to assist the junior detective/investigator to become more confident in their interviewing techniques by explaining some of the major principles behind the model of a PEACE-compliant suspect interview. Some of the potential pitfalls facing interviewers will be addressed, including the use of significant statements and silences, and how to most effectively employ 'special warnings'. It will also provide some guidance to assist the interviewer with legal advisers, before the interview regarding the pre-interview disclosure of information about the investigation, as well as how to deal with some of the strategies employed by legal advisers during the interview itself.

Interviewing suspects is currently a matter for police investigators with the CPS being only marginally involved except in the most serious of cases. CPS lawyers are being asked advice in particular with regard to the amount of disclosure that should be provided to the legal adviser in advance of an interview and this will undoubtedly increase as the prosecution team approach becomes more entrenched. It is not, however, an area in which there is practical expertise among the CPS. It is one thing to look at a suspect interview after it has been completed with a view to assessing its evidential worth in terms of what the suspect has said or not said, and entirely another to actually plan and conduct that interview in the first place. It is absolutely fundamental to the prosecution team approach therefore that the CPS understands the position that the interviewer is in prior to conducting the interview and provide as much support as they can, while at the same time the interviewer understands what the CPS needs from that interview in terms of its proper conduct, its admissibility, and its evidential worth. This requires both parties to learn from and work with each other.

Carrying out an interview of a person suspected of involvement in a criminal offence, under caution, and in the presence of a legal adviser, is one of the most challenging duties that a police officer is likely to encounter. In order to conduct a successful interview the officer is required to display a number of personal skills in conversation and dealing with information, as well as being confident in their knowledge of law and procedure; in particular with regards to Codes C and E of PACE Codes of Practice. Police interviewers' skills are tested in full in the presence of an assertive legal adviser proactively representing the suspect and/or, an appropriate adult, an interpreter, and very often a prisoner who is confident and experienced at the police interview.

5.1.1 **PEACE**

PEACE, developed by Professor John Baldwin in 1992, is the nationally accepted model for investigative interviewing, and it emerged following research into the competency of police interviews which concluded that ineptitude and poor technique were common. As described in 4.2.3 PEACE forms the structured basis of any investigative interview—whether with a suspect or with a witness.

PEACE is an acronym which stands for:

P   Planning and preparation
E   Engage and explain
A   Account, clarify, and challenge
C   Closure
E   Evaluate

This simple structure is the systematic core of any interview and each element will be dealt with in turn. Very important though is to point out that not only does each element of PEACE stand alone as a separate entity in the process, so too do the three parts of the 'Account' phase. As will be seen, it is fundamental to the success of the conversational approach to interviewing that account, clarify, and challenge are dealt with strictly in that order.

5.1.2 The principles of investigative interviewing

At the same time as the PEACE model was produced the Home Office published seven principles of investigative interviewing. These have recently been amended.

POINT TO NOTE—SEVEN PRINCIPLES OF INVESTIGATIVE INTERVIEWING

1   The aim of investigative interviewing is to obtain accurate and reliable accounts from victims, witnesses or suspects about matters under police investigation

2   Investigators must act fairly when questioning victims, witnesses or suspects. Vulnerable people must be treated with particular consideration at all times

3   Investigative interviewing should be approached with an investigative mindset. Accounts obtained from the person who is being interviewed should always be tested against what the interviewer already knows or what can be reasonably established

4   When conducting an interview, investigators are free to ask a wide range of questions in order to obtain material, which may assist an investigation. They are not limited to asking questions aimed at gathering evidence but they should ensure that the questions asked are appropriate to the case and can be justified to others

5   Investigators will not know whether a suspect is guilty of an offence. They have a responsibility, however to provide them with an opportunity to give an account which may include a voluntary admission of guilt

---

6 Investigators are not bound to accept the first answer given. Questioning is not unfair merely because it is persistent

7 Even when the right of silence is exercised by a suspect, investigators have a responsibility to put questions to them

These principles have real significance for the practicalities of interviewing. Interviewing must not be confession driven, the general aim ought to be to discover provable lies and checkable facts. An interviewer who approaches a suspect interview with their mind already made up will be ineffective. Objectivity is vital both as a conversational tool to achieve a level of trust with the suspect, and as part of the ability to assess rationally the suspect's responses. Fairness in the interviewing process is the officer's shield against accusations of oppression. At each stage the interviewer must be able to show both lawfulness and fairness in their approach in order for their actions to be seen by the court as reasonable. The issue of fairness is of particular importance with a vulnerable suspect, and a judge is more likely to exercise powers to exclude evidence in cases where vulnerability has been disregarded or even exploited.

Tenacity is not oppressive, and the courts and juries recognize that suspects will lie in police interviews. It is key to an effective interview to test the account of the suspect and it is the investigator's duty to confront and unravel deceit. It has been suggested by defence lawyers that the right of silence ought to extend to a refusal to be interviewed. This has never been endorsed by any court, and to uncover the truth there is a duty to put questions regardless of the right to silence. Interviewers are often concerned about whether they may ask questions relating to hearsay information or about the suspect's criminal history, and legal advisers will occasionally interfere with the officer's questioning in order to attempt to control what is asked—this should be firmly resisted.

5.1.3 The National Investigative Interviewing Strategy

In 2001, the Association of Chief Police Officers (ACPO) adopted the National Investigative Interviewing Strategy (NIIS), which endorsed the PEACE model for interviewing both suspects and witnesses, and created a five-tier structure of interviewing training and skills. It is important to note that this strategy—as with the PEACE model itself—does not distinguish between suspect interview under caution and witness interviews. PEACE is entirely applicable to any interview both within and outside the police service. Although that is not to say that there are not significant and particular challenges to the officer conducting a suspect interview.

POINT TO NOTE—THE NATIONAL INVESTIGATIVE INTERVIEWING STRATEGY

- Tier 1—Foundation
- Tier 2—Dedicated interviewers
- Tier 3—Specialist interviewers
- Tier 4—Interview supervisors
- Tier 5—Interview advisers

In terms of suspect interviewing, however, at Tier 1 an interviewer is required to be able to conduct a lawful and evidentially admissible interview and training at this level is limited to a day or two. Tier 2 trained officers should form the backbone of investigative interviewers, and after training would be expected to interview competently within the PEACE model at levels of criminality below the most serious cases. A Tier 2 course would normally be expected to last four or five days, although some courses are now ten days in length. Specialist interviewers at Tier 3 would be expected to attend an intensive three-week course, equipping them with the skills needed to conduct the most difficult interviews of people suspected of homicide, serious sexual offences, or acts of terrorism. Tier 4 is not a higher level of interviewing skill, but is intended to ensure interviews are evaluated in order to maintain standards in practice. Tier 5 officers are expected to be trained to interview at Tier 3, but will, additionally, be expected to assist the Senior Investigating Officers (SIOs) in developing interview strategies as well as providing practical assistance to interviewers in planning and preparing for specific interviews of both witnesses and suspects.

5.1.4 Professionalizing Investigative Programme (PIP)

In order to make the NIIS compliant with PIP there has been some reconsideration of the five tiers. This has led to a repackaging of Tier 2 as being the minimum level of training needed for interviewing in cases of serious and complex crime, which may include simple homicide cases. It is generally seen as a basic level of competence demanded by CID roles or other specific investigators. Tier 3 becomes much more of a specialist interviewer. Tier 4 has in some places been abandoned with assessment seen more as a core supervisory role that does not necessarily require specific training.

In training terms there is still work being carried out to fine tune the length of courses and their precise content, in particular the balance between the witness and suspect interview. In the future courses both at Tier 2 and at Tier 3 may be devoted to suspects or witnesses or may incorporate both, nonetheless the core skills will remain largely unchanged.

POINT TO NOTE—PIP INTERVIEWING STRUCTURE

- Volume crime   (Tier 1)
- Serious and complex cases   (Tier 2)
- Specialist interviewers   (Tier 3)
- Interview advisers   (Tier 5)

5.1.5 Interviewing—the two core skills

When police officers are asked to consider the skills of an effective interviewer a number of recurrent themes emerge, such as knowledge, confidence, tenacity, calmness, a good memory, listening and questioning skills, and many others. However, each of the skills necessary may be usefully considered as falling within one, or other—or both—of two key categories: conversation management skills and information processing skills. The success of an interview is entirely reliant upon the interviewer's abilities in these two areas.

Although PEACE provides the structured model, its successful application in a particular case will depend upon the interviewer being able to manage the interview conversationally, while at the same time process, contextualize, and deal with information received from the suspect. These are not easy skills to master, but they can be improved through application and practice.

5.2 The Conversation Model

5.2.1 Conversation—not interrogation

The conversation model of interviewing was formulated in the 1980s by Dr Eric Shepherd as an approach to dealing with resistant interviewees at a time when much more attention was being paid to police practices during suspect interviews.

An interview is defined as a conversation with a purpose, and the use of the term conversational interview may be usefully contrasted with interrogative interview to clearly indicate the general approach of the interviewer. Interrogation carries with it connotations of aggressive, accusatorial, hectoring, and generally bullying behaviour. A number of cases have seen the criminal courts extend the definition of an oppressive interview under section 76 of PACE, from its original wording; 'torture, inhuman or degrading treatment, and the use or threat of violence', to behaviour involving some 'impropriety on the part of the interrogator' (*R v Fulling* [1987] 2 All ER 65). It would be fair to say that today the interrogative style is viewed as both dangerous and ineffective, as cases such as the Cardiff Three (*R v Miller Paris and Abdullahi* [1993] 97 Cr App R 99) have shown, vulnerable suspects can be persuaded by such techniques to make false admissions to murder.

Conversation, however, implies a calm, reasonable, and relaxed interaction between two equals, in which each willingly participates. Achieving a conversational interaction should be the aim of the interviewer from the very outset of their dealings with the suspect, not only because the conversational style is more likely to negate an allegation of oppression, but because the conversational abilities of the interviewer will contribute to whether the suspect will talk or not during the interview. Conversation has rules that have developed socially and to which on an almost instinctive level we all tend to conform. In the conversation model the interviewer understands and uses those rules to encourage the interviewee to respond and to continue to do so.

5.2.2 **Conversational skills**

When asked about good interviewers, police officers frequently talk about individuals who have a good manner with people. Terms such as charisma or character may be used, and their ability to build and maintain rapport is often considered a key skill. However, when pressed we find it more difficult to say precisely what it is that these individuals actually do that creates this effect, resorting to saying that someone just has a way with people. But we need to go a little further than this and rationalize exactly what it is that good conversationalists do. The important question to ask is this: how do they act and what do they do that encourages us to speak with them?

For example, central to whether we feel encouraged to continue to speak to another person is our belief that they are interested in what we have to say. But how is this belief generated, what does the person do to make us think this? Positive indicators would include them focusing entirely on us; looking at us and listening to what we are saying; allowing us to finish what we have to say; and at all times responding appropriately with words and gestures of encouragement. Negative indicators would include not paying attention by doing something else or looking away while we are talking, responding inappropriately and dismissively, or showing signs of impatience or disbelief.

Consider how any kind of communication works in practice. Only in a letter or email does communication take place based upon words alone. In personal contact the words make up a relatively small part of what we communicate to another person, how we say the words and our physical actions while saying them, are much more significant than the words we actually use in putting across a message. If we say to someone, 'That's interesting', but we do not give any life to the words, we will sound insincere, even sarcastic. Similarly if we add enthusiasm in our tone but we look away and are generally inattentive the other person will notice contradictory signals—the words and intonation say interest, but the body language says bored. In cases where there are such contradictory signals we tend to accept the non-verbal signals as indicating the truth.

'Leakage' is the term given to this, where despite what we may say our manner and body language leak our true feelings. This is very important for the police interviewer because it is all too easy to leak a belief in the suspect's guilt and disbelief in what they say. Any such thoughts must be controlled; the impression that must be created is one of objectivity—or a suspension of disbelief—if the interview is to continue. This is a particular problem if the suspect lies and because of other evidence the police officer knows or believes that the suspect has lied. The successful communicator therefore combines the three elements into a consistent message—the words, intonation, and body language all say interested, or I accept what you are saying.

5.2.3 **Response**

A conversation between two people may be seen as an alternate series of responses and each response will have an impact on the conversation. For example, an interested response is likely to maintain a conversation while a bored response is likely to curtail it. What is important is to identify those attributes that the interviewer can display that are most encouraging, and to this end RESPONSE, devised by Dr Eric Shepherd, is a useful acronym.

POINT TO NOTE—RESPONSE	
R	Respect
E	Empathy
S	Supportiveness
P	Positiveness
O	Openness
N	Non-judgemental
S	Straightforward talk
E	Equality

These are attitudes that we respond positively to in a conversation with another person. To make this clear consider how we react when faced with talking to someone who is disrespectful to us, is uninterested in our situation, has prejudged the issue and sees themselves as superior to us. All of these are likely to discourage us from talking to them. Clearly, however, the attitude itself is not enough; one may actually harbour a sense of equality, however, for it to be an effective tool to encourage conversation, there must be a display of behaviour that makes the attitude evident. The question for an interviewer then is not just therefore adopting the proper attitudes, but finding a way of behaving to make the attitude evident.

Respect involves treating the suspect as an individual, showing attentiveness and being neither superior nor subservient. This is often difficult for a police officer who feels a sense of superiority over a criminal suspect, or sees the situation in terms of being in charge and the suspect being under his/her control.

The key point is to consider that a conversation is more likely where a mutual respect exists and so the police interviewer must try to create that impression in their dealings with the suspect.

Empathy is not always easy in the police interviewer/suspect situation. Empathy involves trying to see the world through the eyes of the other person and understanding the situation that they are in. We tend to gravitate towards those with whom we believe we share views and values, those with whom we are most likely to empathize naturally. If we start a new job, for example, we tend to feel most comfortable talking to other new employees, or people of a similar age. Empathy is a fundamental part of rapport.

Supportiveness is closely linked to respect and empathy and is about recognizing the views and rights of the other person and about displaying tolerance towards them.

Positiveness relates more to how we say things, rather than what we say, and involves being enthusiastic and attentive. If we are facially expressive and our voice varies in tone it indicates interest and can be very encouraging. A monotone voice lacking life is a sign of boredom and will adversely affect any conversation because the person you are talking with will feel you are not interested in what they are saying.

Openness indicates honesty while dishonesty breeds evasiveness and secrecy. An open manner in words and style, being ourselves and allowing our own personality to inform the interview, all add to the sense that we are honest and trustworthy people.

Being **non-judgemental** involves accepting the suspect and what they say without prejudice and without showing disbelief, scorn, or ridicule; it is a vital mindset for the interviewer. Regardless of the evidence against a suspect and what is known of their criminal background, what they say must be approached with an open mind, this will encourage the suspect to continue to talk, and will allow for the opportunity to test their account objectively. If an interviewer started by believing what a suspect said but in the end concluded that they were telling lies, it is likely that a jury would come to the same conclusion. If, however, the interviewer started with the belief that the suspect will be telling lies, then any conclusion may be based on where the interviewer started and not on what the suspect said during the interview, and so any belief of the interviewer that the suspect has lied may not be evident to another listener.

Straightforward talk is exactly that—keeping what you say simple and short. Police officers tend to resort to peculiar non-conversational speech in interviews, a mixture of legalese, jargon, and technical language. For example:

> Regarding the motor vehicle that you had in your possession, who is the registered owner?

instead of, more simply:

> About the car Peter, who owns it?

Being able to explain things simply is a skill, and when we consider the caution and the 'special warning' their impact is much greater if they are delivered in a straightforward way.

Equality signals are linked to supportiveness and empathy. We are all more at ease talking with people we feel to be our equals, not speaking down to someone, and not speaking with deference. A classic equality sign is a handshake, something many police officers feel uncomfortable doing with a suspect. However, the legal adviser will almost certainly shake the prisoners hand at the start of their consultation. Other signs would be asking—not telling—the suspect to do something and displaying normal courtesies. Standing if they are standing and sitting if they are sitting.

Many of these are difficult for the police officer who may be dealing with a paedophile, or a violent drug-addicted street robber. But these are the real tests of conversational skill and controlling leakage. Remember showing empathy and respect and displaying equality signals are deliberate acts designed to create a situation in which the suspect is more likely to cooperate with you. They are tools for you to deploy to get what you want from the interview. Of course a suspect interview is unlike a normal conversation in many ways, and the interviewer has a number of obstacles to overcome in order to have a meaningful conversation with a suspect. Some obstacles, however, are more in the mind of the interviewer.

Someone who has rationalized these traits, and understands how they are actually displayed as behaviour, is then able to deploy them deliberately. When we talk about rapport or when we identify someone as a good communicator or good with people, what we are saying is that they have the ability to engage with someone by using behaviour—words, intonation, and body language—in a specific way to achieve their purpose. These are not simply innate personal characteristics with which only some of us are blessed, they are concrete skills that can be practised and learned by anyone, and they are fundamental to your success as an interviewer.

5.2.4 Listening

Listening impacts upon both our ability to engage conversationally with the suspect, and to deal properly with information. If we do not feel we are being listened to we feel disinclined to continue to talk, and if we do not listen closely we do not hear exactly what is being said. The interviewer needs to be able to listen intently to the suspect and identify precisely what they say, because this is the evidence and failure to focus properly on what a suspect says renders the interview process worthless. We are not habitually strong listeners, we are easily distracted and we tend to filter information that we hear for things that interest us.

During an interview, for example, we may be distracted from listening by rehearsing what we are going to ask next or later in the interview, or trying to remember a detail from the case papers while the suspect is talking. Equally, if we decide early in the interview that the suspect is lying and that their account is not credible, we tend to stop listening carefully to it; it is not interesting to us because it is not what we want to hear.

Active listening requires total focus on what is being said and the person saying it. It is not something we could do all the time and socially it is not necessary, however in an interview it is vital to be clear as to precisely what the suspect is saying. The essential difference between ordinary listening and active listening is that with ordinary listening we tend to recall the generality of what somebody has said, while if we actively listen we can—with practice—recall many of the exact words used. If you were asked to speak to someone and then later report back to a third party on what they had said, you would be likely to give a summary in your own words of the gist of their account.

The danger is that an interviewer will edit the suspect's account for what has struck the interviewer as interesting or significant, and will be unlikely to use the suspects own words. Furthermore, because many of us mentally see in images, when we listen to someone giving us an account of something we tend to create a picture or a visual image, and in doing so we will add detail that they have not described. After a short period we may be quite sure that our mental picture is a correct version of their account.

If, however, you were told in advance that you were to report back precisely what the person said in as many of their words as possible, but you were not to make notes then you would—of necessity—engage in concentrated active listening. By doing so you resist the tendency to generalize what they say and focus much more on their actual words. Consider the following:

> This guy was giving it all that, I didn't want to know, but he was right in my face, you know what I mean, he was out of it screaming and shouting, then he just come at me so I done him.

If a suspect to an assault in a pub said this, it would be easy to think it was an admission and yet look again and you will see how little has been said, and how easy it would be for a defence lawyer at court to argue that it does not amount to an admission at all. Self-defence could be raised from 'he just come at me', while 'I done him' might mean anything. Only by focusing carefully on the words used by a suspect can an interviewer identify exactly how much and how little has actually been said, and then move on to look for more detail.

Listening, therefore, is an important conversational skill and we will actively look for signs that what we are saying is being heard by the other person. Indicators that someone is listening to us in the context of an interview include the following:

- showing attentiveness by non-verbal signs;
- maintaining eye contact;
- asking questions that emerge from our answers;
- not interrupting;

- avoiding distractions, such as reading documents;
- summarizing what we have said in our words.

5.2.5 **Batari's Box**

Batari's Box is used as a training aid in various guises and the principles it enshrines are highly significant for the interviewer. Any interaction between two people involves a positioning by each party during the opening exchanges, and this is especially true where they are strangers. How the interaction will go will depend upon the attitude of the parties, but it is rarely a given from the outset. Each party will react to the words and behaviour of the other and this will in turn affect their reaction. So any interaction becomes a spiral of responses which eventually sorts out how the conversation will be conducted.

Figure 5.1 Batari's Box

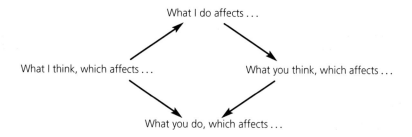

Batari's Box makes explicit the spiral of behaviour between the actions of one party and the thoughts/response of the other. This can be seen working very clearly in a 'no comment' suspect interview. The officer begins in a conversational manner hoping to engage with the suspect, but the suspect has been advised or chosen not to say anything. At this early stage in the interview the two parties are positioning themselves and there is a kind of negotiation going on. The officer is looking for a conversation, while the suspect is looking for the officer to accept their no comment. How this is resolved will depend on the determination of each party to dictate the terms of the interview.

Too often, police officers allow the suspect to dictate these terms and succumb to the suspect agenda. This can be clearly heard in the interview often only a few minutes after the start, when the officer gives up trying to engage with the suspect. What has happened is that the officer has shown insufficient determination. The suspect has resisted the officer's actions—the officer has not been able to resist the suspect's. The effective interviewer understands these principles and looks to dictate the terms of the interaction, not to be dictated to. This means in practice that the police officer needs to be confident and persistent in their efforts to have a conversation with the suspect and be able to resist the suspect's uncooperative responses. Thinking about the start of an interview as a period of positioning will help the interviewer to focus on their aim; the equilibrium will be a conversation.

These principles are not only applicable where there is conflict at the start. Any conversation will develop in accordance to the behaviour of each party. For example, if a police officer asks only short, sharp, and quick-fire questions the suspect is likely to respond in a similar vein. The key is to accept that the interviewer is responsible for the outcome of the interview. The interviewer has broken Batari's Box by refusing to allow the suspect's behaviour to affect their behaviour, while at the same time influencing the suspect.

POINT TO NOTE—CONVERSATION MANAGEMENT

- An interview is a conversation—not an interrogation
- Conversation is generated through RESPONSE
- 'Leakage' must be controlled
- Concentrate on 'active listening'
- Make the suspect respond to the interviewer's behaviour
- Do not let the suspect dictate how the interview will go

5.3 Information Processing

This is the second core skill and functions in tandem alongside conversation management. An interviewer must be able to deal with information. First, they must properly deal with the law and procedures that relate to conducting a suspect interview, then they need to have a full understanding of the matter under investigation including the suspect, and finally, having effectively employed their conversational skills, they need to deal with any additional information they receive during the interview.

Law and procedures are a matter of knowledge and application, and there is no short cut to becoming familiar with the provisions of the relevant sections of PACE Code C—that relate to interviewing, Code E—audio recording interviews, and if necessary Code F—visually recording interviews. Furthermore, it is important to keep abreast of common law developments—stated cases that modify the interpretation of laws—for example the use of bad character evidence is and will continue to be subject to judicial decisions. The CPS should see it as a part of their role to ensure that investigators are kept appraised of such changes and how they may impact upon practical interviewing.

In the planning stage the interviewer will need to develop a clear understanding of the case under investigation such that s/he has little need to refer to documentation during the interview itself, since this is a substantial barrier to engaging with the suspect. A technique for assisting with this involves organizing the disparate material—witness statements, pocket books, intelligence, etc—into a single narrative, like a storyline. Interviewing a suspect and concentrating and absorbing what they say, while at the same time recognizing the context supplied by the interviewer's knowledge of the surrounding circumstances of the case is a difficult skill and requires application and practice. Questions must arise from what the suspect says to the interviewer, any reference to other accounts of the incident must go back to the challenge phase of the interview.

Active listening—as has been noted—impacts upon both conversation management and on information processing. The interviewer's surrounding knowledge should enable them to ensure that the interview remains focused on the relevant issues and they not allow the suspect to take the interview away from the point. This is a common tactic with people engaged in deceit and should be listened for closely.

5.4 **Planning and Preparation**

5.4.1 **Fail to prepare—prepare to fail**

When something goes wrong it tends to be because we did not think about it in advance. If we actually think about the situation we are about to deal with and consider what we need to do and what may happen, we are much less likely to be taken by surprise. The maxim 'fail to prepare—prepare to fail' is perfect for the suspect interviewer, for inadequate preparation results in missed opportunities that may never be recoverable. The essentials of planning and preparation involve four broad areas:

(1) the investigation;
(2) the suspect;
(3) the law; and
(4) practicalities.

5.4.2 **The investigation**

The reason for a person being interviewed under caution is that they are suspected of being involved in a criminal offence, and you must be absolutely clear what material in the investigation indicates their involvement. The starting point for the interviewer's preparation should be to ensure they have a full and clear understanding of why the interviwee is a suspect. What evidence is there that they were responsible and what other information does the interviewer have that points to their involvement? The answers to these questions need to be carefully and objectively considered in advance of any interview.

It is likely that the interviewer will conclude that there is a certain timescale in which the actions of the suspect need to be ascertained, and a series of particular pieces of incriminating evidence or information that they would like the suspect to account for. This should provide the interviewer with both a relevant—or material—timeframe and also key issues that they need to focus upon in their interview. This will give the interviewer aims and objectives for the interview which must be recorded on the interview plan.

What are the circumstances of the offence? If at all possible the interviewer must visit the scene to get a full understanding of what occurred, failure to do this concedes knowledge to the suspect. If the interviewer can see what the suspect would have seen they will be in a strong position to assess the accuracy of the suspect's account and to take them into the level of detail needed in order to show whether someone is being truthful or not.

The interviewer must read all the relevant statements and reports about the case, and in addition to reading each piece of material from start to finish, organize this information into a single chronological account; a timeline. The interviewer must take account of the relevant timeframe for this suspect and then make one set of notes covering all the information relevant to the interview. This is a time consuming exercise but very worthwhile.

In creating this document the interviewer will contextualize the evidence or information with other material and, in the process, develop a far greater understanding of the investigation as it pertains to this suspect. The interviewer will also be able to identify any issues or contradictions in the case. Most significantly for the conversational model, going through this process will help the interviewer to commit the material to their working memory and enable them to conduct the interview with only minimal reference to notes.

5.4.3 The suspect

The interviewer must research the suspect in detail because the information discovered can be used during the interview, in particular at the engaging phase where the interviewer will use their conversational skills. In addition to the material that makes them a suspect there are three general areas that the interviewer will need to know about:

- personal background;
- previous criminal activities; and
- previous conduct at police interview.

Personal background will cover the suspect's domestic circumstances: Are they married? Do they have children? What is their cultural background? Are they working and, if so, as what? Are there any intellectual or health issues that may impact upon the interview? Many police officers engage in rather crude and halfhearted attempts at rapport, because they lack any insight into the individual they are dealing with. Information discovered about the suspect in advance of the interview may be very helpful at that early stage.

Look at any records available regarding their previous criminality arrests, convictions and acquittals. Does their pattern of offending fit the current investigation? Is there evidence of previous criminal behaviour that may be evidential in your case? Do they act alone or with others? How have they come to be arrested in the past? Do they tend to plead guilty at court? Have they any experience of prison?

Most important is to find out about their past behaviour at interview. The best guide to future conduct is past conduct. Do they tend to answer questions or not? If the answer to that is sometimes, then can the interviewer discover what makes the suspect more and less likely to say anything? Are they represented by the same legal advisers at each arrest? Do they pose any risk to the interviewer at interview? Do they tend to provide pre-prepared statements during interview? If possible speak with other police officers who have interviewed the suspect or listen to tapes of the interview. Insights gained here will help the interviewer to prepare for the likely direction that the interview will take, however do remember that the interviewer controls the interview and must be persistent and resist the suspect dictating how it will go.

5.4.4 **The law**

What the interviewer discovers about the suspect may have legal implications in particular if the suspect is a juvenile, or if there are indications that the suspect is mentally disordered or mentally vulnerable. If the interviewer suspects this to be the case or is told in good faith then the suspect should be treated accordingly (PACE Codes of Practice C1.4). In these circumstances an appropriate adult will be required to be present at any interview.

The role of an appropriate adult is to:

- advise the interviewee;
- observe whether or not the interview is being conducted properly and fairly; and
- facilitate communication with the interviewee.

In the case of a person who is mentally disordered or otherwise mentally vulnerable, 'the appropriate adult' means:

- a relative, guardian or other person responsible for their care or custody;
- someone experienced in dealing with mentally disordered or mentally vulnerable people but who is not a police officer or employed by the police;
- failing these, some other responsible adult aged 18 or over who is not a police officer or employed by the police.

PACE Code C Annex E, para 2

Equally, if the suspect does not speak English or appears to be deaf they will require an interpreter. Interpreters present particular difficulties for the interviewer (see 5.9.2).

The interviewer will need to be aware that the suspect's continued detention has to be reviewed by the custody officer for it to be lawful. An interview conducted while a suspect was unlawfully detained will certainly be excluded as unfair, if not oppressive.

Significant statements and silences

An interviewer must be able to identify whether the suspect has made a significant statement or a significant silence:

> The interviewer shall ask the suspect whether they confirm or deny that earlier statement or silence and if they want to add anything.

PACE Code C11.4

These are defined in PACE Code C as follows:

> A significant statement is one which appears capable of being used in evidence against the suspect, in particular a direct admission of guilt. A significant silence is a failure or refusal to answer a question or answer satisfactorily when under caution, which might, allowing for the restriction on drawing adverse inferences from silence . . . give rise to an inference under the Criminal Justice and Public Order Act 1994, Part III.

Code C11.4A

These are often misunderstood, and many interviews begin with whatever the suspect says at the time they were arrested, regardless of whether it meets this definition. These comments may well be relevant but they are not significant. A significant statement or silence needs to occur in the presence and hearing of a police officer or other police staff, so an admission of guilt to a third party is not a significant statement. It also needs to amount to evidence against them, so a denial or alibi is not a significant statement regardless of whether the interviewer can prove it to be false. An outright admission would clearly be a significant statement, but so would something mitigating, for example: 'I didn't mean to hurt him' or 'I was only the driver'. A significant statement need not be made under caution, but in practice will often be after caution and/or arrest.

A significant silence is not answering a question that might lead to an inference, under the Criminal Justice and Public Order Act 1994. In practice this means a question on arrest relating to any 'special warning' material.

POINT TO NOTE—SPECIAL WARNING MATERIAL

Any object, mark or substance, or marks on such objects found at the time of their arrest:

- on their person;
- in or on their clothing or footwear;
- otherwise in their possession; or
- in the place where they were found.

Section 36

and/or

Their presence at or near the scene at or about the time of the offence.

Section 37

A significant silence can only occur under caution. However, because the significant silence relates to what is said under caution—normally at the time of arrest—and not in an interview, the special warning itself does not need to be given. For example, if an officer in an assault case cautions a suspect and asks why he has blood on his shoes, and the suspect refuses to answer, it would amount to a significant silence. Alternatively, if someone is found in the garden shed at the scene of a house burglary and on arrest and caution they refuse to account for their presence there, it would also amount to a significant silence.

In addition, an interviewer needs to ensure that any relevant comments made by the suspect have been properly dealt with. Anything said by a suspect—including unsolicited comments—must be noted, timed, and signed by the officer. The suspect should then be given the opportunity to read the note and sign it as correct or indicate how they think it is inaccurate as soon as practicable (Code C11.13). This should normally be done in advance of an interview, however if not then the interviewing officer needs to deal with it during the interview itself. There is no requirement that a relevant comment needs to be put at the start of the interview, this only applies to a significant statement or silence.

Regardless of whether the suspect has been asked at the time of arrest, the interviewing officer must identify any special warning material—as outlined above—in order to deal with it in accordance with the Codes of Practice should the situation arise during the interview and in that instance the special warning must be delivered lawfully. How this should be dealt with will be covered in more detail at 5.6.4, 'Challenging', where any special warnings should be introduced.

Points to prove and defences

The elements of the offence for which the suspect has been arrested must be considered in order to identify points to prove. This is particularly important with the inferences available should the suspect not answer any questions. In a case of theft, for example, the interviewer will need specifically to cover:

dishonesty, appropriation, property belonging to another, and an intention permanently to deprive the owner. Whatever offence the interviewer is investigating they will need to know the elements of the offence and the available defences. If the interviewer fails to explore a particular defence at the interview stage they may well find it becomes an issue later at trial, because they have left the door open.

CPS Charging Standards (Oxford: Oxford University Press, 2005)—an A5 size book—is available at every police station and contains clear details of the elements of each offence which covers both the points to prove and the defences open in law. This should be the first point of reference for the interviewer in the planning stage. If a copy is not available then a CPS lawyer should be consulted.

5.4.5 **Practicalities**

Here the interviewer should consider the other issues relating to the interview. Will the interviewer conduct the interview with another officer? If so, the interviewer should ensure that the other officer is fully briefed with what the interviewer wants them to do. Many interviews have floundered because of lack of coordination between officers. If the interviewer is the primary interviewing officer they are in control and should get agreement from their colleague that they will follow the interviewer's instructions. The interviewer may ask their colleague to deal with the tapes and to keep an eye on the clock to ensure the tape changes are carried out smoothly and in good time. The interviewer may ask that they keep control of any exhibits that the interviewer wishes to introduce and to make notes during the interview.

The interviewer must ensure that their colleague does not interrupt them and take control of the interview, and the interviewer needs to make it clear if and when they will hand over questioning. It is good practice for the lead interviewer to concentrate on engaging with the suspect while the second officer carries out any administrative duties. The lead interviewer may wish the secondary officer to have a copy of the interview plan to ensure that they cover all that they want to in that interview. Although it is important to consider whether, in a complex case, it would be better to carry out a series of interviews concentrating on a specific area at a time.

Consider the time leading up to the interview. Will the interviewer have an opportunity to collect the suspect from their cell and bring them to the interview room or to meet their legal adviser? Where will any consultation take place between the interviewer and legal adviser, and then the suspect and the legal adviser? It is sometimes the case that both these consultations occur in the interview room, and that the interviewer waits until the legal adviser tells them that they are ready to interview at which time the interview begins. This is not good practice because the interviewer has lost control of the room and the interview. Once the consultation has ended the interviewer should ensure that the suspect is returned to their cell and the legal adviser is shown out of the custody area until the interviewer is ready to begin.

The interviewer should ensure that they know the interview room, how any equipment works, and whether it is functioning properly. Often interview rooms are left in a sorry state, and the interviewer should not be averse to clearing away rubbish and tidying the room, remember the room will reflect on them. Be aware that if the tape machine fails during the interview the interviewer may try replacement tapes and if that solves the problem they should explain what they have done and carry on with the interview. If that is not successful the interviewer will need the custody officer's authority for the interview to continue with a written record being made (Codes E3.3 and E4.15).

The interviewer must break for 15 minutes every two hours and the suspect must be allowed a 45-minute break at meal times unless it would delay their release (Code C12B). The interviewer should be aware of any custody review that is due, as it may be preferable to delay an interview or to conduct a review a little early to prevent disruption.

5.4.6 Seating

It is well worth thinking about who sits where and why in the interview room. In the past a desk between the interviewer and the suspect was necessary in order for contemporaneous notes to be made of the interview, equally early tape recorders needed a microphone to be clipped to the interviewer and the suspect and this dictated that they both sit adjacent to the tape machine. Today the only consideration ought to be: what will help the interviewer to maintain a conversation with the suspect?

Figure 5.2 Interview room seating:1

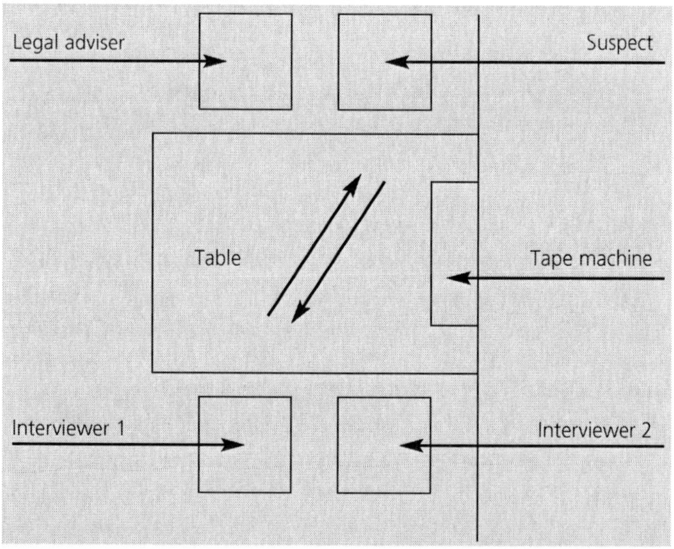

Figure 5.2 illustrates what is often encountered, with the primary interviewer facing the suspect diagonally across the desk, while the secondary interviewer

deals with the tapes. There may be variations where the legal adviser and the suspect are different, and if there is only a single interviewer, they will tend to sit alongside the machine. This configuration may have its origin in the time when it was necessary to clip a microphone to the suspect, today this is unnecessary.

Figure 5.3 Interview room seating:2

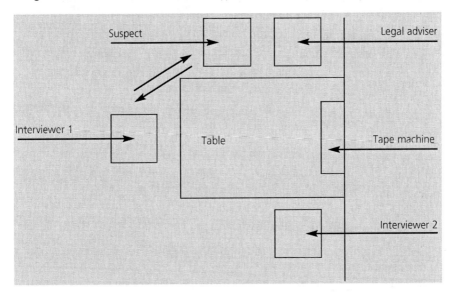

However, the interviewer should consider what would be the most effective configuration for the conversational model. The interviewer wants to engage conversationally with the suspect, and wants to be the focus of their attention. The interviewer does not want any artificial barriers and wants to sit at an angle most conducive to them talking together. If the interviewer is faced with this room layout then they should aim for the configuration in Figure 5.3.

Talking across a desk formalizes the process, while the face-to-face configuration is confrontational. Watch people talking together casually and it is apparent that a comfortable angle develops in which they tend to be slightly offset to each other. If the lead interviewer moves their chair out so that they are not behind a desk, then the suspect turns away from the legal adviser to engage with them, while the secondary officer is less of a distraction.

This is a more conversational arrangement and will help the interviewer to engage with the suspect. If the chairs are fixed, the interviewer should consider taking another chair into the interview room. If the layout is different, the interviewer should consider how best they can use the room to help achieve a conversational feel to the interview. In future it is likely that interview rooms will not be constructed in accordance with this model and many police services already have a less formal layout for their suspect interview rooms.

5.4.7 **The interview plan**

A written interview plan needs to be produced in all cases in order to focus the mind on the purpose of the interview. It should begin with a clear aim, which in most cases will be to establish whether the suspect was involved in the offence for which they were arrested. Thereafter there will be specific objectives that will be tied to the evidence or information that indicates why they are a suspect. For example, there may be an eye witness who saw the suspect near to the scene at around the time of the offence, so an objective would be to find out what they were doing there at that time. A search of their home address may have recovered property stolen from the offence, so an objective would be to obtain an explanation for their possession of the item. Some plans refer to these as the **facts established** and the **facts to be determined.**

The plan should cover the points to prove and the defences open to the suspect. Also whether significant statements or silences have been made, and whether there is scope for the use of special warnings during the interview. Consideration should be given to using exhibits, photographs, or plans during the interview, and/or providing materials to allow the suspect to draw a sketch.

5.4.8 **Preparing pre-interview disclosure**

One of the most difficult areas for police officers is dealing with pre-interview disclosure. This is the information the interviewer will be providing to the suspect through their legal adviser in advance of an interview. There is a clear tension between the interviewer and the legal adviser in that the legal adviser will want to know everything that the interviewer knows before taking instructions from the suspect, while the interviewer would generally prefer not to give away what they know in advance.

In 1993 a Royal Commission recommended that the PACE Codes be amended to encourage police to inform a suspect's legal adviser of at least the general nature of the case. This has never been implemented and the current position has been endorsed by case law, most importantly in *R v Argent* [1997] 2 Cr App R 27. The legal adviser has every right to inspect the custody record which shows the reason and grounds for arrest and any authorizations, but they have no legal entitlement to any more material.

A very important case dealing with this was *R v Imran and Hussain* [1997] Crim LR 754. In this case the interviewing officers did not tell the legal adviser representing Imran that he and others had been caught on video committing a robbery. Not knowing about the existence of the video Imran lied about what had happened and the video was used to prove those lies. Imran's defence argued that this was unfair and the case went before the Court of Appeal to consider whether it was proper or not to withhold such information from the legal adviser prior to the interview. The Court of Appeal agreed with the trial judge who had said:

> It is totally wrong to submit that a defendant should be prevented from lying by being presented with the whole of the evidence against him prior to interview.

The defence had argued that principles dealing with the disclosure of evidence that applied after charge should in fairness be applied before interviewing. Since the defence must be informed about all the evidence against a defendant once that person has been charged, it must therefore be fair to disclose all the evidence before interview. This was entirely rejected by the court who said that it lacked reality to apply rules that related to the prosecution of a person at the time of investigation.

However, defence arguments at court that no inference should be taken from a suspect's silence are invariably based upon lack of disclosure prior to interview. The court in considering these arguments will look at how reasonable the disclosure was and how reasonable the legal advice was that followed. In practice the legal adviser needs sufficient disclosure to be able to take meaningful instructions from the suspect, and little or no disclosure will always result in advice to say nothing.

It is therefore not the law and it is not good practice to disclose all the information in the interviewer's possession to a suspect before an interview. Quite the contrary, it is good practice to ensure that there is information withheld from a suspect so that they are not given the opportunity to lie around the evidence that the interviewer has.

So how does the interviewer decide what to disclose and what not to disclose? This will clearly vary from case to case, however a useful approach is to start with noting everything that the interviewer knows about the offence and in particular what implicates the suspect. The interviewer should then ask themself what do they have that the suspect may not know they have. For example, a suspect in an assault will know what the victim is likely to have said but may not know that there is an independent witness or CCTV footage. In a burglary case the suspect may not know if fingerprint or DNA evidence has been found.

Some or all of the information that the interviewer has identified in this way may be withheld from initial disclosure, and it is very often worthwhile thinking about phasing the disclosure or drip-feeding, providing limited disclosure initially and more later. This approach was specifically supported by the Court of Appeal in *Imran and Hussain*. It will require careful planning and the preparation of two or more sets of written disclosure and the interviewer must be able to explain their decisions if necessary at court. It is useful therefore for the interviewer to keep a note of their decisions to cover this possibility.

The interviewer must, however, be very careful not to lie to or mislead the legal adviser since this will render any subsequent interview inadmissible. The strength of evidence must not be overstated, for example a fingerprint on a bottle in a building does not mean the interviewer can prove the suspect was inside the building—although it is a strong inference. Equally, it must not be implied that there is evidence which does not exist, such as an eye witness or a forensic link between the suspect and the crime.

Once the interviewer has decided what to disclose they should prepare written documents to serve on the legal adviser. This process will create at least three documents: the interviewer's notes of what is not being disclosed initially and in each case why it is not being disclosed; an initial pre-interview disclosure for service on the legal adviser; and a second disclosure to be introduced at some stage during the interview. It is worthwhile considering whether the legal adviser can be supplied with any supporting material to assist, such as copies of exhibits, plans or photographs. Any such material should be listed on the written disclosure.

What information is disclosed before interview and what information is subsequently disclosed during interview will—in the event of the suspect being charged—be recorded on a new form MG6A (see 6.13).

Checklist—Planning and preparation

- Why am I interviewing this person about this offence?

- Attend the scene

- Read all statements and reports

- Organize relevant material into a single chronological event line

- What is the suspect's background?

- What is the pattern of their criminal behaviour?

- How do they behave in police interviews?

- Is the suspect a juvenile, mentally disordered or mentally vulnerable?

- Do I need an interpreter?

- Is their detention/continued detention lawful?

- Are there any significant statements or silences?

- Is there any 'special warning' material?

- Have I written an interview plan?

- Have I consulted with the CPS about the elements of the offence for which they have been arrested and any legal defences?

- Have I briefed interviewer number two?

- Do I have access to any property, photographs, and plans that I need for the interview?

- Is the interview room clean and fully operative?

- Is a custody review due?

- Have I prepared a written pre-interview briefing for the legal adviser?

5.5 **Engage and Explain**

5.5.1 **First impressions**

This part of PEACE deals with first contact with the suspect—assuming another person was the arresting officer—and the opening of the interview up to and including asking the opening question. In this example we will be collecting the suspect from the cell before the interview, however the principles hold good whatever the circumstances of the interviewer's first contact.

It takes only a very short time to form a first impression of someone and once formed it takes a considerable amount of time to reconsider that impression. The opening few minutes of the interviewer's contact with the suspect is therefore very important since the interviewer is unlikely to have the time to modify that impression if they have not created the one that they want. In the conversation model there are characteristics—RESPONSE—which if we are able to display we know will help us have the kind of interview that we want. On entering the cell consider shaking hands with the suspect; it displays equality and because it tends to be something that people respond to without thinking it is unusual for a suspect to refuse.

Personalizing yourself by using your name rather than your rank and asking the suspect what they would like to be called, reinforces your respect and openness. Use their name often—it is one of the most important words to us. Explain what is going to happen and enquire after their welfare, whether they have eaten, washed and spoken to a family member of friend—assuming this right has not been withheld. At all times the interviewer's tone and style should reinforce their words—beware of leakage. Be clear that it is not the case that the interviewer should appear to be their friend. The aim is to be honest, open, professional, and above all objective.

Effort invested at this stage will be rewarded, the suspect will feel less threatened and is more likely to respond normally. One of the conversation rules is that once we start talking with someone there is pressure on us to continue, this is why good interviewers will actively work on generating a cooperative manner with the suspect in advance of the interview itself. It is easier not to cooperate with someone one does not get on with.

Equally important is the principle of reciprocity. This is something which we all instinctively understand, and amounts to simply this: if someone does me a favour I feel indebted and obliged to return the favour. This applies even with people we do not like. We feel we owe someone and we wish to be freed of that obligation and the only way to do so is to return the favour. Of course the opposite also applies, if someone does us a disservice we feel justified in responding in kind. The interviewer should recognize the impact of this principle and take responsibility for everything to the suspect's benefit. The simple act of bringing a suspect a drink or offering the chance to wash or make a phone call may be dressed up to look like a favour which obligates the suspect to the interviewer.

The suspect may not be particularly open to these overtures, and may be hostile, however the good interviewer will understand the principles behind Batari's Box and will not allow the suspect's hostility to set the tone. Becoming agitated is a sign of weakness and the good interviewer will continue to employ RESPONSE signals in order to dictate the interview tone.

5.5.2 **The introduction**

Once in the interview room open the tapes in the presence of the suspect and get them in the machine as soon as possible. It is very important that the interviewer maintains the relaxed conversational informality into the interview room and throughout the process.

The Codes of Practice tell us what needs to be said at the outset of a taped interview and to help us there is often a crib-sheet taped to the desk. **Do not read it out**. It is vital for this model that an interviewer is able to deliver the interview opening while looking at and engaging with the suspect, aiming for a conversation not delivering a set of instructions.

The following must be covered:

- that the interview is being tape recorded;
- the interviewer's name and rank and that of any other interviewer present— (this is subject to a proviso if the interviewer feels they would be in danger by giving their name);
- ask the suspect and any other person present to introduce themselves;
- state the date, time, and place of the interview; and
- tell the suspect that they will be entitled to a copy of the interview tape.

We all have personal styles and there is no single correct way to say each of these things, the key is to de-formalize as much as possible and to keep it conversational. Rather than:

> Right, this interview is being tape recorded

instead, say:

> Peter, that buzzer noise means that the tapes are working OK, have a look there Peter, can you see them going round? Yes . . . good, and that means everything is now being recorded.

Take every opportunity to encourage the involvement of the suspect with the conversation. Some officers mention the microphones on the wall and the machine counter. These are all opportunities to set the tone for the interview.

> My name's Paul, Paul Hughes, and I'm a Detective Sergeant, but Peter please call me Paul, and this is Martin Jones, he's another Detective here. Peter what's your full name please?

This is not intended to be followed verbatim, the key is to think about what the interviewer must covered but to do it in a conversational style appropriate to their personal manner. When it comes to introducing the legal adviser the interviewer should wait until they deal with the suspect's right to legal advice.

5.5.3 The caution

Since the Criminal Justice and Public Order Act 1994, the caution has become a powerful tool to encourage a suspect to talk to the interviewer at interview. Too often it is simply read from the crib sheet as if it were a chore. This is a missed opportunity; the caution needs to be delivered with the intent to make the suspect think about the situation they are in. It needs to be delivered clearly and slowly and then explained in order to ensure that there is no misunderstanding.

The suspect should be told that what the interviewer is about to say is very important:

Peter I want to make sure that you know what your rights are while you are here.

This displays respect and supportiveness. They should then be cautioned slowly and in full before the interviewer explains what it means. Do not simply ask whether the suspect understands and disregard whatever the legal adviser says about the suspect's comprehension. Assume in every case that the interviewer needs to explain it fully and so after the formal caution just say simply:

Now. Peter, I am going to explain what that means.

Most police officers believe that they could explain the caution without much preparation, in truth few can do so effectively and none without thinking about it. A public speaker was reputedly requested to deliver a speech, and asked in response how long did he have to talk. When asked why he needed to know, he replied that if they wanted him to talk for two hours he could start straightaway, if they wanted him to talk for 20 minutes he needed a day to prepare, but if they wanted him to talk for five minutes he needed a week. Being short and concise is impactive but it takes careful preparation. Consider explaining the first part of the caution:

You do not have to say anything.

The interviewer could take this opportunity to reinforce that it is entirely up to the suspect whether s/he talks with them during the interview and regardless of whatever advice s/he may have had, a court will see it as their decision. In *R v Howell* [2003] EWCA Crim 1 the Court of Appeal held that taking legal advice to remain silent at interview did not mean the jury could not draw an adverse inference. In other words the suspect will be responsible for the decision s/he makes and it will not be enough for the suspect to say at court s/he was taking legal advice.

The most important part of the caution is the middle section and this must be explained carefully and concisely:

But it may harm your defence if you do not mention something that you later rely on in court.

The primary inference—there are others—that may be drawn in a no comment interview when the defendant later gives evidence—or her/his lawyer alludes to a defence—is that it has been invented since the interview, and it has been tailored to fit around the prosecution evidence and therefore the evidence the defendant giving is not true. Accordingly this should form the basis of the interviewer's explanation, keep it in simple words, concise and short. It might be useful to think about if you were explaining to a jury:

> Peter there is a but, if you end up in court talking about this and you say things that you haven't told me, the court might think you're telling lies, you've made it up in the meantime, because if it was true you would have told Paul when you could. If it was true you would tell me now.

And the last part of the caution means that whatever is said and—crucially—whether nothing is said can be given in evidence.

Again this is not prescriptive, we each have a personal style and there are many ways to deliver this effectively—the key is to think about using the caution to make an impact on the suspect and drive home in clear and simple terms what it means. It is a powerful tool and the interviewer should take full advantage of it.

5.5.4 **Free and independent legal advice**

If the interviewer forgets to say what the time or date is, or to introduce their colleague, although it will be a breach of the Codes, it is unlikely to render the interview inadmissible. If the interviewer forgets to caution or remind the suspect of their right to legal advice the interviewer will lose their interview.

FILA is a useful term to remember (Free and Independent Legal Advice):

> Peter, you are entitled to free and independent legal advice. I can arrange this for you at any time, and whatever you decide now you can change your mind. I can arrange for you to speak to a legal adviser on the phone or I can get someone here for you.

If they have a legal adviser present the interviewer should still explain their entitlement and then ask the legal adviser to introduce themselves and explain their role. Most legal advisers will do so anyway so the interviewer has maintained control.

5.5.5 **Reasons, routines, and expectations**

Conversation requires empathy and openness, so at this stage the interviewer will be explaining what is going to happen:

> While we are talking Peter . . .

During this phase the interviewer's conversational skills are important. Look for opportunities to involve the suspect in conversation, use their name often and refer to talking together about what happened. Behave as if that is what is going to happen and the suspect will be under pressure to conform. Do not underestimate the power of suggesting by your words and manner that you will be talking.

The **reason** for the interview is that the suspect was arrested on suspicion of involvement in a particular crime and they now have an opportunity to say what they wish to about that. If necessary explain any legal terms, what is arson or kidnapping, do not assume they know what GBH means in law. The interviewer should tell the suspect that the interviewer is very interested in what they have to say, that they do not know what happened and they just want to find out the truth.

Routines will cover such things as tape changes, the showing of exhibits, maps or photographs, breaks, referring to or making notes. Again use this as an opportunity to talk with the suspect, not to give them instructions. The difference will be more in manner and tone than words.

Expectations is about negotiating an agreement about how the interviewer and the suspect will be talking with each other. It gives the interviewer an ideal chance to talk about listening carefully and not interrupting one another. Get the suspect to agree about how you will both behave towards each other, not interrupting or over-talking and listening and responding in a respectful way.

5.5.6 Route map and the opening question

The route map amounts to the identification of no more than five areas of conversation pertinent to the interviewer's case leading to an opening question designed to elicit a first account—the first thing that they say about the reasons they are a suspect, accounting for the evidence or information that suggests their involvement.

In a case of domestic violence committed at the family home after a night's drinking, the interviewer's route map might be: the general relationship between the two parties, the suspect's actions last night, and then what happened when they arrived home:

> Peter, we're going to talk about you and Sue, how long you've been together, how you get on and that, OK?
> We're also going to talk about yesterday, about what you did all day.
> And what happened last night when you got home.

This simple three-step approach focuses the suspect on the issues that the interviewer wishes to address and draws him towards the incident itself. As the interviewer is speaking the suspect will be thinking about the things the interviewer is raising and when they finish she will be already thinking about the events once she got home. At this point the interviewer will need to deal with any significant statement or silence that they identified in their planning stage. The suspect should be asked whether they wish to confirm or deny the statement or silence and if they wish to add anything further.

The interviewer's opening question should be planned in advance and they may wish to deal with the background material first—'So Peter tell me about you and Sue'. Alternatively the interviewer might want to go straight to the main issue—'Tell me what happened when you got home then Peter'. The interviewer needs to use their judgement about the best opening approach based upon the particular nature of the case and the individual that they are interviewing.

Checklist—Engage and explain

- How can I make a good first impression?
- Get the tapes open and in the machine as soon as possible
- Do not read from the crib sheet
- De-formalize your words and style
- Use your name and their preferred name frequently
- Explain the tape process
- State the day, date, time, and location
- Explain the caution carefully
- Explain FILA—Free and Independent Legal Advice
- Introduce the legal adviser if present
- Give the reason for the interview
- Explain routines
- Mutually agree on your conduct
- Identify three to five areas you wish to talk about, focusing on the offence
- Prepare your opening question

5.6 Account, Clarify, and Challenge

5.6.1 Question types

In order to find out information the interviewer will need to ask questions. Behind that simple observation is a host of factors. The simple question 'Why?', may be delivered with accompanying intonation and body language that totally change its nature as a question, for example from sympathy to condemnation. The six questions commonly recommended—what, how, who, when, where, and why—may easily be delivered in an aggressive and even oppressive manner, so here the interviewer's conversational skills are imperative.

Questions need to be short and simple to be clear. Police interviewers have a tendency to use formalities like 'motor vehicle', 'registered owner', or 'public house', this is unnecessary and not conversational and should be avoided. Open questions are productive questions, they elicit more information and allow greater areas to be explored, for example 'And what happened then?'. Closed or narrow questions, by contrast are relatively unproductive, for example, 'So did you . . .' just gives an option to the suspect and will most likely elicit a yes or no response. However, such narrow questions may be necessary to clarify a particular issue, but the interviewer should return to open and productive questions as soon as possible.

Questions can be asked by repeating part of what has been said, either words in the middle or something at the end:

> So I just had to defend myself you know he was coming right at me I was scared.

A response could be to ask 'Defend yourself?' or 'Scared?', either way a question comes from the previous question and encourages the suspect to give more information. It is not necessary to use actual words at all, nods or quizzical looks can be questions in terms of eliciting more. Silence is very effective where an open question is asked and the suspect has responded but there is clearly more that could be said. It works because conversation is a turn-taking process and the turn is handed back and forth, however the interviewer can decide to not take their turn by keeping quiet and this puts pressure on the other party to continue.

Avoid leading questions, for example 'Was the car blue?'. Equally avoid option questions, for example 'Was the car blue or black?'. A much better question would be: 'What does the car look like?'; and if necessary 'What colour was the car?'.

It is very important to ask questions that emerge from the suspect's answers where possible. The investigative material will dictate what needs to be covered, but it should not dictate the actual questions asked. If, for example, in a domestic assault case in exploring whether there is any history of violence in the relationship, listen to what the suspect says about their partner instead of simply asserting that the victim says s/he has been attacked by the suspect before.

5.6.2 **The first account**

In the planning stage having considered what implicates the suspect, a material timeframe will be identified, which contains all the things that the suspect needs to account for: why they are suspected of involvement. The first account will be the first thing the suspect says about what links him to the offence. It may amount to denials, an alibi, an excuse, or a defence, whatever is said is the foundation of the interview. It might include what he says about his presence in a particular building—if you have fingerprint evidence—or what he says about stolen property he has in his possession.

At this stage the approach is a gentle, encouraging one—being really interested in what they have to say, while suspending any disbelief in what they are saying. It may be that their account is absolutely at odds with the investigation so far, but at this point it must be accepted. The purpose is to commit them to an account no matter how general or how contrary to other information. Resist any desire to challenge—this will come later.

It would be better from a conversational point of view not to make notes while carrying out the interview; they are a barrier to listening and to engaging in conversation. If there is a another interviewer in the room, they may make notes, but the first interviewer must remember what the suspect is saying. To this end what they say should regularly be summarized back to them, and—when they are talking about the most significant issues—in their own words if at all possible. As has been said this will help commit what they say to memory and help to analyse precisely what they have said and what they have not said, and it will ensure that the interview is based upon the suspect's account and not other material. Once they have covered their first account go back through it with the suspect and get him to commit himself to it. This process may well generate more material that needs to be clarified.

5.6.3 Topics and probing

Once the interviewer has covered their material timeframe they will have an explanation for all the reasons that the interviewer suspect him. Now they need to divide their account into topics, which may reflect their route map, and might have been supplemented by what the suspect has said. In the case of the domestic assault the following topics may have emerged or been identified from the suspect's account:

- The history of the relationship
- The argument three days ago
- Yesterday morning at home
- Immediately prior to Peter going out
- Peter at the pub
- The journey home
- At home
- Going to hospital
- Arrest

Each topic area must be dealt with in turn and the relevant material obtained before moving on to another topic. The reason for this is to enable the interviewer to keep to a simple structure and not to be confused by flitting from one point to another across the whole account. If while asking about the history of the relationship the suspect begins to talk about going to hospital after the assault, while it is interesting and relevant and should not be ignored, the interviewer should return to deal with the history completely before moving on. Otherwise the interviewer will forget where they are and miss parts of the account.

Each topic area will have material relevant to the investigation, and in some there will be little that is at issue, while in others there will be a great deal. The interviewer should probe each topic for fine grain detail so far as it is relevant to the case. It is in this fine grain detail where the suspect will find it most difficult to lie and to sustain those lies, and where the interviewer is most likely to uncover inconsistencies in their account. In terms of relevance the historical relationship might have little that requires detail, however the events in the house once the suspect got home will need the interviewer to elicit a moment-by-moment account from the suspect.

Each topic should be probed to the degree relevant with summaries as and when needed and certainly at the conclusion of dealing with the topic. It should then be closed and linked to the next topic, until each has been dealt with to an appropriate level of fine grain detail:

> Ok Peter I don't need to ask you anything else about what happened at the pub, can we talk now about when you left the pub to go home, tell me about that.

When people tell lies they tend to try and get away with generalities, and they will continue to lie to us if they believe that we accept what they say. With a lying suspect the interviewer needs to come across as someone who is accepting what s/he is being told, because if the interviewer makes it plain—through leakage— that they do not believe what the suspect is saying, they will have no motivation to continue to talk to the interviewer.

The difficulty for the interviewer is to be sufficiently encouraging and RESPONSE(ive) so that the suspect keeps talking, while at the same time making the suspect tell lies in fine grain detail rather than the broad generalizations that they find relatively easy and will have prepared for. Lying in such detail is very difficult and this is where they will make mistakes and be caught out and provide the interviewer with material for their challenges.

5.6.4 Challenging

Challenging the suspect is the penultimate phase of the interview because when we are challenged we become less communicative, and premature challenges— made before the topics have been explored in detail—will result in a less conversational interview thereafter. Therefore it is important to be aware of what constitutes a challenge. Only when the interviewer is content that there is nothing more that the suspect can be persuaded to say to about the offence should they be challenged.

A challenge amounts to taking issue with what the suspect is telling the interviewer and it can take many forms. At one extreme is the firm assertion—'You are a liar'—but at the other extreme a simple comment, like 'Really', can be delivered in such a way that its meaning—*I don't believe you*—is clear. Police interviewers often challenge prematurely because they recognize immediately when a suspect is saying something that is contrary to other evidence in their possession. The temptation is always to take issue with it straightaway, but if that can be resisted the suspect may go onto tell more lies that can be proved. Ultimately it is far better to be able to show systematic lying throughout an interview rather than just one or two occasions that may be easier to explain in court.

Officers frequently assert 'I know you're lying' towards the end of interviews; this is however not effective challenging. The challenge should not be an assertion like this but more of an explanation that would hopefully lead anyone listening to reach the same conclusion. If the interview has been conducted without pre-conceptions the interviewer may well conclude, based upon how the interview has progressed, that the suspect is lying, but this will be based on specific things that the suspect has said. The interviewer should take the suspect through the reasons why s/he has reached that conclusion. In this way the challenge phase can be understood as summarizing the evidence produced from the interview.

There are two types of challenge material: internal challenges which would deal with anything the suspect said that was inherently contradictory or incompatible, and external challenges which are based on differences between the suspect's account and material from other sources, such as witnesses or forensic evidence. Internal inconsistencies are most likely to occur when the suspect's more general and vague initial account is later explored in detail in the topic phase. They are the most powerful challenges. The suspect may need to adjust their account to cope with the need to produce more detail, or simply make mistakes about what they have said. It is difficult to make up lies in detail and even more difficult to remember exactly what you have said:

> Earlier you said that you spent all day yesterday at home playing computer games, then later you said that you went out to see a friend. Why didn't you tell me that in the beginning?

External challenges involves putting material to the suspect:

> You said you don't know Michael but your fingerprints are in his house, how is that?

Challenges should build up to the strongest, and they should be delivered as an enquiry rather than an assertion:

> Peter, I just don't see how that can be right, because . . .

The key is for the interviewer to be objective in their assessment of what the suspect has said and what other material the interviewer has. If the interviewer can do this then their challenges will be clear and others will come to the same conclusions that they have.

5.6.5. 'No comment' interviews

Despite all the efforts during the engage phase the suspect is not answering questions or is saying 'no comment'. In this case the interviewer needs to remember Batari's Box and work hard at conversational skills. This should be seen as a struggle over how the interview is going to proceed, with each party seeking to dictate. When listening to tape recordings of 'no comment' interviews it is often very clear at which point the officer gives up trying to engage the suspect, and this can be after a relatively short time. The practical difficulty is that the interviewer is having a one-sided conversation, getting nothing back from the suspect. The pressure that the interviewer feels at this stage is testament to the power of the conversation rule that conversation requires cooperation.

One approach is for the interviewer to say to themselves that the suspect is answering—but in their head only. With a difficult suspect who says 'no comment' without listening to the question, the first job is to get them to listen. This will be achieved by being measured and persistent, and giving the suspect time to answer as though s/he were actually speaking. It will become clear when a suspect is actually listening and this should be seen as the first 'victory'. Once a suspect is listening, and if the interviewer's account of the offence is good they will be taken back to the event in their mind.

Without a first account there is only the external investigative material to rely upon, this should therefore form the basis of the interview. Try to take the suspect through the relevant events, reliving them in detail. This works well if the interviewer has a good idea of what they are likely to have done, for example an assault case where there is a full victim's account. Cover the whole material timeframe and ask about where they are implicated in the offence. Behave as if they are talking, work hard at engaging and take it slowly and methodically.

This is an example of where your knowledge of the scene would be vital. You can see what they would have seen and you can talk about it:

Peter what did you see . . .
In the hallway . . .
Through the glass door . . .
As you came up the path. . .

Pause after each question/statement as though getting an answer. Treat this as the first account and then select and probe a topic in the same way as a talking interview. This approach calls for great tenacity and is physically tiring, but if any approach will persuade the suspect to say something this will. It can result in a good deal of pressure to talk and anything less from the interviewer is handing over control to the suspect.

In particular, where the suspect has not answered any questions the interviewer must ensure that they have had an opportunity to respond to all the material the interviewer has which implicates them in the offence. This is very important in order to ensure that an inference from silence is available at court. The inference will only be given to the jury if the suspect mentions something at court which they did not at interview. However, the onus is on the interviewer to ensure that the suspect had the opportunity to mention it.

This is best achieved by a direct question. For example, in a case of theft, if the interviewer does not prepare the elements of the offence and therefore does not specifically ask the suspect whether s/he believed they had an honest right to take the property, the suspect has the opportunity at court to say that s/he did have an honest belief that the property was his/hers and that if the officer had asked him/her that question s/he would have answered. If, however, the interviewer specifically asks the question—'Did you honestly believe the property was yours?'—and this elicits no response, it makes it much more difficult for the suspect to avoid the inference at court.

5.6.6 **Delivering special warnings**

Special warnings can be delivered if the suspect is refusing to say anything, or refusing to say anything about certain important evidence, as outlined at 5.4.4. The special warning exists because it relates to powerful evidence that in all reasonableness requires an explanation—'Why do you have blood on your shoes?'—'Where did you get that injury?'—'Where did you get the credit card?'—'What were you doing in the garden?'.

It is important to realize that an inference may be drawn in the case of a special warning if the suspect refuses to answer at interview regardless of whether the suspect later comes up with an explanation for it. It is distinct from the caution where an inference may only be drawn if the suspect fails to mention something that s/he subsequently uses in court.

The special warning must be delivered in accordance with PACE—although ordinary language may be used. The officer must lay out the elements of the special warning as follows:

(a) what offence is being investigated;
(b) what fact they are being asked to account for;
(c) this fact may be due to them taking part in the commission of the offence;
(d) a court may draw a proper inference if they fail or refuse to account for this fact;
(e) a record is being made of the interview and it may be given in evidence if they are brought to trial.

PACE Codes of Practice C10.11

It will normally be the case that a special warning will be administered in a 'no comment' interview. Therefore the suspect will already have been asked to account for the specific fact—and refused to do so—before the officer uses the special warning. Think about the conversation model and deliver the warning in a way that drives home to the suspect and anyone else listening the significance of their failure to account for the fact:

Peter, as you know I am investigating the attack on your wife, she has serious head injuries.
You have blood on your shirt and on your shoes.

> It might be that the reason you've got blood on your shirt and shoes is that you attacked your wife and caused those injuries.
> If you don't tell me where this blood is from, a court might think it is because you did attack your wife and it is her blood.
> Peter everything we stay is being taped and can be given in evidence.

Part three of the special warning is worth particular attention. Frequently interviewers will tell the suspect that **they** believe the fact is due to the suspect's involvement in the offence rather than the way it is laid out in the Codes of Practice. This should be avoided because what the interviewer thinks is irrelevant, what they can show is all that matters. The correct way to deal with it is objectively, as if it is the only reasonable conclusion.

The interviewer should find a way to make their delivery of the special warning impactive, and this will only come through planning. It is a missed opportunity to think only about going through the legal requirements in order to secure the inference at court. Deliver it with intent—focus the mind of the suspect on the consequences of not explaining.

If a suspect is not answering questions or does not account for something where a special warning may not be given, consider reminding the suspect of the caution. This can be delivered in similar terms and, although the inference available to the court is different, it may still be delivered in a way that demands an answer. For example, in circumstances where a suspect's fingerprints or DNA is found at a scene and they will not account for it a special warning is not available. However, it may still be dealt with in a similar way to a special warning, by reminding the suspect of the caution:

> Peter, I am investigating a burglary at 25 Acacia Avenue.
> Your fingerprints/DNA have been found inside that address.
> It might be that your fingerprints/DNA are there because you did that burglary.
> Peter if you don't tell me how your fingerprints/DNA came to be in that house, a court might think it's because you did do that burglary.
> And if later you tell the court why your fingerprints/DNA are in that house but you don't tell me now, they might not believe you Peter. They might think if it was true there's no reason not to have told me. If it was true they might expect you to have told me now.

Clearly, in this example, no inference will be available at court unless the suspect supplies an explanation and the judge rules that it was a 'failure to mention'—during the interview—'something later relied upon'.

Checklist —Account, clarify, and challenge

- The first account is the first thing the suspect says that accounts for your suspicions

- Speak in a relaxed informal style

- Do not interrupt the suspect

- Ask open questions if possible

- Actively listen

- Ask questions that come out of what they say

- Avoid making notes if possible

- Have the suspect commit to an account

- Identify a chronological list of relevant topics

- Go through each topic in turn—do not leave it until you are finished

- Identify what is relevant to your enquiry in each topic

- Search for relevant fine grain detail

- Lying is very difficult in detail—do not let them off the hook

- Do not challenge until you have covered all of your topics

- Challenge objectively

- Internal challenges first, external second

- If 'no comment' work hard on engaging

- Ensure they have the opportunity to account for all your suspicions

- Give the special warning with impact

5.7 Closure and Evaluation

5.7.1 Closure

Before concluding the interview it is useful to consider the interview plan in terms of its purpose, aims, and objectives. Has the interviewer covered everything that they planned to? Has the suspect accounted for the interviewer's suspicions? If not, have they said all they are willing to say?

PACE Code E4.17 states that at the conclusion of the taped interview the suspect must be told that they have the opportunity to clarify or add to anything they have said. Should the suspect introduce any new material at this stage, do not be afraid to deal with it as a first account and go back to the start of the structure.

The conversation model applies throughout the process and at this stage the conversational rule that applies is that departing should not offend. We all know how there are times when we wish to disengage with someone we have been talking to. If we are in a group we may be able to slip away, however if it is just us and one other person we feel obliged to not be rude. We therefore look for an opportunity to part that is not offensive, for example by saying: 'Please excuse me I just need to get a drink/go to the toilet/speak to . . .'.

In the interview it may well be that the interviewer will need to speak to the suspect again so it would be foolish to undermine all the efforts they have invested in setting up a mutually respectful relationship. The suspect should be left feeling that they have been dealt with professionally and fairly because, even if nothing comes from the interviewer's efforts on this occasion, they might well find they reap the benefits in future dealings.

If the interviewer is asked by the suspect or their legal adviser what will happen next the interviewer must give truthful answers, but they must never discuss bail or possible sentencing. PACE requires the interviewer to ensure that the tapes are sealed in the presence of the suspect and they have the opportunity to sign the seals. If they refuse to do so an inspector or, if not available, the custody officer should be asked to enter the interview room and sign the seal.

5.7.2 Evaluation

Evaluation tends not to be given the attention it requires, in particular the performance of the interviewers. The interview may be evaluated from two perspectives: the impact of the interview on the investigation—both evidentially and in terms of information—and the quality of the interview.

Evaluating the interview as it relates to the investigation amounts in the first instance to identifying what evidence—if any—has been generated against the suspect. Have admissions been made? If so, what exactly has the suspect said and does it actually amount to an admission? 'I took the money' may be part of a dishonesty defence, while 'I punched him', may involve self-defence. The CPS/police partnership approach at this stage is vital and where there is any doubt as to what the suspect means that part of the interview should be transcribed in full. Details of how to complete the records of interview forms may be found at 6.26. If what the suspect has said falls short of an admission, have they supplied facts which may be corroborated by other means—witnesses or forensic evidence for example—or have they said things which may be proved to be lies? Is there sufficient evidence to request a CPS charging decision?

These may well open new lines of enquiry and if they are arguably reasonable the interviewer will be obliged to ensure that they are carried out. Since the Criminal Procedure and Investigation Act 1996, if a line of enquiry emerges from an interview or is suggested by the legal adviser and it is reasonable the interviewer has no discretion but to pursue it. This will also be the case where the interview has not produced any admissions or mitigation from the suspect, but where the suspect or the legal adviser suggests someone else was responsible.

In the second instance, how has the interview changed the complexion of the investigation? Does it now need to refocus, because the suspicions which led to the suspects arrest have now been accounted for, does the interview eliminate this suspect?

The quality of the interview as a professionally conducted process should also be examined, and the National Investigative Interviewing Strategy originally envisaged a strong Tier 4 structure to ensure proper evaluation of performance. It is already the case in some places that Tier 4 is becoming marginalized. This is a pity because workplace supervision is fundamental to the success of the strategy. In the past a lack of post-training supervision has led to a reversion to old practices and the Tier 4 was specifically designed to address this issue.

Regardless of supervision, self-evaluation is critical to improvement: the interviewer should learn the lessons from their performance. The interviewer must take responsibility for how the interview went. There is nothing pre-determined in an interview; the interviewer needs to believe that they can influence the suspect to give them what they want by their approach. Go back to planning and preparation—did something happen that the interviewer was not prepared for? Did the interviewer fail to engage with the suspect? The interviewer should listen to theirself, what they said and how they spoke to the suspect. The interviewer should not rely on their recollections about what went on; critically listening to oneself conducting an interview is massively enlightening. The interviewer should identify what they did well, what they did badly, and how they can improve both.

Checklist—Closure and evaluation

- Cover your interview plan
- Give the suspect the opportunity to clarify or add anything
- Departing must not offend
- Truthfully answer the suspects questions about what happens now
- Do not discuss bail or sentencing
- Ensure tapes are sealed and signed
- Evaluate the evidence against the suspect
- What new lines of enquiry have opened?
- How did you do?
- What went well and what went badly?

5.8 **Dealing with Legal Advisers**

5.8.1 **General**

The first principle of investigative interviewing as enshrined in the Home Office Guidelines is—as we have seen—to obtain accurate and reliable information in order to discover the truth. As well as being concerned with fairness to the suspect this involves a duty to the victim and to the public at large. The only role of a legal adviser in a police station is to protect and advance the legal rights of their client. There is no commensurate duty of fairness to the victim or the public or to uncovering—or assisting in uncovering—the truth of the matter being investigated.

The legal adviser's responsibility is to the suspect, and according to the Law Society the aims of the legal adviser include: to influence the police to accept the suspect is not guilty; to influence the police not to charge the suspect; to influence the police to make the most favourable case disposal decision for the suspect; and to create the most favourable position for the suspect if they are charged. In short, the legal adviser will endeavour to ensure that the outcome of the interview is in the best interests of the suspect. This conflict of roles is behind the tension between police officers and legal advisers at police stations, and the interviewer needs to understand this tension and deal with it professionally.

5.8.2 **The pre-interview briefing**

The first contact between the legal adviser and the interviewer is likely to be pre-interview disclosure. At this stage the interviewer should have carefully considered what disclosure is going to be provided and whether it will be phased, and will have produced document(s) detailing that disclosure. If the interviewer has engaged in the process described earlier—where decisions have been taken what **not** to disclose rather than what to disclose—the interviewer will be in a position where s/he does not wish to provide any further disclosure beyond what has been prepared.

However, the legal adviser will want to know everything that the interviewer does prior to taking instructions from the suspect and despite the legal position being that the interviewer is not obliged to supply any disclosure before interview, the legal adviser will attempt to persuade, cajole and intimidate police interviewers into supplying them with as much information as possible. *Defending Suspects at Police Stations: The Practitioner's Guide to Advice and Representation* (5th edn, Legal Action Group, 2006) by Ed Cape and Jawaid Luqmani explains to the legal adviser in detail what material they should ask for at this stage and provides a detailed list of what may be expected to exist, it also provides a conversation management model of interviewing for the legal adviser to deploy against the police interviewer to assist in obtaining more information.

Police interviewers must accept that legal advisers will often engage in these tactics to disrupt the planned disclosure and that such tactics must be resisted. A simple method for the interviewer to achieve this is the adoption of the WRITE model:

W	Written disclosure
R	Record questions asked by the legal adviser
I	'I have given you what I consider to be appropriate disclosure I would now like to interview your client'
T	Take your time
E	Engage professionally with legal adviser

The legal adviser should be supplied with a copy of the disclosure prepared earlier. Some officers ask the legal adviser to sign a copy of this, but the legal adviser is not obliged to sign it and will most likely be supplied with a copy in any case. In this event, it may be prudent to consider starting the interview by reading the disclosure provided.

Accept that the legal adviser will not be satisfied with the disclosure provided and will—as the Law Society recommends—ask further questions in an attempt to elicit more information. The interviewer should make a written contemporaneous note of what the legal adviser asks, in much the same way as the legal adviser will be doing. This will enable the interviewer to deal with any questions that may arise at court should the defence seek to argue that disclosure was inadequate. It may also give an insight into how the case is viewed by the legal adviser and what they believe to be significant.

Having carefully considered disclosure there will be nothing that the interviewer will wish to disclose further, and therefore the answer to each question from the legal adviser should be: 'I have given you what I consider to be appropriate disclosure, I would now like to interview your client'—or something very similar. It will feel awkward to keep giving the same answer because the legal adviser will use conversation management tools to put the interviewer under pressure to depart from their position, however it is important to be resolute and stick to the plan.

Take your time. The interviewer should not allow him/herself to become flustered by the questions or exasperated with the legal adviser and should not attempt to force the legal adviser to stop asking questions by leaving. They will appeal to reasonableness and may sound very persuasive, they will try to persuade the interviewer that they cannot take instructions based upon what has been disclosed, and they may imply that unless more information is provided it will be a 'no comment' interview. The interviewer must not, however, be persuaded to move from their planned position, and should continue to listen and note the questions asked until the legal adviser has finished.

The interviewer should engage professionally with the legal adviser throughout this process and accept that they are both professionals with different responsibilities and that the legal adviser—like the interviewer has duties and a job to do. There is substantial potential for conflict but the interviewer must deal with the legal adviser calmly and with respect in order to ensure that the interview is not disrupted unnecessarily.

Some legal advisers may wish to tape record this process and will bring small tape recorders for this purpose. If this is the case the interviewer should consider using a tape recorded interview room so that each party may have a copy of the tape at the conclusion. However, tape recording the process should not be a substitute for written disclosure or for making contemporaneous notes of the legal adviser's questions.

5.8.3 During the interview

At the introductions stage of the interview the interviewer should say to the suspect:

> Now, Peter, can I ask your legal adviser to introduce him/herself and explain to us what his/her role is here today.

Many legal advisers take this opportunity to make an opening statement that includes explaining that they will intervene if they consider it necessary during the course of the interview. Interviewers should remember that they are not constrained by the rules of evidence and that they have both a right and a duty to put questions properly to the suspect. In addition the Home Office Principles point out that persistence is not oppressive. Remember too that the role of the legal adviser is not to advise the interviewer, but to give advice to the suspect.

To this purpose the interviewer should resist engaging with the legal adviser during the course of the interview. This includes commenting upon any legal advice that appears to have been given, for example not to answer questions. The reasonableness of any legal advice will be a matter for the court. Equally the interviewer should resist any attempt by the legal adviser to control the interview. If the legal adviser interrupts—but their behaviour falls short of disruption—they should simply be asked whether they wish to advise the suspect.

The interviewer must accept that when they introduce material that has not been supplied to the legal adviser in advance, phased or drip-fed disclosure, the legal adviser will always ask that the interview is stopped in order to allow a further private consultation. The interviewer can seem to be in control of this inevitability by saying—at the time the new material is introduced—that this is not information that has been disclosed beforehand and that they will break off the interview to allow a consultation.

5.8.4 Pre-prepared statements

The courts have treated pre-prepared statements at interview as being a means of mentioning facts later relied on in court. This means that if a suspect provides a pre-prepared statement but declines to answer questions or say anything at interview, it may be that no inference may be drawn at court. In the case of *R v Knight* [2003] EWCA Crim 1977, the Court of Appeal found that the purpose of the adverse inference provision was to obtain the early disclosure of the suspect's account and not the scrutiny and testing of it during a police interview. They observed that a pre-prepared statement does not provide automatic immunity from an adverse inference, it would depend upon the depth of the statement compared with the account at trial. However, this does not affect the interviewer's duty to carry out a full interview with the suspect even if a pre-prepared statement has been supplied.

This tactic has proved popular with legal advisers and interviewers should be prepared to receive one. In some cases the statement will be provided at the outset of the interview, in others towards the end. In some cases it is supplied at charge, although the Law Society advises that it should be provided during interview to meet properly the provisions of the Act.

It may be that the legal adviser will provide a written copy of the statement to the interviewer, in these circumstances the suspect should be asked to read it aloud. If they refuse and the legal adviser declines to read it the interviewer should read it out before asking the suspect whether it is correct. It may be that the legal adviser reads a statement but refuses to provide a written copy. In this case the suspect should again be asked whether it is correct. Once the content of the statement is on tape it is evidential so it is not necessary for the statement itself to be produced as an exhibit.

Regardless of whatever method the statement is introduced the interviewer should stop the interview in order to have time to consider the contents and how it impacts upon the case and the interview plan. The reason for the interview being stopped should be fully explained. If the legal adviser has declined to provide a written copy a transcript of the statement may be obtained during the break in the interview.

5.8.5 Disruptive behaviour

Interviewers need to understand that much of the activity of legal advisers that they feel is disruptive amounts to legitimate active defence on behalf of the suspect. Interventions in order to clarify or challenge improper questioning is quite proper, as is advice not to answer particular questions. However, if the legal adviser's 'approach or conduct prevents or unreasonably obstructs proper questions being put to the suspect or the suspect's responses being recorded' (PACE Code C.6D), only then may the legal adviser be required to leave the interview.

The examples of such behaviour are answering the questions on behalf of the suspect or providing written answers for the suspect to read, however there is the potential for other kinds of behaviour to be considered just as improper. It is a serious step to take and the decision must be made only by a superintendent or, if one is not readily available, an inspector. In order to satisfy a court it will be necessary for that officer to witness the behaviour.

5.9 **Other Considerations**

5.9.1 **Bad character interviews**

The Criminal Justice Act 2003 made significant changes to the admissibility of evidence relating to the defendant's character and there are a number of ways in which evidence of a defendant's bad character may be used at a trial. One provision allows evidence that shows the defendant has a disposition towards misconduct, and this often amounts to evidence that the defendant is inclined—or has a propensity—to commit the sort of offence with which s/he is charged and/or evidence that s/he is untruthful. Misconduct means committing offences or other reprehensible behaviour.

Evidence of a defendant's previous convictions will be admissible, for example, if they show that s/he is inclined to commit the type of offence with which s/he has been charged. If the current charge is an assault outside a nightclub and the defendant has a conviction for an assault outside a nightclub, it is good evidence of their inclination to commit this sort of offence. If they have a conviction for a dishonesty offence, however, it does not tend to show an inclination to commit acts of violence, unless it was a case where violence was a feature, such as a robbery. So in some cases the conviction itself will be good evidence, while in many others it will be the circumstances of the offence that show the defendant's propensity.

With the inclusion of reprehensible behaviour, the Act takes it further than just the defendant's convictions: any bad behaviour is admissible to show the necessary propensity. So an acquittal may still provide evidence that the defendant is violent, or as may a case of assault where the victim declined to substantiate the offence. Indeed historic evidence of violence that has never before been brought to police notice may be admissible.

Clearly then there is scope for the interviewer to use bad character material during suspect interviews. It will normally be the case that the interviewer will suggest to the suspect that their previous behaviour shows that the offence for which they have been arrested is 'in character'.

The Law Society guidance for legal advisers at police stations states that the interviewing officer should be asked the following questions if they intend to deal with bad character material:

- What information do the police have about the suspect's previous convictions or other misconduct, including its source, its extent, and the precise details?
- What is the specific purpose of the questions?
- Under what gateway of admissibility are they relevant?

Interviewing officers should therefore be prepared to deal with these questions and interviewers should consider obtaining the assistance of the CPS.

The first concerns the actual information that the interviewer has, and in particular can the interviewer show that it is capable of being adduced in evidence. Bad character evidence needs to be proved in the same way as any other evidence in a case, a certificate of conviction does not prove the facts of the case. It may be necessary to obtain further witness statements from victims or witnesses in order to be able to prove specific facts from previous cases that show the suspect's propensity. This is not to say that a suspect cannot be asked about things that cannot yet be proved, but the interviewer will be in a stronger position when talking about material s/he knows will be admissible.

The second question should focus the interviewer on what the material proves and that will often be a propensity to commit like offences. For example—the purpose of interviewing the suspect about the circumstances of his conviction in 2002 for robbery is that it shows a preparedness to carry and use firearms—assuming that the current case is one of possession of a firearm. The interviewer should be clear about what specifically the bad character material is thought to show.

There are seven 'gateways of admissibility' under which bad character evidence may be admitted in court—assuming it can be proved evidentially. At court the CPS is required specifically to apply for the inclusion of bad character evidence in the case under one of these gateways, although this is not a requirement at interview (see 6.27). Gateway 4 or D is:

> Evidence going to a matter in issue between the defendant and the prosecution.

So unless the suspect agrees that s/he has a propensity to commit like offences then that propensity will be a matter in issue. For the interviewer the relevance of the questions goes to whether the suspect is inclined to commit these acts—violence, theft, sexual assault, deception or whatever s/he is under investigation for and that propensity is a matter at issue. Therefore, in almost every case, the answer to the third question posed by the legal adviser will be Gateway 4.

The Law Society recommend that the legal adviser press for a separate bad character interview to that dealing with the main offence. Although current guidelines suggest that bad character can be dealt with at the end of the main interview, having a separate bad character interview will actually help the interviewer by limiting how much ground is needed to be covered. The Law Society guidance states that it will very often not be in the suspect's interests to answer questions about bad character, and that it is unlikely that any inference would be drawn from such a refusal. So interviewers should prepare for a 'no comment' response from the suspect.

5.9.2 Interpreters

Interpreters bring particular problems for interviewers in terms of conversation management and the interaction between the interviewer, the interpreter, and the suspect needs to be carefully managed to reduce these problems to a minimum. There is always a danger that the interpreter effectively conducts the interview by conversing with the suspect while the interviewer has a too passive role. The interviewer must realize that the focus of the interview should be the relationship between the suspect and the interviewer and that the interpreter is merely a conduit.

The interpreter must be briefed to recount precisely what both the interviewer and the suspect say, without summary or embellishment. This can sometimes be helped by the interviewer breaking up the questions and having the interpreter translate in sections taking two or three phrases to complete the entire question. The interpreter should be instructed to deal with the suspect's answers similarly translating as things are said and not necessarily waiting for a complete response. After a short period the suspect will become used to this process.

Equally the interpreter should be seated out of the suspect's eye line so that the suspect is engaged with the interviewer and not the interpreter. The interviewer should engage with the suspect throughout and maintain eye contact both while speaking and while listening to the interpreter's translation. Remember conversation involves conveying a message through a combination of words, intonation, and body language. There is much the interviewer can do in their manner, behaviour, and response to mitigate the problems of the interpreter.

5.9.3 Oppression and unreliability

Section 76 of PACE described oppression as including torture, inhuman or degrading treatment, and the use or threat of violence. Case law has since redefined oppression more in line with its dictionary meaning, and it is now understood as the exercise of authority or power in a burdensome, harsh, or wrongful manner; unjust or cruel treatment (*R v Fulling* [1987] 2 All ER 65). In that case the trial judge ruled that the interviewer frequently interrupting the suspect, shouting rudely, and using obscenities all amounted to oppressive conduct. It is not necessary for the defence to show an interview is oppressive; if the issue is raised it is for the prosecution to prove that it was not. If a judge finds that an admission has been obtained through oppressive conduct by the interviewer, s/he must exclude the confession regardless of whether it is true or not; the judge has no discretion under section 76.

In addition to problems of oppression, any confession may be inadmissible because it was obtained in circumstances which were likely to make it unreliable. These could include any offering of an inducement, such as bail or a particular form of case disposal; failure to caution the suspect or inform them of their legal rights; failure to provide proper rest periods; failure to provide an appropriate adult, or failures by the suspect's legal adviser properly to protect their interests.

Oppression and unreliability, however, invariably emerge from the confession-driven interrogative interviewing style, in which there is a presumption that the suspect needs to be cajoled or persuaded to conform to the interviewer's pre-conceptions. The conversation management model of interviewing is effective in combatting the threat of oppressive behaviour and obtaining unreliable admissions by having its basis in an open, objective, and non-judgemental approach to the interview process.

5.9.4 Evidential records of Interviews (ROTIs and ROVIs)

This is dealt with in detail in Chapter 4. However, the interviewing officer is responsible for completing the evidential record of the interview. Unless the case is a serious one that calls for a full transcript there will be a need for an accurate and balanced summary of what took place during the interview to allow the CPS to consider case disposal: what if any charges are appropriate and what defences are suggested or made out by the suspect?

The evidential record may form the basis of fact on which the CPS makes the decision to prosecute and how they present the case. It is important that any good work at the preparation stage and during the interview is not undone by the presentation of an inadequate record of interview that allows those admissions to be misrepresented. Any mitigation offered or any aggravating features must also be recorded preferably in the actual words used by the suspect, such as remorse or planning, since this material will often form the basis of submissions and decisions as to sentence.

Special warnings given should be recorded in full to ensure compliance with the requirements of the relevant sections of the Criminal Justice and Public Order Act because no inference will be given if the special warning is not properly administered. The suspect's response—or lack of response—should also be recorded fully. Equally any questions that go to the heart of the matter under investigation and any responses should be recorded in order to deal with any issue around the failure to mention facts later relied on in court.

5.10 Conclusion

PEACE together with the conversation management model provides the interviewer with the tools to conduct a thorough and professional suspect interview. It is an ethical approach to a historically difficult and contentious area. Do not be fooled into thinking it is a model that is in any way easy on the suspect. It is very difficult for a suspect to lie their way through an interview conducted in accordance with this structure, especially in the fine grain detail of the account phase.

Information processing and conversational skills are not talents that individuals are born with. They may be learned and practised and there is no single way to conduct a good interview, for each interviewer will bring their own personality and character to the process.

The key question that an interviewer should ask themselves at each point is: What can I do that will help me to talk with this person and encourage them to talk with me?

Manual of Guidance: Anatomy of a Police File

6.1 **Introduction**

This chapter goes through the Manual of Guidance's series of forms in detail, explaining the particular purpose of each one and the problems which may arise in relation to them. It emphasizes the importance of correct submission of information to the CPS explaining why the CPS needs the forms and quite detailed background information in relation to each of them. Heavy reliance has obviously been placed on the Manual of Guidance itself throughout this chapter.

6.1.1 **The Manual of Guidance—What is it?**

The Manual of Guidance (MOG) has been prepared jointly by the police and the CPS and is an essential part of the joint prosecution team approach. It offers guidance on the preparation, processing, and submission of prosecution files. Indeed every piece of paper submitted by the police should be in accordance with the MOG.

A small handbook has been produced as a portable document for all police officers to carry with them to assist them in preparation of prosecution files ('the mini MOG'). A new version of the manual itself is in the pipeline which may well accommodate recent initiatives, such as the streamlined process (see Chapter 9).

This manual is accessible and user-friendly and provides step-by-step instructions, clear guidance, and helpful tips on the completion of every one of the MG forms. It also provides detailed advice for police officers in relation to their obligations in the charging centre, disclosure and obligations towards victims and witnesses.

The MG forms are the chosen method of communication between police officers and the CPS and their proper and detailed completion enables both to work smarter and more effectively in order to prosecute crime.

POINT TO NOTE—MINI MOG

Good file preparation and supervision is essential to ensure that the case progresses smoothly and is fit for purpose. Every step in the preparation of the file is inextricably linked to the next, and your role in getting case files 'right first time' is vital to reduce delays and duplication of effort throughout the system.

There are over 20 MG forms. The last update of the MOG forms was in March 2007. All forces are required by the Director's Guidance on Charging to use the current edition. However, practices vary across forces depending upon what has been loaded onto the particular force computer. This in itself is unsatisfactory. The electronic version on the Home Office website is presently the 2004 version.

Obviously not every form will be relevant to every type of case; however, some are essential for every case, eg the MG1: File Front Sheet. Some of the MG forms may be seen by the defence, eg the MG5: Case Summary, but it is to be noted that many of them are restricted to CPS/police eyes only.

This therefore allows the police to give the CPS additional confidential information, to which the defence do not have access since they are not disclosable, eg the MG6: Case File Information form.

Which forms are used in each type of case is not a personal decision to the officer but is a policy laid down in joint CPS and police guidelines. Occasionally these are subject to alteration by local agreements. These forms have been devised to cover nearly all eventualities. As the CJS has developed so have the MG forms, so that there are now forms also covering conditional cautioning and applications under the Powers of the Criminal Courts Act 2003.

It is vital that police officers familiarize themselves with the nature and purpose of all the forms. All relevant information intended to be put on each and every one of these should be present. Where it is not, the CPS is at a total disadvantage when both reviewing the file and subsequently presenting it in court. Lack of awareness of the specific contents of each form has in the past led to lost opportunities at court and a breakdown of communication of important facts. This results in inefficiency and waste of resources leading to increased administrative burdens with memos flying between the police and the CPS.

6.2 **MG1: File Front Sheet**

6.2.1 **Essentials**

This form is the front page of the case file. It tells the CPS at a glance the reference number, the type of file that is being submitted, details about the defendant, and whether or not it is a special category of case or offender. Additionally it informs the CPS that the officer in the case has complied with his disclosure obligations and that the case has been put through a supervisor who has authorized submission to the CPS.

6.2.2 **The form itself**

File type: expedited/evidential/full

The number of forms to be filled in and the amount of evidence required to be submitted in each particular case is largely dependent on the Director's Guidance on Charging and on what type of plea is anticipated in the magistrates' court.

Far less of a file is required for anticipated guilty pleas which will hopefully be disposed of summarily and speedily shortly after submission. However, where a case is likely to go to Crown Court, or be contested, far more information and evidence is required. Any files submitted to the custody sergeant must subsequently have passed the 'threshold test' prior to charge.

The file requirements where the streamlined process (see Chapter 9) is in operation may vary. Police officers must ensure that they are familiar with such requirments in relation to different types of cases, and the Borough in which they work.

Expedited files must be used for cases which are straightforward and likely to be guilty pleas, or cases where all the evidence is not yet available in a case and the custody officer wants the defendant to be remanded in custody. In this situation all the key evidence in the case may not be available but what is essential is that there is sufficient information for the courts to be able to hear a case and sentence the defendant or that there is sufficient information for the duty prosecutor to apply a 'threshold test'.

Key witness statements do not necessarily have to be in the usual MG11 format. They could comprise the police officer's EAB or a video (CCTV) if that was the key evidence. Other evidence, if not readily available can be summarized as can the interview (admissions of the defendant) in the MG5.

Other MG forms may also have to be submitted with the Expedited Report. If it is a custody case, the officer must also complete an MG7 (Remand Application) outlining the objections to bail. If it is an anticipated guilty plea, and there are offences to be taken into consideration, an MG18 will need to be completed, together with an MG19 (Compensation Claim) if a claim for compensation is to be made.

Evidential files are to be submitted in all other cases, ie those likely to be contested and/or going to the Crown Court, including all indictable cases where it is not a custody case. Prior to charge this is called an Evidential Report and requires more information.

The main difference is that all key witness statements in MG11 format are included as are copies of all documentary exhibits and an interview record (summary sufficient). Unused material must also be included together with the crime report and incident log. In some cases there are local protocols for submission of disclosure schedules even at this early stage but this is not a national requirement.

Other essential forms at this stage will include the MG10 (Witness Non-Availability) to be able to set a trial date; the MG6 (Confidential Case File Information); MG2 (Special Measures Assessment) if there are vulnerable or intimidated witnesses, and an MG16 if 'bad character' is relevant to the offender and an application to admit it is anticipated.

Figure 6.1 is taken from the *Statutory Charging Manual* and illustrates the requirements for Expedited and Evidential Reports pre-charge.

Figure 6.1 Expedited and evidential reports

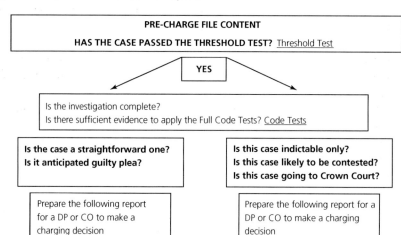

PRE-CHARGE FILE CONTENT

HAS THE CASE PASSED THE THRESHOLD TEST? Threshold Test

YES

Is the investigation complete?
Is there sufficient evidence to apply the Full Code Tests? Code Tests

Is the case a straightforward one? **Is it anticipated guilty plea?**	**Is this case indictable only?** **Is this case likely to be contested?** **Is this case going to Crown Court?**

Prepare the following report for a DP or CO to make a charging decision	Prepare the following report for a DP or CO to make a charging decision

PRE-CHARGE **EXPEDITED REPORT**	PRE-CHARGE **EVIDENTIAL REPORT**

EXPEDITED REPORT

- A KEY witness statement or index notes
- Other compelling evidence, e.g. CCTV
- If witnessed by more than four officers a key statement and a summary of other evidence may be enough
- Summary of interview (SDN)
- PNC of suspect(s) previous convictions/ cautions/reprimands/final warnings
- PNC pre-cons of key prosecution witnesses MG3 – with case outline and suggested charges
- Any other information that may have a bearing on the code tests must be included
- MG7 – Remand application form (if appropriate)
- MG18 – Offences to be taken into consideration
- MG19 – Compensation form

EVIDENTIAL REPORT

- ALL KEY witness statement(s), or index notes
- Copies of key documentary exhibits
- Any unused material likely to undermine the case or assist the defence
- PNC of suspect(s) previous convictions/ cautions/reprimands/final warnings
- PNC pre-cons of key prosecution witnesses
- MG3 – with case outline and suggested charges
- Summary of interview (SDN/ROTI/ROVI)
- MG5 – Case summary unless set out in MG3
- MG6 – Case file information
- Crime Report and Incident Log Witnesses (Disclosure schedules are not required at this stage)
- MG2 – Initial witness assessment (if appropriate)
- MG10 – Witness non-availability (if appropriate)
- MG16 – Bad character/dangerous offender (if appropriate)
- MG18 – Offences to be taken into consideration (if appropriate)
- MG19 – Compensation form

A KEY WITNESS STATEMENT IS A STATEMENT OF A WITNESS PROVIDING EVIDENCE THAT IS NECESSARY TO PROVE SOME OR ALL OF THE ELEMENTS OF THE ALLEGED OFFENCE

NB A full file is a completed file that makes the case totally trial ready where all the relevant forms should be included including all unused material schedules, witness list and all relevant statements and exhibits.

Full File is the term used when a file has absolutely everything required in it and is 'trial ready'. Such a file is submitted post-charge for contested and Crown Court cases.

All statements (not just key ones) including continuity ones, and all documentary exhibits will be on the file. Additionally, where applicable, all relevant MG forms, including disclosure schedules (MG6B, MG6C, MG6D, MG6E) and fully updated witness list (MG9) and exhibit list (MG12).

Each case must have a police unique reference number (URN), which must be allocated at the earliest opportunity and completed in every case and be put on to all forms. The URN in fact comprises of four different elements: (i) the service PNC code; (ii) the division or sub-division; (iii) a numeric identifier; and (iv) the year. For example:

URN	01	QA	00429	07
	Met police	Harrow Division	Number allocated	Year

An offender charged with linked offences (ie founded on the same facts and forming part of a series of offences of the same or similar character) can be submitted as a single URN. However, this is not the case where the offences are not linked in any way. Care must then be taken when dealing with multiple offenders (the MOG offers further guidance on this).

Case types

Certain types of case are required to be flagged up so that they can be monitored and receive priority and other special attention, for example:

- child abuse cases—those involving neglect, physical injury, sexual or emotional abuse, where the victim is under 18;
- hate crime cases—those including any incident perceived by the victim or another to have been motivated because of disability, gender, homophobia, race or religion;
- domestic violence (DV) cases—those including any incident or threatening behaviour, violence or abuse (psychological, physical, sexual, financial or emotional) between adults who are or have been intimate partners or family members regardless of gender or sexuality.

In the following two types of cases it is important that they are highlighted so that the police officer and the prosecutor are mindful of obligations to bring these to the attention of the court:

- **Drugs test (Cozzart)**: If this box is ticked it means that the adult offender has tested positive for a Class A drug where a sample has been taken under section 63B of PACE for drug related or 'trigger' offences, and that certain other conditions have been met. On this information being put before the court the defendant in effect loses his right to bail and may only be granted bail if there is no significant risk. (It also means that the police officer should have completed a form D2 indicating the results of the test. This pro forma should also be submitted with the file for the first court hearing.)

- **POCA**: This refers to the powers under the Proceeds of Crime Act 2003 in respect of offences committed after 24 March 2003 where there is a financial benefit and the prosecutor can then apply for a restraint/confiscation order or seizure of cash, etc. It is important for prosecutors to have this information from the outset of the case since it may well affect where the case should be heard. All such cases should go to the Crown Court. It also means that the police officer should have completed a form MG17 (Proceeds of Crime Act (POCA) Review) and should have attached it to the case papers.

Details of defendant

Where there are more than two defendants, a further MG1 needs to be completed since all the details in this box relate to the specific defendant, ie anticipated plea, name, date of birth, gender, occupation, nationality. Additionally this box covers the following:

- PPO—this means the defendant is a prolific and other priority offender, targeted locally as a persistent offender. If this is the case and 'yes' is highlighted then he/she will receive priority attention, and be fast tracked, as well as alerting the prosecutor immediately to his/her previous convictions and other considerations.
- Ethnicity code—there are two such codes and both must be completed. The '6+1 police determined PNC ethnicity code' and the '16+1 self determined classification' is categorised in a table on the reverse of the MG1 form.
- Religion/belief and disability—again these are categorized on the back of the MG1 form for ease of reference.
- Number of TICs—this means offences to be taken into consideration. If this box is ticked then an MG18 should have been completed by the police officer and it is also helpful for this to be mentioned in the body of the MG3/MG5 case summary.
- Other pending cases—if there are any other pending cases then the OIC should provide details to the CPS on the MG6 case file information form or on the MG7 (Remand Application Adult/Youth), if relevant, to a remand in custody. Where details of any offences for which the defendant is on bail are not on the printout it is important that the information is provided to the prosecutor viz: date bail granted, from which court or police station, date of surrender, charges, conditions of bail, etc.
- Previous convictions/simple cautions/conditional cautions/reprimands/final warnings/ Police Notice for Disorder (PND).

A Police National Computer (PNC) check must be carried out in every case and an indication given here as to the existence or otherwise of convictions and cautions, etc. A Phoenix printout plus copies should also be attached to the file (obtained from the PNC) that is accessed through a terminal in the computer assisted despatch (CAD) room.

Young offender

This section is particularly relevant to Persistent Young Offenders (PYOs) but also requires information about the parent and guardian if different from the name on the charge sheet.

PYO: The initial function of identifying a young offender who is also a PYO falls to the police. Such an offender is aged between 10 and 17 and has been sentenced by any criminal court in the UK on three or more separate occasions for one or more recordable offences and who is, within three years of the last sentencing occasion subsequently arrested and charged or has an information laid against him/her for a further recordable offence.

Such offenders are closely monitored (as a result of them being 'flagged' cases) and they are prioritized and fast tracked by the court to be dealt with within 71 days. The CPS needs to know that the offender is a PYO. This information will be passed on to the court and will be relevant at a number of stages of the criminal justice process including consideration of bail and sentencing.

Disclosure certification

This is rarely completed by the OIC but is important particularly where a remand in custody is sought. It relates to the officer certifying that s/he has considered any unused material in the case and does not consider that there is anything which might assist the defence particularly in the early stages of the case prior to the Criminal Procedure and Investigations Act 1996 (CPIA 1996) being triggered.

Such information could relate to previous convictions for prosecution witnesses, lost evidence amounting to an abuse of process, reluctant and hostile witnesses. This information should be recorded on the MG6.

In these circumstances the Crown Prosecutor will be obliged to notify the defence at the first opportunity. This does not mean that the prosecutor would be not opposing bail but it is necessary for such information to come from the prosecutor not the defence and be put before the court in order for proceedings to be fair.

Supervisor authorization

It is important that any file submitted to the CPS has been seen by a supervisor who should ensure, inter alia, that all parts of the MG1 (including the disclosure certification) are filled out and the file is correctly flagged. The supervising officer by signing his/her name, rank, and number is effectively endorsing that in accordance with the Code for Crown Prosecutors s/he believes there is a realistic prospect of conviction and that it is in the public interest to proceed and that the correct type of file has been submitted with the necessary MG forms. Such supervision also allows for efficient effective communication in the event of problems with a file.

Termination and no consultation

Where the police officer does not require to be consulted about the case if the CPS decides to terminate it, then this box should be ticked. Best practice dictates that in nearly all cases there will be close liaison between the CPS and the police prior to any course of action being taken.

KEY CONSIDERATIONS—MG1

- Includes URN
- Informs the CPS on type of file
- Provides offender details
- Indicates special category case
- Demonstrates officer's compliance with disclosure duties
- Authorizes submission to the CPS by supervisor

RESTRICTED (when complete)

MG1

FILE FRONT SHEET

Page No. .... of ....

File type: Expedited / Evidential / Full   CPS Office: ....   URN

Child abuse ☐   Hate Crime (*specify*............................)   DV ☐   Drugs Test ☐   POCA ☐

Defendant ( ) Anticipated plea: Guilty / Not Guilty

Surname: .... **Forename(s)**: ....

D.O.B: ....   M / F   PPO Y / N   Occupation: ....

Ethnicity Code: PNC ☐ 16-point +1 ☐   Nationality: .... Religion / Belief: (*specify*................)

Disability (*self-determined specify*...........................)   No. of TIC(s) ☐   Other pending cases   Y / N

Circle if: Previous convictions / simple caution(s) / conditional caution(s) / reprimand / final warning / PNDs

Young Offender: Persistent Young Offender Y / N

Parent / Guardian full name and address if different from charge sheet:..

....

Defendant ( ) Anticipated plea: Guilty / Not Guilty

Surname: .... **Forename(s)**: ....

D.O.B: ....   M / F   PPO Y / N   Occupation: ....

Ethnicity Code: PNC ☐ 16-point +1 ☐   Nationality: .... Religion / Belief: (*specify*................)

Disability (*self-determined specify*...........................)   No. of TIC(s) ☐   Other pending cases   Y / N

Circle if: Previous convictions / simple caution(s) / conditional caution(s) / reprimand / final warning / PNDs

Young Offender: Persistent Young Offender Y / N

Parent / Guardian full name and address if different from charge sheet:..

....

I certify that, to the best of my knowledge and belief, I have not withheld any information which could assist the defence in the early preparation of their case, including the making of a bail application.

Officer in case: ....   Rank / Job title: ....   No. ....

Station: ....   Tel. No. ....

Signature: ....   Date: ....

Supervising officer authorising submission to CPS

Supervisor: ....   Rank / Job title: ....   No. ....

Signature: ....   Date: ....

If CPS consider termination of case and consultation not required, tick ☐

2006/07 (1)   **RESTRICTED (when complete)**

HATE CRIME CATEGORIES

Hate Crime	Disability
	Gender
	Homophobic
	Race
	Religious

16 POINT +1 SELF-DETERMINED ETHNIC SYSTEM

Major Categories	Sub-groupings	HO Code
White	British	W1
	Irish	W2
	Any other White background	W9
Mixed	White and Black Caribbean	M1
	White and Black African	M2
	White and Asian	M3
	Any other mixed background	M9
Asian or Asian British	Indian	A1
	Pakistani	A2
	Bangladeshi	A3
	Any other Asian background	A9
Black or Black British	Caribbean	B1
	African	B2
	Any other Black background	B9
Chinese or other ethnic group	Chinese	O1
	Any other ethnic group	O9
Not stated		NS

RELIGION / BELIEF CATEGORIES

Religion / Belief	Buddhist
	Christian *(includes Catholic, Protestant, C of E etc)*
	Jewish
	Hindu
	Muslim *(Islamic)*
	Sikh
	Other *(specify)*

6.3 **MG2: Special Measures Assessment**

6.3.1 **Essentials**

This form is an essential part of both the police officer's and the CPS's obligations under the Code of Practice for Victims of Crime, considering their needs from the outset of a case. The completion of this form allows tailored support to individual victims and witnesses to enable them to give the best evidence in court. It is to be noted that when the form is completed it is restricted and will not be disclosed to the defence.

Together with the back of the MG11 (Witness Statement), this form provides the witness care unit and the CPS with sufficient information, if correctly completed, to access accurately the witness needs and views and make a special measures application and or/hold an early special measures meeting (ESM) with the witness where appropriate. The extension of some special measures (eg video evidence in chief/TV link) in recent legislation has made the detailed completion of this form even more significant.

One of these forms should be completed in respect of each vulnerable or intimidated witness. Generally the form would be completed after a statement has been taken from a witness (together with the back of the MG11—'Does the witness require Special Measures Assessment as a vulnerable or intimidated witness?'). However, officers should be aware of the guidance contained in 'Achieving Best Evidence' and in some circumstances they may also wish to consult the CPS prior to a statement being taken or a video interview.

It is vital that the needs of the witness are picked up at the earliest stage and that the form is filled out by the OIC with detailed knowledge of the witness. A form where relevant should be submitted to the duty prosecutor at the police station at the point of charge in any contested and Crown Court case. This form notifies the CPS that there is a vulnerable or intimidated witness within the definition laid down by the Youth Justice and Criminal Evidence Act 1999, sections 16 and 17, and the Victim's Code.

6.3.2 **The form itself**

Step 1—Identification of witness

This first step identifies the type of witness that may require special measures:

- Vulnerable witnesses eligible on the grounds of age (under 17) or incapacity (mental disorder, learning disability, physical disability, or disorder).
- Intimidated witnesses eligible on grounds of fear and distress about testifying including victims of domestic violence and sexual complainants.

The relevant box should be ticked (see further 4.4).

Step 2—Eligibility for 'special measures'

All except children and complainants of sexual offences have to show that unless the special measure is granted the quality of their evidence is likely to be diminished by reason of their disability. The court will take into account their views (see Step 5). Expert evidence may also be required in some cases but it is very helpful if the police officer obtains a separate statement from the witness covering specifically the nature of the disorder or fear and how it will affect them giving evidence.

The form also includes reference to factors in Step 2 (the box on the right-hand side at (e)) viz; circumstances of offence, age of witness, social and cultural background/ethnic origins, domestic and employment circumstances, any religious beliefs or political opinions, any behaviour towards the witness by the accused, his/her associates, family, or anyone else.

Step 3—Special measures

This step requires any child (under 17) who is in 'need of special protection' to be identified. In such cases children giving evidence in offences involving sex, violence, cruelty, or abduction are automatically presumed to give evidence in chief by pre-recorded video and cross-examination by live TV link. The quality test is applied unless the witness is a child in need of special protection as above.

At the bottom of page 1 of the MG2 all the potentially available special measures are then listed and the relevant ones should be ticked. It is to be noted that video-recorded cross-examination is not yet available, and video-recorded evidence in chief is only available in specific circumstances. Use of 'intermediaries' to assist a vulnerable witness to give evidence is a relatively new concept and in many cases such a go-between does prove invaluable and should be considered. It is important that again the officer justifies in as much detail as possible why a particular measure is likely to improve the quality of the evidence of the witness.

Step 4—Supporting evidence

Any evidence that can be obtained to support the application should be submitted if available. As previously indicated in Step 2 a supporting statement from the witness themselves, in addition to any medical or professional evidence, often assists.

Step 5—Views of witness

The views of the witness themselves are a vital consideration for both the court and indeed should be considered by the police and the CPS at the outset. Counsel often prefer vulnerable and intimidated witnesses to give live face-to-face evidence rather than via a link or behind screens. It is important therefore that the witness's own preference is not ignored or undermined here.

Step 6—Views of interested parties

The views of other interested parties (parents, carers, doctors, guardians) should only be completed where appropriate and may already have been submitted in Step 4 supporting evidence, eg developmental stage/attention span, etc. A parent's/police officer's view about how the child should give evidence could also be recorded here and other information from which the CPS can make a decision whether a statement from that person may be required.

Step 7—Other agencies involved

The provision of details of any other agencies involved with the witness and contact details are designed to assist the prosecutor in contacting anyone either to obtain further information or appropriate assistance. It is essential in any event in all such cases that the CPS is kept informed of any 'work in progress' (eg counselling) with the witness.

Step 8—Explanation if no child witness video

This step acts as a reminder to police officers of the necessity for a detailed explanation where a statement in exceptional circumstances is taken from a child witness rather than via an ABE interview.

Step 9—Requirement for ESM

This is a reminder to officers that they should also have ticked Box 4 on the MG6 (Case File Information Form) where an ESM is required. This asks 'any vulnerable and intimidated adult witnesses—is a special measures meeting required?—complete MG2'.

In fact, police officers often tick this Box 4 in order to identify such a witness rather than request an ESM meeting between the witness and prosecutor. Presently such a meeting is not the norm in most cases. However, on receipt of the MG2 the prosecutor in liaison with the officer may decide whether such a meeting is appropriate and at what stage it should be held in all circumstances of the case (see further 4.4).

KEY CONSIDERATIONS—MG2

- Considers witness's needs from the outset
- Identifies witnesses in need of special protection
- Provides the CPS with information to apply for special measures
- Records views of witnesses and others
- Suggests an ESM if appropriate

MG2

SPECIAL MEASURES ASSESSMENT

(Youth Justice and Criminal Evidence Act 1999)

Name of witness: .... URN

Age: .... **Date of Birth**: ....

STEP 1   Identification of Witness *(one form per witness)*

This Act aims to assist certain vulnerable groups of witnesses to give evidence at court with the assistance of 'Special Measures'. Tick to show which of the group(s) below apply to this witness.

Vulnerable

a) Child under 17

b) Witness with a mental disorder

c) Witness with learning disabilities

d) Witness with a physical disability / disorder

Intimidated

e) Witness in fear or distress about giving evidence

f) Complainant in sexual case

STEP 2   Eligibility for 'Special Measures'

a) and f) are automatically eligible for Special Measures. **Go to Step 3.**

For b), c), d) and e), explain briefly below the nature of the vulnerability, fear or distress and show how this is likely to diminish the quality of their evidence in terms of their evidence being complete, coherent and accurate. Coherence refers to their ability to understand the questions put to them and to give an appropriate answer. **Note guidance in respect of e).**

Nature of disorder / impairment or witness fear / distress and effect on evidence. (Expert advice may need to be sought.)	**e) Consider and note these factors** • The circumstances of the offence. • The age of the witness. • Their social and cultural background / ethnic origins. • Their domestic and employment circumstances. • Any religious beliefs or political opinions. • Any behaviour towards the witness by the accused, his / her associates, family or anyone else.
....	

STEP 3   Special Measures

If a child witness is under 17, tick to show if the case is:

a) Sexual offence

b) Offence involving violence, cruelty or abduction

c) Any other offence

If either **a)** or **b)** apply, then the child witness is **'in need of special protection'** and the admission of a visually recorded interview if available, is mandatory and any other evidence must be given by a live link.

Which Special Measure(s) is / are likely to improve the ability of the witness to give evidence, and why? Consider: the needs of the witness, age, development or disability, communication difficulties, the state of mind (distress, shock); the type and severity and/or the circumstances of the offence (offender known to the witness); the purpose and likely value of a visually recorded interview on this occasion, perceived fears about intimidation and recrimination.

Special Measures	Tick if required	State how this will improve the quality of the witnesses evidence
Screens		
Live link		
Evidence in private		
Removal of wigs and gowns		
Visually recorded evidence		
Video cross-examination		
Intermediaries		
Communication aids		

2006/07 (1)

STEP 4 Please attach copy of supporting evidence, e.g. birth certificate, medical report (if available).

STEP 5

Give the views of the witness as to why the measures sought are required.

....
....
....
....
....
....

STEP 6

If appropriate, what are the views of interested parties? e.g. parent, carer, doctor, nurse, guardian, etc.

....
....
....
....
....
....

STEP 7

Details of other agencies involved, e.g. Social Care Services, CPS, Schools, etc. (include results of any communications and contact numbers, details and addresses).

....
....
....
....
....

STEP 8

If you decide not to collect evidence from a child witness by visual recording, explain why:

....
....
....
....
....

STEP 9
Please indicate on form **MG6** if a Special Measures meeting is required.

Assessing Officer (print name, rank / job title, number): .... Date: ....

Contact details (telephone, mobile, e-mail): ....

6.4 MG3: Report to Crown Prosecutor for Charging Decision. Decision Log & Action Plan

6.4.1 Essentials

This form was reformatted in 2007 to reflect directly the details recorded on Compass (ie CMS—the CPS computer case management system). It basically now allows more space and runs into four pages. It is the mandatory report form that must be completed by police officers and submitted in respect of any suspect where either a charging decision or advice is required from the CPS or prior to pre-charge consultation when a meeting with a duty prosecutor in other than straightforward cases is required (sometimes a verbal report may suffice, dependent on the nature of the case).

The form provides the prosecutor with an outline of the circumstances of the case and the proposed charges thereby allowing the prosecutor to make an informed review decision. It further lists all the material provided to the prosecutor. In turn the prosecutor provides the police with a detailed charging decision or advice and the form acts as an audit trail for all parties and evidence of decision making. The prosecutor then follows this up with an action plan agreed with the police in relation to work outstanding and further investigation.

The MG3 records the first consultation with the police. Any subsequent consultation requires a form MG3A to be completed—'Further Report to the Crown Prosecutor for a Charging Decision' similar in format to the original form. The MG3 is in two parts, Part A (the first two pages) is to be completed by the police officer and Part B (the last two pages) is to be completed by the duty prosecutor. It is to be noted that the URN must again be recorded on top of the form for performance and case management purposes.

The form can be handwritten (if legible) by the officer but the most effective method is for electronic completion. It may then be submitted electronically (eg for advice over the phone by CPS Direct) or handed over with the case papers to the prosecutor or submitted in advance for a subsequent decision. Similarly the prosecutor will complete Part B of the form following a consultation meeting when making a charging decision. Once the case has been registered on CMS a copy of the completed form will be printed off and given to the police officer.

It is to be noted this form is restricted and does not appear on the disclosure schedule and is not disclosable to the defence.

6.4.2 The form itself

Part A—Report to Crown Prosecutor (for police completion)

(i) Suspect details

The MG3 can be used for up to two suspects. Any more and additional copies of the form need to be used. The details of the suspect need to be entered in full. If advice is sought at the pre-arrest stage and the identity of the suspect is not yet known then 'not known' should be entered—it should not be left blank.

'Ethnicity' must be recorded using the 16+1 self-determined classification system as seen from the MG1.

As for the MG1, here it is important to flag up, by ticking the appropriate box, whether the defendant is a PPO, PYO, or a youth offender (YO).

Bad Character Evidence/Dangerous Offender: The form must be specifically marked 'yes' or 'no' if there is any relevant 'bad character evidence' of the suspect or if s/he may potentially be a 'dangerous offender'.

If either of these circumstances apply then a form MG16 (Evidence of Defendant's Bad Character and/or Dangerous Offender) must also be completed and submitted. That form has been specifically devised for the purpose of putting all relevant information of these two features in a case. They will be dealt with in detail when considering the MG16 at 6.27.

Suffice to say here that 'bad character' as laid down by the Criminal Justice Act 2003 does not only relate to a defendant's previous convictions but can also relate to any other relevant 'reprehensible' conduct by the defendant.

Similarly whether or not the courts may consider them a dangerous offender is dependent on the type of offence they are up before the court for in the present case (ie it must be any either-way offence involving sex or violence) and whether, because of their past conduct (either in the form of previous convictions or past behaviour) it is anticipated that they may be dangerous and therefore subject to more onerous penalties within the CJS on sentencing.

In both situations it is important that the prosecutor is aware of this information at the earliest opportunity. Bad character is relevant to the review process itself and if it is to be used the prosecutor must make a written application to the court in advance. The fact that the defendant is a dangerous offender is generally only relevant at the sentencing stage but it could also be relevant at the first appearance before the court. In the case of a YO, representations as to mode of trial must refer to whether or not they are a dangerous offender.

These two important features in a case will therefore, act as a reminder to the officer that further work needs to be done where the answer is 'yes'.

(ii) Material provided to the CPS

It is very important that details of all information submitted to the prosecution are entered here including the date of creation of the material. It is obviously dependent on the type of file being submitted and the type of case as to what that material supplied actually is. The list acts as an aide memoire to the officer of most types of material. This information will form the basis of the decision of the prosecutor at that time so on subsequent review it is very helpful to know what exactly that information was when a review decision was taken.

It is to be noted that where statements (MG11s) are submitted the name of the witness should also be entered.

In addition to usual items of evidence, ie statements, forensics/expert evidence, pocket notebooks/incident report books, police incident logs, videos/photos and previous convictions or disposals, three specific forms are also mentioned:

- The MG2 (see 6.3)—Special Measures Assessment, already considered, for vulnerable and intimidated witnesses.
- The MG13 (see 6.24)— Application for Order(s) on Conviction relates primarily to ASBOs (anti-social behaviour orders) where the officer has considered, usually after discussion with the CPS, that it is an appropriate case to seek an ASBO on conviction of the defendant.
- The MG17 (see 6.28)— Proceeds of Crime Act (POCA) Review relates to potential applications under the Proceeds of Crime Act 2003 where there has been a cash seizure or the restraint and confiscation of the defendant's assets are to be considered. This form has to be completed for the review stage (with views of the financial investigation unit (FIU)) in order for the prosecutor to take immediate action.

(iii) Contact details of the officer

These must be filled in and it is helpful if the officer includes a mobile number/email address as well in the details. It must be highlighted if the OIC is in fact a different officer from that officer completing the MG3.

(iv) Outline of circumstances and decision/advice sought

The second page of the MG3 (expanded from the previous version) provides a clear space for the officer to submit a full outline of the key points of the circumstances of the case and spell out the decision which s/he is seeking (eg to charge) or the type of advice sought. A separate additional sheet can be completed if necessary.

The form itself lists a number of factors which the police officer must consider when completing this section. This list is not exhaustive but it is essential that officers have a full understanding and detailed knowledge of their case prior to its submission to a prosecutor. Such considerations highlighted include:

- any time limits on proceedings if applicable;
- the strength and weaknesses of the case;
- any possible lines of defence (including anything said by the defence representative);
- an assessment of the witnesses—their reliability and credibility. Are any of them vulnerable/intimidated (MG2 should also be submitted)?;
- public safety issues, eg opposing bail (MG7 required); dangerous offender (MG16 required);
- disclosure issues—Is there anything that needs to be disclosed immediately to the defence that undermines the prosecution case or assists them?—Is there other confidential information you wish to tell the CPS about?—In which case submit it on an MG6;

- any financial or asset recovery issues (ie MG17 to complete if POCA 2003 applies);
- orders on conviction (MG13 if ASBO or other order considered); and
- any public interest issues (relating to the offender or the offence itself, eg a local protocol requiring prosecution save in exceptional circumstances because of the nature of the offence).

It is helpful if all the officer's 'thoughts' on the case are on paper rather than left in the officer's head for subsequent discussion with the prosecutors. No stone should be left unturned as it were. It is vital that the prosecutor takes an informed decision based on quality information submitted.

(v) Supervisor's comments

This ensures first that the file has been through a supervisor prior to submission to the CPS and also allows the supervisor to provide any additional comments which may assist either the officer in the case in his/her line of enquiry or the duty prosecutor in coming to a decision.

Part B—Charging decision/advice & case action plan (for CPS completion)

Additional guidance has been provided to prosecutors to ensure that all such forms are completed to a consistent minimum national standard. In particular they are reminded that Part B does not merely just provide a record of the decision for the officer but it also explains the thought process behind that decision and provides a clear audit trail of decision making, and outstanding actions for police officers and other Crown Prosecutors alike.

(i) Full Code Test/Threshold Test/Investigative Advice

These tick boxes allow the prosecutor to immediately highlight which particular test they have been applying to the review of the file. Something in the past which was not always clear from the MG3.

The Full Code Test: This is applied where all the required evidence is available, and there is a realistic prospect of conviction, and it is in the public interest to proceed.

The Threshold Test: This is applied where all evidence is not available and a remand of the suspect in custody is sought. A lower standard of proof is required here of reasonable suspicion that the defendant has committed the offence and that there is a likelihood of further evidence being available and it is in the public interest to proceed.

It is important that if this box is ticked then an action plan needs to be completed with a specific review date when the full code test should be applied to the evidence submitted by the police officer.

Investigative Advice: This, as has already been seen in 3.3.4, is best practice requiring police officers to refer cases at the earliest opportunity to the CPS.

(ii) Charging decision and advice, specifying or attaching charges

It can be seen that the form is then broken down for the Crown Prosecutor into a number of separate headings, which the prosecutor (or custody officer making a charging decision) must consider in every case. This should ensure that any decisions taken cover all the relevant and key issues required.

It is helpful if the prosecutor indicates that they have considered all the evidence submitted, eg that they have watched a specific video (ABE or CCTV) in coming to their decision and read all the evidence submitted by the officer.

Case Analysis/Evidential Issues: The way in which prosecutors analyse a case 'thinking trial' from the outset has already been considered in Chapter 2. The prosecutor should pinpoint the key issues in the case from the outset so that anybody can see at a glance what the case is about.

Evidential Criteria: The prosecutor must then deal with the evidential criteria identifying the evidential issues in the case and setting out factors that point to guilt. The prosecutor should also set out how any apparent defence can be overcome. Any particular evidential problems/issues should be noted with advice on how they can be remedied. If there is insufficient evidence to proceed then the specific weaknesses must be identified.

Guidance on the completion of the MG3 from the Statutory Charging Manual

Public Interest: This is the second part of the Code test in the Code for Crown Prosecutors and must be considered in every case when there is enough evidence. Often the seriousness of the offence or the circumstances of the defendant determine whether it is in the public interest to proceed. The Code also outlines common public interest factors both for and against prosecution. The prosecutor must balance these factors and note clearly in their review how they reach their overall assessment in the particular case.

Mode of Trial: This must be addressed in any either-way case in accordance with published mode of trial and sentencing guidelines. This will indicate to the prosecutor any representations which may be made at court as to whether or not the case is so serious that it should only be heard in the Crown Court because the magistrates' powers of punishment are insufficient. It is also helpful where the offence is indictable only (especially if an unusual one) to indicate as such in this section.

Police officers will be able to recognize which type of file is required post-charge when it is indicated where the case is to be heard.

ECHR: This relates to the European Convention on Human Rights with which all prosecutions must comply. Often no ECHR points arise in a case, especially where all procedures have been correctly complied with by the police. However, even this should be noted. If such a point is anticipated, the prosecutor should endorse the file with the relevant case law to show how the point can be overcome.

Understanding and knowledge of the evidential, public interest and ECHR factors that may impact on a case will allow police officers to be in a better position to carry out any required outstanding action in a case.

NWNJ: This stands for 'No Witness, No Justice' and is part of an ongoing campaign re-enforced by the Victim Code to consider the needs of victims and witnesses from the outset in a case. If the victim is vulnerable/intimidated an MG2 should have been completed by the officer and the prosecutor will be considering making an application for special measures and whether in the particular case an ESM or even a pre-trial interview with the witness is required to provide them with further support and encouragement. In the latter case it will also give the CPS an idea as to the potential strength of their performance in court.

Instructions to Court Prosecutors: This section was devised primarily to assist Associate Prosecutors (APs) who have been granted rights of audience in the magistrates' court to act on behalf of the CPS. The prosecutor could here inform the AP that they must oppose bail and subsequently make a bail appeal if the magistrates grant it.

Other Case Issues: There are some offences which require either the consent of the DPP or the Attorney General prior to charge. In the former case any Crown Prosecutor is authorized to give such consent but the consideration and the giving of it must be specifically noted on the file. The space also allows the prosecutor to include any other comments on the case or highlight potential problems.

Charge(s): Where the prosecutor has decided that a charging decision can be taken then the prosecutor must specify the charges to be preferred and draft them where necessary for the police (see further 3.6.3—The charges (and charging standards)).

Monitoring Codes—Prosecutor to indicate general nature of decision and advice (page 4)

The final page of the MG3 consists of a number of codes, A–N, to indicate the nature of the decision/advice given in each case. Only one box is to be ticked for each case and the outcome must be recorded against each suspect. A further code is required to indicate whether a NFA decision was based on evidential or public interest criteria (this affects police recording detection rates). The correct completion of these codes is essential for record-keeping and statistical purposes. Full details can be found in the MOG or Statutory Charging Manual.

Further action agreed (see also 3.6.4—Action plans)

In many instances an action plan may be agreed between the officer and the prosecutor. This is basically a request to police for further investigation or information and will list outstanding evidence still to be obtained. This will often be required before any charging decision or final advice can be given. It is important that such action plans are case-specific, focused, detailed, and realistic, taking into account police resources.

All such action plans must be action dated, ie time bound so that an action/ review date in relation to each task must be agreed. If there is presently insufficient evidence to charge an agreed date for a charging review after all the evidence and information requested has been provided by the officer should be made. A decision to charge will not be taken until all agreed actions have been completed.

Again it is to be noted that there is a place to highlight specifically that the case is one where POCA 2003 considerations are appropriate and an MG17 should have been completed. It should be referred to the FIU for investigation as an asset recovery case and consideration given to the need for a restraining order.

In relation to PYOs there is a 71-day target in a contested case. Any action date needs to take this into account. Similarly the 'return bail date' also to be completed in this section should take such factors into consideration when setting dates for submission of evidence to be supplied by police. Obviously all review target dates should fall prior to any return bail dates where possible.

Further consultation needed pre-charge

In cases where the prosecutor has requested further evidence prior to charge the 'yes' will be circled and the officer will then be required to complete a form MG3A to update the prosecutor on the progress of the enquiry. The prosecutor must clearly print their name and provide contact details and date the completion of the MG3.

Investigation stage at which advice sought/How advice delivered

These two sets of boxes will be completed where the box 'investigative advice' has been ticked. This allows subsequent monitoring of the effectiveness of pre-investigative advice.

As previously mentioned a copy of the completed MG3 will be given to the officer and a copy will be prominently attached to the case file for ease of reference as well as being recorded on CMS. A fully endorsed MG3 is an extremely useful tool for both police officers and prosecutors, saving duplication of time and effort in being able to see at a glance the key issues in a case and any outstanding ones.

MG3A: Further report to Crown Prosecutor for charging decision

This replicates the MG3 and is to be used where there has not been a charging decision and the prosecutor has required further investigation and evidence from the police.

The suspect's name and URN will go on the top of the file together with the date of completion of the MG3 (or MG3A if one has already been completed). Again there is a space for the supervisor's comments and for the officer to provide his/her contact details.

If the prosecutor considers a charge is now appropriate the second part of the MG3A will be completed as usual by the prosecutor including the monitoring codes, etc. If further action is still required then a time bound action plan will be agreed. Any subsequent MG3As or further reviews must be placed in date order on the file.

KEY CONSIDERATIONS—MG3

- Informs the CPS of proposed charges and outline of circumstances
- Enables prosecutor to make informed decision about the case and charges
- Highlights key issues in the case
- Ensures an audit trail of decision making
- Provides police with an agreed action plan

Not Disclosable

REPORT TO CROWN PROSECUTOR FOR CHARGING DECISION
DECISION LOG & ACTION PLAN

Page No. .... of ....

REPORT TO CROWN PROSECUTOR
(FOR _POLICE_ COMPLETION)

URN

Suspect (   )

Surname: ....   Forename(s): ....

D.O.B: .... M / F   Ethnicity code (self determined 16 point +1): ....

PPO ☐   PYO ☐   YO ☐   Bad Character Evidence Y / N   Dangerous Offender Y / N

Custody Ref: ....   Return bail date: ....

Proposed charges: ....

....

Suspect (   )

Surname: ....   Forename(s): ....

D.O.B: .... M / F   Ethnicity code (self determined 16 point +1): ....

PPO ☐   PYO ☐   YO ☐   Bad Character Evidence Y / N   Dangerous Offender Y / N

Custody Ref: ....   Return bail date: ....

Proposed charges: ....

....

Material provided to CPS *(indicate if attached)*

	Date of item		Date of item
MG2 Special measures Assessment (VIW)		**MG13** Order(s) on Conviction	
Statement of:		Pocket note book / Incident report book:	
Statement of:		Police incident log:	
Statement of:		Video / photographs:	
Interview record:		Previous convictions / disposals:	
Forensic / expert evidence:		**MG17** POCA Property or Financial gain	

Contact details
Officer completing: .... Rank / Job title: .... Signature: ....

Station: .... Tel: .... Mob: .... E-mail: ....

OIC name *(if different from above):* .... Date: ....

REPORT TO CROWN PROSECUTOR
(FOR _POLICE_ COMPLETION)

URN

Outline of circumstances and decision / advice sought *(unless verbal report given)*
(Consider: time limit on proceedings (if applicable); strengths and weaknesses of case; possible lines of defence; witness assessment; public safety / bail issues; disclosure; any financial or asset recovery issues; orders on conviction; public interest.)

(Continue on separate sheet if necessary)

Supervisor's comments *(if applicable)*

Supervisor's name *(print)*: .... Signature: ....

**CHARGING DECISION / ADVICE & CASE ACTION PLAN
(FOR _CPS_ COMPLETION)**

URN

Full Code Test ☐　　　　　Threshold Test ☐　　　　　Investigative Advice ☐

Charging decision and advice, specifying or attaching charges _(refer to documents / evidence seen, decision on offences)_

Case Analysis / Evidential Issues

Evidential Criteria

Public Interest

Mode of Trial

ECHR

NWNJ _(consider pre-trial interview with witness)_

Instructions to Court Prosecutor

Other Case Issues _(DPP consent, etc.)_

Charge(s)

(Continue on separate sheet if necessary)

CHARGING DECISION / ADVICE & CASE ACTION PLAN
(FOR _CPS_ COMPLETION)

URN

Prosecutor to indicate general nature of decision and advice *(Tick one box only)*							
Code	Advice / Decision	Suspect ( )	Suspect ( )	Code	Advice / Decision	Suspect ( )	Suspect ( )
A	Charge + request Evidential File			G	TIC		
B	Charge + request Expedited File			H	Request further evidence to complete Evidential Report		
B2	CC non-compliance – charge + request Expedited File			I	Request further evidence to complete Expedited Report		
C	Simple caution			J	Early advice further action necessary		
D	Conditional caution			K	No prosecution – Evidential		
D2	CC non-compliance – No prosecution			L	No prosecution – Public Interest		
E	Reprimand			M	Other		
F	Final warning			N	Refer for POCA investigation		
If 'K', enter Evidential code:				If 'C, D, E, F or L', enter Public Interest code:			

Further action agreed:

Action date by:

1.

1.

2.

2.

3.

3.

4.

4.

POCA case (**MG17**) Y / N   Charging review / action date: ....

Return bail date: ....   PYO Provisional trial date: ....

Further consultation needed pre-charge: Y / N   *(If further consultation necessary, use continuation sheet **MG3A**)*

Prosecutor name *(print)*: .... Contact details: .... Date: ....

Investigation stage at which advice sought:

Pre arrest ☐   Post Arrest ☐   Post Interview ☐   Post bail for further enqs. ☐   Bail for charging decision ☐

How advice delivered:

Face to Face ☐   Video Conferencing ☐   Telephone ☐   CPS Direct ☐   Written ☐

Not Disclosable
FURTHER REPORT TO CROWN PROSECUTOR
FOR CHARGING DECISION

Page No. .... of ....

FOR **_POLICE_** COMPLETION

Suspect's name: ....

URN | | | |

Decision / Advice now sought following completion of MG3 / MG3A dated ....

Supervisor comments *(if applicable)*

Supervisor name *(print name)*: .... Signature: ....

Contact details

Officer completing: .... Rank / Job title: .... Signature: ....

Station: .... Tel: .... Mob: .... E-mail: ....

OIC name *(if different from above)*: .... Date: ....

**CHARGING DECISION / ADVICE & CASE ACTION PLAN
(FOR _CPS_ COMPLETION)**

URN

Full Code Test ☐   Threshold Test ☐   Investigative Advice ☐

Charging decision and advice, specifying or attaching charges *(refer to documents / evidence seen, decision on offences)*

Case Analysis / Evidential Issues

Evidential Criteria

Public Interest

Mode of Trial

ECHR

NWNJ *(consider pre-trial interview with witness)*

Instructions to Court Prosecutor

Other Case Issues *(DPP consent, etc.)*

Charge(s)

(Continue on separate sheet if necessary)

Page No. .... of ....

CHARGING DECISION / ADVICE & CASE ACTION PLAN (FOR *CPS* COMPLETION)

URN

Prosecutor to indicate general nature of decision and advice *(Tick one box only)*							
Code	Advice / Decision	Suspect ( )	Suspect ( )	Code	Advice / Decision	Suspect ( )	Suspect ( )
A	Charge + request Evidential File			G	TIC		
B	Charge + request Expedited File			H	Request further evidence to complete Evidential Report		
B2	CC non-compliance – charge + request Expedited File			I	Request further evidence to complete Expedited Report		
C	Simple caution			J	Early advice further action necessary		
D	Conditional caution			K	No prosecution – Evidential		
D2	CC non-compliance – No prosecution			L	No prosecution – Public Interest		
E	Reprimand			M	Other		
F	Final warning			N	Refer for POCA investigation		
If 'K', enter Evidential code:				If 'C, D, E, F or L', enter Public Interest code:			

Further action agreed:　　　　　　　　　　　　　　　　　　　　　**Action date by:**

1.　　　　　　　　　　　　　　　　　　　　　　　　　　　　　　1.

2.　　　　　　　　　　　　　　　　　　　　　　　　　　　　　　2.

3.　　　　　　　　　　　　　　　　　　　　　　　　　　　　　　3.

4.　　　　　　　　　　　　　　　　　　　　　　　　　　　　　　4.

POCA case **(MG17)** Y / N　　　　Charging review / action date: ....

Return bail date: ....　PYO Provisional trial date: ....

Further consultation needed pre-charge: Y / N　*(If further consultation necessary, use continuation sheet MG3A)*

Prosecutor name *(print):* .... Contact details: .... Date: ....

Investigation stage at which advice sought:

Pre arrest ☐　Post Arrest ☐　Post Interview ☐　Post bail for further enqs. ☐　Bail for charging decision ☐

How advice delivered:

Face to Face ☐　　Video Conferencing ☐　　Telephone ☐　　CPS Direct ☐　　Written ☐

6.5 **MG4: Charge(s)**

6.5.1 **Essentials**

This form records the specific offences that a person has been charged with. It records the defendant's reply after charge and records the grant of unconditional bail to the defendant. A copy of this form is provided to the person charged.

6.5.2 **The form itself**

Preliminaries

The name, address and contact details of the suspect should be recorded at the top of this form.

The custody number as well as the URN and the date of arrest must also be recorded. This is one form where the arrest/summons number should also be included (A/S No). This assists in the tracking of prosecutions and supports the collection of management information.

Again usual details about the suspect, their gender, date of birth, whether they are a PPO, PYO or YO should also be completed. Additionally, ethnicity and whether or not an interpreter is required and the language/dialect (including the name of the interpreter) should be noted. (It is the responsibility of the police to obtain any relevant interpreter for the defendant's first appearance before the court.)

The charges

The form contains the caution given prior to charge in relation to the defendant's right not to say anything after charge. The precise wording contained in the PNLD should be followed together with the offence code. However, in some cases the CPS may have formulated the charge in any event.

Any reply to the charge must be contemporaneously recorded. All charges must be numbered sequentially. The charge form must then be signed and dated by the suspect (and appropriate adult if necessary), charging officer and details of the OIC and the fact that the charge was accepted and the date.

Post-charge unconditional bail

This part of the form is only to be filled out if the defendant is to receive unconditional bail post-charge. It notifies the defendant of the next court date and warns him/her that if s/he fails to attend s/he will commit an offence.

Copies

A copy of the form should be provided to the person charged, a copy attached to the custody record, and two more made available for the CPS file and at court.

KEY CONSIDERATIONS—MG4

- Records specific offences with which defendant is charged
- Refers to caution to defendant prior to charge
- Contemporaneously records defendant's reply to charge
- Contains information on post-charge unconditional bail

MG4

CHARGE(S)

Surname: ....

Forename(s): ....

Address: ....

....

....

....

Postcode: ....

Contact telephone number: ....

Custody no.

First arrest date: .... URN

PPO ☐ YO ☐ PYO ☐ A/S No.

M ☐ F ☐ Date of birth

Ethnicity Code: PNC ☐ 16-point (self-determined) system

Interpreter: language / dialect ....

Name of interpreter

You are charged with the offence(s) shown below. You do not have to say anything. But it may harm your defence if you do not mention now, something which you later rely on in court. Anything you do say may be given in evidence.

Sequential No.	Charge(s)	CCCJS Offence Code
	Continuation charges: Yes ☐ No ☐	

Reply (if any): ....

....

Signed (person charged): .... Signed (appropriate adult): ....

Officer charging   Surname: .... Rank: .... No: .... Station: ....

Officer in case   Surname: .... Rank / Job title: .... No: .... Station: ....

Charge accepted Surname: .... Rank / Job title: .... No: .... Time: .... Date: ....

FOR POST CHARGE UNCONDITIONAL BAIL ONLY (for all other types of bail use MG4A)

I understand that I am granted bail and must surrender to the custody of .... Magistrates' / Youth Court

at (full address) .... on .... time ....

I have been informed that if I fail to do so I may commit an offence and be fined, imprisoned or both.

Signed (person bailed): .... Signed (appropriate adult): ....

Officer granting   Surname: .... Rank: .... No: .... Time: .... Date: ....

File copy ☐   Court copy ☐   Custody record ☐   Person charged ☐

2006/07 (1)

6.6 **MG4A: Bail—Grant/Variation**

6.6.1 **Essentials**

This form was originally and mostly used by the custody officer for the grant of conditional bail, recording details of the bail conditions, and noting any subsequent bail variation. There are now three tick boxes for the type of bail granted including pre-charge unconditional bail (note post-charge unconditional bail was indicated on the MG4) as well as pre-charge conditional and post-charge conditional bail.

6.6.2 **The form itself**

The police station and the name of the suspect, the custody number, and URN are again recorded here at the top of the form.

Grounds for imposing conditions

The appropriate box must be ticked in order to justify conditions being applied to the bail in accordance with PACE, viz: it is necessary to prevent the suspect failing to surrender to custody, committing a further offence whilst on bail, interfering with witnesses or otherwise obstructing the course of justice or for their own protection or their own welfare/interest if it is a child or young offender.

Conditions and variations

Conditions

The actual conditions must be recorded in detail together again with the reasons against each condition as to why they appeared necessary. For example:

Condition of residence—reason—to prevent him failing to surrender
Curfew—reason—to prevent him committing further offences on bail at night

If the conditions involve a security or surety an MG4C should also be completed (see later).

Variations

Where bail is to be varied the number of each bail condition to be varied should be entered along with the varied conditions and the reasons for the variation. In this instance it is only necessary to list the conditions which have been varied. Where an MG4, a computer generated form, is used it is helpful to print out all the conditions of bail following an application for variation.

If all conditions have been removed the reason(s) why should be written and explained in the right-hand column.

Where it is the surety or security that has changed this should be written in the left-hand column and a new MG4C completed.

Declaration

The declaration wording for the granting of bail back to the police station or court reminds the suspect that s/he may commit an offence if s/he fails to surrender and may be arrested if s/he fails to comply with the conditions and that the suspect has the right to apply to the police or the court for variation of any of his/her conditions. Further that s/he has received a copy of the form.

Return dates for bail to the police station or court should be inserted where appropriate.

Signatures

Both the suspect and the officer must fill in the form and it should be dated.

Copies

Again there should be four copies: one for the person bailed, one for the custody record, one for the file, and one for the court.

KEY CONSIDERATIONS—MG4A

- Used by custody officer to grant pre-charge conditional/unconditional bail and post-charge conditional bail
- Records details of bail conditions
- Outlines reasons for imposing conditions
- Makes note of bail variations post-charge
- Highlights if surety/security imposed

MG4A

BAIL – GRANT / VARIATION

Variation No ....

PRE-CHARGE UNCONDITIONAL ☐   PRE-CHARGE CONDITIONAL ☐   POST-CHARGE CONDITIONAL ☐

Station: ....

Surname: .... Forename(s): ....

Custody No. ☐ ☐ ☐

URN ☐ ☐ ☐

Grounds for imposing conditions

The above named person has been granted bail subject to the following conditions (number each separately).
These conditions are imposed because they appear necessary to prevent that person from:

Failing to surrender to custody   Committing an offence whilst on bail ☐

Interfering with witnesses or otherwise obstructing the course of justice ☐   For that person's own protection ☐

For that person's own welfare or own interests (if child or young person) ☐

No.	Condition / variation	Reason(s) why conditions appear necessary
		Continued on separate **MG4A**: Yes ☐ No ☐

If this record is not part of the custody record, a note of the reason(s) must be made on the custody record.

I understand that I am granted bail **with conditions / without conditions** and must surrender to the **court / police** station specified. I have been informed that if I fail to surrender to custody I may commit an offence and be fined, imprisoned, or both; that if I fail to comply with any of the conditions set out above, I may be arrested; and that if I wish to vary any of the conditions I may apply to either the police station or court specified, stating my reasons. I have been given a copy of this form.

Details of court / police station (Grant of bail only)

.... Magistrates' / Youth Court / Police Station

at *(full address)* ....

....

on *(date)* .... at *(time)* ....

Signed *(person bailed)*: .... Signed *(appropriate adult)*: ....

Officer granting   Surname: .... Rank: .... No: .... Time: .... Date: ....

If bail is unconditional or varied enter "all previous conditions cancelled, released on unconditional bail".
*If surety or security is changed enter "surety / security changed" and complete **MG4C**.*

File copy ☐   Court copy ☐   Custody record ☐   Person bailed ☐

2006/07 (1)

6.7 MG4B: Request to vary conditional bail

6.7.1 Essentials

Only the defendant can request to vary his/her conditional bail from the police station, either pre- or post-charge. It is this form that has to be completed. It cannot apply if the defendant has been through court which has then imposed conditional bail. Only a court could then vary those conditions. This form is to be completed by the police officer at the request of the defendant and passed to the custody officer for a decision.

6.7.2 The form itself

The following need to be included:

- Is this the first or subsequent request to vary police bail conditions?
- Specify the type of conditional bail: pre- or post-charge.
- Again specify police station, defendant's name, custody number and URN.
- Describe what variation has been reported by the defendant and the reason given by the defendant for seeking the variation.
- It is important that the police officer specifies where the necessary enquiries have been made to verify the defendant's reasons given for the request, eg s/he has obtained a job and requires his/her curfew to be lifted or s/he requires to change address because his/her tenancy has finished.
- The decision section is completed by the custody officer who will either refuse the application and get the defendant to sign it and date it or grant the application in which case a further form MG4A will be completed by the custody officer spelling out the new bail conditions and variations.
- Again four copies are required to be submitted.

KEY ISSUES—MG4B

- Allows defendant to request variation of police bail conditions
- Only to be used prior to defendant's court appearance
- Outlines variation required and reasons for it
- Confirms necessary enquiries made by police
- Records decision of custody officer

REQUEST TO VARY CONDITIONAL BAIL

Request No ....

PRE-CHARGE CONDITIONAL ☐　　　　　POST-CHARGE CONDITIONAL ☐

Station: ....　　Custody No. ☐☐☐

Surname and initials: ....　　URN ☐☐☐☐

Current no.	Variation requested	Reasons given for request

Continued on separate **MG4B**: Yes ☐　No ☐

I request that the conditions of my bail be varied as above for the reasons stated above.
I have not had an application to change my current bail conditions heard by a court.

Signed (person bailed): ....　Signed (appropriate adult): ....

Time: .... Date: ....

Enquiries made to verify reasons given for request.
Show where recorded if not on custody record or state not appropriate ....

DECISION (complete section A or B)

(A)　Application refused

The conditions of bail set out on form **MG4A** ....　remain unchanged

Signed: .... Surname: .... Rank: .... No: ....

I have been informed that my bail has not been changed. I have been given a copy of this form. I understand that this does not prevent me from making further applications to either the police station or court specified, for the conditions to be varied.

Signed *(person bailed)*: ....　Signed *(appropriate adult)*: ....

Time: .... Date: ....

(B)　Application granted

Conditions of bail are varied as specified on form **MG4A** ....　(complete **MG4A**)

File copy ☐　　Court copy ☐　　Custody record ☐　　Person bailed ☐

2006/07 (1)

6.8 **MG4C: Surety/Security—(For Police Conditional Bail Only)**

6.8.1 **Essentials**

This forms records any details and undertaking from any surety or security. It is to be used only in conjunction with the MG4A (and any other bail conditions) since it will be a condition of bail imposed by the police. The custody officer may require a surety/security to ensure the attendance of the defendant at the police station or court following release from police custody.

6.8.2 **The form itself**

Police custody number and URN need to be inserted and the name of person to be bailed (for ease of reference).

Surety

A surety is a specified person who gives an undertaking to ensure that a defendant will turn up to meet his/her bail date at court or the police station. It is authorized by section 3(4) of the Bail Act 1976. That is the surety's only obligation. S/he is not expected to prevent further offences or stop the defendant from interfering with witnesses. It will therefore only be used where the custody officer has concerns about the defendant's failure to appear.

In practice the surety has to agree to forfeit a sum of money if the defendant fails to appear at the relevant time. No actual sum of money is provided at that time; indeed consideration can be given to other goods that have a realizable value from the surety. However, the custody officer must assure him/herself that the surety does have sufficient funds up front to provide if necessary.

The custody officer (see section 8 of the Bail Act 1976) decides whether a person is suitable as a surety by considering the proposed surety's financial resources, the means by which the surety would pay the sum of money if the defendant failed to appear, and the character and previous convictions of the surety and their relationship with the defendant. In this regard the surety should usually be an adult with a permanent address who is a likely person to secure the attendance of the defendant. S/he must have sufficient means to pay if the defendant subsequently fails to attend. The surety has to sign a declaration here to the effect that s/he acknowledges his/her liability to pay £X if the defendant fails to surrender.

A surety is allowed to be relieved from his/her obligations but s/he needs to notify the police in writing by making a statement outlining the reasons why. If this happens the police may decide to arrest the defendant under the Bail Act 1976.

The surety must also be informed of any variation of police bail conditions (failure to do so may affect the decision on seizure of monies owed).

Generally the recognisance will be taken by the custody officer with the surety appearing before him/her in person. A record of the acceptable surety and their details will then be entered on the MG4C.

Security

A security as opposed to a surety is an actual sum of money or other security that is lodged upfront with the custody officer against the defendant's surrender to custody. Therefore, money in this instance actually changes hands prior to the defendant's failure to appear. Again it is a custody officer's decision based on his view that the defendant may fail to appear only.

A security is normally provided in cash, albeit exceptionally goods may be offered as a security, but cheques and credit cards, etc are not acceptable. The custody officer must satisfy him/herself that the security provided belongs to the provider. In deciding the amount of security the custody officer will take into account the likely penalty at the end of the day for the offence. Again where a security is acceptable and has been lodged a record of the details of this security should be entered on the form MG4C.

Four copies of the MG4C are required: one for the security provider/surety, one for the custody record, one for the case file, and one for the court.

KEY ISSUES—MG4C

- Records details and undertakings of surety/security
- Used in conjunction with MG4A
- Outlines obligations of surety if defendant fails to appear
- Confirms acceptance of security by police

SURETY / SECURITY – (for police conditional bail only)

Station: ....

Custody No.

URN

Person to be bailed

Surname: .... Forename(s): ....

Surety

I have been informed that the above named will be bailed on my surety and must surrender to the custody of:

.... Magistrates' / Youth Court / Police Station

at *(full address)* ....

on .... at .... am / pm

I acknowledge my liability to pay £ .... to the court if the above named person fails to surrender to custody as shown above.

I have also been told that:

(i)   If I later decide that the above named person is unlikely to surrender to custody and for this reason wish to be relieved of my obligations as a surety, I need to notify a police officer in writing.

(ii) I will be informed if the above named person requests the police to vary any of the bail conditions.

Signed *(surety)*: .... Time: .... Date: ....

Surname: .... Forename(s): ....

Address: ....

....

Recognisance taken by:

The above recognisance was taken by me and I gave the surety a copy of this record.

Officer: Signature: .... Time: .... Date:...........................

Surname: .... Rank: .... No:...........................

Additional surety on separate **MG4C**   Yes ☐   No ☐

Security

Because it appears that the above named person is unlikely to surrender to custody, security of .... has been accepted from:

Surname: .... Forename(s): ....

Address: .... for the

surrender of the person bailed to the custody of .... Magistrates' / Youth Court / Police Station

on .... at *(time)* .... am / pm

Security taken by:

Signed: .... Surname: .... Rank:.................... No:..................

I acknowledge my liability to forfeit the security if the person to be bailed fails to surrender to custody as shown above.

Signed *(provider of security)*: .... Time: .... Date: ....

Additional security on separate **MG4C**   Yes ☐   No ☐

MG4A Variation number *(if applicable)* ☐

File copy ☐   Court copy ☐   Custody record ☐   Surety / Security provider ☐

2006/07 (1)

6.9 **MG4D and MG4E: Postal Requisition Forms (not dealt with in detail)**

These forms are specifically designed for postal charging which is still in the pilot phase and may be rolled out throughout England and Wales in the future. They are not dealt with in this chapter.

6.10 **MG4F: NFA Letter Template**

6.10.1 **Essentials**

Under section 37B(5) of PACE, where a decision has been taken to employ NFA in any case by the CPS (or police) it is the obligation of the custody officer on this form to notify the suspect of the same.

6.10.2 **The form itself**

The form tells the suspect the reason why such a decision to take no further action has been taken in relation to specific offences as set out on the top of the form. The reasons either relate to insufficiency of evidence such that there is not a realistic prospect of conviction or where there is sufficient evidence, that it is not in the public interest to proceed with the prosecution (albeit the police may retain the suspect's details).

The form itself highlights the fact that if the decision by the prosecutor is clearly wrong it can be reconsidered. Moreover, it warns that in some circumstances where further evidence comes to light the decision may change or an aggrieved party may themselves instigate criminal or civil proceedings irrespective of the CPS decision in the case.

It reiterates that the decision only relates to offences specified at the top of the form and that any bail conditions in respect of other offences will still apply. It also reminds the suspect that the aggrieved party may themselves wish to pursue a criminal or civil action.

Finally it requires the custody officer to sign the letter (with a copy to parent/ guardian if applicable).

KEY ISSUES—MG4F

- Police notification to suspect of NFA decision and reason why
- Spells out offences to which decision applies
- Highlights circumstances in which decision can be changed
- Informs suspect that aggrieved may still pursue own action

Notification of No Further Action (NFA)
Section 37B(5) PACE 1984

Dear Sir / Madam,

I refer to the offences for which you were recently arrested on *[date ....]*, the details of which are:

Offence 1:	Date:
Offence 2:	Date:
Offence 3:	Date:
Police Station:	Custody Record No:

The Crown Prosecution Service has decided that no further action will be taken at this time in respect of the offence(s). After consideration of the evidence and other information that is currently available the decision was that:

☐ There is insufficient evidence to provide a realistic prospect of conviction.

☐ There is insufficient evidence to provide a realistic prospect of a conviction currently, but the case will be kept under review since further evidence may become available in the future, as a result of which a decision to charge may be made.

☐ Although there is sufficient evidence to provide a realistic prospect of a conviction, a prosecution is not needed in the public interest. You should note that the police may contact you further to inform you that your name will be retained on their records as being responsible for committing the offence(s).

A decision not to charge may be reconsidered if a review of the decision indicates that it was clearly wrong and should not be allowed to stand.

This notice only applies to the offence(s) specified above. If you are currently on bail to return to the police station in respect of these offence(s) it will not be necessary for you to return. It is important to note that any bail conditions imposed in relation to any other offences will still apply.

The fact that no further action is being taken at this time does not prevent an aggrieved party pursuing criminal proceedings or civil remedy.

Yours faithfully

[Signed Custody Officer]

cc: Parent / Guardian *(if applicable)*

6.11 **MG5: Case Summary**

6.11.1 **Essentials**

Traditionally, and certainly prior to the MG3, this was an extremely important form and it was essential for it to be completed in every case. It was the only place where the circumstances of the case were outlined and on which prosecutors relied, especially if there was a guilty plea, to read out the summary to the court for sentencing purposes.

In the past, it must be said, prosecutors placed far too greater reliance on often inaccurate and misleading case summaries. The emphasis within the CPS is now to provide a detailed and accurate picture to the court on a guilty plea not placing a heavy reliance totally on the MG5 when presenting facts to the court.

It is, however, incredibly useful to the CPS if the MG5 tells a chronological story to the reader. Furthermore, it reduces the time taken in reviewing a case and certainly preparing the case for court when the case summary does represent a clear and accurate picture of all the circumstances.

The MG5 is usually provided to the defence in their advance disclosure package. It is important therefore, that any confidential information about the case is submitted separately on the MG6 (Case File Information) and that there are no personal opinions of the officer or remarks which the defence could take exception to included on the MG5.

POINT TO NOTE—STREAMLINED PROCESS (SP)

A new structured **Police Report** (a revised and improved MG5) replaces the MG5 discussed here for all areas where SP is in operation. However the key tips on the completion of the form remain the same. See further 9.3.

6.11.2 **The form itself**

As stated, the MG5 must tell a story, so it must have a beginning, a middle, and an end.

The introduction will spell out the nature of the offence.

The middle will summarize what actually happened, who did what and how the offence was witnessed. This is particularly important where there is more than one offender involved to provide details of what each offender did. Similarly, multiple offences should be dealt with separately. Everything should be listed in chronological order, without lengthy quotes from statements—short and sweet.

The end will usually be comprised of details of the arrest of the defendant, subsequent charge, caution and reply, followed by a short descriptive note (SDN) of the contents of the interview. A phrase like 'he fully admitted the offence' is simply not sufficient. The SDN is discussed (at 6.26.2). Suffice to say it must contain the following:

- a brief account of any admissions (eg 'he agreed that when he took the items he did not intend to pay for them');
- any mitigating or aggravating features (eg 'the defendant explained that he needed the items stolen for his children and had no funds to pay for them' or 'the defendant admitted the theft was pre-meditated before she went out shopping');
- the defendant's version or explanation if different from that put forward by the police (eg 'the defendant only admitted to taking one of the three items the subject matter of the charge and said that she could prove she had paid for the other items in an earlier visit to the store');
- the conduct of the defendant in interview can also be included (eg 'x showed no remorse; was upset and sorry for his actions');
- the start and end times of the interview should also be included.

Tick boxes

The bottom part of the MG5 relates to tick boxes, which alerts the prosecutor to the need for an application to the court for an order on the conviction of the defendant. These relate to an Exclusion, Restraining Order or an ASBO (in which case an MG13 (Application for Order(s) on Conviction) must be completed).

Order on conviction

An Exclusion Order is, for example, an order excluding a person from licensed premises or sporting grounds (eg football banning order). An ASBO relates to anti-social behaviour orders (see 6.24.2). A Restraining Order is made under the Protection of Harassment Act 1997. This is soon to be extended to all offences, even available on the acquittal of a defendant in appropriate circumstances under the Domestic Violence Crime and Victims Act 2004, section 12(5).

Forfeiture/Destruction Order

A Forfeiture or Destruction Order relates, for example, to a court order to destroy drugs or an offensive weapon, the subject matter of the charge or forfeiture of illegal possession of property to which the defendant is not entitled.

Compensation

A Compensation Order (in which case MG19 (Compensation Claim) must also be completed) can be made on conviction where there has been some personal injury, loss or damage to any person for an offence charged or taken into consideration. Relevant supporting documents must be attached to the MG19 with full details of the person to be compensated.

POCA case Property or Financial gain

A POCA application can be made in relation to property or financial gain (in which case an MG17 must be completed) where a defendant can be shown to have benefited from his/her crime and the courts can make a confiscation order. This is now a very important weapon against criminal activity and the FIU should always be consulted first

Where there is no attached separate MG form in relation to the above it is vital that full information in support of such an application is within the body of the MG5. In any event brief details are helpful for a quick overview of what is required, and why the order is thought necessary. This also puts the defence on notice of the same.

KEY ISSUES—MG5

- Structured and tells a story
- Summarizes all key relevant issues
- Provides an accurate account with times and dates
- In chronological order
- Without lengthy quotes
- Does not contain personal opinions
- Provides an SDN of interview
- Does not contain confidential information
- Has the relevant box been ticked and supporting information supplied if seeking an order from the court?

MG5

CASE SUMMARY   URN

R v ....   Page No. .... of ....

Order on conviction e.g. Exclusion / ASBO / Restraining order – complete **MG13** ☐   Forfeiture / Destruction order ☐

Compensation – complete **MG19** ☐   POCA case Property or Financial gain – complete **MG17** ☐

Date of completion: ....   (✓) box if required

2006/07 (1)

6.12 **MG6: Case File Information**

6.12.1 **Essentials**

This is an incredibly important form which surprisingly is often left blank or is inadequately completed by police officers. It is a confidential form; it is not disclosable to the defence and is specifically designed in the form of key questions and headings to remind police officers of all potential outstanding relevant information in relation to evidence, background information, and case management issues. Such information, when provided, greatly assists the prosecution in their effective review and subsequent prosecution of the offence.

The back of the form is blank to allow the officer to put as much information as possible about points identified on the front of the form. The list, however, is not an exhaustive one and officers are to be encouraged to complete the rear, including opinions, thoughts, and problems which need to be addressed on any aspect of the case. There is never too much information on the MG6 from the prosecutor's point of view. Only one form needs to be completed in relation to each file regardless of the number of defendants.

6.12.2 **The form itself**

The URN and the defendant's details must be included as always at the top of the form and there is a reminder that the form is confidential, ie for police and CPS eyes only.

The form then asks the question: 'Is the investigation complete?'. If the answer is 'no' then the officer must highlight, on the rear of the form, what is outstanding and other further lines of enquiry to be completed.

The officer must specify whether the Investigation commenced on or after 4 April 2005. This was inserted so that it was immediately obvious to both the officer and the CPS which disclosure regime applied to the particular case. This is dealt with in the disclosure chapter (Chapter 7) and in relation to the completion of the disclosure schedules at 6.15.2.

Medical/Forensic/Visually Recorded Evidence and Disclosure

As stated in the body of the MG6 itself, four questions must be answered in relation to medical, forensic and visually recorded evidence and disclosure. They must be completed in every case where they are relevant. The format of this form was changed in 2004 to cater for section 51 indictable offences which were fast tracked directly to the Crown Court. It now provides target dates on all the main types of evidence and material that generally tend to hold up a case and may not be immediately available, ie forensics, medical evidence, videos, and disclosure issues.

This information is required by the prosecutor to put before a judge at the first preliminary hearing of an indictable case which sometimes occurs within two weeks of the defendant's first appearance in the magistrates' court. The judge then decides a date by which full papers are to be served in the case and makes decisions on case management issues, based on the information about outstanding evidence provided to the court by the prosecutor. It is imperative therefore that an updated MG6 is provided in relation to expected target dates for outstanding evidence and that they are clear and firm.

Medical Evidence

It is to be noted that this can relate to the defendant or victim or witness in relation both their physical or psychiatric health.

The officer must indicate whether medical statements are required, whether they have been obtained and, if not, the target date for them and whether they may be a problem in relation to this. There often is and it is therefore helpful for the OIC to outline his/her efforts to obtain these statements to date.

Forensic Evidence

Again the officer must indicate, if relevant, whether or not the items have been sent for examination and the delivery date for receipt of the report together with any additional information where items have been subsequently sent and also an explanation for the late submission.

It is important to note that whenever work is submitted for scientific examination a form MG21 (previously an MGFSP) must also be completed. This is a detailed form (discussed at 6.32) and a copy of it should be attached to the MG6 so that the prosecutor has access to the information provided.

Indeed best practice suggests that officers discuss the submission of the form with the prosecutor so that all necessary information is provided to the forensic team from the outset and all the right questions are asked of them (in the 'points to prove' section).

Visually Recorded Evidence

The officer is required to indicate whether or not all the evidence has been viewed and copied, if not, then the target date for completion must be provided, and whether or not the reviewing or recording of material may be a problem. The evidence could be in the format of ABE tapes for vulnerable and intimidated witnesses or CCTV evidence.

There have been a number of problems encountered in the past with multiplex video tapes and their viewing by both the CPS and the defence. Any such anticipated problem should be highlighted here.

Disclosure

This section is often left blank but applies in every case since it requires the officer to indicate whether s/he has complied with his/her disclosure obligations and submitted the relevant completed and signed disclosure schedules (MG6C, MG6D and MG6E). This is in relation to unused material in the case which does not form part of the actual evidence against the defendant but may be relevant and to which statutory obligations of disclosure may arise under the CPIA 1996 (as amended).

It further requires the officer to highlight any anticipated complications in relation to unused material (eg materials in a large scale enquiry which have been retained but not examined).

Additionally the officer is reminded of his/her obligation to pursue reasonable lines of enquiry by the indication of whether or not there is any 'third party material in the case'. If there is, the prosecution must be informed at the earliest opportunity to make a decision as to whether or not the CPS should make an application to obtain it (again discussed in detail in Chapter 7).

Ticking the relevant box (18 boxes)

These boxes act as an aide memoire to the police officer of all key issues to be considered in any case. Where a box is ticked the officer should then fill out the details on the back of the form cross-referencing it to the relevant tick box question on the front. These tick boxes are not exhaustive but do highlight the main issues generally arising in any case which require any information to be communicated to the prosecutor.

1. Victim personal statement taken/to be taken?

This is an additional statement to the main witness statement which can be made at the same time as the original witness statement or subsequent to it. Its purpose is to explain to the court the effect of the crime on the individual victim and to discuss any other concerns which they may have, eg with regard to the offender's bail.

On the back of the MG11 (Witness Statement) the witness is requested to indicate whether the officer has explained the scheme to him/her and has provided them with the relevant leaflet on it. Although this scheme is optional for victims, it is good practice for police officers in all cases where there are individual victims to explain the importance of making such a statement and provide them with the opportunity to do so.

In the past there has been a reluctance of officers to obtain such statements from victims since they are of the opinion that because they are disclosable to the defence they may be quoted in court by the prosecutor, thereby highlighting the victim's vulnerability to the defendant. However, they are useful important documents in alerting the court to the long-term effects of the crime on the victim and are highly relevant for sentencing purposes. In the short term also, the victim's attitude to the defendant being allowed bail is an important factor to inform the court.

The VPS is a statement separate from the victim witness statement forming part of the evidence in the case. The ticking of the box will alert the prosecutor to look for it (perhaps to read out to the court in relation to an objection to bail or in sentencing). If a VPS has not been taken the prosecutor may then send the officer a memo requesting him/her to speak to the victim in order for one to be completed.

2. Witness (including expert) statements still to be taken?

This information assists the prosecutor in case progression issues. By indicating any outstanding statements to be taken and timescales this will prevent the prosecutor sending a memo to the police asking for the same information and may also assist the prosecutor in requesting an adjournment from the court in order to obtain them.

3. Photographs of the injuries? (include date when available)

Forces are provided with digital cameras in which case photographic evidence is usually already on the file. Where other evidence is anticipated it is useful to know here what that photo is likely to show and its anticipated date of arrival.

4. Any vulnerable or intimidated adult witnesses. Is a Special Measures meeting required? Complete MG2

Such witnesses have already been subject of detailed consideration in relation to the completion of an MG2 at 6.3. This will provide supporting evidence to the prosecutor to consider and make an application for special measures when a witness gives evidence in court. The ticking of this box which often occurs prior to the completion of the MG2, allows the prosecutor then and there to consider the necessary support required for such a witness at the earliest opportunity and reminds officers and CPS alike of their obligations towards them.

5. Are there child witnesses/victims?

It has already been seen that a witness under 17 is a 'vulnerable' witness so the same comments apply as above. Furthermore the CPS have an additional policy document in relation to child witnesses reminding prosecutors of the special treatment required towards them in each case.

6. Have any witnesses refused to make statements (include names and evidence they could give)

The CPS is often notified by the defence that there were further witnesses to an offence but there are no statements from them. This is totally unsatisfactory. Where witness details are known it is vital the CPS is provided with as much information as possible as to what they might have said and the reason for their refusal to make a statement. In most situations such information is subsequently disclosable to the defence.

It will always be desirable to try and persuade a witness with relevant evidence to give that evidence for the prosecution or at least to make some form of statement even if they will not subsequently come to court. Then if the defence do manage to call them that statement can be put to them in cross-examination, and the prosecution are not caught unawares.

7. Is this a special category case, eg hate crime/domestic violence, etc? Attach relevant incident reports

If this is a special category of case then this should have already been flagged up at the top of the MG1 since it requires additional specialist handling by the police and the CPS alike. In such cases there may well be some intelligence which the officer can impart to the prosecutor in relation to background and surrounding circumstances.

In domestic violence it is often the case that there have been previous call outs in respect of the same parties so any relevant incident reports should be submitted and highlighted here also.

8. Strength and weaknesses of evidence and/or witnesses?

It may be the prosecutor's job to review the evidence in the case but it is the officer in the case who has had the contact with the witness and the defendant and is best able to assess their reliability and credibility and any prevarication or unwillingness to attend court or anti-police attitude on their part—indeed any issues that may affect their veracity. Similarly, anything in relation to the defendant which has been said outside the interview or in his/her demeanour or behaviour at any time.

This is a golden opportunity for the officer to put his/her personal, informed opinions about the case highlighting any anticipated problems which may not be readily visible from the submission of the case papers themselves and it should not be readily ignored by the officer.

9. Are there specific problems/needs of prosecution witnesses, eg interpreters?

The requirements of professional and expert witnesses must always be considered. Here the police officer can comment on their availability, preferences and contact details if they are required to come to court and give evidence.

Prosecution witnesses may need interpreters in which case language and dialect must be specified. Witnesses may have disabilities requiring a sign language interpreter or other special assistance in which case details can be inserted of what action has been taken and what arrangements should be provided.

10. If no MG19 on file and compensation is an issue, enter victim's name and address, approximate value

This information should be on the MG19 but where an application for compensation is appropriate and no MG19 has been received back from the witness the officer should have ticked the box on the MG5 and the prosecutor will then look to this section for any additional information. The victim's confidential details and approximate values can be inserted on the back of the MG6 so that they can be given to the court who may award compensation if sentencing occurs on the first hearing. It will be more likely to be granted if the prosecutor can provide some indication of the amount involved and other relevant information even without an MG17.

11. Issues of bad character and/or dangerous offender. Complete MG16

Again here a separate form, MG16, needs to be completed if these apply. However, it is useful if the box is ticked if either is relevant as a reminder to the prosecutor so that even if the form MG16 has not been completed they are alerted to the same.

A comment on the relevance of previous convictions (eg offences with similar modus operandi) or additional information in possession of the officer about the defendant's previous conduct should be cited in case the prosecutor wishes to place that information before the court or ask for further enquiries to be made.

12. Further persons to be arrested/interviewed/undergo ID procedure?

Where further offenders are still outstanding, any information concerning these enquiries and anticipated timescales should be included here. Additionally, any information relating to the defendant him/herself and the holding of ID procedures should be included. The prosecutor may wish to tie up future defendants with the one before the court and adjourn the current case for this to take place.

13. Others charged whose details do not appear on this file?

It is essential that any information about anyone else connected with the same offence (eg an adult bailed but charged with a PYO who is already before the court) is given to the prosecutor from the outset. Problems are often caused where cases are not adjourned for defendants to be linked up and separate files with separate reviewing prosecutors then go through the system.

14. Other person(s) yet to be charged?

The same applies as for question 13 insofar as a suspect may have been granted pre-charge police bail for further evidence to be obtained and it is anticipated that they are likely to be charged with the same offence or connected offences relating to the particular file in question.

15. Others receiving caution/final warning/reprimand out of the same incident? (include names, offences and reasons)

It is often embarrassing for the prosecutor to find out from the defence in open court that another 'joint offender' was cautioned in respect of the same offence but that their client is up before the court. Ticking this box and providing the relevant information means that the prosecutor is appraised of it prior to court and will be in a position to explain to the court how the offender differs to the one in the dock and why that course of action was taken.

16. Matters of local/public interest?

This is important where, for example, an offence although not serious in itself is a particular problem in the area in which it was committed or a prosecution would have a significant positive impact on maintaining community confidence.

Both these situations are highlighted in the Code for Crown Prosecutors as public interest factors in favour of a prosecution so they are relevant to the actual review of the case as well as circumstances, which the prosecutor may well wish to point out to the court as aggravating factors in relation to the sentencing of the defendant.

17. If POCA case, has financial investigation commenced? Complete MG17

Wherever the defendant has benefited from his/her criminal conduct and there is the opportunity for the court to make an order against the defendant the powers available under POCA 2003 will be considered. Again a separate detailed form should be completed if this is the case—the MG17. In fact early advice should be sought from CPS in relation to all aspects of this, however, this tick box reminds the CPS about POCA 2003 (in addition to the tick box on the MG5) and notifies them whether the FIU are already involved and from when.

18. Are there any other applications/orders on conviction required? MG13

Again this acts as a reminder to both officers and CPS that further relevant information can be provided on the back on the MG6 in the absence of completion of the MG13 at that stage.

It is to be noted that question 10 (MG19—Compensation Claim); question 11 (MG16—Evidence of Defendant's Bad Character and/or Dangerous Offender); question 17 (MG17—Proceeds of Crime Act (POCA) Review) and question 18 (MG13—Application for Order(s) on Conviction) are all inserted as a reminder to officers and prosecutors for the provision of necessary information in the absence of completion of a specific form and to alert them to the same.

As indicated, the back page of the form is to be completed with cross reference to the particular question answered out of the 18 tick boxes or to provide other relevant information to the prosecutor. The officer completing this form must then sign and date it.

The supervising officer should ensure that the MG6 is properly completed to take account of all reasonable lines of enquiry and that relevant agreed targets for the submission of evidence has been correctly identified.

KEY ISSUES—MG6

- Confidentially informs the CPS of all background information
- Assists the prosecutor in reviewing and prosecuting the case
- Provides target dates and information on awaited evidence (medical/forensic/video) and disclosure issues
- Tick boxes act as aide memoir to the police/CPS on all key issues
- Back of form blank—to be completed with additional information and cross-referenced to tick boxes

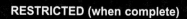 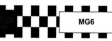

CASE FILE INFORMATION
Not Disclosable   URN

This document is for internal use only. It should be regarded as a memorandum between the police and CPS.
It may well contain confidential information, and therefore must not be disclosed to the defence.

Defendant's surname: .... Forename(s): ....

Is the investigation complete? **Y / N**   Investigation commenced on or after the 4th April 2005 **Y / N**
<u>The following four questions **MUST** be completed in all cases where relevant</u>

Medical Evidence *(physical or psychiatric injuries of defendant / victim / witness)*
Are medical statements required? **Y / N**. If **Yes**, have they been obtained? **Y / N**
If **No**, target date to obtain: ....
Is obtaining medical evidence a problem? **Y / N**. If **Yes**, give brief details: ....
....

....

Forensic Evidence *(attach copy of MG21 / MG21A)*
Have items been sent for examination? **Y / N**. If **Yes**, delivery date for receipt of report (if known): ....
Are extra items to be sent? **Y / N**. If **Yes**, give brief details including reasons for later submission: ....
....

....

Visually Recorded Evidence
Has all evidence been viewed and copied? **Y / N**. If **No**, target date for completion: ....
Is viewing and copying the recorded material a problem? **Y / N**. If **Yes,** give brief details: ....
....

....

Disclosure
Have all **MG6C, D** and **E** Schedules been completed and signed? **Y / N**
Are there any anticipated complications regarding unused material? **Y / N**. If **Yes**, give brief details: ....
....

....

Is there any third party material in this case? **Y / N**. If **Yes**, give brief details: ....
....

....

Where applicable, tick the relevant box(es) and record details on the reverse of this form.

		✓			✓
1	Victim personal statement taken / to be taken?		10	If no **MG19** on file and compensation is an issue, enter victim's name and address, approximate value.	
2	Witness (including expert) statements still to be taken?		11	Issues of bad character and / or dangerous offender. Complete **MG16**.	
3	Photographs of the injuries? (include date when available).		12	Further persons to be arrested / interviewed / undergo ID procedure?	
4	Any vulnerable or intimidated adult witnesses. Is a Special Measures meeting required? Complete **MG2**.		13	Others charged whose details do not appear on this file?	
5	Are there child witnesses / victims?		14	Other person(s) yet to be charged?	
6	Have any witnesses refused to make statements (include names and evidence they could give)		15	Others receiving caution / final warning / reprimand out of the same incident? (Include names, offences and reasons).	
7	Is this a special category case, e.g. hate crime / domestic violence, etc? Attach relevant incident reports.		16	Matters of local / public interest?	
8	Strengths or weaknesses of evidence and / or witnesses?		17	If POCA case, has financial investigation commenced? Complete **MG17**.	
9	Are there specific problems / needs of prosecution witnesses, eg, interpreters?		18	Are there any other applications / orders on conviction required? **MG13**	

Date form completed:...

CASE FILE INFORMATION
Not Disclosable

Page No. .... of ....

URN

Officer completing: .... Rank / Job title: .... No: ....

Signature: .... Date form completed: ....

6.13 **MG6A: Record of Pre-interview Briefing**

6.13.1 **Essentials**

This is a relatively new form which enables a chronological log of the brief information provided to the accused or their lawyers. This will assist the prosecution to use adverse inferences (under section 34 of the Criminal Justice and Public Order Act 1994) in respect of the defendant's failure to mention facts when questioned in interview, or rebuttal of subsequent defences. The level of disclosure, to be given to the suspect pre-interview is a decision for the police officer.

Defence lawyers will often argue that the reason the defendant went no comment at interview was because of inadequate disclosure by the police and that it would be unfair to draw an inference from that silence.

What is required is a 'fair' disclosure to enable the suspect to obtain a balanced picture of the case against him/her. This must be decided on a case-by-case basis dependent upon the complexity, seriousness, and nature of the case itself. The case law is discussed in more detail at Chapter 7. Detailing the disclosure that was provided will allow the CPS to be better prepared to counter defence arguments at court.

Care should be taken in recording everything that the legal adviser was told about the case prior to interview. In addition, as more information is revealed to the legal adviser during the interview—drip feed disclosure—this too should be fully recorded on the form. Once fully completed the MG6A should show precisely what the legal adviser was told. Eventually all the relevant information in the officer's possession will probably be disclosed during the interviewing process, accordingly all this information should be laid out on the MG6A, including the order and the time the information was disclosed and the method.

There is always going to be a difference of opinion between defence solicitors and police officers about the amount of pre-trial disclosure they should receive. Police officers may find it useful to peruse a book written specifically for defence solicitors providing detailed advice of how they should behave at the police station. It is always useful to appreciate how one's 'opponent' is being briefed! See R Ede *Defending Suspects at Police Station* (5th edn, Legal Action Group, 2006).

6.13.2 **The form itself**

The suspect's name and name of solicitor and firm representing him/her must be completed at the top of the form.

List of information provided to suspect of defence solicitor/legal representative

What is required here is the time and date of the pre-interview briefing, the name of the person briefed and a description of the information/material including how it is given (ie verbally, audio or visual, eg CCTV).

Signatures

The solicitor must then be invited to sign the form after the last entry of information given. The officer him/herself should sign it with his/her rank/job title and station and the OIC, if for any reason it is different to the officer briefing the solicitor.

A copy will be given to the defence and a copy retained by the police for the file.

KEY ISSUES—MG6A

- Provides information on case against suspect prior to interview
- Police to make decision on level of disclosure
- Fair disclosure is essential
- Enables the CPS to draw adverse inferences
- Prevents later arguments about what has been disclosed

MG6A

RECORD OF PRE-INTERVIEW BRIEFING   Page No. .... of ....

URN

Suspect(s) Surname: .... Forename(s): ....

Solicitor / Legal Representative: .... Firm's name: ....

List of information provided to suspect or defence solicitor / legal representative

| Time and date | Person briefed | Description of information / material
(include how given: verbally / written / audio / visual) |
|---|---|---|
| | | |

After last entry invite solicitor / legal representative to sign receipt of information

Officer completing:...   Rank / Job title:..

Station:..   Date:..

Officer in case *(if different from above)*:..

2006/07 (1)

6.14 **MG6B: Police Officer/Staff Disciplinary Record**

6.14.1 **Essentials**

This form is completed personally by the person subject of any finding or conviction against them who makes any statements in relation to any case whether or not as a witness they form part of the prosecution case.

This form should be completed where a full file of evidence is submitted to the CPS. It is vital that the police officer or other member of police staff, eg the police community support officers who are witnesses in a case, notify the CPS in this regard. Detailed procedures (agreed between ACPO and CPS) govern how such relevant information should be revealed to the prosecutor.

Note that revelation to the prosecutor does not mean automatic disclosure to the defence. However, if the CPS is unaware of the information it could subsequently be fatal to the conviction if it came to light. It is a CPS decision whether or not the information provided satisfies the 'disclosure test' and therefore must be disclosed to defence.

Police officers and other staff members should refer to their Professional Standards Department if they are unsure as to whether or not to complete the form and further assistance can be found in the prosecution team Disclosure Manual at chapter 18. Moreover, on the back of the MG6B there are detailed instructions as to how to complete the form itself and the type of information which it is necessary to provide on it. Negative returns of form MG6B are not required.

This form will never be sent to the defence and there is no need to include this material on the schedule of unused material. It will be treated in the strictest confidence by the CPS.

6.14.2 **The form itself**

Types of findings

At the top of the form are six potential options of types of findings so that the officer can tick the appropriate box.

1. *I have a disciplinary finding of guilt/have failed to meet the appropriate standard of conduct at a misconduct hearing*

Further guidance is provided at paragraphs 2–5 of the notes on the back of the MG6B.

The only exception to the above are disciplinary findings which have been expunged in accordance with police regulations (but if relevant may be required to be revealed to the prosecutor); disciplinary findings in respect of charges arising out of neglect of health, improper dress or untidiness or entering licensed premises; disciplinary findings resulting in non-relevant cautions (ie where officer's integrity, honesty or credibility is not an issue in relation to a particular case). In any event cautions can only be revealed within the first 12-month period.

2. I have a criminal conviction/criminal caution

Further guidance is provided at paragraph 6 of the notes on the back of the MG6B.

This will include all recordable convictions (as defined in PACE, section 27) where spent or otherwise including foreign ones; or criminal cautions for recordable offences (bindovers are to be recorded as criminal cautions); penalty notices for disorder for recordable offences.

The PNC printout should be attached to the MG6B in this instance.

3. I have been charged with a disciplinary offence/notified of a failure to meet the appropriate standards indicated below but the case has not yet been concluded

Further guidance is provided at paragraph 7 of the notes on the back of the MG6B and the Police (Discipline) Regulations 1985 and the Police Conduct Regulations 1999/2004 are set out on the bottom of the back of the MG6B form. Police officers should note that there are new national professional standards Codes of Conduct in the pipeline which will come into force by the end of 2008.

If disciplinary proceedings have been commenced the prosecutor should be notified of that fact on this form (save for exempted disciplinary matters as indicated at 1, ie neglect of health, etc).

Where an officer has been notified under Regulation 9 of the Police Conduct Regulations 1999/2004 they need only reveal that fact to the prosecutor where it is considered relevant to the case if the proceedings have not yet been completed.

4. I have been charged with a criminal offence indicated below but the case has not been concluded

Again the CPS should be informed of this fact where the person has been charged or summonsed using the MG6B to provide the details.

5. I have an adverse judicial finding against me

Further guidance is provided at paragraph 8 of the notes on the back of the MG6B.

An adverse judicial finding (AJF) is a finding by a civil or criminal court expressly or by inevitable inference that a police witness has knowingly, whether on oath or otherwise, mislead the court.

Such AJFs are recorded in full by the prosecuting advocate or force solicitor in a civil case and forwarded to the professional standards department. The officer in this situation should refer to them directly for guidance in relation to the MG6B and case law dictates they must be revealed to the prosecutor in all cases.

Whether or not they will then be disclosed to the defence is dependent on a case-by-case basis relating to the specific issues in the case and what is in dispute between the prosecution and the defence. The CPS will decide the extent of any disclosure to the defence dependent on whether or not it satisfies the disclosure test and will write separately to the defence in this regard. Subsequently it will be the responsibility of the prosecution advocate, where AJFs are disclosed, to determine whether they may be deployed in cross-examination and accordingly what the CPS response will be to that deployment.

6. I have been given a relevant formal written warning or relevant caution

Further guidance is provided at paragraph 9 in the notes on the back of the MG6B.

Generally notification of formal written warnings and cautions are not required as a matter of routing to the CPS. However, in some circumstances it may have a bearing on the particular circumstances of the case, for example being relevant to an officer's credibility.

At paragraph 18.14 of the Disclosure Manual the example is given where an officer has received a warning because of an irregularity in exhibit handling and an exhibit in the instant case is in issue. This will be a situation where the caution should be revealed to the CPS. In any event they are disregarded after a 12-month period.

Change of circumstances (refer to paragraph 10 on the back of the MG6B)

Since there is a continuing duty of disclosure on the prosecutor in respect of all unused material any change of circumstances in relation to disciplinary and/or criminal records, etc must be notified to the CPS as soon as possible (initially via the MG6). It is important that information on the MG6B is totally up to date.

Information on the MG6B

The form has four columns on page 1:

- the date of finding/charge or notification;
- the nature of offence/allegation or details of the conduct which (it is alleged) failed to meet the appropriate standards;
- the punishment/sanction;
- the date of expunction, where appropriate.

These are self-explanatory but details given to the CPS in column 2 must be sufficient to enable them to make an informed decision as to the relevance of the information to the proceedings in question. The CPS will return the form if these details are insufficient and they cannot decide its relevance and the disclosure test in the particular case.

Declaration

At the bottom of the MG6B the police officer/police staff member must sign and date a declaration to the effect:

This information is true to the best of my knowledge and belief and I am aware that I have a continuing obligation to provide updated information should circumstances change.

Back of the MG6B

As previously indicated the back of the MG6B contains guidance as to the completion of the MG6B and also reminds officers to consult the Prosecution Team Disclosure Manual and Professional Standards Department if in any doubt as to the forms completion.

KEY ISSUES—MG6B

- Informs the CPS of any disciplinary/criminal/AJF against police staff
- Police responsibility to submit the form
- Professional Standards Department can assist on completion
- Detailed instructions provided on back of form
- Confidentiality assured
- CPS decision as to relevance and disclosure to defence

POLICE OFFICER / STAFF DISCIPLINARY RECORD

Page No. .... of ....

URN

Name: ....   Rank / Job Title: .... No: ....

Station / Unit: ....

1. I have a disciplinary finding of guilt / have failed to meet the appropriate standard of conduct at a misconduct hearing. *(See note 2-5)*. ☐

2. I have a criminal conviction / criminal caution *(see note 6)*. ☐

3. I have been charged with a disciplinary offence / notified of a failure to meet the appropriate standards indicated below but the case has not yet been concluded *(see note 7)* ☐

4. I have been charged with a criminal offence indicated below but the case has not yet been concluded. ☐

5. I have an adverse judicial finding against me *(see note 8)*. ☐

6. I have been given a relevant formal written warning or relevant caution *(see note 9)* ☐

(Please tick as appropriate)

Date of finding / charge or notification	Nature of offence / allegation or details of the conduct which (it is alleged) failed to meet the appropriate standards	Punishment / Sanction	Date of expunction

This information is true to the best of my knowledge and belief and I am aware that I have a continuing obligation to provide updated information should circumstances change.

Signature: ....   Date: ....

The Guidance in the Prosecution Team Disclosure Manual or Professional Standards Department should be consulted if an officer or member of Police staff is in any doubt about how to complete this form.

1.   Please print details and give enough detail to allow CPS to make an informed decision about disclosure.

2.   Police officers / members of police staff making a statement, whether the statement forms part of the prosecution case or not, should reveal to the prosecutor any disciplinary findings of guilt or failures to meet the appropriate standards recorded against them, unless the findings have been expunged. Police officers / members of police staff nevertheless should reveal details of any expunged disciplinary matter when requested by the prosecutor, or if considered relevant to the case.

3.   Findings of guilt or failures relating to 'Neglect of Health', 'Improper Dress or Untidiness' and 'Entering Licensed Premises' under the Police (Discipline) Regulations 1985 and disciplinary hearings resulting in non relevant cautions (Police Conduct Regulations 1999 / 2004) are exempt from revelation unless specifically requested by the CPS. *(For relevant cautions see paragraph 9.)*

4.   Where a finding of guilt or not meeting the appropriate standard results in a fine or a reprimand it shall be expunged after three years; and five years for any other form of punishment, provided that during the relevant period the officer / member of staff is free from further punishment other than a disciplinary caution. (Reg. 17(2) Police Regulations 1995.) For members of Police Staff local rules will apply.

5.   If the finding of guilt or failure to meet the standards is likely to be expunged by the time the case comes to trial and the officer's / member of police staff's evidence can be heard, the fact that it is likely to be expunged in the near future should still be revealed to the prosecutor.

6.   Police officers / staff making a statement, whether the statement forms part of the prosecution case or not, should inform the prosecutor of the existence of any criminal convictions or cautions using this form, attaching the Police National Computer (PNC) Printout for that officer / staff if the offence disclosed is a recordable offence. This is for all offences recorded on the PNC whether spent or otherwise, as well as convictions and cautions in Scotland and other foreign countries. Bindovers should be recorded as cautions. Where an officer / member of police staff has been charged or summons for a criminal offence but the proceedings have not been completed, the prosecutor should be informed on this form **MG6B**.

7.   When an officer / member of police staff has been served with a notice under Regulation 9 of the Police (Conduct) Regulations, or are under investigation for any disciplinary matter, they are not required to reveal the fact to the prosecutor, unless considered relevant to the case. If disciplinary or failing to meet the standards proceedings have commenced, the fact should be reported on this form (unless it is a finding or failure of the misconducts listed in paragraph 3).

8.   An adverse judicial finding is a finding by a court that a police witness, whether on oath or otherwise, has knowingly misled the court. This may be stated expressly by a court, or may be inferred from the particular circumstances of a court's proceedings. This will include civil as well as criminal hearings. If the officer / member of police staff is subject to an adverse judicial finding, the relevant Professional Standards Department (PSD) should be contacted in order that it can provide guidance on the completion of this form.

9.   Officers / members of police staff are not routinely required to provide details of formal written warnings or cautions that arise out of disciplinary hearings unless the nature of the written warning or caution may have a bearing on the present case. For example, a written warning or caution would be relevant if the officer's honesty, integrity or credibility were an issue. For those purposes all written warnings and cautions are disregarded after 12 months, but if in doubt, advice should be sought from the relevant PSD.

10. The prosecutor must be notified immediately of any change in circumstances.

Police (Discipline) Regulations 1985

1. Discreditable conduct
2. Misconduct towards a member of a police force
3. Disobedience to orders
4. Neglect of duty
5. Falsehood or prevarication
6. Improper disclosure of information
7. Corrupt or improper practice
8. Abuse of authority
9. Racially discriminatory behaviour
12. Damage to police property
13. Drunkenness
14. Drinking on duty or soliciting drink
16. Criminal conduct
17. Being an accessory to disciplinary offences as set out above

Police Conduct Regulations 1999 / 2004

1. Honesty and integrity
2. Fairness and impartiality
3. Politeness and tolerance
4. Use of force and abuse of authority
5. Performance of duties
6. Lawful orders
7. Confidentiality
8. Criminal offences
9. Property
10. Sobriety
11. Appearance
12. General conduct

NOTE: Offences under paragraphs 10 (Neglect of health), 11 (Improper dress or untidiness) and 15 (Entering licensed premises) of the Police (Discipline) Regulations 1985, have been deliberately omitted.

6.15 **MG6C: Police Schedule of Non-sensitive Unused Material**

6.15.1 **Essentials**

This schedule informs the prosecutor of the existence of all non-sensitive unused material relevant to the case and where the property is located if inspection is required. The prosecutor must then review the material and record the result of that review on the form making a decision as to whether or not it is disclosable to the defence. The form itself is then disclosed to the defence with the decisions of the prosecutor endorsed on it.

The importance of disclosure of unused material is considered in Chapter 7, but the importance of these forms—MG6C and MG6D (non-sensitive and sensitive 'schedules' as they are called)—cannot be over-emphasized. Without a comprehensive list of unused material from the police officer the CPS simply cannot fulfil their own obligations under the CPIA 1996, and will fail to meet defence requests and the case may be lost.

The disclosure officer's duty

It is the duty of the disclosure officer to reveal to the prosecutor on the schedule all items of relevant unused non-sensitive material which had been recorded and retained by him/her in the course of the investigation. It is the prosecution role thereafter to determine whether any of the unused material needs to be disclosed to the defence because it satisfies the 'disclosure test', ie that it is material which might reasonably be considered capable of undermining the case for the prosecution or assisting the case for the defendant.

The prosecutor is assisted in this task by the detailed completion of the schedules themselves and also the officer's comments on the MG6E (discussed at 6.17) which highlights the unused material which in the officer's view fulfils the disclosure test.

When to submit?

Usually the duty on the prosecution to disclose unused material via the schedule to the defence is only triggered after a not guilty plea in the magistrates' courts or after service of the papers for the Crown Court. However, the police officer must consider unused material from the outset of an investigation and is required, for example, in CJSSS and on the submission of a file prior to a charging decision to submit as a minimum unused material which fulfils the disclosure test even if schedules are not completed at that time. Local protocols in some areas do demand completed schedules from the outset. There are, therefore, major advantages for the disclosure officer in starting the schedules at an early stage.

The prosecutor's duty of disclosure is a continuing one for the duration of criminal proceedings against the accused. Therefore any new material coming to light must be treated in the same way as earlier material and the schedules continually updated by means of continuation sheets. This will especially be the case after the receipt of a defence statement and potential further enquiries by police officers in the light of them.

Since the Code places the responsibility for creating the schedules in the first instance on the disclosure officer and keeping them accurate and up to date the prosecutor will never amend the MG6C schedule itself. The schedules will therefore be returned to the disclosure officer for this action to be done.

6.15.2 **The form itself**

The top of the form states 'The Disclosure Officer believes that the following material, which does not form part of the prosecution case, is not sensitive'.

If the officer has any doubt about any material s/he should retain it and seek the advice or assistance of the prosecutor at the earliest opportunity (paragraph 6.1 of the Codes of Practice; paragraph 31 of the Attorney General's Guidelines on Disclosure).

Sensitive material is listed on the MG6D but unused material containing sensitive information, eg names and addresses, etc can be inserted on the MG6C as long as the sensitive information has been edited out. The prosecutor should be informed of the nature of edited material if it is not obvious on the MG6. The responsibility for only serving such edited documents on the defence when directed by the CPS rests with the police officer. However, only straightforward editing should be done by them without prior consultation with the CPS.

The left hand side of the form is for the police officer to complete, the right hand side for the prosecutor.

Description and relevance

The form itself states that the disclosure officer 'should give sufficient detail for the CPS to decide if the material should be disclosed or requires more detailed examination'. Police officers are then referred for further guidance to the Attorney General's Guidelines on Disclosure (2006) and the Prosecution Team Disclosure Manual (2006 (continually updated) on the internet at Chapter 6 and 7).

POINT TO NOTE—DETAILED DESCRIPTIONS

It is crucial that descriptions by disclosure officers on non-sensitive schedules are **detailed, clear and accurate.** The description may require a summary of the contents of the retained material to assist the prosecution to make an **informed** decision on disclosure ...

Attorney General's Guidelines on Disclosure, para 29 (emphasis added)

Each item on the disclosure schedule must be listed separately and numbered consecutively. Sometimes because of the nature of the enquiry there may be items of a similar or repetitive nature. These can be block listed and described by quantity and generic title. However, if any of the items among them satisfy the disclosure test they must be listed and described individually.

In theory, the prosecutor should be able, by reading the description given by the officer in the schedule to decide whether s/he needs to see the particular material or make a decision as to non-disclosure from the nature of the description alone.

A **copy** of any material which the police officer considers satisfies the disclosure test (as s/he will outline on the MG6E) should be submitted with the schedule as an aide to the prosecutor. Best practice dictates that copies also of the custody record, crime report, and log of messages received should also be attached.

This schedule is the 'spine index' for the prosecutor—getting disclosure right involves the police officer in the first instance providing the necessary detailed accurate analysis of the materials submitted in the schedule. It is simply inadequate to refer to a document by a form or number which may be meaningless outside the police service (instead of writing CAD message, s/he should write: 'log of messages number 345 containing a first description of the subject' or alternatively: 'initial police call to the incident'.

As they are compiling their list officers should be mindful of the fact that first the lawyer will be reviewing it on the information they provide and then secondly the defence will receive the form as their only knowledge of unused material in the case.

Poor completion of the schedules merely wastes time and resources since both the prosecutor and the defence are likely to request further information about the item and/or request to see them because they are unclear as to the relevance of the material listed.

Additionally the disclosure officer is required to put the location of the item, ie where it can be found—in the box marked 'location'. Where copies have been submitted to the CPS with the schedule it should also be indicated in the box provided.

The prosecutor's duty—for CPS use

The right hand part of the form requires the prosecutor to enter one of three letters and any comments prior to sending the form to the defence.

D = Disclose to defence

Those items which satisfy the disclosure test, ie undermines the prosecution case/assists the defence, must be disclosed to the defence on an objective test—a copy will be attached.

I = Defence may inspect

This is as above, but the item cannot be copied and must be inspected usually at the location indicated (the police station).

CND = Clearly not disclosable

In the prosecutor's opinion the unused material neither undermines the prosecution case nor assists the defence case and therefore the defence are not entitled to see it.

The prosecutor will consider the case against each accused separately. Material satisfying the disclosure test is likely to be different in each case and different for each accused. The prosecutor will also bear in mind in reaching any decision: the nature and strength of evidence against the accused; the essential elements of the offence alleged; the evidence on which the prosecutor relies; any explanation put forward by the accused; and what material or information has already been disclosed.

The Disclosure Manual at Chapter 12 gives detailed examples of when the disclosure test may be fulfilled because material potentially weakens the prosecution case, is inconsistent with it, or assists the accused or raises a fundamental question about the prosecution.

It is important that officers submit copies of all items considered to fulfil the disclosure test since the prosecutor's duty is to inspect, view, or listen to any material in this regard prior to making that final decision. If it is not sent to the prosecutor there will be further delay while it is requested. The CPS and the disclosure officer should consult regularly and be in close liaison throughout the disclosure process.

Comment

In the comments section the prosecutor will give brief reasons for the decision where, for example, the disclosability or otherwise of the material may not be apparent from the description or perhaps the prosecutor has decided to disclose material not identified by the disclosure officer on the MG6E and satisfying the disclosure test or for reasons where it is thought it might otherwise be helpful.

Signatures

The form requires the signature and date of the disclosure officer on submission. Each completed form should be individually signed and dated. A signature date from the reviewing lawyer at the date of review taking responsibility for the schedule when it is sent out to the defence is also required.

The prosecutor will send out an accompanying letter with copies of the items to be disclosed on the schedule which meet the disclosure test. A copy of the endorsed schedule will also then be sent to the disclosure officer so that s/he is aware, for example, of any items the defence are entitled to inspect.

KEY ISSUES—MG6C

- Informs the CPS of existence of all non-sensitive unused material relevant to the case
- Provides clear detailed accurate descriptions
- Copies attached of material satisfying disclosure test
- Enables the CPS to make decisions on what to disclose to defence
- Shows results of the CPS review of unused material
- Endorsed form disclosed to defence

MG6C

POLICE SCHEDULE OF NON-SENSITIVE UNUSED MATERIAL

Page No. .... of ....

R v ....

URN

The Disclosure Officer believes that the following material, which does not form part of the prosecution case, is NOT SENSITIVE.

FOR CPS USE:
* Enter: D = Disclose to defence
  I = Defence may inspect
  CND = Clearly not disclosable

Item No.	DESCRIPTION AND RELEVANCE Give sufficient detail for CPS to decide if material should be disclosed or requires more detailed examination. (For further guidance refer to the Prosecution Team Disclosure Manual and Attorney General's Guidelines)	LOCATION State precisely where the item can be found / located	*	COMMENT

Signature:

Name:

Date:

Reviewing lawyer signature:

Print name:

Date:

2006/07 (1)

6.16 **MG6D: Police Schedule of Sensitive Unused Material**

6.16.1 **Essentials**

The purpose of this form is to inform the prosecutor of all sensitive material relevant to the case and the reasons for its sensitivity such that it should be withheld from the defence because it is not in the public interest to disclose it. The prosecutor in turn will then decide whether or not they agree it is sensitive and whether in the circumstances a public interest immunity application (PII) is required before a court.

Confidentiality

This form is totally confidential for the eyes of the police and CPS only. It certainly should not be disclosed to the defence and there are stringent procedures to be followed depending on the nature of the information revealed on the MG6D for the handling and storage of the form. In most cases the MG6D is handed to the CPS in a sealed envelope and will then go in a separate locked cabinet with the Branch Crown Prosecutor and not in the file itself. A protective marking will be applied to the form consistent with the level of sensitivity of its contents.

In exceptional circumstances where the material is so sensitive such that 'compromising the material would lead directly to loss of life or directly threaten national security' (eg investigations into organized crime/terrorist activity) a separate 'highly sensitive' MG6D should be completed and dealt with through direct contact with the CPS prosecutor. Some police forces may wish to apply the same procedures to CHIS material (covert human intelligence source).

Even if there is no sensitive material of any description the officer is still obliged to submit and sign a blank MG6D along with the MG6C and MG6E and endorse it to that effect.

If an MG6C entry has been edited for personal data such as a name, address, or contact number, and the fact that it has been so edited is clear, then it is not necessary to make those details the subject of a separate MG6D entry. However, if a document has been described on an MG6C but there is sensitive material on the document which is something more than just personal details then that sensitive material should be dealt with by an MG6D entry.

In practice the investigating officer or disclosure officer (after speaking to their supervisor) will contact the reviewing lawyer (or his/her supervisor) direct in order to discuss at an early stage face to face, full details of the sensitive material to assist the prosecutor in reaching a decision.

6.16.2 **The form itself**

Description

Again each item of material should be listed separately and numbered consecutively. In relation to sensitive material it is highly likely the prosecutor will want to inspect all sensitive material that might undermine the prosecution case or assist the defence. Arrangements will have to be made for the prosecutor to do so in a way that is appropriate according to the nature of the material.

POINT TO NOTE—DETAILED DESCRIPTIONS

Some items by their very nature will reveal why disclosure should be withheld. Others require more explanation. Careful attention to this element of the schedule will avoid further enquiries and consequent delays. Both the 'description of the item' and the 'reasons for sensitivity' sections must contain sufficient information for the prosecutor to make an informed decision as to whether or not the material itself should be viewed. Schedules containing insufficient information will be returned by the prosecutor.

Disclosure Manual, para 8.6

Reason for sensitivity

The officer must also record the reason for the item's sensitivity again without disclosing the nature of the source or its identity, eg description—informant providing information for search warrant; reason for sensitivity—informant may be in danger if identity revealed/would prejudice administration of justice and others coming forward if identity revealed, ie the officer must identify the pubic interest that would be prejudiced (see further Disclosure Manual, para 8.4).

It is important to note that the sensitivity of the schedule and the sensitivity of the information may differ. It may be possible to describe a highly sensitive piece of information on the schedule without disclosing the information itself (eg a name which makes the material sensitive). The contents of the schedule alone determine the security marking where no material is submitted with it, otherwise, if the material actually accompanies the schedule.

On submission of the form, the officer must sign and date it also.

Decision of prosecutor—for CPS use

A decision endorsed on the form save in the most straightforward cases will generally only be made by a prosecutor after a conference with an officer in the case and his/her supervisor and inspection of the relevant material. Senior officers and senior lawyers should be represented at any conference held (including handler/controllers if there is an informant).

In reaching such a decision the prosecutor will carefully examine all the circumstances of the case, the nature of the sensitive material and why it is considered that real harm will be caused to the public interest by disclosure. They will further consider the consequences once the disclosure test has been passed of revealing the item to the defence, the material itself, the category of material, the fact that an application is being made at all, the significance of the material to the issues in the trial and the involvement of any third parties in bringing the material to the attention of the police. Finally, should the material be made the subject of a court order for disclosure what the police view is regarding the continuance of the prosecution in that event.

The prosecutor will either indicate Yes/No in agreeing whether or not the material is sensitive and then endorse Yes/No in respect of whether or not a court application is appropriate.

The courts have encouraged prosecutors not to make unnecessary PII applications just because there is sensitive material but to come to an informed decision themselves and seek a direction from the court only where they believe the disclosure test has been satisfied **and** material is also sensitive.

POINT TO NOTE

Neutral material or material damaging to the accused need not be disclosed and unless the issue of disclosability is truly borderline, should not be brought to the attention of the court [per House of Lords in *R v H and C*]. This places a heavy onus on the police and prosecutors to be aware of all factors which might affect the legality or admissibility of evidence from sensitive sources or procedures.

Disclosure Manual, para 8.23

The prosecutor will then endorse their own views on the material before signing the form itself.

Applications

Where an application to the court is to follow, the prosecutor, usually in conjunction with prosecution counsel, will decide the type of application to be made. It is important that the police and the CPS are careful to maintain the confidence of the court by making the appropriate form of application.

Such applications will be in writing and the officer may be required to attend court to give evidence in support of the application. A summary of the facts of the case will be required, a list of trial issues which the prosecutor has been able to identify and a summary of the defence case which has been advanced, usually in a defence statement.

A specimen form of background submission is attached at Annex D7 of the Disclosure Manual. The Disclosure Manual at Chapter 13 outlines the detailed requirements for the nature and form of the submission to the judges.

The disclosure officer or rather his/her supervisor will be required to sign the form with the prosecutor but the responsibility for that form and contents rests solely with the latter.

KEY ISSUES—MG6D

- Informs the CPS of existence of all sensitive material relevant to the case
- Outlines reasons for sensitivity
- Comprehensive detailed information required
- Form is totally confidential
- Consultation and conference with the CPS/counsel required
- Enables the CPS to decide whether to make PII application to court

MG6D

POLICE SCHEDULE OF SENSITIVE UNUSED MATERIAL
Not Disclosable

Page No. .... of ....

R v ....

URN

The Disclosure Officer believes that the following material, which does not form part of the prosecution case, is SENSITIVE.

*Tick if copy supplied to CPS

Item No.	Description	Reason for sensitivity	*	Agree sensitive Yes / No	Court application Yes / No	CPS views
				FOR CPS USE		

Signature:

Date:

Name:

Reviewing lawyer signature:

Print name:

Date:

2006/07 (1)

6.17 **MG6E: Disclosure Officer's Report**

6.17.1 **Essentials**

The MG6E must accompany every MG6C and MG6D schedule submitted from the officer. This will include, for example, after service of the defence statement and reconsideration of the material, any subsequent submission of an amended schedule by the officer. Its purpose is essentially threefold:

- The officer must highlight on the form all material that in his/her opinion is capable of passing the 'disclosure test' and why s/he has come to that view. The MG6C itself should not be marked or highlighted in any way since that is provided to the defence.
- It requires the disclosure officer to sign a certification in all cases that s/he has complied with his/her duty of disclosure.
- On the back of the form it reminds the officer to provide the prosecutor with copies of certain items in line with paragraph 7.3 of the Code of Practice.

6.17.2 **The form itself**

The form itself is not disclosable. It is a confidential memo in effect between the police and the prosecution assisting the prosecutor in forming opinions regarding the unused material in the first instance.

The top of the form reminds the officer of the purpose of the form as stated above.

The following items are listed on the schedule(s) for this case and relate to:

- Material which might reasonably be considered capable of undermining the case for the prosecution against the accused, or of assisting the case for the accused
- Material required to be supplied under paragraph 7.3 of the Code . . .

In both situations the officer should indicate in the column marked 'Schedule' which schedule s/he is referring to, ie MG6C or MG6D and enter the item number from the schedule (under 'item no') which corresponds exactly with the number from the schedule.

Reason

The officer must then under this heading explain why s/he has come to the view that the material may undermine the prosecution case and/or assist the defence in providing as much information as possible. This will involve the officer in a proper and full consideration of all the relevant material in order that s/he can reach an informed decision him/herself.

The Code of Practice and Disclosure Manual outline examples of such potential material—basically that may have an adverse effect on the strength of the prosecution case or tends to show a fact inconsistent with it or matters which assist the defence, for example; in cross-examination or in their ability to support a submission that could lead to the exclusion of evidence (see further Attorney General's Guidelines on Disclosure).

Where the relevant item for disclosure is attached, the box on the MG6E should be appropriately ticked. Best practice as previously indicated wherever possible is to submit copies of these items to the prosecutor so that they can make their final decision with all the relevant information before them.

Certification in all cases

The disclosure officer must certify the following and sign and date it to provide an assurance to the prosecutor on behalf of the police investigation team that all relevant material has been considered and revealed to the prosecutor:

> To the best of my knowledge and belief, all material that is or may be relevant has been retained and made available to me. It has been inspected, viewed or listened to and revealed to the prosecutor in accordance with the Criminal Procedure and Investigations Act 1996 as amended, Code of Practice and the Attorney General's Guidelines.

The disclosure officer must provide different certifications in the course of the disclosure process to cover revelation of all relevant retained material: whether the material satisfies the disclosure test, whether the material satisfies the disclosure test as part of a continuing duty.

The signed and dated MG6E must be used again to provide certification to the prosecutor where the defence statement is submitted even if there is no change to the officer's original opinion.

The same section must also be filled in as an option where the disclosure officer believes there is no material fulfilling the disclosure test. In the past officers as a matter of course often submitted a blank MG6E without exercising their mind specifically in relation to the issues herein addressed which was most unsatisfactory:

> *I have reviewed all the relevant material* **OR** *I have considered the defence statement and further reviewed all the relevant material (delete as applicable)* that has been retained and made available to me and there is nothing to the best of my knowledge and belief that might reasonably be considered capable of undermining the prosecution cases against the accused or assisting the case for the accused.

Paragraph 7.3 items (on the back of the MG6E) states:

> At the same time as complying with the duties in paragraphs 7.1 and 7.2, the disclosure officer must give the prosecutor a copy of any material which falls into the following categories (unless such material has already been given to the prosecutor as part of the file containing the material for the prosecution case):

- information provided by an accused person which indicates an explanation for the offence with which he has been charged;
- any material casting doubt on the reliability of a confession;
- any material casting doubt on the reliability of a prosecution witness;
- any other material which the investigator believes may fall within the test for prosecution disclosure in the Act.

Thus, the back of the MG6E reminds the police officer that copies of the above should always be provided to the prosecutor and listed on the MG6E even if the officer does not believe that those items fulfil the particular disclosure test.

KEY ISSUES—MG6E

- Highlights material capable of undermining prosecution case or assisting defence
- Assists the CPS in applying disclosure test
- Form not disclosable to defence
- Reminds disclosure officer to provide the CPS with copies
- Signed certificate demonstrates disclosure officer's compliance with duty of disclosure
- Must accompany every disclosure schedule submitted by disclosure officer

---

DISCLOSURE OFFICER'S REPORT
Not Disclosable

Page No. .... of ....

URN

R v ....

The following items are listed on the schedule(s) for this case and relate to:
- Material which might reasonably be considered capable of undermining the case for the prosecution against the accused, or of assisting the case for the accused
- Material required to be supplied under paragraph 7.3 of the Code (see overleaf)

*Enter C or D to denote schedule **MG6C** or **6D** and enter item no. from schedule*

* Schedule	Item no.	Reason	Tick if attached

Certification in all cases:
To the best of my knowledge and belief, all material that is or may be relevant has been retained and made available to me. It has been inspected, viewed or listened to and revealed to the prosecutor in accordance with the Criminal Procedure and Investigations Act 1996 as amended, Code of Practice and the Attorney General's Guidelines.

Signature of Disclosure Officer: .... Name: .... Date: ....

I have reviewed all of the relevant material, **OR** *I have considered the defence statement and further reviewed all the relevant material (delete as applicable)* that has been retained and made available to me and there is nothing to the best of my knowledge and belief that might reasonably be considered capable of undermining the prosecution case against the accused or assisting the case for the accused.

Signature of Disclosure Officer:......................... Name: .... Date: ....

CRIMINAL PROCEDURE AND INVESTIGATIONS ACT 1996 (S.23(1))
CODE OF PRACTICE

Revelation of material to the prosecutor

Paragraph 7.3 states:

'At the same time as complying with the duties in paragraphs 7.1 and 7.2, the disclosure officer must give the prosecutor a copy of any material which falls into the following categories (unless such material has already been given to the prosecutor as part of the file containing the material for the prosecution case):

- information provided by an accused person which indicates an explanation for the offence with which he has been charged;

- any material casting doubt on the reliability of a confession;

- any material casting doubt on the reliability of a prosecution witness;

- any other material which the investigator believes may fall within the test for prosecution disclosure in the Act.'

6.18 **MG7: Remand Application Adult/Youth**

6.18.1 **Essentials**

This form should provide the prosecutor at the charging centre (making the decision whether to object to bail) and subsequently the prosecutor in court with enough information first to decide that objections to bail are appropriate and secondly to enable the prosecutor at court to put forward those objections to the court with sufficient information to back up any points made.

At the charging centre a properly completed MG7 may 'persuade' the prosecutor to apply 'the threshold test' where all the evidence is not available and authorize charge and put the defendant before the court. In a busy remand court, the prosecutor is heavily reliant on this form containing all relevant information.

Therefore it is extremely important that the instructions on the completion of this form are carried out to the letter and that all comments by the officer and points raised are fully backed up with supporting evidence. Hearsay is admissible but wild unsupported allegations about the defendant are not.

This form is confidential between the prosecutor and the police although the Probation Service may receive a copy of it where a bail hostel place (in bail information schemes) is being considered for the defendant to assist them in assessing his/her suitability.

6.18.2 **The form itself**

Preliminaries

As with the other forms, the URN should be at the top followed by the defendant's name.

The relevant box should be ticked if s/he is either a PPO or PYO which immediately alerts the prosecutor to detailed consideration of his/her previous convictions.

If the defendant is a youth his/her date of birth should be given together with information as to whether or not the Youth Offender Team (YOT) has been consulted. In fact they should be consulted in every case and prosecution policy would be to speak to them in advance of any objections to bail to find out their views or proposals for the youth.

The officer must then point out whether there is a vulnerable or intimidated victim. If there is, an early VPS is helpful to the prosecutor to put before the court in support of the application (the relevant box should have been ticked at number 1 of the MG6).

The time and date of arrest for breach of bail where this is applicable should also be inserted here (in which case there should also be an accompanying MG8).

If the defendant has been arrested on warrant, that information should be detailed here, ie 'arrested on warrant' and a statement attached outlining the circumstances of arrest providing as much detail as possible and including the number of attempts made, for example to execute a fail to attend warrant and the result of each attempt.

The recommendation is for a remand

The next three tick-boxes indicate, if ticked, that a remand **in custody** is sought (ie objections to bail) or a remand to **police custody** (ie to the cells) is sought under section 128(7) of the Magistrates' Courts Act 1980—24 hours maximum for a youth but three days for an adult offender. This is commonly called a 'three day lie down'. In this instance the prosecutor will need to speak to the police officer directly since it is an unusual course of action and the request must be related to ongoing investigations into offences other than the one for which the defendants stands charged. The defendant must then be brought back before the magistrates as soon as enquiries have ceased.

This may be used, for example, to clear up offences to be taken into consideration. It must not be because the police officer wants time to hold an identification parade on the charged offence or for any other reason of convenience. This is probably one of the only occasions when a prosecutor may actually call the police officer into the box to provide the court with further information as to the reason for the remand request.

The third tick box, **Local Authority Accommodation/Secure Accommodation**, relates solely to the YO. Custody is always to be considered as a final option as far as youths are concerned, especially when they are very young. The court may remand a YO to local authority accommodation when bail is refused. Conditions can be imposed in relation to this remand on behalf of the local authority and the local authority must always be consulted first.

It is to be noted that 17-year-old youths are treated as adults in respect of all remand provisions, albeit they appear in the youth court. They, therefore, do not go to local authority accommodation.

The court has the power, after consultation with the local authority, to impose a security requirement, ie a remand to secure accommodation. This applies to boys aged 12–16 and girls aged 15–16. In practice there is usually little secure accommodation for girls available. Certain conditions must apply in order for the court to be able to impose such a requirement. These are in fact laid out in the tick boxes 6–8 on the MG7 (to be discussed shortly). Suffice to say that the prosecutor will only apply for such a secure order where all other options have been considered and it has been decided that they are inadequate to protect the public from serious harm or to prevent commission of further offences.

Boys aged 15–16 are in fact usually kept in prison or a remand centre rather than secure local authority accommodation, unless the court believes that due to their physical and emotional immaturity or propensity to harm themselves it would be undesirable for such a remand. It is noteworthy that no girl under the age of 17 may be remanded to a prison.

In relation to this application the CPS is a party to the proceedings and will generally have liaised with the local authority and will be making the application. This is to be distinguished from the situation where the local authority can itself apply for a secure accommodation order in certain circumstances.

Reason(s) for opposing bail

The first four 'reasons' are laid down in the Bail Act 1976 and the prosecutor at court must demonstrate to the court that in the words of the Bail Act there are 'substantial grounds' to believe that the defendant, if granted bail, would (1) fail to surrender, (2) commit further offences whilst on bail, (3) interfere with witnesses or obstruct the course of justice, or (4) for the defendant's own protection.

POINT TO NOTE

The Criminal Justice and Immigration Act 2008 (s 52, Sch 12) amends the Bail Act 1976 to restrict the grounds on which a person charged with an imprisonable summary offence (including low value criminal damage) may be refused bail.

The restrictive grounds for refusing bail which previously applied only to non-imprisonable offences now apply to imprisonable summary only offences. However the Act adds three new grounds on which bail may be withheld from someone charged with an imprisonable summary only offence:

1. The defendant if released on bail will commit an offence resulting in physical or mental injury to any person, or that it will put any person in fear of such injury
2. The court does not have sufficient information to make the remand decision
3. If the exceptions to drug users in certain areas apply

Bail decisions taken by police under PACE are not affected by this but any information that the police can provide, particularly in respect of the first ground, wil assist the prosecutor, for example in common assault domestic violence cases.

Youths only

Tick boxes (5)–(8) apply in relation to **youths** only in addition to the above. This is primarily because of detailed legislation relating to YOs as laid down in the Children and Young Persons Act 1969 (CYPA 1969) (as amended).

Tick box (5) states that the welfare of a youth offender is always a prime consideration and it is possible therefore to remand a defendant for his/her own welfare into local authority accommodation (under the Bail Act 1976).

Tick boxes (6)—(8) however relate solely to the conditions which must be met under section 23(5) of the CYPA 1969 (as amended) in order for a secure accommodation order to be applied for by the CPS and so that the court can impose a security requirement on the offender.

Tick box (6) states that the defendant must have been charged with or previously been convicted of a violent or sexual offence or an offence punishable in the case of an adult with 14 years' imprisonment or more.

An additional alternative requirement to (6) within the legislation but not on the form is as follows: being convicted of one or more imprisonable offences which taken together with any other imprisonable offence of which he/she has been convicted amounts to 'a recent history of repeatedly committing imprisonable offences whilst on bail/remand in local authority accommodation'. Obviously any information with regard to that condition could also be put forward where it is detailed to the prosecutor.

In addition to (6) above tick box (7) relates to the condition that any security requirement can only be imposed where either the court is of the opinion that only secure accommodation is adequate 'to protect the public from serious harm' from the youth or tick box (8) that only secure accommodation would prevent the commission by him/her of imprisonable offences.

As previously explained where these conditions are met a remand to local authority accommodation with a security requirement can be given by the court in respect of girls between 15 and 16 and boys aged between 12 and 16 years.

It must be stressed that both the police officer and the prosecutor should have liaised in advance with YOT in relation to a youth offender as to the most suitable course of action for him/her. This will be dependent on the age and gender of the youth and the nature of the offence and his/her previous record as well as the availability of secure accommodation so the court's options may be limited.

Substantiation of the grounds

The officer must here supply sufficient details to the prosecutor in relation to the boxes which s/he has ticked to provide supporting evidence to the court to back up all the reasons put forward. Unfortunately, it is this hurdle at which the officer often falls down, providing insufficient information and often requiring the case to be put back while the police liaison officer at court tries to contact the OIC or the court may well refuse a request for an adjournment and then the defendant is bailed because of the prosecutor's inability to substantiate claims s/he has made.

In the 'old days' the officer him/herself used to say to the prosecutor 'just put me in the box and I will tell the court'. Those days are long gone. The officer must have all available information on the MG7 or attach documentation (or on the MG6 if confidential). Experience teaches that an officer 'put into the box' can then be subject to detailed cross-examination by the defence brief which can prove highly unsatisfactory. It is much better that the prosecutor with full knowledge of the Bail Act 1976 can put forward relevant objections in an appropriate manner in line with the legislation.

The most common grounds for opposing bail relate to: (i) failing to surrender and (ii) committing offences on bail. The types of behaviour/circumstances which may amount to these reasons are as follows, albeit this is not an exhaustive list.

Fail to surrender to custody

- Convictions for absconding/failure to attend in the past
- Of no fixed abode (Why? Since when? Has the defendant put forward an unsuitable address and, if so, why?)
- Lack of community ties/associations (explain: Is s/he a foreigner? Unemployed? No family, etc)
- Access to travel documents (nature of offence—forged documents; nature of job, eg travelling abroad)
- Defendant's behaviour related to the offence (eg s/he tried to resist arrest or ran off)
- Nature of the offence itself (serious and therefore likely to attract custodial sentence; strength of evidence against defendant)

Commit offences on bail

- Defendant's previous convictions (highlight the relevance to the prosecutor, eg demonstrating persistent continuing offending, similar modus operandi, offences committed on bail—in which case details of offence, dates and conditions; defendant in breach of sentence/licence—again details)
- Lifestyle (eg drug addict, alcoholic, unemployed, ie needing to commit crime to support habit, self, family or out of control)
- Attitude of defendant to previous court orders (eg breach of probation/bail; comments of OIC).

Tick boxes (3), interfering with witnesses or otherwise obstructing the course of justice, and (4), for the defendant's own protection, are more difficult to substantiate and less readily employed by the prosecutor in court.

Interfere with witnesses or otherwise obstruct the course of justice

- Nature of offence (eg domestic violence/sexual offence)
- Intimidated victims (has the box been ticked on the MG6 at 1 and provision of a VPS with victim's concerns to show the court?)
- Previous for witness intimidation (or threats made to witnesses in existing case)
- Potential for interference in recovery of property, arrest of accomplice, interference with ongoing investigations (explain how and why)

For the defendant's own protection

- Nature of offence (eg rape of child) such that community seeks revenge (provide full details)
- Circumstances relevant to the offender (eg medical history, suicide attempts suggesting self-harm)

Finally the police officer should give additional information not already provided in relation to the estimated date by which the full file will be submitted so the court will be aware how long it is likely that the defendant will be remanded in custody if bail is refused.

Suggested conditions

Even where the officer only wants a remand in custody it is useful if the officer here suggests potential appropriate conditions in the event of bail being granted. Any conditions put forward must be necessary to prevent the defendant from doing any of the grounds of the Bail Act 1976 as listed.

It may be useful, for example, to remind the prosecutor to ask for a doorstep condition. This means that the defendant must present himself to a police officer at the door of his residential premises if required to do so during the hours of curfew where a condition of residence/curfew has been imposed. Alternatively the police officer might provide further information about the victim or the family (eg school address of children) to obtain a condition not to go near them. Similarly, information on any sureties put forward by the defendant and the officer's views thereon would be useful too. It is to be noted that the condition of 'signing on' at the police station, often favoured by magistrates in fact causes difficulties for busy police officers dealing with members of the public. Alternative conditions already mentioned such as 'doorstep curfews' appear to be more effective.

Details of co-defendant(s)

Information about co-defendants (potential or actual) with details of their court hearing dates is useful so that in their application the prosecutor can attempt to tie up parties so that they can all be dealt with together.

Signature

The officer must sign and date the form as must the supervisor (who could also record any further comments where necessary and sign and date it).

KEY ISSUES—MG7

- Important form where police wish to remand defendant in custody
- CPS decision whether to object to bail in court
- Grounds for opposing bail to be substantial with supporting evidence
- Suggests conditions of bail if bail granted
- All information must be on the form for the CPS

REMAND APPLICATION ADULT / YOUTH Page No. .... of ....

(This form may be copied to the Probation Service)   URN

Defendant surname: .... Forename(s): .... PPO ☐ PYO ☐

D.O.B. *(Youths only)* .... YOT consulted *(Youths only)* Y / N   Vulnerable / intimidated victim Y / N

Time / date of arrest for breach of bail *(if applicable)*: ....

The recommendation is for a remand (tick ✓ one box only):

In custody ☐   Police custody ☐   Local Authority Accommodation / Secure Accommodation ☐

Reason(s) for opposing bail

1. Fail to surrender to custody   ☐   6. Charged with or convicted of a violent / sexual   ☐
2. Commit offences on bail   ☐   offence equivalent to 14 plus years imprisonment in
3. Interfere with witnesses or otherwise   ☐   the case of an adult *(Youth only)*
   obstruct the course of justice   7. The only way to protect the public from serious   ☐
4. For the defendant's own protection   ☐   harm *(Youth only)*
5. For the defendant's own welfare   ☐   8. To prevent the commission of imprisonable offences ☐
   (Youth only)   *(Youth only)*

Give full details to substantiate each ground for opposing bail or seeking a remand in custody.
Provide an estimated date by when a full file will be submitted.

....

....

....

....

.... *Continue on separate sheet*

If bail is granted despite the recommendations for a remand in custody, suggest here any conditions of bail
considered appropriate with reasons (include sureties).

....

....

....

....

.... *Continue on separate sheet*

Give details of co-defendant(s) – name(s), court(s) and hearing date(s) – in this or other outstanding cases.

....

....

Officer in case: .... Rank / Job title: .... No: .... Date: ....

Supervisor's name: .... Rank / Job title: .... No: .... Date: ....

6.19 **MG8: Breach of Bail Conditions**

6.19.1 **Essentials**

It is vitally important that the court is provided with full information about the circumstances in which someone has been brought there. As has been seen the officers are to be encouraged to include any attempt made to execute a fail to attend warrant on the MG7 by attaching an additional statement. The MG8 if utilized and completed correctly by the officer provides sufficient information for the prosecutor where there has been a breach of bail to put all the relevant details before the court enabling them to determine the truth of the allegations and make a correct decision on the bail/custody dilemma before them.

Unfortunately, in some areas this form is little used resulting in defendants brought before the court being unnecessarily and often wrongly re-bailed because of the paucity of information in the prosecutor's hands.

The MG8 has been designed to provide all necessary information to the prosecutor: the original charges, conditions imposed, and evidence of how those conditions are alleged to have been breached. Their submission and completion allows the prosecutor to do their job and in most cases remand the defendant in custody.

6.19.2 **The form itself**

Appearance within 24 hours of arrest

The defendant must appear in court within 24 hours of arrest. This at the top of the form and immediately reminds both police officers and prosecutors alike of the time limits placed on bringing a defendant before the court within 24 hours of his/her arrest by the Bail Act 1976, section 7(4). If this is forgotten by either the police or the prosecutor the defendant will simply walk free since any further detention or attempt to deal with him/her for the breach is unlawful.

Preliminaries

The defendant may have been conditionally bailed by the police post-charge or s/he will have already been before the court and granted conditional bail by them.

The fax number of the originating criminal justice unit (CJU) needs to be provided since the form at the conclusion of the breach hearing is to be faxed to the police at the originating CJU for their information.

A person is brought before the court where s/he is arrested for breach bail. This can therefore be a different Borough or Court from that from which s/he was originally bailed. It is important therefore that records are updated at the place or origin for his/her next appearance in court.

The URN here will depend on whether the defendant has merely breached his/her bail in respect of the original offence or has at the same time committed a further new offence for which s/he has now also been arrested. In the former case the original URN should be completed in the box. In the latter case a new URN (for the new offence) would be raised. Then the original URN would be inserted into the lower box marked 'original URN' (if different from above).

Details of the defendant—name, address, date of birth—need to be inserted. Ticking the relevant box if s/he is a PPO/PYO/YO to alert the prosecutor to his/her status and previous convictions and manner of dealing with him/her is essential.

The police station or court from which s/he was bailed and the date of the next due appearance must also be inserted on the form.

Time and date of arrest for breach of bail

It is absolutely vital that this is accurate and that everyone is aware of the time by which the defendant must be brought before the court, ie within 24 hours of arrest. The court must then deal with the defendant there and then and must not adjourn the case.

Where the defendant is brought before a different court from that from which s/he was originally bailed it is important that information is given to the prosecutor as to where exactly s/he was bailed from and his/her next court appearance date. When s/he has been dealt with for the breach of bail then the court will then remand him/her to that originating court for his/her next appearance date.

Details of original charges and circumstances of the offence leading to the conditional bail

The officer must complete this section, and/or tick the box and attach an MG4/MG5/MG7 (or even the original file) if available. As much relevant information should be submitted to the prosecutor as possible. Where the police do not submit an MG8 details of the original offence and charges are often left out of the file leading to problems for the prosecutor at court.

Current conditions of bail should be listed in full (not just the one(s) breached) and an MG4A attached if available.

Full details of the alleged breach are required. Officers should attach a statement or evidence and arrest book (EAB) and any other supporting evidence clearly highlighting the circumstances of arrest and specifically including any other attempts made to arrest the defendant for breach of bail. The officer in the case must sign and date the form.

This is particularly important where the defendant denies the breach and a 'mini-trial' takes place there and then. The prosecutor is allowed to read as evidence the statement of the officer or details provided. Where the defendant has decided to bring live witnesses to court to support his/her case it is obviously essential that the detail is there for the prosecutor to rebut the defence of the accused in cross-examination or provide the court with additional information regarding the defendant's behaviour in relation to previously granted bail.

The officer in the case must sign and date the form.

Result of breach hearing

It is again important that the result is notified immediately to the originating CPS/CJU—by fax if necessary—so that the PNC can be updated. The prosecutor should also sign the form and date prior to sending.

Furthermore the prosecutor is obliged to notify the OIC immediately if bail is granted under the Victim Code where there is a vulnerable or intimidated witness involved so that the officer can notify that witness on the day.

KEY ISSUES—MG8

- Provides all necessary information to the CPS as a breach of bail
- Acts as aide memoire to officers of what is required
- Inclusion of details of original charges, current bail conditions, details of alleged breach
- Enables the CPS, if correctly completed, to prosecute a breach
- Allows notification of result of hearing to be sent asap

MG8

BREACH OF BAIL CONDITIONS

(The defendant MUST appear in court within 24 hours of arrest)

POLICE POST-CHARGE CONDITIONAL BAIL ☐   **COURT CONDITIONAL BAIL** ☐

Insert fax number of originating CJU

URN

Defendant surname: .... Forenames: ....

Date of birth: .... PPO ☐   PYO ☐   YO ☐

Address (if not shown elsewhere): ....

....

Court / Police Station: .... Date of Appearance: ....

Time and date of arrest for breach of bail: ....

Original URN (if different from above)

Bailed from: .... Court / Police Station on: .... (date)

To appear at: .... Court on:.. (date)

Give the details of the original charge(s) / offence(s) and the circumstances of the offence(s) that led to
Conditional Bail or where available include copies of **MG4, MG5** and **MG7** / the original file – *(tick if attached)* ☐

....

....

....

....

List current conditions (in full – or where available) include copy of **MG4A** / the original file – *(tick if attached)* ☐

....

Give details of the alleged breach(es): ....

....

....

....

....

....

....

Officer in case: .... Date: ....

Result of breach hearing:

....

....

....

Signature of prosecutor: .... Date: ....

(This form must be faxed back to the originating CJU at the conclusion of the breach hearing)

2006/07 (1)

6.20 **MG9: Witness List**

6.20.1 **Essentials**

This form tells the prosecutor, the WCU and the Witness Service who are the witnesses in the case, their details, whether or not a statement has been provided, whether they are vulnerable/intimidated and whether or not they have previous convictions. This form is to be submitted when a full file is sent to the CPS so in this instance most statements should be attached to the file.

It is helpful if the witness list is in the same sequence as the MG11s (Statements) submitted and that they basically tell a story, viz victim/main witness; other civilian witnesses; police officers in order of witnessing arrest, ie arresting, interviewing, exhibiting; OIC; expert witnesses, (technical/forensic).

6.20.2 **The form itself**

Preliminaries

The form contains names and addresses of witnesses as well as information about previous convictions. The Witness Service is entitled to a copy of this form but a witness has to authorize release of their details, consent being recorded on the back of the MG11. The column on the right-hand side marked '♣' provides information containing their previous convictions and should be edited off the document where relevant.

The date of the completion of the witness list needs to be completed so that a prosecutor can see if the list is up to date and when the PNC checks were made. A revised witness list should in fact be prepared (with statements and accompanying MG20) if additional statements are to be submitted.

Again the URN must be completed.

Columns for completion

Witness No.: obviously the witness numbers will be in chronological order but here, if the witness is vulnerable or intimidated a 'V' has to be inserted into this column to alert the prosecutor, the WCU and Witness Service of this fact (in which case an MG2 should have been completed).

Statement No.: this speaks for itself but where there is more than one statement from a witness the number of statements should be indicated.

*: this column must be ticked if the statement is attached.

♣: this column is ticked to indicate whether or not the witness has any previous convictions. If it is ticked a copy of their Phoenix print out should be attached to the file and as previously stated this information should not go out to any third party without prior authorization from the CPS but may be highly relevant in relation to the disclosure of unused material.

Witness details

The witness details comprise their name, address, occupation, date of birth and means of communication with them, ie phone, mobile, pager, email where appropriate.

KEY ISSUES—MG9

- Informs the CPS , WCUs and Witness Service of witnesses in case
- Informs the prosecutor of statement numbers and whether or not attached
- Indicates vulnerable/intimidated witnesses
- Provides witness details including previous convictions

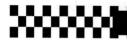

The whole column marked ♣ must be expunged before passing to a third party.

WITNESS LIST

Page No. .... of ....

Date of completion: ....

URN | | | | |

R v ....

★ Tick if statement attached

♣ Previous convictions? Enter Y or N

Wit. No.	Witness Details (In the 'Wit.No' column enter 'V' if the witness is a victim, 'Vu' if vulnerable or intimidated)	Statement Number	★	♣
	Name:			
	Address:			
	.... Post Code:			
	Occupation: .... Date of Birth:			
	Telephone No. (Home): .... (Work):			
	Mobile / pager no: .... E-mail address:			
	Name:			
	Address:			
	.... Post Code:			
	Occupation: .... Date of Birth:			
	Telephone No. (Home): .... (Work):			
	Mobile / pager no: .... E-mail address:			
	Name:			
	Address:			
	.... Post Code:			
	Occupation: .... Date of Birth:			
	Telephone No. (Home): .... (Work):			
	Mobile / pager no: .... E-mail address:			
	Name:			
	Address:			
	.... Post Code:			
	Occupation: .... Date of Birth:			
	Telephone No. (Home): .... (Work):			
	Mobile / pager no: .... E-mail address:			

6.21 **MG10: Witness Non-availability**

6.21.1 **Essentials**

This is a very important form because it provides the prosecutor at court with the ability to set trial dates in the knowledge that witnesses will be available. It is therefore vital that it is accurately and fully completed. With the emphasis within the CJS of the setting of trial dates at the first hearing it is important that it is submitted with all files as best practice especially where the streamlined process is in operation (see Chapter 9). It further provides reasons for police non-availability where the court requires an explanation.

It is essential that this form is kept up to date and is re-submitted where there has been an adjournment or witness availability has changed and the MG10 was completed some time previously.

This form is a restricted document and is retained by the prosecution and not disclosed to third parties since it would basically provide evidence of when some-one was not at home. Hence civilians do not have to have the reason for their absence explained on the form albeit the court often requests it.

6.21.2 **The form itself**

Preliminaries

The form requires the name of the defendant and the court to be submitted as well as the names of witnesses and their witness number. This number then readily identifies them for ease of reference in the columns below for completion.

Non-availability dates

The relevant columns and boxes must be marked with a cross where any witness is **not** available. For police officers only there are codes which are marked in place of an X to identify the reason for their non-availability:

R = Rest day
L = Leave
C = Course
N = Night Duty
S = Sickness
O = Other

Details should be provided at the bottom of this form where the Code C, S, or O has been ticked since the court will enquire further, especially where they are having difficulty fixing a court date. In practice the court is more likely to ignore rest days and night duty and courses in spite of prosecution objections if an early trial date needs to be fixed. For avoidance of doubt it is helpful if witnesses with 'no dates to avoid' or, for example, experts wanting to be called am or pm are indicated accordingly. However, the prosecutor will put as much information as they have about unavailability before the court.

The 'month' should be written at the head of each of the columns together with each individual witness number underneath and then the relevant days of the month marked with an X or a code as indicated where the witness is **not** available.

Signature

The person completing the MG10 should sign and date it. The information as to availability will have to be taken from the officers' EABs and the back of the MG11 witness statements.

KEY ISSUES—MG10

- Provides the CPS with detailed picture of witness availability
- Explains reasons for non-availability
- Must be kept updated
- Enables the CPS to set trial dates in court
- Assists case management

MG10

WITNESS NON-AVAILABILITY

Page No. .... of ....

URN				
Crown Court No.				

R v .... at: .... Magistrates / Youth / Crown Court

Witness (names)*　(　) .... (　) ....

*Insert no.　(　) .... (　) ....

　(　) .... (　) ....

Mark dates when police and other witnesses are NOT available. Codes for police non-availability:
R = Rest day　L = Leave　C = Course　N = Night duty　S = Sickness　O = Other

Date	Month *Witness No	Date	Month *Witness No	Date	Month *Witness No	Date	Month *Witness No	Date	Month *Witness No	Date	Month *Witness No
1		1		1		1		1		1	
2		2		2		2		2		2	
3		3		3		3		3		3	
4		4		4		4		4		4	
5		5		5		5		5		5	
6		6		6		6		6		6	
7		7		7		7		7		7	
8		8		8		8		8		8	
9		9		9		9		9		9	
10		10		10		10		10		10	
11		11		11		11		11		11	
12		12		12		12		12		12	
13		13		13		13		13		13	
14		14		14		14		14		14	
15		15		15		15		15		15	
16		16		16		16		16		16	
17		17		17		17		17		17	
18		18		18		18		18		18	
19		19		19		19		19		19	
20		20		20		20		20		20	
21		21		21		21		21		21	
22		22		22		22		22		22	
23		23		23		23		23		23	
24		24		24		24		24		24	
25		25		25		25		25		25	
26		26		26		26		26		26	
27		27		27		27		27		27	
28		28		28		28		28		28	
29		29		29		29		29		29	
30		30		30		30		30		30	
31		31		31		31		31		31	

'O', 'C' and 'S' codes – give full details:

_____

Name of person submitting form and date

2006/07 (1)

6.22 **MG11: Witness Statement**

6.22.1 **Essentials**

The MG11 is double-sided, the front of the form records the written evidence of the witness whilst the back of the form has a number of sections for completion relating to personal details about the witness themselves, the additional care, if any, they require and their consent to those details being revealed to a third party.

6.22.2 **The form itself**

Preliminaries

The front of the form (and continuation sheet) contains, at the top, the legislation and criminal procedure rules by which such a statement may be admitted as evidence. Only a statement in this format complies with the requisite evidential and procedural rules and can be 'served section 9' and can be accepted by the defence in certain circumstances. (CJ Act 1967, s 9; MC Act 1980, ss 5A(3)(a) and 5B; Criminal Procedure Rules 2005, Rule 27.1). This includes an EAB where the section 9 declaration is signed.

The URN of the case, the name of the witness, age if under 18 or 'over 18', and their occupation must be inserted at the top.

Declaration

The top of each MG11 statement contains a formal declaration which the witness must sign and date. This specifically states:

> This statement (consisting of .... page(s) each signed by me) is true to the best of my knowledge and belief and I make it knowing that, if it is tendered in evidence, I shall be liable to prosecution if I have wilfully stated in it, anything which I know to be false, or do not believe to be true.

The witness has declared that they are telling the truth and if not they know they can be prosecuted for it.

Visual recording

A vulnerable and intimidated witness may have their evidence in the first instance visually recorded in which case the box should be ticked, but the officer may also compile an MG11 from the video recording and ensure the witness agrees with it and signs it. If the witness statement is not going to be used as evidence because the video is to be played in court, the unused statement should be listed on the MG6C disclosure schedule.

Then comes the body of the statement which may obviously continue on more than one page. Tips on the taking of a witness statement are provided in Chapter 4. The witness must sign and date every page of their witness statement.

The back page of the MG11

This needs to be filled out in every case even where, for whatever reason, the officer after an ABE has done a witness statement.

Witness contact details

The name, address, date of birth, gender, any former name and ethnicity code (16+1) and religion/belief of the witness should be inserted here. Additionally, means of contact (phone/mobile/email) and preferred method of contact and best time of contact should be provided. This information is not just for convenience of contacting the witness but will also indicate how they wish to be treated, eg because of religion/belief.

Dates of witness non-availability

These must be completed for this information to be transferred on to the MG10. Where there are no dates to avoid it should be recorded here. This section must be completed otherwise a trial date could be set when a crucial witness was unavailable.

Witness care

This section is crucial to allow the prosecution team to comply with obligations under the Victim Code and ensure that the witness is fully informed and supported throughout their experience within the criminal justice process. There are four questions asked:

a) **Is the witness willing and likely to attend court?:** if not then reasons should be given in detail and also recorded on the MG6, 'confidential information form' for the prosecutor to consider whether a witness summons may be appropriate together with officer's views.

b) **What can be done to ensure attendance?:** this could relate to special measures in court, eg screens or TV link or could be something as simple as money to attend court or someone to look after a child.

c) **Does the witness require a Special Measures Assessment as a vulnerable or intimidated witness?:** if yes an MG2 should be submitted. However, this is a reminder to the officer from the outset of his/her obligations to vulnerable/intimidated witnesses and is helpful to the prosecutor.

d) **Does the witness have any particular needs? If 'Yes' what are they?:** this could relate to any witness and any type of additional needs, eg a hearing or eye impairment or other physical disability (eg wheelchair access), child care problems or language difficulties requiring an interpreter or intermediary.

Witness consent

This is for the witness to complete and sign (and appropriate adult where necessary with contact details):

a) The Victim Personal Statement scheme (victims only) has been explained to me

b) I have been given the Victim Personal Statement leaflet

Any individual victim or small business proprietor/partner can make a VPS (or relative/partners of homicide incidents; carers of children or adults with learning difficulties). This has already been explained in relation to tick box 1 on the MG6. It is entirely up to the victim whether or not they make one and if they don't make one initially they can always make one at a later stage prior to sentence of the defendant.

Such an additional statement is also taken on an MG11 and can be clearly indicated as such as the end of the original witness statement if taken at that time or on a subsequent MG11 where made later.

The purpose of the statement is to provide further information which can be put before the court about the effect of the crime on the victim or, for example, the effect of the defendant being granted bail and details of their vulnerability etc.

    c) I have been given the leaflet 'Giving a witness statement to the police—what happens next?'

Every witness should be given this automatically and this again acts as a reminder to the police officer to fulfil his obligations.

    d) I consent to police having access to my medical record(s) in relation to this matter.

This is a very important box and must be ticked as 'yes' where there is relevant medical evidence available or it is the type of case where it is likely (eg a sexual offence) that access to the medical records of the witness will be required. The access at this stage will be for the prosecution team's eyes only. Where consent is not given it may be extremely difficult to proceed with a particular case.

    e) I consent to my medical record in relation to this matter being disclosed to the defence.

This section, if marked 'yes', allows the defence to have access to the witness's medical records where relevant and authorized by the CPS without the prosecution having to make further application to the court in this regard.

    f) I consent to the statement being disclosed for the purposes of civil proceedings if applicable, eg child care proceedings, CICA.

This may be necessary where there are child care proceedings or Criminal Injuries Compensation and the ticking of this box will mean that the prosecutor does not have to apply to the court for permission to do the same where appropriate.

    g) The information recorded above will be disclosed to the Witness Service so that they can offer help and support, unless you ask them not to.

The Witness Service now has access, in order for them to do their job, to witness details and information. If the witness does not wish them to assist this box must be ticked, otherwise they will be provided automatically with such details (subject to the exception previously mentioned in relation to previous convictions) in order that they can provide the witness with help and support.

Now that all areas have WCUs (see 4.5.1) they will be the first point of contact for the witness prior to referral to the Witness Service.

The person taking the statement must sign and date the MG11 indicating the time and place where it was taken.

MG11T

This is a continuation sheet for the witness statement to be completed after the first page of the MG11 has been written. The latter will contain the back page and all witness details.

KEY ISSUES—MG11

- Records written evidence of a witness
- Contains formal legal declaration
- Signature on every page
- Identifies needs of vulnerable/intimidated witnesses
- Informs the CPS about VPS
- Provides consent to disclosure of medical records
- Allows the Witness Service to contact witness

WITNESS STATEMENT

CJ Act 1967, s.9; MC Act 1980, ss.5A(3) (a) and 5B; Criminal Procedure Rules 2005, Rule 27.1

URN

Statement of: ....

Age if under 18: ....*(if over 18 insert 'over 18')*   Occupation: ....

This statement (consisting of   page(s) each signed by me) is true to the best of my knowledge and belief and I make it knowing that, if it is tendered in evidence, I shall be liable to prosecution if I have wilfully stated in it, anything which I know to be false, or do not believe to be true.

Signature: ....Date: ....

Tick if witness evidence is visually recorded ☐   *(supply witness details on rear)*

....

....

....

....

....

....

....

....

....

....

....

....

....

....

....

....

....

....

Signature: .... Signature witnessed by: ....

2006/07 (1)

Witness contact details

Home address: .... Postcode: ....

Home telephone No: .... Work telephone No: ....

Mobile / Pager No: .... E-mail address: ....

Preferred means of contact *(specify details)*: ....

Best time of contact *(specify details)*: ....

Male / Female   Date and place of birth: ....

Former name: .... Ethnicity Code (16 + 1): .... Religion / Belief (*Specify*....................)

DATES OF WITNESS NON-AVAILABILITY: ....

....

Witness care

a) Is the witness willing and likely to attend court? Yes ☐ No ☐ If 'No', include reason(s) on form **MG6**.

b) What can be done to ensure attendance? ....

c) Does the witness require a Special Measures Assessment as a vulnerable or intimidated witness?
   Yes ☐ No ☐ If 'Yes' submit **MG2** with file.

d) Does the witness have any particular needs? Yes ☐ No ☐ If 'Yes' what are they? *(Disability, healthcare,
   childcare, transport, language difficulties, visually impaired, restricted mobility or other concerns?)*

   ....

Witness Consent (for witness completion)

a) The Victim Personal Statement scheme (victims only) has been
   explained to me: Yes ☐ No ☐

b) I have been given the Victim Personal Statement leaflet   Yes ☐ No ☐

c) I have been given the leaflet "Giving a witness statement to the police –
   what happens next?"   Yes ☐ No ☐

d) I consent to police having access to my medical record(s) in relation
   to this matter *(obtained in accordance with local practice)*   Yes ☐ No ☐ N / A ☐

e) I consent to my medical record in relation to this matter being disclosed
   to the defence: Yes ☐ No ☐ N / A ☐

f) I consent to the statement being disclosed for the purposes of civil
   proceedings if applicable, e.g. child care proceedings, CICA   Yes ☐ No ☐

g) The information recorded above will be disclosed to the Witness
   Service so that they can offer help and support, unless you
   ask them not to. Tick this box to decline their services: ☐

Signature of witness: .... PRINT NAME: ....

Signature of parent / guardian / appropriate adult: .... PRINT NAME: ....

Address and telephone number if different from above: ....

....

Statement taken by *(print name)*: .... Station: ....

Time and place statement taken: ....

WITNESS STATEMENT

CJ Act 1967, s.9; MC Act 1980, ss.5A(3) (a) and 5B; Criminal Procedure Rules 2005, Rule 27.1

URN

Statement of: ....

Age if under 18: ....*(if over 18 insert 'over 18')*   Occupation: ....

This statement (consisting of   page(s) each signed by me) is true to the best of my knowledge and belief and I make it knowing that, if it is tendered in evidence, I shall be liable to prosecution if I have wilfully stated in it, anything which I know to be false, or do not believe to be true.

Signature: .... Date: ....

Tick if witness evidence is visually recorded ☐   *(supply witness details on rear)*

Signature: .... Signature witnessed by: ....

2006/07 (1)

MG11T(CONT)

Page No. .... of ....

Continuation of Statement of: ....

Signature: ....   Signature witnessed by: ....

2006/07 (1)

6.23 **MG12: Exhibit List**

6.23.1 **Essentials**

This form tells the prosecutor which exhibits are to be produced in the case, who produces them and where they are located. All items should be on the exhibit list in the order that they are exhibited in the statements. This means every relevant item, not just the interview!

Officers should submit photocopies of all paper exhibits at the earliest opportunity. This is particularly important in even the smallest fraud case and causes delay and much prosecution and defence consternation when such exhibits are not properly copied and readily available from the start. Small exhibits, such as offensive weapons, can also be photocopied to assist the prosecutor and the court even though they may well be brought to court for any trial taking place.

6.23.2 **The form itself**

The name of the defendant and URN must go on the top of the form as usual.

There are then a number of boxes for completion:

- **Police property reference**: the number used to identify the item in the police property store.
- **Description as per label (indicate if copy)**: the description here has to be the same as is entered onto the exhibit label to avoid subsequent confusion arising at court. If the item is a copy this should also be indicated.
- **Exhibit reference no.**: each item has to be given an exhibit reference number which is the initials of the person producing it together with a sequential number, eg YM/1, YM/2. Where two people have the same initials it is helpful if the second letter of the surname is also added, eg YMo/1 (Y Moreno); YMa/2 (Y Matthews), etc.
- **Person producing and current location of exhibit**: it may well be the case that someone else may be required to obtain an exhibit at any time so it is important that the location of the exhibit is accurately completed here.
- ***: this box should be ticked where the exhibit itself or a copy is attached. Generally speaking the police should retain the original exhibits unless requested by the CPS or required for court.

Date of completion

This date will enable supervisors or the CPS to see clearly if additional exhibits have been added at a later date. In this case an additional exhibit list should be submitted under cover of an MG20.

KEY ISSUES—MG12

- Informs the CPS of exhibits to be produced, who produces them and where located
- All exhibits to be included
- Copies of documentary exhibits to be submitted
- Correct exhibit number vital

MG12

EXHIBIT LIST

Page No. .... of ....

R v ....

URN

* Tick if exhibit attached

Police property reference	Description as per label (indicate if copy)	Exhibit reference no.	Person producing and current location of exhibit	*
			Person producing: Current location:	
			Person producing: Current location:	
			Person producing: Current location:	
			Person producing: Current location:	
			Person producing: Current location:	
			Person producing: Current location:	
			Person producing: Current location:	
			Person producing: Current location:	
			Person producing: Current location:	
			Person producing: Current location:	
			Person producing: Current location:	
			Person producing: Current location:	

Date of completion: ....

2006/07 (1)

6.24 **MG13: Application for Order(s) on Conviction**

6.24.1 **Essentials**

This form has recently been adapted to include orders other than ASBOs, ie Restraining Orders and Sexual Offences Prevention Orders. All these orders can be made by the court on the application of the prosecutor when the defendant has been convicted of a particular relevant criminal offence. The courts can also make an order of their own volition. Its main use, however, is primarily in relation to the obtaining of an ASBO on conviction for any offence. The form should provide the CPS with sufficient information for them to make such an application to the court. It covers the conditions sought and should include necessary evidence and the substantive grounds to support them.

Prior to the completion of this form, the tick box at the bottom of the MG5 'Order on Conviction' should in any event have been ticked. Additionally the tick box on the MG6 at 18 should also have been ticked and relevant information put on the back of the MG6 for the prosecutors. Confidential observations of the officer can be inserted here since they may be third parties who do receive a copy of the MG13.

Best practice indicates that early advice from both the duty prosecutor and, in relation to an ASBO, an anti-social behaviour coordinator is first sought. The duty prosecutor may advise on the appropriateness of seeking an order and also assist in formulating suitable conditions. The best time to submit the MG13 is therefore at the point of charge.

The prosecution's ability to request an order is activated on a guilty plea or guilty verdict at trial. It is important that the completed form is available from the first appearance. An MG13 could in theory be submitted any time prior to a trial (but not between trial and sentence). The prosecutor, however, would be unable to make a proper application without sufficient notice and in any event advance notice should in all cases be given to the defence. The courts have indicated in practice they will refuse to hear such an application if no formal notice has been given to them.

The MG13 is usually kept confidential between the CPS and the police but it may be copied to the Probation Service and occasionally to the defendant.

It may be useful to serve on probation in the circumstances where the court has given an indication that a community penalty is likely. It would then be important that any prohibitions in an order did not impede the defendant's ability to comply with the conditions in the community penalty. It will be up to probation to inform the CPS and the police of their proposals for programmes for the defendant in such a community penalty.

In practice the completed MG13 is rarely served on the defendant or his/her representative, since they will subsequently be served with a copy of the draft order when finalized by the CPS which may differ from the proposed condition s/prohibitions put forward by the officer on the MG13, especially if it has been completed without assistance of the CPS.

6.24.2 **The form itself**

The name of the defendant and URN must go on the top of the form as usual.

Type of order

This should be specified where indicated albeit it may be obvious from the type of offence committed by the defendant against whom an order is sought.

The main orders are as follows.

ASBOs

These are orders sought under section 1C(2) of the Crime and Disorder Act 1998 (as amended by the Anti-social Behaviour Act 2003). The 'CRASBO' (as it is colloquially known) has been highly publicized and may be imposed after a conviction where the defendant has acted (in theory at any time since 1 April 1999) in a 'manner that caused or was likely to cause harassment, alarm or distress' to anyone outside his household. Furthermore the order is necessary to protect the public from further anti-social acts by the defendant. The order prohibits the defendant from doing anything described in the order.

The court can make an order of its own volition but if it is not anticipated the case would then have to be adjourned for the CPS to obtain necessary evidence to support it. The court should only consider an ABSO after it has decided the appropriate sentence. It is not an alternative sanction, rather an additional one, and should be viewed as outside the actual sentencing process. It is to be noted that applications can be made in civil proceedings for ASBOs but that is a different process albeit police can apply for one of these also.

Restraining Orders

These can be made presently under the Protection from Harassment Act 1997. The court has the power when dealing with a defendant convicted of an offence to make a restraining order under section 5 of the Act. The purpose of the order is to protect a specified person from further conduct from the defendant amounting to harassment or conduct causing a fear of violence. Again the order prohibits the defendant from doing anything described in it.

It is noteworthy that section 12(5) of the Domestic Violence, Crime and Victims Act 2004 will make such orders available in all types of cases and even on acquittal where it is necessary to protect the victims when it comes into force.

SOPOs

These Sexual Offence Prevention Orders were created under the Sexual Offences Act 2003 (ss 104–113) replacing the Restraining Order under the old legislation in respect of sexual offences only. The court must be sentencing the defendant in respect of a specific sexual or violent offence such that s/he becomes a 'qualifying offender'. However, it must also be 'satisfied that it is necessary' to make such an order for the protection of the public (or any particular member of the public) from serious sexual harm (psychological or physical) from the defendant. Again the SOPO prohibits the defendant doing anything described in the Order for a minimum period of 5 years.

Evidence in support

The form spells out that 'detailed evidence' must be given 'to support the necessity for each condition/prohibition shown below'. The form then requires:

- the number of the condition/prohibition;
- the proposed condition/prohibition, including the timescale where appropriate; and
- the evidence to support the application.

Proposed condition/prohibition

It is important that any conditions or prohibitions are not drafted too widely and that they are tailored to the particular circumstances of the case. The defendant him/herself must obviously know what s/he can and cannot do and the prosecutor, in the event of a breach, must be able to prove it.

POINT TO NOTE

The Manual of Guidance says compliance of conditions with the following is essential in relation to ASBOs. This guidance has been endorsed in subsequent case law:

- Only impose prohibiting and not positive requirements
- Cover the range of anti-social acts committed by the defendant
- Relate clearly to the acts complained of
- Be realistic, reasonable, and proportionate
- Be clear, concise, and easy to understand
- Be specific about time and place
- Be specific when referring to exclusion from an area and include street names and clear boundaries including maps
- Ensure non-association with named individuals where appropriate
- Be clear, in terms which make it relatively easy to determine and prove a breach

---

The proposed conditions therefore must be proportionate to the type of behaviour complained of and necessary to deal with particular anti-social or sexual behaviour of the defendant. They must also be certain. It will be open to a defendant to argue when prosecuted for a breach that s/he had a reasonable excuse for non-compliance if a particular condition/prohibition is drafted without all these factors being taken into consideration.

For example, in a recent case dealing with street drinkers it was suggested that 'not being in a state of drunkenness in a public place' was a preferred prohibition to one of 'not consuming intoxicating liquor in a public place'. In the latter situation a witness would have to prove: (a) that the substance being consumed was alcohol; and (b) effectively see the person drinking from the specific bottle in order to prove it. However, the demeanour, behaviour and smell of the defendant is far easier to prove in relation to 'a state of drunkenness'.

The more certain and specific the prohibition the better, eg not to enter any shop or commercial premises from which the defendant has been barred and not to associate with specific persons in any public place. Geographical limits are to be preferred for practical reasons, as is specification of the type of behaviour prohibited, eg lewd or obscene acts.

It is to be noted that the courts do not generally favour an attempt to impose a prohibition which prevents an offender from committing a specific criminal offence, eg assaulting a particular person, since this can be dealt with within the criminal law itself. An ASBO preventing a defendant from committing any criminal offence was certainly held to have been too wide.

As previously stated SOPOs last for a minimum of 5 years. ASBOs and Restraining Orders are time-bound but in relation to ASBOs all the conditions do not have to run for the full term of the ASBO itself.

Evidence

It is this section which police officers often find difficult to complete but which is most pertinent to the prosecutor. It is to be stressed that it is evidence that is required not opinion so any allegation inserted into this column must be backed up totally and in detail by supporting evidence. The courts have decided that albeit these are civil types of proceedings the criminal standard of proof applies. However, importantly, hearsay evidence is admissible but not 'unreliable tittle-tattle' (per Pilcher J in *R(W) Acton Youth Court* (2006) 170 JP 31 at 24).

The prosecution may be required to make a hearsay application in advance where evidence is given. Ultimately it will be for the court to decide what weight is to be attached to any particular evidence submitted in the form of hearsay.

The OIC will usually submit an MG11 (Witness Statement) with an overview of all aspects of the case detailing previous convictions of the defendant, why an order is deemed necessary, and other evidence of the defendant's anti-social behaviour ranging back as far as the 1 April 1999 when the legislation came into force. It is important that detailed previous convictions are provided containing more information than a Phoenix printout (analogous to completion of the MG16 see below) so that a clear link between the conditions/prohibition sought and those previous convictions can be demonstrated. In practice the more recent, the more similar, and the more prevalent, the more probative they become.

Additionally, details of any pending cases should be included and confidential information can go onto the MG6. The more detail and information the better for both the CPS in the making of the application and the court in assisting their subsequent decision making.

A draft copy of the order should be prepared by the CPS for service on the defendant and the court in advance of the hearing.

Warning to defendant

This is included to inform the defendant that the information on the MG13 is merely a guide and may vary from the actual conditions applied for in court or subsequently imposed by them where they have received a copy.

The MG13 is an extremely useful communication tool between the police and the CPS and should be viewed as such.

Signatures

The OIC, supervisor, and duty prosecutor will sign and date the MG13 where one has been submitted in advance and in fact discussed with the duty prosecutor in the charging centre.

Breaches

Where an order is breached it becomes a criminal offence. It is important for the OIC to ensure that the defendant accepts that s/he is the person subject of the order, that s/he understands the conditions particularly those breached and if possible details of any defence to be raised are obtained from him/her.

Since it is a criminal offence a proper MG file should then be submitted by the police containing all the evidence in the case. It is also vital that the MG5 contains a summary of the proceedings in which the order was made and what was in the court's mind when making the order, ie why they made it in the first instance. If the CPS is not given the full background information then it is unlikely that the court will be able to pass a meaningful sentence subsequently.

As a rider it is to be noted that the number of ASBOs handed out has been declining and that more than six out of ten are breached by offenders. Many ASBOs issued in the future may be accompanied by parenting orders with parents forced to take responsibility for their offspring's behaviour and some commentators are saying this is the end of the line for the ASBO.

KEY ISSUES—MG13

- Informs the CPS that police wish to apply for an order on conviction
- Specifies the type of order, eg ASBO
- Details the conditions sought
- Provides supporting evidence to substantiate application
- Enables the CPS to make informed application to the court

MG13

APPLICATION FOR ORDER(S) ON CONVICTION

Page No. .... of ....

(This form may be copied to the Probation Service)   URN

Defendant surname: .... Forename(s): ....

Specify type of Order *(e.g. ASBO, Restraining, Sexual Offences Prevention Order, etc):* ....

....

Give detailed evidence to support the necessity for each condition / prohibition shown below:

No.	Condition / Prohibition *(include timescale where appropriate)*	Evidence

Warning to defendant:

The above conditions / prohibitions are given as a guide and may vary from the actual conditions applied for at court.

Officer in case: .... Rank / Job title: .... No: .... Date: ....

Supervisor: .... Rank / Job title: .... No: .... Date: ....

Duty Prosecutor: .... Date: ....

2006/07 (1)

6.25 **MG14: Conditional Caution**

6.25.1 **Essentials**

This form provides details of the offence(s) for which the offender has been conditionally cautioned. It demonstrates by his/her signature that they agree to it and the conditions outlined on the form, and furthermore that they understand the implications of non-compliance. The conditional cautioning form was first introduced in December 2004 when certain pathfinders' sites began operating conditional cautioning as a pilot scheme. It has now been rolled out across England and Wales.

The conditional caution introduced by the Criminal Justice Act 2003 created a new disposal option for the prosecution team and provided an opportunity to divert an appropriate offender from court in specific circumstances. This scheme does not replace the non-statutory police caution commonly called the 'simple caution' but is a further tool to be utilized in the handling of low level offenders. It provides a swift, effective alternative to the formal court process for offenders who are prepared to both admit to their guilt and agree to comply with specified conditions in straightforward cases which are of sufficient seriousness to warrant some form of prosecution. At the same time it helps improve victim satisfaction and assists offenders to deal with any underlying problems which drive their offending behaviour.

Guidance to police officers and Crown Prosecutors on the operation of this scheme is to be found in the Statutory Code of Practice for Conditional Cautioning and in the Director's Guidance on Conditional Cautioning (5th edn, October 2007). Such cautions are limited to offences specified in Annex A of the Guidance which are mainly summary offences (excluding most motoring offences) and specified either way offences (eg possession of drugs, theft, obtaining by deception). The scheme is not appropriate for the more serious violent and persistent offender. The disposal should only be used where it provides an appropriate and proportionate response to the offending behaviour.

ACC Francis Hapgood, ACPO lead for conditional cautioning, states:

> The conditional caution is a valuable new tool for the police officer that will augment current pre-court disposal and broaden our opportunities when responding to offending. Police officers will have a key role in the operation of the conditional cautioning scheme as they will have first hand knowledge of the circumstances surrounding both the offence and the offender.

Conditions imposed in the scheme must be either rehabilitative, eg an offender with a small quantity of drugs could be cautioned and subsequently have to attend the drug dependency course or drug education, or reparative, eg an offender makes good damage s/he has caused or pays compensation or apologizes to the victim.

A conditional caution is usually proposed by the custody sergeant prior to charge once the threshold test is met (ie that there is a reasonable suspicion that the offender has committed the crime and that it is in the public interest to proceed) and it appears to the custody sergeant that a conditional caution is the most appropriate method of proceeding.

If the custody officer concludes that there are factors preventing referral of the case to the CPS s/he should record these on the custody record, eg defendant on bail; likelihood of re-offending; only a partial admission. In this situation the custody officer could then proceed to charge in accordance with the Director's Guidance on Statutory Charging, where s/he has the authority to do so.

Checklist—Necessary requirements for a conditional caution

- Offender aged over 18 years of age at time of disposal

- The offence is one to which Annex A of the Director's Guidance applies

- There is sufficient evidence to bring the charges (on the full code test)

- CPS concludes that the public interest can be met by an out of court disposal

- In this case the most likely outcome of attending court will be a minor penalty

- The use of reparative and rehabilitative conditions is felt to be the most effective way of dealing with the offending behaviour and/or recompensing the victim

- Views of individual victims should be considered wherever possible

- The offender has **admitted** the offence in a PACE interview and agrees to accept the caution and carry out the conditions

Admission?

There has been some discussion as to what amounts to a PACE-compliant admission for the purposes of a conditional caution; ie whether or not it has to be recorded as an 'audio taped interview' as opposed to other forms of recording on admission. The Director's Guidance on Conditional Cautioning at paragraph 4.23(b) requires a custody officer to 'determine whether the suspect has made an admission that complies with PACE 1984'. The Conditional Caution Code of Practice (paragraph 4:1) however, refers to an admission made under caution in 'interview' and to a 'clear and reliable admission' under a cautioned interview.

It is clear that in respect of either-way offences to be conditionally cautioned all admissions must be supported by an audio-taped interview. For summary only offences there is a discretion with police officers such that in these minor offences where they do not usually interview the suspect the other forms of admission laid down in Home Office Circular 16/2008 on 'Simple Cautions for Adult Offenders' (see 16, 18 and 19) are acceptable as admissions for a conditional caution also. This requires an unsolicited admission made to an officer recorded in his/her notebook, or by the custody officer in the custody record—in both cases signed by the accused as an accurate record. Best practice, however, for a number of summary offences, eg common assault, still suggests the holding of an audio-recorded interview so there is no doubt about the admission in the circumstances.

CPS decision

It will be the CPS (including CPS Direct via the telephone) who will then agree that such a caution should be administered and also what relevant conditions should be applied to it after referral by the custody officer. It is possible that the CPS will also refer a case back for a conditional caution even where the police have not considered it in the first instance.

POINT TO NOTE—DIRECTOR'S GUIDANCE ON CONDITIONAL CAUTIONING

Paragraph 3.1: 'the decision to offer a conditional caution and the conditions to be attached can only be made by a crown prosecutor.'
Paragraph 3.2: 'police officers and crown prosecutors should work together to ensure that a conditional caution should be considered wherever it is appropriate.'

Where an offender does not provide informed consent to the conditional caution s/he will then be prosecuted for the offence, the offender can him/herself refuse a caution and ask for a prosecution. However, where the offender accepts a caution and complies with the conditions the prosecution will not proceed. If the offender does not satisfy the conditions imposed s/he will be prosecuted in most cases for the original offence. This is a decision of the CPS taking into account whether the offender has a reasonable excuse for non-compliance.

A conditional caution is not a conviction but is entered on the PNC and may be cited in any subsequent court proceedings, therefore, forming part of the offender's formal criminal record.

Information to be provided to the CPS

Essentially these are cases which the police have authority to charge so the evidential part should have been sorted out by the police prior to CPS involvement so the approval process can be simplified. It is anticipated that consultation between the CPS and the police will take place while the defendant is in custody or within 72 hours if possible, usually by referral to the charging lawyer in the charging centre.

> **POINT TO NOTE**
>
> Simplified documentation . . . should facilitate the proportionate preparation of sufficient information for the decision-making and speedy disposal of cases suitable for conditional cautions.
>
> Director's Guidance on Conditional Cautioning, para 2

Paragraph 6 of the Director's Guidance lays down the information to be provided by the police termed the '**conditional cautioning referral papers**'. Obviously a draft MG14 forms an essential part of this. However, in addition, any witness statements and/or MG5 summary including the SDN of the admission and record of the offenders previous convictions or cautions should also be submitted to the CPS.

The decision of the CPS will be subsequently recorded on the MG3 and the MG14 will be amended where suggested conditions are subsequently altered by the CPS.

> **POINT TO NOTE**
>
> The maintenance of confidence in the conditional cautioning system is dependent on the accurate and timely supply of all relevant information in each case. In any case where relevant information is found to be missing during the referral the process may be suspended while the required information is obtained.
>
> Director's Guidance on Conditional Cautioning, para 6.3

6.25.2 The form itself

As usual the URN and A/S No together with the defendant's details must be inserted at the top of the form.

The form then requires sufficient details of the offences and date of arrest to be included, although as previously indicated it is usual to submit an MG5 with key witness statements and SDN of interview as well as the defendant's previous convictions to the prosecutor. This information should clearly indicate that the offender has made a full and clear admission of the offence. Additionally any views expressed by the victim as to any proposed conditions or by the offender indicating a willingness to comply with any conditions should also be noted on the M14.

Signature

The key element of page 1 of the MG14 is the signature of the offender at the bottom of the page indicating that s/he admits to the offences set out on the form and accepts the relevant information in respect of them and that s/he understands s/he has the right to legal advice prior to doing so.

It is imperative there must be informed consent of both the caution and the conditions so that the offender understands the implications of accepting a conditional caution and also how to satisfy the conditions. Such legal advice before and during the interview process should protect the suspect from any potential pressure.

It is very important that the officer in charge is not considered to have induced the offender in any way so the possibility of a conditional caution should never be mentioned to any offender prior to admitting the offence.

In practice the form will be submitted in draft to the CPS with the details of the offences for which the conditional caution is required and a suggestion of the appropriate conditions. This form may then be subsequently amended by the CPS prior to its being shown to the offender for his signature.

Conditions

The officer will put forward on the back page of the MG14 proposed conditions and compliance requirements including completion and progress dates.

Conditions imposed must be proportionate to the offence, appropriate, clear, practicable, achievable, and verifiable and reflect what is available locally. They must also have rehabilitative or reparative objectives. Restrictive conditions can be used but only alongside rehabilitative or reparative ones. Multiple conditions can be given but proportionality is to be remembered. Generally any time for compliance should not exceed 16 weeks so that a prosecution may still take place in summary cases where there has been non-compliance. In relation to any unpaid work suggested as a condition it should not generally exceed 20 hours.

Annex B of the Director's Guidance on Conditional Cautioning provides further guidance on the selection of appropriate conditions. It makes clear that reparative conditions are to make good the loss sustained by the victim or community and to repair relationships. Individual victims should where possible be consulted and suitable conditions canvassed. Payment of financial reparation should only be included where a victim requests it. Any decision inviting a victim to participate in the conditions must only be made if the victim has been consulted and agreed. Such information should go on the MG14.

Examples would include the payment of compensation (and the Director's Guidance includes compensation guidelines for personal injury received), personally repairing or making good damage, undertaking unpaid work on community property related to the harm caused, writing a letter of apology, participating in restorative justice, and mediation.

Rehabilitative conditions are all about stopping or modifying the offending behaviour or reducing the risk of offending behaviour. Examples include not committing further offences for a defined period of time and attending a drugs/alcohol referral programme specifically related to the nature or cause of offending behaviour.

Restrictive conditions must be clear and unambiguous and may be included as part of a package of measures designed to rehabilitate offenders or to make good harm caused. Examples include: not contacting a named person or going to a named specified location or staying out of a particular establishment. Such conditions, however, must not restrict access to home, work, education, place of worship, or access for necessities of every day living.

Compliance

It is important when looking at the conditions to also consider the most suitable method of assessment of compliance with them taking into account the local infrastructure and the types of conditions being offered (see para 5.19 of the Director's Guidance on Conditional Cautioning).

The 'authorized person' administering the caution must provide the offender with a named contact and telephone number in the event of difficulties in complying with the conditions or any other problems. That person will also act as the focal point of contact for partner agencies involved in the monitoring of conditions imposed. S/he will, for example, notify the courts of any compensation order details since they will act as collection agents for compensation and forward monies to the victim even though they will not enforce payment of the compensation itself. This point of contact will also actively monitor compliance of the conditions and completion dates.

Evidence required

In practice the arranged monitor/local contact named on the MG14 will confirm to police the satisfactory attendance and completion of conditions. In some circumstances the offender him/herself may be required to provide evidence of the satisfactory completion of those conditions and where it is appropriate and practical the 'evidence required' section on the right-hand side of the form will be filled out and forms part of the condition itself.

There is no formal investigation of compliance with conditions but where the officer in the case or monitor becomes aware of non-compliance the offender should be spoken to immediately and given the opportunity to provide an explanation first.

Ultimately the offender can be arrested for non-compliance under section 24A(i) of the Criminal Justice Act 2003 in order to ascertain whether or not s/he has a reasonable excuse and the case will be referred back with the views of the police officer to the CPS for a decision. The CPS can then vary the conditions, take no action, or prosecute for the original offence depending on the excuse provided and the degree of non-compliance.

Declaration

The rest of the MG14 on the back page contains a declaration by the offender basically saying that s/he understands the following:

- that s/he can be liable for prosecution if s/he does not comply with the conditions and that the MG14 signed by him/her can form part of the evidence in the case;
- that s/he will notify the named contact as soon as possible if s/he either changes address or is unable to comply with the conditions;
- that a record of the conditional caution will be kept;
- that the conditional caution can be disclosed in relation to employment sought or future criminal proceedings;
- that if s/he has been conditionally cautioned for an offence under the Sexual Offences Act 2003, Schedule 3, s/he may go on the 'sex offenders register';
- that information on his/her compliance may be provided to coordinators by service providers;
- that a victim could take out a private prosecution or civil action against him/her and that the police could disclose his/her details to the victim for this purpose.

It is to be noted in this latter instance that in such circumstances it is highly likely in practice that the CPS would take over and discontinue such a private prosecution which it has authority to do. To allow a private prosecution to continue after the administration and acceptance of a caution would breach the principle of finality and would risk undermining the integrity of the cautioning regime.

Once the offender has read the declaration or had it read and explained to him/her the offender must then sign again when the caution has been administered.

The administration of the caution

Paragraph 8 of the Director's Guidance on Conditional Cautioning spells out the procedure for the administration of a caution. When the CPS has confirmed a conditional caution as appropriate a police officer 'an authorized person' as permitted under section 22(4) of the Criminal Justice Act 2003 will proceed to administer the caution.

In line with the declaration, s/he will inform the offender of the evidence against him/her and the decision made by the CPS. S/he will explain the conditional caution and the implications of accepting it and explain the requirements for and consequences of making a further admission of the offence at this stage and that the signature of the defendant may be used in evidence should the case result in a prosecution.

It must be made clear to the offender that s/he should not admit offences simply to receive a conditional caution and effectively walk out of a police station. S/he must further ensure the offender has had the opportunity for legal advice prior to his/her agreement and that s/he does in fact admit the offence still and is willing to comply with the conditions.

S/he should ensure that s/he understands the effects of the caution together with the consequences of failure to comply with any of the conditions.

Review date

The bottom of form MG14 on the back page must be completed by the OIC or authorized person on the review date indicating whether there has been full compliance with the conditions or non-compliance. In the latter case the officer should provide details of this and any explanation for non-compliance which will be forwarded to the CPS for their final decision.

KEY ISSUES—MG14

- Valuable new alternative disposal system for low grade offences
- CPS make final decisions
- Provides details of cautioned offences and conditions attached
- Demonstrates fully informed agreement of offender to caution and conditions
- Spells out to offender the implications of non-compliance
- Confirms conditional caution administered
- Allows for review of compliance on review date

MG14

CONDITIONAL CAUTION

URN

A/S No.

Offender's surname: .... Forename(s): .... D.O.B.: .... Male / Female

Ethnicity Code: PNC .... 16-point +1: ....

Address: .... Postcode: ....

Tel no: (home) .... (work): .... (mobile): ....

Details of the offence(s) *(Include facts <u>as if charged,</u> date(s) of offence / arrest and if necessary continue on MG(c))*

Sequential No	Offence	CCCJS Offence Code

I admit to the offence(s) set out above. I understand I have the right to legal advice.

Signature of person cautioned: .... Date: ....

2006/07 (1)

MG14

A agree to comply with the following conditions of the caution:

Condition(s)	Compliance requirements, including completion / progress check dates	Evidence required
1.		
2.		
(Continue on a separate sheet if necessary)		

Contact details for reporting compliance with the conditions ....

Offender Declaration – I understand the following:

1) That if I fail within the agreed time to comply with, or to complete, any of the conditions attached to this caution, I will be liable for prosecution for the offence(s) outlined above and this signed form may be presented as part of the case against me in a court of law;

2) I will inform the contact shown above without delay if: I am unable to comply with any of these conditions and explain why or I change my normal place of residence, as recorded overleaf.

3) A record of this conditional caution will be kept;

4) That the conditional caution may be disclosed, when appropriate, to certain potential employers, or in connection with any future criminal proceedings;

5) Where one or more of the above offence(s) is listed in Schedule 3 of the Sexual Offences Act 2003 and the relevant age and disposal thresholds are met that I will become subject to the notification requirements of Part 2 of that Act (commonly known as the Sex Offenders Register).

6) Information on my compliance may be provided to the co-ordinators by the service providers, DIP, et al.

7) I understand that a victim may still take out a private prosecution or civil action against me. The Police may disclose my details to a victim for this purpose.

Signature of person cautioned: ....

Signature of appropriate adult *(where applicable)*:...

Caution administered by: .... Rank / Job title: .... No: ....

Station: ....

Signature: .... Tel. No.: .... Date: ....

For completion by the Officer in the Case / authorised person on the review date

I hereby certify that the conditions shown above have / have not been completed satisfactorily *(attach any relevant evidence in support of this)*.

Name of officer / authorised person finalising the caution: .... Rank / Job title: .... No.: ....

Station: .... Signature: ....

Tel. No.: .... Date: ....

2006/07 (1)

6.26 **MG15: Record of Interview**

6.26.1 **Essentials**

This form is used for recording the content of both audio and visually recorded interviews of suspects as well as visually recorded interviews of vulnerable/intimidated and significant witnesses. (The latter will be dealt with below.)

POINT TO NOTE—THE MAIN PURPOSE OF THE WRITTEN RECORD OF INTERVIEW

- To provide a balanced, accurate and reliable summary of what has been said
- To enable police supervisors to assess the evidence
- To enable the Crown Prosecutor to decide (where there is a suspect):

  - whether or not a prosecution should proceed
  - whether the proposed charges are appropriate
  - what lines of defence to anticipate
  - what mode of trial is appropriate

- To assist in the conduct of a case by the prosecution, the defence and the court where the record of interview has been accepted by the defence
- In the case of vulnerable and intimidated witnesses to prevent and protect them from giving live evidence in court
- In respect of significant witnesses, to demonstrate the integrity of the way in which the evidence has been gathered

MINI MOG, 38

Type of format

The reader is referred to Chapter 5 for a detailed discussion of interviews.

The top of the MG15 describes the different types of written record that can be used: contemporaneous notes; SDN; ROTI (record of taped interview); ROVI (record of visually recorded interview).

In fact out of these the SDN is the shortest version of interview record allowed and may be submitted in expedited file cases, ie custody cases, anticipated guilty pleas, and for CJSSS.

The ROTI and ROVI are usually prepared for full evidential file cases and will often suffice if properly completed by the officer. However, a superintendent can authorize a verbatim full transcript or the CPS can specifically request one in relation to any case.

Contemporaneous notes are fairly scarce with modern technology recording the interview and the officer making notes usually only of salient points rather than a fully contemporaneous record. This could happen where the suspect merely wishes to make a statement and the officer records it.

6.26.2 **SDN**

This is a brief account in the third person of certain aspects of the interview sufficient for expedited files only. These can be handwritten and in fact the SDN can be entered onto the MG5 case summary rather than the MG15. If this is the case start and end times of the interview should also be inserted.

Contents of SDN are as follows:

- main salient points necessary to prove offence (eg intent/dishonesty/knowledge of key facts/present at scene of crime, etc);
- admissions (but more detail than merely 'D fully admitted offence');
- aggravating factors (eg vulnerable victim/abuse of position of responsibility/ showed no remorse;
- D's version different/D's explanation (if it amounts to a defence ROTI required, eg 'I hit him because he hit me first' = self defence/'I forgot to pay' = denial of dishonesty for theft—therefore not guilty plea);
- mitigating circumstances (eg illness/remorse/unemployment);
- significant silence (failure to answer questions which deal with the material part of the allegation);
- special warning (and response made if appropriate);
- TIC offences;
- evidence of bad character if applicable;
- summarizing (what has been admitted/denied at the end of the interview).

Poorly compiled SDNs will result in delays since the defence will merely apply for an adjournment to listen to the tape.

6.26.3 **ROTI (record of taped interview)**

The ROTI should be typed and prepared for full file situations. They will always be on the MG15 and will be produced as an exhibit in the interviewing officer's statement. Where two officers are involved in the interview only one should exhibit it, the other will merely say that s/he was present at the interview and make reference to the tape exhibit.

A record of interview must include:

- all admissions and questions and answers leading up to them (including ambiguous ones);
- statements and questions about intent, dishonesty, possible defences;

- knowledge of key facts—the points to prove the essential elements of an offence;
- defences and alibis;
- presence at scene of crime on this and other occasions;
- information about any other person's involvement;
- special warnings and responses given;
- details of any TIC offences.

The form itself (ROTI)

The following details must be inserted at the top of the form for the purposes of the ROTI:

- the full name of the defendant/witness;
- the time, date, and duration of the interview;
- the name and status of all those present at the interview (including second interviewing officer, appropriate adult, defence solicitor, etc);
- the reference number of audio tapes.

Additionally the top right hand box must be signed by the officer who is going to produce the interview as an exhibit with the number of pages of which the interview consists and the exhibit number given to it by that officer. The officer will also be required to sign the bottom of every page of the MG15 which is used.

The text

Obviously the top of the form must be completed correctly but in addition the text must state the fact that a caution was given and the fact that the suspect was reminded of their right to free legal advice. Also, if appropriate, the fact that any significant statement or silence before the interview was put to the suspect. The MG6A should also have been completed relating to the pre-interview disclosure given to the suspect and/or his/her representative.

On the left hand side of the MG15 are two columns 'tape counter times' and 'person speaking'.

Tape times will be helpful for ease of reference when preparing the written record if counter times are noted for all the key salient points and admissions, defences, etc as well as TICs.

Person speaking is again helpful for ease of reference. It is important to know who is asking a question or intervening since it could for, example, be a defence solicitor speaking at a crucial stage rather than a suspect.

The ROTI will suffice only when it contains all the material listed above. The information and descriptions given must be sufficient to allow the prosecutor to decide whether or not the suspect should be charged and whether or not those charges will adequately reflect the gravity of the offence as disclosed.

6.26.4 ROVI (record of visually recorded interviews with vulnerable, intimidated, and significant witnesses)

The ROVI is in fact a revised version of the interview summary, formerly known as an 'index', that police were required to compile since the 'Memorandum of Good Practice' was published in 1992 on how such interviews should be conducted. ACPO published new guidance on ROVIs in May 2007 which also took into account the revised 'Memorandum of Good Practice' called 'Achieving Best Evidence' also published in 2007.

Vulnerable and intimidated witnesses have been defined elsewhere at 4.3.2 and 4.3.3. In certain circumstances they are entitled to provide their main evidence in chief by means of video link.

Significant witnesses (or key witnesses)

- are those who have or claim to have witnessed visually or otherwise an indictable offence, part of such an offence or events closely connected with it (including any incriminating comments made by a suspected offender either before or after the offence); and
- stand in particular relationship to the victim or have a central position in an investigation into an indictable offence.

The purpose of recording the evidence of a significant witness is to demonstrate the integrity of the way in which that evidence has been gathered. It will only be used in serious cases and on the authority of a senior officer in charge of an investigation.

Currently there is no statutory provision for video recordings of interviews with significant witnesses to be played as evidence in chief until section 137 of the CJA 2003 is implemented.

Purpose of ROVI

This is not a statement, transcript, replacement for a video or an exhibit. However, ROVIs are necessary in every case where a vulnerable/intimidated or significant witness is interviewed on video (or audio if a significant witness) irrespective of whether or not a transcript is subsequently created.

POINT TO NOTE

The overall function of a ROVI is to contribute towards the effective investigation and management of a case by guiding investigating officers and prosecutors through their viewing of the interview.

ACPO Guidance on completion of ROVI, Annex D, para 5

The ROVI will assist the prosecutor at the pre-charge investigation stage to make informed decisions on, for example, any further enquiries to be conducted by the officer. At the post-charge stage it will enable the prosecutor (and defence) properly to prepare the case and make decisions relating to the editing of the interview.

The form itself (ROVI)

Obviously the form MG15 should be used and typed if possible. All the fields at the top of the form should be completed as per the ROTI. It is important that all time entries are recorded in hours, minutes, and seconds using the clock shown on the video with the speakers identified against the relevant time entry and text.

However, since it will not be an exhibit the top right hand box should be crossed out but it will be provided to all parties in the proceedings.

ROVIs should be as succinct as possible with most of it indirect speech. Direct speech should only be used if, for example, potentially ambiguous language is reported. Background material of no apparent relevance should be summarized in general terms only.

The content of the finished ROVI should, as far as possible, give a chronological account of the conduct of the interview and include the following:

- rapport (engage and explain) including ground rules and where appropriate truth and lies. Simply identifying the rapport stage took place will usually be all that is required in a ROVI;
- identification issues such as detailed descriptions or identifying features of suspects. This should include the identification points raised in *R v Turnbull* [1977] QB 224;
- details of the location of the event witnessed;
- points to prove the offences;
- details of time, frequency, dates and locations and those present when the offence(s) occurred;
- extent of any injuries;
- any threats and admissions made;
- key statements made by witness, the suspect or other witnesses;
- anything that negates potential defence (eg consent);
- any aggravating factors (including racial, homophobic, gender, etc);
- any corroborative evidence identified (witnesses, CCTV, forensic, etc); and
- any issue that undermines the prosecution case or supports the defence case.

ACPO Guidance 2007, para 10

ROVI procedure with

Depending upon the circumstances, the SIO still has the discretion to transcribe the interview at an early stage of the investigation. However, charging decisions by the prosecutor will be based on the ROVI and the viewing of the video recording itself. If a not guilty plea is entered the CPS are responsible for sending the video for transcription (unless police have already done it) but the ROVI will suffice for a guilty plea.

The CPS should then make an application to the court for the video recording to be played as evidence in chief (under s 27 of the YJCEA 1999) and will serve both the video and transcript on defence. The video itself will be the exhibit in the case and the transcript provided as unused material. Where the application is unsuccessful the witness will have to give live evidence in chief. In these circumstances the preferred option is for the witness to make a brief section 9 (CJA 1967) statement (MG11) confirming what they said in interview is an accurate account of the evidence. The transcript should be checked by the OIC also. The witness's and interviewer's MG11s, together with the transcript, will be adduced in evidence and the video itself will be unused material.

An alternative option is for a full CJA statement (MG11) to be prepared from the video recording as soon as possible. The OIC can do this but the witness should then be asked to review it and invited to make corrections, alterations, or additions where necessary and agree its contents and sign the MG11. That witness's MG11 will then be adduced in evidence and the video will then be unused material.

6.26.5 **Contemporaneous notes**

The top of the form and signature of the officer at the bottom should also be completed here. This will be a rare course of action because of the requirement of Code E of PACE whereby effectively every interview is taped. However, it could arise where a suspect asks the police officer to write down a statement for him/her. This should be clearly indicated at the beginning prior to the exact words spoken by the person being written down. No editing and paraphrasing must take place. All questions put (eg to make it more intelligible) and answers given must be recorded contemporaneously and all on form MG15. At the end the suspect should be asked to read it or have it read to him/her and make any corrections and alterations and then sign it to the effect that it was made of his/her own free will, that s/he has read it (or had it read to him/her) that it is true and that s/he has been able to add, alter or correct anything s/he wants.

KEY ISSUES—MG15

- Records content of audio/visually recorded interviews of suspects
- Records visually recorded interviews of vulnerable/intimidated/significant witnesses
- Comprises either SDN, ROTI, ROVI, contemporaneous notes
- Provides balanced, accurate, reliable summary of what has been said
- Enables the CPS and defence to proceed with case without full transcript
- Supports vulnerable/intimidated witnesses to give evidence via video link

MG15

RECORD OF INTERVIEW

URN

Contemporaneous Notes / SDN / ROTI / ROVI (delete as applicable)

Person interviewed: ....

Place of interview: ....

....

Date of interview: ....

Time commenced: .... Time concluded: ....

Duration of interview: ....

Audio tape reference nos.: .... Visual image reference nos.: ....

Interviewer(s): ....

Other persons present: ....

Police Exhibit No:

Number of Pages:

....
Signature of interviewer producing exhibit

Tape counter times	Person speaking	Text

Signature(s): ....

2006/07 (1)

Person interviewed: .... Page No. .... of ....

Tape counter times	Person speaking	Text

Signature(s): ....

2006/07 (1)

6.27 **MG16: Evidence of Defendant's Bad Character and/or Dangerous Offender Information**

6.27.1 **Essentials**

The form came into existence as a result of the Criminal Justice Act 2003. This Act implemented a new statutory scheme from 15 December 2004 for dealing with the admissibility of bad character evidence in relation to both defendants and non-defendants (ie witnesses). It also introduced a new sentencing framework in respect of all offences committed on or after 4 April 2005. This included an entirely new scheme for sentencing offenders who have been assessed as dangerous and have committed a specific sexual or violent offence. The form allows the police to provide the CPS with evidence of either a person's bad character, or evidence that a person is potentially dangerous to the public, which is relevant for sentencing purposes.

Admissibility of bad character

Basically the law has been fundamentally changed so that bad character evidence relating to the defendant can be admissible if it is relevant to the issues in the case and it satisfies certain criteria. This is subject to the court's discretion to exclude it if it would be fair to do so. Juries will, therefore, no longer have the wool pulled over their eyes and bad character can be used along with other evidence to help prove the guilt of the defendant and/or rebut any defence raised.

A large number of cases in the Court of Appeal since the beginning of the new legislation have clearly demonstrated that the courts have taken a broad approach to the interpretation of it and in a considerable number of cases bad character has become the 'norm'. It is therefore a very important evidential tool for both police officers and prosecutors and the opportunity to utilize it should not be lost.

The seven gateways

Section 101(1) of the CJA 2003 provides an exhaustive list of seven gateways via which the defendant's bad character can be admitted. The CPS will make an application under one or more of these gateways where appropriate and are totally reliant on the quality of the information received from the police in this regard. A detailed application can go a long way to ensuring that the courts do not exercise their discretion to exclude the evidence.

POINT TO NOTE—SEVEN GATEWAYS OF ADMISSIBILITY (S 101(1) OF THE CJA 2003)

1   All parties agree
2   Evidence is adduced by the defence
3   Important explanatory evidence
4   Relevant to any matter in issue between prosecution and defence—this can include propensity to commit offences of the same kind or propensity to be untruthful
5   Is of substantial probative value between co-defendants
6   Is necessary to correct a false impression
7   Where defence attacks another's character

The working of the gateways is quite complicated and outside the scope of this book. However, when in doubt the police officer should always refer to the CPS for advice on these complex provisions.

Interestingly, even if bad character cannot be fitted into a gateway under section 101(1) it may still be admissible under old common law rules if it is deemed not to be bad character but is still relevant to an issue in the case. It is also admissible in any event where the court decides that the behaviour 'has to do' with the facts of the offence itself.

Definition of bad character

What is important for police officers to note is the wide definition of bad character provided by the legislation and as interpreted by decided cases. It is not confined to previous convictions but also includes 'a disposition towards misconduct' and 'any other reprehensible behaviour'. Bad character therefore can include potentially any of the following:

- previous convictions;
- cautions;
- reprimands;
- final warnings;
- TICs;
- concurrent charges;
- acquittals;
- discontinuances;
- previous defences used;
- behaviour after the offence for which the defendant stands charged;
- ASBOs; and
- disciplinary records.

It may also cover incident reports in relation to the defendant, eg of domestic violence or of racial or a public order nature. It covers previous allegations against the defendant but the court is wary where it could be untrue. The court will not allow a trial to be side-tracked by satellite issues regarding the credibility or otherwise of the reprehensible behaviour being put forward in evidence.

Proving bad character

Since bad character is a piece of evidence it has to be proved like any other. More detailed information is required than is available on the PNC printout, the CPS and the court will want details of the circumstances of the offences themselves which are not allowed to be given in the court by the OIC. The CPS will give guidance at the pre-charge stage if further enquiries need to be made and also as to the manner in which the evidence will be actually proved in court. Usually it may require a statement from a complainant who has personal knowledge of, for example, an allegation (which itself could be admitted via the hearsay provisions of the CJA 2003). The court often expects the defendant to admit a minimum of undisputed facts in relation to the particular behaviour or conviction, which then are submitted as a 'section 10 admission' at trial.

The message, therefore, is to research the bad character in question and provide full information to the CPS on the MG16.

Dangerous offenders

The provisions within the CJA 2003 are important because they can potentially apply to every either-way or indictable only sexual or violent offence (called a 'specified offence' listed in Sch 15 to the CJA 2003). Where the defendant has committed such an offence and s/he satisfies the test of dangerousness then s/he can receive a severer sentence from the court.

The test of dangerousness requires the court to undertake a risk assessment of the offender's future conduct: is there a significant risk to members of the public of serious harm occasioned by the commission by him/her of further specified offences? The court will also take into account previous convictions and any 'pattern of behaviour' which goes to suggest the offender is a significant risk and a danger to the public.

Sections 13–18 of the Criminal Justice and Immigration Act 2008 amend the public protection legislation such that it has removed the previous rebuttable presumption of dangerousness where an adult suspect has a previous conviction for a sexual or violent crime.

The judiciary are given more discretion as to the final penalty where all the provisions are met and there is now a 'seriousness threshold' to be passed before such a public protection sentence can be imposed in the first instance (a notional term of at least 2 years' duration).

Timings

The MG16 was devised to cover both bad character and dangerous offenders, such that an officer should submit evidence of these at the earliest opportunity.

Best practice dictates that in relation to bad character the form should be completed and submitted with the MG3 at the charging centre since it is relevant to the review of the case by the Crown Prosecutor as it can be evidence against the defendant to prove his guilt.

It is essential that as a matter of course every police officer considers whether bad character is relevant to an issue in the case while planning their interview strategy and as part of their pre-interview disclosure where relevant. Where the bad character has been put to the defendant in interview, the defendant's responses to it are helpful to the CPS in assessing how the bad character can subsequently be used in court and how it can be proved.

In nearly all situations, the CPS is required to provide written notice to the court of their intention to adduce bad character.

In relation to dangerous offenders, the magistrates cannot impose any of the new sentencing options. However, they will consider the question of dangerousness after a guilty plea or conviction. In relation to a youth the issue of dangerousness may be decided at the mode of trial stage. It is therefore, also vital for officers to be just as proactive in collating and evaluating information in relation to potential dangerousness at the earliest opportunity even though it is not essential for the actual review of the file in most cases.

6.27.2 The form itself

The form requires the defendant's name, date of birth, and arrest number to be inserted.

It reminds the police officer that the form should be submitted at the pre-charge stage with form MG3 for the prosecutor in relation to bad character. Evidence on the MG16 submitted post-charge would usually relate to dangerous offenders being relevant to the mode of trial or sentencing process.

Evidence of bad character (BC) (evidence for trial)

This box acts as an aide memoire to the police officer of the definition of bad character including 'relevant evidence or disposition towards misconduct or other reprehensible behaviour'. It further states that this can relate to either:

- the commission of an offence of the kind charged, including previous convictions for offence(s) of the same or similar description (same charge/indictment) or category;
- the commission of any other related type of offences (even where not of similar description or same category); or
- the defendant's untruthfulness is his/her propensity to tell lies. This may be shown, for example, by convictions for perjury or deception.

As previously indicated the bad character definition is extremely wide and may cover a host of situations in addition to those mentioned in the aide memoire at the top of the form.

Dangerous offender (DO) information (information for sentencing—specified offences of sex/violence)

The form reminds the officer that usually the information required will be for sentencing purposes in relation to specified offences of sex/violence. It has been noted already that in practice the CPS may require that information at an early stage.

The form tells the officer to 'list below information that may be taken into account by the sentencing court when assessing whether the defendant poses a significant risk to the public of serious harm'.

Brief details of charge(s) or proposed charge(s)

By listing the offences which the offender is to face it should alert the officer's mind to the 'relevant' issues in the case in relation to bad character or remind the officer to check that the offender faces 'specified offences' in relation to dangerous offenders.

The officer will then indicate whether the information s/he is putting on the form is relevant to bad character or dangerous offenders by ticking the relevant column.

Relevant evidence/information

Again the officer is provided with an aide memoire of the type of information which may be relevant under this head which s/he should insert into the box provided or additionally attach the relevant documentation to the MG16. The detailed information required has already been the subject of discussion (above).

Such information will include previous convictions but more detailed information than contained on the PNC printout (eg MO; concurrent charges; TICs; cautions, reprimands and final warnings; previous defences used if known).

Evidence or information (other than convictions) includes outstanding investigations, acquittals, discontinuances, previous allegations made against the defendant, incident reports including domestic violence and race.

Finally, the officer in the case and the reviewing lawyer should both sign and date the MG16.

KEY ISSUES—MG16

- Remember BC at the interview stage
- Research BC/risk of dangerousness where potentially relevant
- Submit MG16 at pre-charge stage to the CPS
- If in doubt ask the CPS
- Provide full information on the MG16
- Good MG16s will allow the CPS to do their job properly and use that information in court

EVIDENCE OF DEFENDANT'S BAD CHARACTER AND / OR DANGEROUS OFFENDER INFORMATION

Defendant's full name: ....

DOB: ....

URN

A/S No.

This evidence / information will be revealed to the Duty Prosecutor with Form MG3 for pre-charge advice / charging decision or, where appropriate, post charge.

Evidence of Bad Character (BC) (Evidence for trial)

List below relevant evidence of, or a disposition towards misconduct or other reprehensible behaviour relating to:

Omission of offences of the kind charged, including previous convictions for offence(s) of same or similar description (same charge / indictment) or category;

The commission of any other related type of offences (even where not of similar description or in same category);

The defendant's untruthfulness, e.g. conviction for perjury offences, deception.

Dangerous Offender (DO) Information (Information for sentencing – specified offences of sex / violence)

List below information that may be taken into account by the sentencing court when assessing whether the defendant poses a **significant risk to the public of serious harm.**

Brief details of charge(s) or proposed charge(s)	*BC	*DO	**Relevant Evidence / Information**
			• Previous convictions: include more detailed information than contained on PNC printout, i.e. MO, concurrent charges, TICs, Cautions, Reprimands and Final Warnings, previous defences used if known. • Evidence or information (other than convictions): includes outstanding investigations, acquittals, discontinuances, previous allegations made against the defendant, incident reports including domestic violence / racial etc.
			(Attach relevant documentation)
			(Attach relevant documentation)
			(Attach relevant documentation)

Officer completing form (rank, number or job title)

Name: .... Date: ....

Duty Prosecutor / Reviewing lawyer

Name: .... Date: ....

*May be applicable to BOTH Bad Character and Dangerous Offender provisions (tick as appropriate)

2006/07 (1)

6.28 **MG17: Proceeds of Crime Act (POCA) Review**

6.28.1 **Essentials**

The Proceeds of Crime Act 2002 (POCA) came into force on 24 March 2003, and is specifically designed to take the profit out of crime and hopefully disrupt organized crime by taking away the financial lifeblood of such criminals. Given that 70% of recorded crime is acquisitive, the new legislation was aimed at attacking criminality by removing that profit motive.

The new MG17 was devised at the end of 2006 to raise the profile of POCA investigations and meet the operational need to codify relevant information between agencies. The form includes detailed explanatory notes on the reverse of it, but as will be seen, the officer in the case must go to the FIU and the CPS from the outset wherever POCA is being considered.

Prior to 2003, the law had developed in a piecemeal fashion and was not widely used or enforced. Whenever a police officer thought about confiscation, it was usually only in relation to drug trafficking offences. POCA therefore gives direct effect to the asset recovery strategy, providing new stronger powers for investigators and prosecutors: extending cash seizure and investigatory orders for police; enabling restraint orders to be obtained from the start of an investigation; ensuring the Crown Court becomes the one-stop-shop for all preliminary applications; order and enforcement in relation to criminal confiscation and redefining money laundering offences and closing identified loopholes. It also established an asset recovery agency known as ARA. This role has now fallen to the recently created Serious Organised Crime Agency (SOCA) governed by the Serious Organised Crime and Police Act 2005 (SOCPA) with the function of investigating and recovering criminal assets by the introduction of a civil recovery scheme where a criminal prosecution could not be brought for whatever reason.

Implications for the prosecution team

Both police officers and prosecutors alike should be thinking about 'spotting a POCA' as a matter of course in relation to all types of acquisitive crime, even when the value involved is relatively small.

To assist the prosecution team in this task, there is a local unit of experienced financial investigators (FIU/called Payback Units in the MPS) to whom all queries should be referred at the outset and whose early advice and direction is invaluable. Moreover, a number of police officers and prosecutors have received training on the legislation and it is important for the police to seek early CPS advice in far more cases than they have done in the past, and seek more restraint and confiscation orders than previously.

Seizure of cash and potential restraint orders are matters which need to be considered pre-charge in appropriate cases emphasizing that timely consideration of POCA issues is essential. Moreover the choice of the charges can themselves affect which confiscation legislation applies and whether the extended benefits provisions apply. This essentially Draconian legislation provides potent tools for the prosecution team which should be used to full advantage in the fight against crime.

6.28.2 **The form itself**

One form per defendant is required. The URN number, name and address of the defendant and whether or not there is a pending prosecution is required to be inserted at the top of the form.

Three sections

The form is basically divided into three sections:

- **Section 1—Confiscation Assessment** is completed by the police officer and really acts as an initial aide memoire to that officer as to whether or not POCA applies in the first instance. It will require the officer, if answering in the affirmative to any of the nine questions asked, to refer immediately to the FIU if s/he has not already done so.
- **Section 2—Initial Assessment** is to be completed by the FIO after an assessment of the case and informs the prosecutor of the state of play.
- **Section 3—Request confiscation statement or JARD closure** sets the whole process in motion, as it were, or stops it. JARD, Joint Asset Recovery Database, assists everyone in the collation of information and subsequent enforcement. This is a national database shared by many law enforcement agencies and seeks to 'flag up' duplicate investigations being conducted on the same individual throughout England and Wales. Entries are made for cash seizures, confiscation and laundering investigations.

The explanatory notes on the back of the form briefly explain the terminology used in POCA—for example, 'lifestyle offences'.

The form is 'restricted' and therefore not disclosable to the defence.

POINT TO NOTE

'CPS policy is that POCA should be used as a matter of course, even where the value involved is relatively small. The FIU/Payback Units will carry out an enquiry to determine if a realistic order can be made'.

'POCA does not only apply to drug trafficking'.

'POCA applies only to offences committed on or after March 24th 2003. In some cases therefore, earlier legislation in relation to confiscation and asset recovery need also to be considered, which is not dealt with here'.

Explanatory notes POCA Form MG17

Section 1—Confiscation assessment (for police completion)

There are nine questions for the officer in the case. If s/he answers any of them in the affirmative, s/he must immediately refer it to the FIU and the MG17 form should be attached to the MG3 for pre-charge advice or a decision from the prosecutors. The officer should be considering whether or not the suspect is suitable for a confiscation investigation or not. Confiscation follows conviction and should be considered wherever the defendant has benefited from his/her acquisitive crimes.

Following conviction, but not necessarily, as potential confiscation investigations can run parallel to criminal investigations, the police may undertake such investigations in order to assess a criminal's benefit from crime. The benefit figure can then be calculated back over a period of up to six years and can be considerably more than that for which the criminal has been convicted. This very much depends on the criminal lifestyle that the defendant has led and will usually be determined by the court. The court can make a confiscation order, which is a value order, ie an order made in a sum of money. Financial Investigators will attempt to identify all realisable assets that may be used to satisfy any such orders. Failure to satisfy the order will result in a default sentence being served in full and this is in addition to any other sentence to be served. The debt remains outstanding until paid in full.

1. **Does the evidence reveal any 'criminal lifestyle' offences, eg trafficking of drugs, people or arms, prostitution and child sex; directing terrorism, money laundering, copyright offences, blackmail?**

The above is taken from the definition of criminal lifestyle offences within Schedule 2 to POCA. It further includes all attempts, conspiracies and incitement to commit any of those offences. There is no minimum benefit in a Schedule 2 offence under the Act.

The three key questions for the officer are:

1. whether the offence itself is acquisitive;
2. whether any benefit has been derived from the crime;
3. whether a lifestyle type offence under Schedule 2 to POCA has been committed.

2. **Did the suspect obtain any property or financial gain?**

The key thread running through these offences enabling a confiscation order to be applied for is the obtaining of a benefit.

The suspect will have 'benefited' from the offence(s) whenever s/he has obtained property or a pecuniary advantage, however briefly, and this is so even if the suspect was immediately apprehended and the property has been recovered (Note 4). This line of thinking can even be used in murder investigations where the suspect has benefited from their crime, eg a hit man.

The confiscation process at the Crown Court is dealt with on the balance of probabilities and is used to determine any matter relevant to the confiscation process. This includes whether the defendant has a criminal lifestyle, the benefit from criminal lifestyle, the benefit from general criminal conduct, or the amount to be recovered.

Such criminal lifestyle therefore is established by committing:

- either one of the specified list of offences in Schedule 2 to the Act (above);
- an offence over a period of at least 6 months and the defendant has benefited from conduct which constitutes the offence (see below); and
- conduct forming part of a course of criminal activity (see below).

3. **Could the suspect be charged with 4 or more offences in the current proceedings that will amount to a total benefit, including TICs, of at least £5,000?**

4. **Has the suspect been convicted on at least 2 occasions within the last 6 years of any offence where the total benefit including TICs and the current offences are at least £5,000?**

5. **Has the suspect benefited by at least £5,000, including TICs, from any offending committed over a period of at least 6 months?**

These cover the definition laid down in section 75 of POCA which sets out other potential lifestyle offences where the conduct of the suspect is alleged to be 'part of a course of criminal conduct'. In such non-criminal lifestyle offences, the relevant benefit figure will relate to the offence itself and the value of any TICs and must be over £5000.

In lifestyle cases, assumptions will/will not apply dependent upon whether convicted of a Schedule 2 offence or as defined in section 75 of POCA. The officer must not try and assess the value of the benefit or presume that an offender cannot satisfy the order. Again, the FIU should be consulted.

Where the court decides the defendant has a criminal lifestyle, it may assume all the property transferred to or held by or expended by him/her in a six-year period ending on the date when the current proceedings began resulted from criminal conduct and is therefore eligible to be included in the amount to confiscated. If there is no finding of criminal lifestyle, then only the benefit from the current offence (ie the particular criminal conduct) can be considered when assessing the recoverable amount.

6. Are money-laundering charges being considered in this case?

Money laundering is the term used to describe the method by which criminals process 'dirty' money from illegal activity through a succession of transfers and deals so as to obscure the source of the illegally acquired funds and give the money the appearance of legitimate or 'clean' funds or assets.

> ### POINT TO NOTE—MAIN OFFENCES OF MONEY LAUNDERING
>
> - Concealing, disguising, converting, or transferring criminal property (s 327).
> - Arranging to facilitate the acquisition, retention, use or control of criminal property on behalf of another (s 328).
> - Acquiring, using or having possession of criminal property (s 329).

Note that sections 327 and 328 are 'lifestyle' offences, but section 329 is not. Where it is a potential issue, the case must be taken not to limit the court's powers to maximize confiscation. However, to charge section 327 or section 328 simply to attract the 'lifestyle' provisions could be an abuse of process and traditional legislation, such as the Theft Act (handling stolen goods) must always be considered.

The Crown Prosecutor must show beyond reasonable doubt that the property in question has a criminal origin. 'Criminal property' is anything that represents, in whole or part, benefit from criminal conduct, ie not just money. For example, evidence of the defendant living beyond his/her means.

These offences can apply to the original offender who is able to launder his/her own proceeds of crime as well as to anyone else who deals with these proceeds of crime, either directly or indirectly on their behalf.

Money laundering can be charged as a stand-alone offence or in conjunction with others. Significant attempts to transfer or conceal property should normally merit a separate charge of money laundering. Therefore a money laundering charge ought to be considered where the proceeds are more than de minimis and a defendant charged with the underlying offence has done more than simply consume his/her proceeds of crime. All the three money laundering offences carry heavier penalties than most underlying ones. It is to be noted that potentially all handlers and thieves are also money launderers and can qualify for confiscation if convicted.

7. Are the victim(s) claiming compensation?

Here, compensation can be awarded out of confiscation amounts and before any order is paid—it is not related to compensation for personal injury arising from assault or criminal damage allegations.

8. Has there been a cash seizure in excess of £1,000?

POCA gives powers to the police to seize cash including any type of currency, cheques, bearer bonds, bank drafts, etc which have been derived from or intended for use in crime, and subsequently to secure its forfeiture in civil magistrates' courts proceedings.

POINT TO NOTE—WHEN CASH SEIZURE IS ALLOWED

- There is reasonable belief you have found £1000 or more
- When you have found the cash, you are carrying out a lawful search or are lawfully on the premises where the cash was found
- The suspect is unable to offer you a credible explanation for their possession of the cash and you are unable to verify the explanation
- You believe that the cash may represent the proceeds of crime, or was intended for use in the commission of crime

MINI MOG, 48

Seized cash may not be detained for more than 48 hours, excluding bank holidays and weekends except by order of a magistrate. The officer will need to contact the FIU for advice. A magistrate may then make such an order if satisfied that there are reasonable grounds for the officer's suspicion and that the continued detention is justified for the purposes of investigating its origin or intended use.

Cash can still be forfeited at court even if no criminal charges are brought, or for whatever reason a criminal case does not proceed. The CPS are not involved in part of the cash seizure process and if legal issues arise it is highly recommended that advice is sort from the force solicitor at the earliest opportunity. In this situation, the CPS has neither the power nor a duty to act in such proceedings. However, if the CPS advises a criminal prosecution, then the money seized is likely to form an exhibit in the case, or be held with a view to the court making a confiscation order following conviction.

In these circumstances, the CPS would provide advice to the police on the basis that the issue arises from a criminal offence and is ancillary to contemplated or ongoing criminal proceedings. Conversely, if the CPS advises against prosecution, then either the cash will be returned, or purely civil forfeiture proceedings will continue without CPS involvement.

9. Is a restraint order necessary?

A restraint order prevents assets belonging to the defendant being dissipated without the permission of the Crown Court. This is so that there are sufficient assets to pay any confiscation order that might be made. The order is against the defendant, not the assets. The defendant is allowed to use his/her property as long as s/he does not diminish the value of it. However, if s/he deals with the property in an unauthorized manner, s/he will be in contempt of the court order and can be sent to prison for breaching it.

A restraint order can be made when there is a reasonable cause to believe that the alleged defender has benefited from his criminal conduct and either: a criminal investigation has started, or criminal proceedings have started, or the offender absconds, or there is an application for the reconsideration of the 'available amount' or 'benefit'.

Thus restraint orders can be obtained from the start of an investigation prior to any criminal proceedings commencing.

The court is unlikely to grant an order unless there is a real likelihood of dissipation of the defendant's assets. Decided cases, however, indicate that where an offence involving dishonesty is charged, there is an inference that assets are likely to be so dissipated.

Time is obviously of the essence, when considering a restraint order. Where the officer in consultation with the CPS considers it to be appropriate, s/he should refer it immediately to the FIU for a witness statement and the prosecutor will then prepare a draft order to annex to that statement following a standard template, and will then conduct the application.

10. Next Hearing Date

This merely requires the officer to insert the next hearing date in the magistrates' or Crown Court and sign and date Section 1 of the MG17.

Section 2—Initial assessment (for FIU completion)

The FIU may well be involved prior to any part of the MG17 being completed. However, wherever an affirmative answer has been given to any of the questions 1–9 in Section 1 by the OIC that will then be referred to the FIU for their assessment.

While FIU views about the merits of an application will be considered, they are not conclusive. Financial investigating officers have obtained an enormous amount of experience since POCA was implemented and their expertise is invaluable in such cases. Certainly, their views will be of great assistance to the prosecutor in any decision as to whether or not to pursue a confiscation order.

The FIU will answer questions 11–17 in Section 2:

11. **The case is suitable/not suitable for confiscation proceedings.**
12. **An initial entry has been made/not been made on the JARD system.**
13. **Assets have/have not been identified.**
14. **Restraint may/may not be appropriate in the case.**
15. **Timetable for completion of a financial statement following conviction would be . . .**
16. **There are/are no cash seizure proceedings pending.**
17. **There are/are no forfeiture proceedings pending.**

The FIU will then sign and date Section 2, providing his/her contact details.

It is vital that the FIU's assessment is completed prior to the first court appearance and a prosecutor may require an adjournment pending a reply. This is because POCA at section 70 provides a mandatory power to commit to the Crown Court where the prosecution requests committal with a view to confiscation. The court must say whether it would have committed for sentence in any event.

Note also that POCA applies to youths, but committal of youths would only be considered in exceptional circumstances.

Section 3—Request confiscation statement or JARD closure (for CPS completion)

The prosecutor based on the information on the MG17, his/her own knowledge of the circumstances of the case and the FIU's assessment which will often be given face to face, will then decide whether confiscation is appropriate and request a statement from the FIU to be used in the application to the court by the completion of box 18. The Crown Court will then set out a timetable for confiscation.

If the prosecutor decides not to pursue a confiscation order, s/he must give his/her reasons in box 19 and will then indicate the JARD entry may be closed. Such reasons might include: low value of benefit and no identifiable assets; stolen property recovered and no lifestyle assumptions.

KEY ISSUES—MG17

- Potent new legislation for the prosecution team
- Spot a POCA in any acquisitive case
- Has any benefit (however small) been derived from the crime?
- Think: 'Is your prisoner suitable for a confiscation investigation?'
- Is this a money laundering case?
- Should I be seizing the cash?
- Think ahead about a restraint order
- POCA does not only apply to drug trafficking
- Always involve FIU/CPS at an early stage

PROCEEDS OF CRIME ACT (POCA) REVIEW
(one form for each defendant)

Defendant

URN

Surname: .... Forename(s): ....

D.O.B.: .... Pending cases Y / N

Address: ....

.... Postcode: ....

Section 1 – Confiscation assessment *(for Police completion)*	
If __Yes__ to any question immediately refer to FIU and attach to MG3 / MG3A for pre-charge advice / decision	
1. Does the evidence reveal any 'criminal lifestyle' offences, e.g. trafficking of drugs, people or arms, prostitution and child sex; directing terrorism, money laundering, copyright offences, blackmail?	**Y / N**
2. Did the suspect obtain any property or financial gain?	**Y / N**
3. Could the suspect be charged with **4 or more** offences in the current proceedings that will amount to a total benefit, including TICs, of at least £5,000?	**Y / N**
4. Has the suspect been convicted on at least **2 occasions within the last 6 years** of any offence where the total benefit, including TICs and the current offences are at least £5,000?	**Y / N**
5. Has the suspect benefited by at least £5,000, including TICs, from any offending committed over a period of **at least 6 months?**	**Y / N**
6. Are money laundering charges being considered in this case?	**Y / N**
7. Are the victim(s) claiming compensation?	**Y / N**
8. Has there been a cash seizure in excess of £1,000?	**Y / N**
9. Is a restraint order necessary?	**Y / N**

10. Next hearing date: .... at .... Magistrates / Crown Court

OIC *(print name)*: .... | Date: .... | Tel: ....

CPS lawyer *(print name)*: .... | Date: .... | Tel: ....

Section 2 – Initial Assessment *(for FIU completion)*

11. The case is suitable / not suitable for confiscation proceedings.

12. An initial entry has been made / not been made onto the JARD system. (JARD Case No ....)

13. Assets have / have not been identified.

14. Restraint may / may not be appropriate in the case.

15. Timetable for completion of a financial statement following conviction would be ....

16. There are / are no cash seizure proceedings pending.

17. There are / are no forfeiture proceedings pending.

FIU Officer *(print name)*: .... | Date: .... | Tel: ....

Section 3 – Request confiscation statement or JARD closure *(for CPS completion)*

18. Defendant convicted of: ....

....

The timetable for confiscation is: ....

19. Reasons for not pursuing confiscation: ....

....

CPS Lawyer *(print name)*: .... | Date: .... | Tel: ....

EXPLANATORY NOTES

1   **CPS policy is that POCA should be used as a matter of course even where value involved is relatively small. The FIU will carry out an inquiry to determine if a realistic order can be made.**

Whilst there is no lower limit to the amount of benefit that will trigger POCA please refer to Local Protocol for local arrangements. **ALL** lifestyle cases should be considered as confiscation cases save for drug trafficking cases if the amount trafficked is minimal e.g. passing minor amounts to friends.

POCA does not only apply to drug trafficking

2   POCA applies to offences commited on or after the 24th March 2003. Confiscation may still be possible under earlier legislation and asset recovery should still be considered.

3   'Criminal lifestyle' offences are defined in POCA Schedule 2 and include: drug, people and arms trafficking, money laundering, directing terrorism, copyright offences, counterfeiting coins and notes, prostitution and child sex and blackmail together with attempts, conspiracies and incitement in respect of these offences.

Criminal Lifestyle, can also be found when:

- Offences form part of a course of criminal activity (benefit from FOUR OR MORE offences in these proceedings), where the benefit amounts to at least £5,000 or
- Benefit of at least £5,000 from at least TWO PREVIOUS CONVICTIONS on separate occasions in the last six years.
- Benefit of at lease £5,000 from OFFENCES COMMITTED OVER A PERIOD OF AT LEAST SIX MONTHS.

4   The suspect will have benefited from the offence(s) whenever he / she has obtained property or a pecuniary advantage, however briefly and this is so even if the suspect was immediately apprehended and the property has been recovered.

5   In 'lifestyle cases' assumptions will apply. **DO NOT** try to asses the value of the benefit or presume that the offender cannot satisfy an order. **Seek assistance** from the OIC or the FIU.

6   The money laundering provisions refer to 'criminal property' not simply money. If there is evidence of the defendant living beyond his / her means, charges under sections 327, 328 or 329 POCA 2002 should be considered.

7   If a restraint order has already been obtained, confiscation proceedings will usually follow.

8   If there is no restraint order in place is there a possibility that assets will be dissipated before a confiscation order is made? If so, seek comment from the FIU about the matter.

9   In some cases, you may need to seek an adjournment pending a reply from the FIU. POCA 2002, s.70 contains a mandatory power to commit if the Crown requests committal with a view to confiscation. The Court **MUST** say whether it would have committed for sentence in any event. This power only applies where all offences for which the Prosecution are seeking Confiscation occurred on or after the 24th March 2003.

10   POCA applies to the Youth Court but commital of a youth should only be requested in exceptional circumstances.

11   This question is not referring to compensation for personal injury arising from assault or criminal damage allegations. Compensation can be awarded out of confiscate assets.

12   Whilst FIU views about the merits of an application will be considered, they are not conclusive.

13   Reasons for not pursuing a POCA application might include:

- Low value of benefit and no identifiable assets
- Low value of benefit, stolen property recovered and no lifestyle assumptions
- A compensation order would fully or substantially deprive the defendant of the benefit
- Street level drug dealing by user, no identifiable assets.

6.29 **MG18: Offences Taken into Consideration**

6.29.1 **Essentials**

The MG18 provides the prosecutor, court, and defence with details of the offence(s) that the defendant has admitted and wishes the court to take into consideration (TICs) when sentencing. It also shows the defendant admits them and consents to have them dealt with by way of TIC. Five copies of the form should be provided to the CPS (for court and defence).

There has been a major problem with the recording and use of the TIC system, as it is called, in the past caused by both police officers and prosecutors. A new form has been devised and new guidance issued (May 2007) to counter this but it requires the cooperation of the police and the CPS for it to work properly. It is particularly important that a proactive approach is taken to TICs by investigators and prosecutors in every case (especially PPO cases) given that the Court of Appeal has so clearly confirmed the relevance of TICs in the sentencing process (*R v Miles* [2006] EWCA Crim 256) and the recognized benefits to the CJS generally.

The TIC system means that a defendant may ask a court when it passes sentence to 'take into consideration' other offences of a similar nature. There is no statutory basis for this but it is a useful and well-recognized practice. The criteria for including such offences as TICs are that the defendant admits the offence(s) and consents to it (them) being 'TICed'; that the court has jurisdiction (eg a magistrates' court cannot TIC an indictable offence); and finally that the offences are similar to the one for which the defendant is convicted.

In the case of multiple offenders a number of new rules have been introduced recently (see ss 17–21 of the Domestic Violence, Crime and Victims Act 2004). If police officers are in any doubt they should be discussing strategy at an early stage with prosecutors as to the appropriateness or otherwise of TICs and also whether the TICs should be followed up and charged if subsequently denied at court.

The CPS as endorsed in the Code for Crown Prosecutors 2006 (para 10.4) will now robustly prosecute such outstanding offences where they are subsequently denied and where there is sufficient available evidence to do so. For police officers therefore, it is important that there is such evidence before an offence is 'TICed' and put on the form. Furthermore, police officers should use every available opportunity from the defendant's first booking in at the police station to encourage such admissions. Police stations have posters and TIC notices available which draw attention to the advantages of starting life 'with a clean sheet' as it were. However, it is important that police officers never offer an inducement to a defendant (eg that s/he will be bailed) in return for an admission of a TIC.

The TIC form, MG18, once completed should be available at the very first hearing so that if the case is concluded there and then they can be addressed. Moreover, a victim can receive compensation for a 'TICed' offence (where relevant an MG19—Compensation Claim should be completed). Statistically it will also count as a sanction detection.

There is a specific form of wording which should be employed when formally putting charges and TICs to the accused:

> On the information currently available it appears appropriate to charge you with (x) and have (y) taken into consideration at sentencing. If you accept the offences to be taken into consideration now, but refuse them later in the proceedings, you may be prosecuted for these offences. Do you understand?

6.29.2 **The form itself**

Police station, URN, and name of defendant must be inserted at the top of the form followed by the offence(s) for which the defendant is charged, the hearing date, and which court.

Information of the accused

Then follow five points for the 'information of the accused' in plain English:

- explaining the TIC system to him/her;
- telling the defendant that if s/he subsequently withdraws his/her admission it may result in further prosecution(s) in relation to the TIC(s);
- explaining to the defendant that s/he can volunteer information about TICs either in writing at the bottom of the form (headed 'statement the accused may wish to volunteer') or by letter or in a separate statement to the police;
- telling the defendant to sign all the sheets in the schedule of TICs attached to the front sheet and to sign the specific receipt below (entitled 'receipt to be signed by the accused').

Receipt to be signed by the accused

Highlighted in a box this section acknowledges that the defendant has received a copy of the document and must be signed and dated (as well as all schedules attached) and indicating who it was 'in the presence of', ie before which police officer.

Statement the accused may wish to volunteer

This section must also be signed and dated stating who it is in the presence of. The defendant will not always add anything to what s/he has already said in interview. If the admissions are in the course of the interview (usually at the end) it is helpful if police officers can add a short descriptive note on the MG15 showing admissions made to each listed TIC and the number of TICs taken from the schedules is marked in the margin against each admission.

Schedule of offence(s) taken into consideration

The second part of the form at page 2 is the part the officer will complete with full details of the TICs together with a column for completion at court. The top of the form will again contain details of the defendant's name, URN, and the A/S No also.

There are seven columns for the officer to complete in relation to each individual TIC admitted.

The number of each TIC will be written sequentially so as to avoid any doubt when the defendant in court is admitting or denying them. The number should correspond to any additional information put in by the officer as suggested above (eg interview notes). The crime reference number should be inserted along with the place the offence was committed and the date of the offence(s) (in chronological order).

Details of offence(s)

These are important. The form tells the officer to record the PNLD offence code as well as all 'relevant factors'—voluntary admission, vulnerable victim, and if compensation is required (in which case an MG19 should be attached).

The prosecutor at court may be required to outline the relevant facts on any particular TIC so it is in this column that the officer should provide pertinent information including any other evidence, eg forensics that corroborate the offence. This would go to the strength of the evidence against the defendant and indicate to the prosecutor this offence could be charged if the defendant subsequently denies it in court. Any aggravating factor such as vulnerable victims or offence committed on bail or mitigating factor, eg that the defendant admitted TICs at the earliest opportunity, can be noted here also.

Then follows the name of the victim and the value of the property taken/damaged or whether it was recovered.

Court use only

This must be completed by the prosecutor indicating clearly against each TIC whether it was accepted or not. Prosecutors must ensure that a copy of the TIC schedule is returned, with this column completed in every case. They have been remiss on this in the past resulting in extra work for the police administrators in finding out the results. Police also have responsibilities to notify victims of results in these cases.

Prosecuting a denied TIC

With a robust and proactive approach, where a TIC is denied in court immediate consideration should be given to prosecuting the denied TIC. Best practice dictates this decision should have been made between the police and the prosecutor in advance so that they can tell the court and the defendant there and then whether they intend to proceed and lay an information where appropriate to ensure the court finally has adequate sentencing powers. Such a decision will depend on the details of evidence against the defendant revealed by the police, discussions prior to the court hearing with the police and any explanation given to the court by the defendant for his/her denial of the previously admitted offences.

A clear line should be ruled after the last TIC entry on each MG18; this avoids any subsequent claim by a defendant that TICs have been added without their endorsement. The defendant must sign the TIC schedule at the bottom of every page (where more than one sheet).

KEY ISSUES—MG18

- Provides the CPS/defence/court with details of 'TICed' offences
- Shows defendant admits them and consents to having the offences dealt with by way of TIC
- Consider TICs at earliest opportunity
- Do not offer any inducements for a TIC
- Completion of MG18 prior to first hearing
- Full information about TIC offence and other supporting evidence
- Proactive stance of the prosecution where TICs denied

OFFENCES TAKEN INTO CONSIDERATION

URN [ ][ ][ ][ ]

Station: .... Date: ....

To (Surname): .... Forename(s): ....

Memorandum for the Information of the Accused

Charged / indicted Offence(s): ....

For hearing / trial at:. .... on: ....

1. The attached schedule gives particulars of .... offences, which you have admitted committing but have not been charged with.

2. If you plead guilty or are found guilty of any offence(s) with which you have been charged you can, before any sentence is passed, admit all or any of the offence(s) in the attached schedule, and ask the court to take them into consideration.

3. If you withdraw your admissions to these additional offences that you wish the court to take into consideration, those offence(s) may result in further prosecutions(s).

4. If you wish to volunteer any further information concerning any of these other offences you may do so in writing, *either* at the bottom of this form or in a separate letter. If you prefer, you may ask a police officer to take any statement you may wish to give.

5. Please sign **all** the sheets in the schedule containing the offences to be taken into consideration **and** immediately below the last offence recorded. Then sign the receipt below, and keep for your information the copy of this document.

Receipt to be signed by the accused

I have received a copy of this document. Signature: ....

Date: .... In the presence of: ....

Statement the accused may wish to volunteer

....

....

....

....

....

....

Date: .... Signature: ....

In the presence of: ....

MG18

SCHEDULE OF OFFENCE(S) TAKEN INTO CONSIDERATION

Name of accused (Surname): .... Forename(s): ....

URN ☐ ☐ ☐ ☐

A/S No.

Page No. .... of ....

No.	Crime Ref. No.	Place committed	Date of offence	Details of offence(s) For **EACH** offence: • record PNLD offence code • **relevant factors** – voluntary admission, vulnerable victim, etc. • if compensation is required attach **MG19**	Name of victim	Property (a) Value (b) Recovered (c) Damaged	COURT USE ONLY Accepted at court? 'Y' or 'N'

Signature of accused ....

Rule off any remaining space after the last TIC has been entered, and invite the accused to sign beneath the final entry (repeat process where there is more than one sheet).

2006/07 (1)

6.30 **MG19: Compensation Claim**

6.30.1 **Essentials**

This form is given to the victim or witness to complete the details of their loss, injury or damage and will then enable the prosecutor to make an application for compensation at court. Unfortunately they are not always on the file submitted (not necessarily the fault of the police) so it is important that the police tick the relevant compensation box at the bottom of the MG5 where the MG19 is not submitted to alert the prosecutor. Best practice is for this form to be completed at the same time as the statement of the complainant is being taken. At the very least a victim can include in their statement an estimate of their loss or damage although the court prefer only to award compensation when certain rather than estimated costs are claimed and are supported by relevant documentation.

6.30.2 **The form itself**

Where an MG19 is completed it will contain the victim's name and address and is for the eyes of the police, prosecutor, and court only. Information as to victim's details should be included on the MG6 prior to the completion of an MG19.

The police will fill out the top of the form with the name of the defendant, the offence charged and its date and the URN.

Compensation form: Notes for guidance

'Notes for guidance' to victims and witnesses tell them how to complete the forms and stress the need for timeliness in its return to the police within 14 days. Delay may mean an award of compensation is not granted even where merited. It is further stressed that it is the magistrate or judge who has the discretion to award compensation and it is not in the hands of the prosecution team.

Each victim should have been given an explanatory leaflet entitled 'victims of crime' which additionally refers to the fact that a personal injury claim can also be pursued via the Criminal Injuries Compensation Authority.

The form is divided into five sections, A–E, dependent on the type of injury/loss/damage for which compensation is being claimed.

A. Property stolen (and not recovered) or damaged (other than road traffic collisions)

Victims are asked to provide documentary evidence to support their claim, eg copies of receipts, estimates, bills. Originals should be retained by the police with the victim's details edited out so they can be passed on to the defence.

B. Other financial loss (incurred as a result of the offence)

This relates to, for example, loss of earnings (because of injury); taxi fares (because no car after road traffic accident (RTA)), travelling expenses (to hospital). Again these claims should be supported by relevant documentation.

309

C. Personal injury (Also include injury sustained as a result of a road traffic collision)

Again any claim should be backed up by medical evidence. Where the victim has ticked the medical consent box on the back of the MG11 the police can obtain such evidence on their behalf. The nature of their injuries, the medical treatment received and the continuing effects if they have not fully recovered should be documented here.

Additionally the last page of the MG19 must be completed relating to details of doctor, dentist, or any other specialist (in PI cases only) and including details of any attendance at dentist, doctor, or hospital. This information assists the police in obtaining the relevant statements.

D. Road traffic collision/damage

This relates solely to road traffic accidents and the damage caused as a result.

Details of the victim's insurance company should be given as well as costs of repair (with supporting documentation).

A compensation order by the court can only be made for an RTA in respect of an offence under the Theft Act 1968 or where the defendant is uninsured and compensation is not payable by a Motor Insurance Bureau Agreement (limited to £300).

E. Insurance details

These must be given so the victim can make a claim for loss of no claims bonus excess to pay on the policy (as long as the necessary supporting documentation is included).

It is important that victims notify the court of any claims they are going to make in relation to their car hire or medical insurance in this regard.

Finally, the complainant must fill out their personal details on the back page of the form.

KEY ISSUES—MG19

- Allows victim/witness to complete details of their injury/loss/damage
- Provides the CPS with information to make application for compensation at court
- Alerts the CPS by ticking of compensation box at bottom of MG5
- Best practice is to complete MG19 when taking a statement
- Supporting documentation is essential

COMPENSATION CLAIM

For Police Use

R v

URN

Offence:

Date of offence:

COMPENSATION FORM: NOTES FOR GUIDANCE

If you have any queries regarding completion of this form, contact: ....

The offence for which proceedings have been instituted may give rise to the question of compensation. The relevant sections of pages 2-4 of this form should be completed clearly in **BLOCK CAPITALS** and returned to the police in the Freepost envelope provided.

It is very important that this form is completed as soon as possible. If sent to you by post it must be returned within 14 days. Failure to return this form on time may lead to the case proceeding without an application for compensation being made on your behalf. If you do find that you require extra time, please contact the case clerk to see if an extension is possible.

COMPLETE ONLY THE SECTIONS WHICH APPLY TO YOU. THIS FORM MUST BE SIGNED AND DATED ON PAGE 3.

PLEASE NOTE: **The magistrate or judge will decide whether or not to order compensation. We have no authority over this decision.**

Personal injury claims can also be pursued via the Criminal Injuries Compensation Authority – please refer to the enclosed victim of crime leaflet for details.

A. Property stolen (and not recovered) or damaged

(N.B. in the case of road traffic collisions, please complete section D)

Relates to property stolen or damaged that has not been recovered by police. This section does not apply to damage caused in a road traffic collision – please use Section D.

It is important that you provide documentary evidence to support your claim. This means that copies of receipts, estimates or bills should be provided wherever possible. Property recovered by police but not yet returned to you (due to it being used in evidence) should not be claimed for, as this will be restored upon completion of the court case.

Costs of replacement or repair (including VAT).

Description of item(s):

....

....

....

....

....

....

....

Amount:

2006/07 (1)

B. Other financial loss

Relates to other expenses. For example:

- Loss of earnings – if you had to take unpaid time off work due to injuries sustained
- Taxi fares – due to being without your car as a result of a traffic collision / criminal damage
- Travelling expenses – incurred by having to visit hospital / specialists as a result of injuries sustained.

It is important that you provide documentary evidence to support your claim. This means that copies of receipts, estimates or bills should be provided wherever possible.

Details of other financial loss or expenses incurred as a result of the offence:

Description of item(s):	**Amount:**
Total:	

C. Personal injury *(Also include injury sustained as a result of a road traffic collision)*

Relates to injuries sustained as the result of an assault or traffic collision. It is important that you also fill in page 4 of this form, as we will need to obtain medical evidence on your behalf. Please continue on a separate page if the space provided is not sufficient. In serious injury cases, where you may suffer long-term effects, please keep the case clerk informed of your condition as the case progresses.

The police cannot obtain medical evidence on your behalf unless you have authorised us to do so. You MUST complete and sign a form giving us authority to ask for details of your medical condition to be disclosed. We can then contact the hospital, your GP or dentist and ask them to provide a statement detailing your injuries and treatment. The police officer in charge may have already asked you to complete a form. If not, please contact the case clerk as soon as possible.

Nature of injuries:

Details of medical treatment received *(please also complete)*

Have you fully recovered? Yes ☐ No ☐ If 'No', describe continuing ill effects:

D. Road traffic collision / damage

Relates to traffic collisions only. It is important that you provide us with details of your insurance company so we can liaise with them during the prosecution. A copy of this bill / estimate regarding damage MUST be attached.

Description of damage:

....

....

....

....

....

....

....

....

....

....

....

....

....

....

Cost of repair: **Written estimate / bill attached? Yes ☐ No ☐**

Name and address of your insurance company

....

....

E. Insurance details

It is important that you tell us of any claims you have already made or intend to make via your car / home / medical insurance. Please ensure that a copy of your claim form and / or the company's reply is attached to this form.

Loss of 'no claims bonus'?   **Yes ☐ No ☐**   **If 'Yes', please give amount:**

Excess on policy?   **Yes ☐ No ☐**   **If 'Yes', please give amount:**

Confirmatory letter from insurance company attached?   Yes ☐ No ☐

Signed: **Date:**

Personal details of claimant

Name: ....

Address: ....

....

Home telephone: .... **Business:** ....

E-mail address: ....

Details of doctor / dentist (personal injury cases ONLY)

1. Did you attend Accident and Emergency as a result of your injuries?   **Yes** ☐ **No** ☐   If 'Yes', please confirm

Hospital: ....

Date of attendance: ....

Doctor's name if known: ....

2. Were you referred to a specialist / other department?   **Yes** ☐ **No** ☐   If 'Yes', please confirm

Hospital: ....

Date(s) of re-attendance(s): ....

Doctor / dentist's name if known or department: ....

3. Have you seen your GP / dentist in relation to these injuries?   **Yes** ☐ **No** ☐   If 'Yes', please confirm

GP / dentist's name: ....

Surgery address: ....

Date of attendance(s): ....

6.31 **MG20: Further Evidence/Information Report**

6.31.1 **Essentials**

The whole purpose of this form is that it should accompany any additional evidence or information about a case every time such further material is submitted to the CPS. It provides tick boxes (not exhaustive) for the police officer to indicate to the prosecutor what forms/evidence/information are attached to the MG20 and also allows a space for the police officer to provide comments about the case or material submitted or directly answer any memo from the CPS.

Where material is submitted and not accompanied by the MG20 there is therefore no audit trail and in such circumstances vital evidence and information may be lost or not tied up with the correct file. It is therefore a very important form.

This document is again one for police/CPS eyes only and will not itself be disclosed to the defence.

6.31.2 **The form itself**

The completion of the URN, the originating police office for the memo, the defendant's name, next court date and offences (in general terms) must all be inserted here. This will enable the CPS to link up the MG20 and attach contents to the original file and also prioritize it in terms of the next court appearance.

Unfortunately, only too often MG20s arrive late and are not linked up to the correct file in time for the court appearance. However, in the age of IT and indeed Integrated Prosecution Teams (IPT) in some areas, it is hoped such problems will cease.

Submitted as indicated

Then follows a large number of tick boxes against which the officer should tick the relevant box where s/he has attached the documentation listed. These tick boxes cover most of the usual types of additional material, albeit best practice as outlined has indicated that many of the forms (save for updated ones) should have been available from the beginning at the charging centre:

- bad character/dangerous offender (MG16);
- CCTV—tapes/discs;
- case file information (MG6);
- compensation—receipts/estimates (MG19);
- conviction memorandum (certified copy) (necessary if bad character is to be put before the court or in relation to, eg, proof of disqualification);
- custody record (copy) or updated copy;
- DVLA printout (usually obtained by the court);
- defendant previous convictions/cautions, etc (Phoenix printout);
- disclosure schedules (MG6B/MG6C/MG6D/MG6E);

- drink drive forms roadside/hospital/station procedure (MG6DDA-D—not covered in this chapter);
- copy exhibits and exhibit list (MG12);
- forensic evidence (including MG21);
- copy of medical report/surgeon's statement;
- Order on Conviction Application (MG13);
- proceedings/investigations outstanding (officers to provide full details to CPS);
- POCA application (MG17);
- copy Home Office Production Order (HOPO) required when the defendant is already in prison for another offence and has to be produced by that prison before the court;
- record of interview/recorded interviews (MG15);
- special measures assessment (MG2);
- TIC schedule (MG18);
- witness availability list (MG10);
- updated witness list (MG9);
- previous convictions/cautions of witnesses;
- copy statement of witness or original MG11;
- 'Other—specify' (it is useful to complete this tick box even in an abbreviated form where the others do not apply since it acts as a record of what has been provided by the police to both parties).

MG20s can be kept in date order on the CPS file and their proper completion is therefore essential for efficient file handling.

Further information/remarks

This is unfortunately a very small section at the bottom of the form. It is preferable for it to be typed and for a clear indication of where a continuation sheet has been added. Officers sometimes try and scribble (often illegibly), handwritten responses to CPS memos here which are very important to the progress of the case. Far better to start on a separate sheet and type it and merely indicate at the bottom of the MG20 to see the attached sheet. In certain circumstances (eg where a witness withdrawal statement is obtained), protocols (eg for domestic violence/rape) require the officer to complete mandatory detailed information also on the MG20.

Signature

The officer must sign the MG20 along with his/her supervisor who should also check that all relevant documents are attached and that the form is legibly and accurately completed prior to its forwarding to the CPS.

KEY ISSUES—MG20

- Important form acting as audit trail for information from police
- Provides the CPS with further evidence/information concerning a case
- Tells the CPS what forms/material is attached to submission with MG20
- Comments and replies must be clear, detailed, and legible

MG20

FURTHER EVIDENCE / INFORMATION REPORT

To: Crown Prosecution Service   URN

Office: ....

R v ....

Next Court date: .... at: .... Magistrates' / Youth / Crown Cou

Offence(s): ....

Submitted as indicated

Bad Character / Dangerous Offender (**MG16**)	☐	Order on Conviction Application (**MG13**) ☐
CCTV – tapes / discs	☐	Proceedings / investigations outstanding ☐
Case file information (**MG6**)	☐	Proceeds of Crime Act (POCA) (**MG17**) ☐
Compensation – receipts / estimates (**MG19**)	☐	Prisoner production copy order ☐
Conviction memorandum (certified copy)	☐	Record(s) of interview (ROTI / ROVI, etc) (**MG15**) ☐
Custody record (copy) or updated copy	☐	Recorded interviews (video / tape / DVD) ☐
DVLA printout	☐	Special Measures Assessment (**MG2**) ☐
Defendant previous convictions / cautions etc.	☐	TIC schedule(s) (**MG18**) ☐
Disclosure (**MG6B / MG6C / MG6D / MG6E**)	☐	Witness availability list updated (**MG10**) ☐
Drink drive forms roadside / hospital / station procedure	☐	Witness list updated (**MG9**) ☐
Exhibit (copy documents)	☐	Witness previous convictions / cautions ☐
Exhibit list (**MG12**)	☐	Witness statement (copy) – witness (**MG11**) ☐
Forensic Evidence (*including MG21 / MG21A*)	☐	Witness statement (original) – witness (**MG11**) ☐
Medical report / Surgeon's statement (copy)	☐	Other – specify ☐

Further information / remarks (continued on separate sheets if necessary)

All documents indicated above are attached

Officer in case: .... Rank / Job title: .... No.: .... Date: ....

Supervisor's name: .... Rank / Job title: .... No.: .... Date:..................

2006/07 (1)

6.32 **MG21: Submission of Work for Scientific Examination**

6.32.1 **Essentials**

This form is for police to complete to accompany samples submitted for forensic examination and indicate to the scientist the relative priority rating. It provides an audit trail of scientific submissions and circumstances of the case; instructs the FSP (Forensic Science Provider) to provide details of specific points to prove the case and the scientist with target dates for case management together with a list of exhibits submitted for examination.

Mini MOG, 41

The key to successful forensic strategy is early communication. Such early contact with the FSP and the detailed and correct completion of the MG21 is a priority not just for police officers but also for the CPS.

Borough Forensic Managers (BFM) must also play a key role and are the focal point in assisting the prosecution team and pointing them in the right direction in order to ascertain the potential evidential value of the submission.

In the past the CPS have rarely been involved in discussions concerning the submission of forensic evidence, and in very few cases have the FSP been provided with a full picture of the evidence in a case. As a result there has been a failure to maximize forensic opportunities and so ensure that justice is done.

Many Crown Prosecutors have now received training in forensic awareness and forensic opportunities. BFMs now have the necessary level of understanding and expertise to make informed decisions. Police officers and the CPS alike are encouraged to get to know their BFMs and seek their advice at an early stage and discuss all potential issues arising in a case with them prior to submitting them to the FSP.

Protocols

Officers should ensure full awareness of the various protocols in existence relating to, for example, fingerprints and DNA evidence (since 2004) also any local protocols relating to timings of submissions. The evidential protocols require a 'staged approach' to the provision of evidence to the CPS basically separating the identification of evidence sufficient for charging purposes from its subsequent use in court and interpretation.

It is basically a resource issue of both time and money such that the evidence is tailored to the needs of the stage at which the offender is within the criminal justice system. It cannot be emphasized enough that the BFM should be the officer's first point of call where they are in any doubt about the staged approach or the viability of a referral to the FSP. This development is in line with the developments within the CJS generally and the Criminal Procedure Rules (since 2005) which explain the duties of all parties in the case to identify at an early stage those issues which are in dispute in a case and agree all others. There is then an expectation that the trial will only be on those disputed issues.

Stage 1 merely requires enough evidence (hearsay) to identify the suspect sufficient for a charging decision, first appearance, and advanced information to the defence.

Stage 2 depends on what plea is entered. If a guilty plea is entered no further work is needed but if it is a not guilty or no indication and the case has been adjourned for service of the case then this requires a full direct evidential comparison between the defendant and the crime scene sufficient for the usual contested case. Statements from the scene of crime and the FSP and the continuity statements would usually be required.

Stage 3, usually after receipt of the defence statement following re-review of the evidence, will require a full evaluative statement specifically tailored to the issues which have arisen in the case. This may well involve further analysis and interpretation of the sample submitted. Obviously this will involve the FSP receiving a copy of the defence statement in all cases as soon as possible where forensic evidence is involved.

6.32.2 **The form itself**

The MG21 replaces the MGFSP and was redesigned in conjunction with the FSPs. The form is now set out in a chronological sequence with the main administrative elements contained on the front page. It also provides more detail than the previous form and reflects modern terminology familiar to police officers.

Page 1 of the form

This is the administrative section. As usual the URN must be recorded at the top of each page of the form.

1. Police Crime Reference Number

This is the specific crime report number.

2. Scientific Support Reference Number

This is the specific scientific support reference number.

3. FSP Reference Number

This section must be left blank for the FSP to use only

4. Contact Details

This will include not only details of the OIC but also an alternative point of contact, eg the BFM and importantly the contact details of the reviewing CPS lawyer also.

5. Supervisory authority for submission

The signing of this demonstrates that the supervisor both agrees with the priority for the submission shown by the officer subsequently and that s/he authorizes the submission to the FSP.

Where for any reason the case does not proceed and forensic evidence is no longer required it will be the supervisor's responsibility to ensure that the FSP is informed forthwith to prevent unnecessary costs and resources. This is further spelt out in print at the bottom of the page.

6. Budgetary authority for submission

This will come from a supervisor (usually the BFM) but not necessarily the same as at 5. Unauthorized submissions will not be accepted by the FSP. All forensic managers are required to manage their own forensic budget. Authority will be granted based on the evidential value and validity of the submission. Close liaison therefore between the BFM and the CPS is essential since once forensic evidence for a crime has been obtained no further submissions are usually authorized.

Where aspects of the submission are required urgently the box at the bottom of the front page needs to be ticked and section 10 will also need to be completed.

Best practice dictates that in this case the officer in the case will have contacted the FSP personally in advance of the submission of the MG21.

Page 2 of the form

7. Circumstances of Incident(s)

As much information as possible needs to be given to the FSP under this heading. Paying attention to detail is all important.

Thus the date, time, and specific offences being investigated must be inserted a the top of the form including in particular whether a suspect has been identified or not.

Section 7 has three parts, (a)–(c):

a) Give details of surrounding circumstances and MO of offence, include address, location, or vehicle reg. where appropriate

It is important that this section is completed in sufficient detail for the FSP to obtain a clear idea of all the surrounding circumstances of the offence. It may well be appropriate to attach key witness statements to provide a clear picture to the FSP.

Example—poor practice

Circumstances—**suspect broke** into a house and **attacked** a female victim in her bedroom. Victim's flatmate has awoken and **disturbed** the suspect. A **fight** followed and suspect shot victim's flatmate in leg. Suspect has been **arrested**.

The above is an inadequate description which will not assist the FSP or point them in the right direction.

'Suspect'—Full description and clothing worn required.

'Broke'—How precisely did the suspect obtain entry to the premises?

'Attack'—The full nature of the attack and forensic opportunities must be spelled out.

'Disturbed'—What exactly does this mean? Opportunities for DNA/transfer of fibres?

'Fight'—What precisely happened? What are the level of injuries? What is the nature of the involvement of the parties?

'Arrested'—In what circumstances? What did he say? What was his condition?

b) What account (if any) has been given by the suspect(s) [specify who] and include admission, denials, defences, etc.

c) Add any other relevant information eg an account provided by the subject(s) [specify who], other aggravating factors or whether there is a child victim, vulnerable/intimidated witness involved.

By the end of this section therefore, the FSP should have a clear picture essential to grasp the full details and implications of the case. This leads onto the next section which is basically spelling out the right questions to be asking the FSP. This does not involve telling them how to do their job but assists them to focus on the kinds of issues which need to be addressed in each particular case.

8. What are the points to prove?

Best practice suggests it is extremely helpful for the CPS lawyer and BFM to have an input into this section to ensure that all the key evidential points and forensic opportunities are covered. As indicated, in the past the CPS have not had any input until much later in the day, if at all, resulting possibly in the wrong questions being addressed by the FSP.

The reasonable lines of enquiry as well as the evidential points to prove should be outlined in this section. As it states on the form 'these issues should reflect the advice, the case strategy and the decisions that have been agreed between the investigator, prosecutor and where appropriate forensic scientist ... aspects of the examination necessary to support a charging decision' should also be included here.

This section is all about highlighting the key issues and asking the right questions.

POINT TO NOTE

In the example of poor practice above we would specifically need to know:

- whether there is anything linking the suspect to the scene, eg point of entry, handling of victim, fight with flatmate, point of exit, clothing and samples taken on arrest;
- whether there is anything linking the suspect with the gun (eg was it retrieved, is there residue, were bullets found?);
- whether there is evidence that the suspect attacked the victim or the flatmate;
- whether there is evidence that he broke into the house.

It is understood that the FSP prefer open, more general questions thus allowing them also to think outside the box. Where there are specific questions the officer wants addressed it may be best to contact the FSP directly.

Further information that could also be inserted is, for example, the crime scene assessment; whether there are any links between the crime and other crimes or between the suspect and other suspects or crimes; whether the case is linked to a previous submission; whether it forms part of a series of investigations; whether there is any evidence to corroborate/refute a suspect's allegation, eg that sex was consensual or that tears to the clothing tended to show force was used.

The FSP may well be able to put up scientific barriers to counter defence arguments where they have a detailed knowledge of the case.

Page 3 of the form

9. Additional information attached to this form

A list of tick boxes suggests further information that may be relevant to the case whereby the specific box can be ticked and information added describing its nature and relevance is useful.

Sexual offences form (for all sexual offences)		Scene Examiner's Report	
NFFFID Form (national firearms forensic intelligence data base for all firearms offences)		Photographs/Visual records (eg CCTV/ scene video, etc)	
Firearms Safety Form		Plans	
Toxicology Form		Witness/Victim's Statements (often extremely useful)	
DNA Match Report		Critical Success Factor Forms	

Other (please specify): ....

The critical success factor forms are forensic science service forms which assist with brief additional information not contained on the MG21 upon which the FSP will rely according to the samples submitted and type of offence. Indeed they are only available for certain types of offence; non-sexual assaults involving blood and fibres, auto crime, and burglary involving blood and fibres, offences involving broken glass, offences involving footwear impressions.

10. Contact with FSP

The form reminds the officer that 'it is advisable to contact the FSP before submission where there is NO SUSPECT and/or where there is an URGENT aspect to the work'. This is essential. It is always advisable to speak to the BFM/CPS and then contact the FSP directly in order to effectively negotiate a timescale which, once inserted in the form at 12 (key dates) becomes in a sense a form of contract between the prosecution and the FSP.

Then follows a series of **critical questions** which will be relevant to the priority to be given to the forensic submission:

Are aspects of this submission required urgently?—Y/N
If YES to whom does the urgent aspect relate?

The provision of the deceased/victim/witness/suspect number as specified by the officer in the next two sections is required here.

Has the work been discussed with any representative of the FSP?—Y/N

If yes the OIC must provide the time, date and name of the FSP representative.

Specify any related Police or FSP reference numbers of any previous submissions (e.g. related DNA crime stain submission).

Provide details of what was discussed and agreed with the FSP prior to submission.

11. Details of Deceased/Victim/Witness

Full details should be provided including date of birth, occupation, ethnicity code, and PNC warning signs in relation to all of the above and additionally any person subject for elimination. These will be numbered and referred to both above and below in the form by that number.

Page 4 of the form

12. Suspect key dates

This is a very important part of the form. The CPS, OIC and FSP should always agree a specific FSP delivery schedule to ensure all evidence is obtained within the agreed time limits. This section must be completed in respect of each suspect and basically relates to the priority to be given to the submission and subsequent agreement of timescales within which the FSP will complete its examination and deliver the results. Such information should also be inserted onto the MG6 form under Forensic Evidence for the information of the prosecutor at court.

The suspect's usual details—name, date of birth, PNC warning sign, occupation, ethnicity code, date and time or arrest and arrest number, DNA bar code reference—must also be provided.

Where the suspect is a PYO, YO or PPO the relevant box should be ticked which will in effect ensure that timescales given nationally and agreed targets set for completion of such cases are adhered to.

Various options then follow in relation to the state of play of the suspect within the CJS. The relevant box must be ticked and key dates inserted:

- **Known suspect—not yet arrested**
- **Pre-charge—arrested (currently in police custody)**

Both of these will be urgent and require a date to be agreed for despatch of the work after discussion with the FSP as previously indicated.

- **Pre-charge and on police bailed to return**

This will include the return bail date, the date for items to be received by the FSP laboratory and the date agreed with the FSP by which the necessary results to assist the charging decision will be dispatched.

- **Charged and bailed to court**

This will include the date charged, the date fixed for service of the prosecution case, the next key court date, eg court date.

- **Charged and remanded in custody**

This will include the date charged, the date of the next remand hearing, the agreed action date for the full code test (if applicable), the date fixed for service of the prosecution case, the date for items to be received by the FSP and finally the date agreed with the FSP by which the necessary results will be despatched.

In this instance particular regard needs to be paid to the custody time limits, since timeliness of delivery must be in keeping with them. It is important that the FSP is updated about all key dates in the progress of the case at court and in the event of any delays the CPS will have to go back to the court and request an adjournment and explain the reasons for it. The FSP must therefore keep them fully informed of any changes to the timetable of delivery.

- **Post-plea requirement**

Early consultation prior to the setting of court dates is essential where further scientific examination or evaluation is required. Before or after the plea and case management hearing (PCMH), especially where a conference has been held with counsel—to which FSP can be invited to attend in appropriate cases—the reviewing CPS lawyer may have a clear idea of issues to be raised at trial. This may have arisen from the defence statement, a copy of which should be sent to the FSP for their input where appropriate. Additionally witness availability dates should be considered prior to the setting of any fixed trial date. The FSP will also be invaluable with input into how best any forensic evidence may be presented at trial.

Page 5 of the form

Items for scientific examination

This form is to be completed in duplicate. It is vital that all items are properly packaged and labelled to preserve the integrity of the evidence.

Any known health and safety risks must be specifically noted (eg Aids, hepatitis, scabies). Sharp and hazardous items must be appropriately packaged and labelled and marked with the appropriate label.

The officer should consult the BFM if s/he is in any doubt about the handling of samples or their labelling. Poor packaging can result in loss of evidence, secondary transfer, and wastes time and money and can certainly open up opportunities for the defence. Indeed the value that proper packaging gives to the integrity and continuity of the evidence can only be appreciated when it is lost, damaged, or devalued through neglect.

POINTS TO NOTE

- Package and label asap
- Appropriate sized packaging
- What is packaging/what is exhibit?
- Has anything been added to exhibit?
- Do not handle items unnecessarily
- Do not talk, cough, or sneeze over exhibits
- Take exhibit bag to evidence
- Collect all potential evidence
- Handle one item at a time
- Never reopen bags
- Consider storage of packaging materials

Forensic Science Service-CPS course 2007

It is essential that every sample/item submitted is given a separate bar code (DNA) reference or exhibit number, an exhibit bag seal number (the exhibit number recorded must correspond to those on the exhibit label), and further details of the items—with descriptions, where recovered, to whom the item relates, the date and time it was found or taken and finally the name of the person who seized the items also.

Method of delivery

The bottom of the form provides a tick box selection relating to the method of delivery by either: hand, courier, registered/recorded post and requires the name of the person delivering it and a signature to ensure safe delivery and continuity of exhibits. There is a final tick box relating to informing the SIO exhibits officer if they need to be contacted prior to the return of any exhibit to the force.

6.32.3 **MG21A: Submission of Additional Work for Scientific Examination**

This form should be filled out in the event of additional samples being sent to the FSP after an MG21 has already been completed. The information required to be inserted on the form will refer back to the original MG21.

- **Section A—Police and FSP reference numbers must be inserted**
- **Section B—Additional laboratory examination/work required**

  This is as a result of either additional exhibits; additional deceased/victim/witness; further information in the case; additional suspect(s); other reason—in which case it needs to be specified precisely what is required.

  The relevant box in relation to these must be ticked and referred back to the original MG21 or a newly submitted items for scientific examination form in respect of additional exhibits.

- **Section C—Priority and authorisation**

  Again this requires the relevant tick box to be noted depending on the state of play of a suspect in relation to the CJS: no known suspect, known suspect not yet arrested, pre-charge arrested in police custody, pre-charge and police bail to return, charged and bailed to court, charged and remanded in custody, post-plea requirement.

  Both supervisory and budgetary authorization must be obtained in respect of the MG21A also. The box requiring aspects of submission for the urgent consideration of FSP should also be ticked. In which case the FSP should have been contacted prior to submission by the OIC.

- **Section D—Details of further deceased/victim/witness**

  This section must be completed where the relevant box in Section B was ticked if there is an additional person here.

- **Section E—New information relating to the circumstances of the case and additional points to prove**

  This must be filled out in detail as per the instructions in the original MG21 where further information in relation to the case has been received.

  Never think of forensics as something to do with the FSP. The latter should be viewed as part of the prosecution team with all parties including the OIC, BFM, CPS reviewing lawyer and the FSP themselves all working together communicating and sharing information to enable all forensic opportunities to be obtained in any particular case.

KEY ISSUES—MG21

- Provides audit trail of scientific submissions to the FSP
- Tells the FSP relevant priority rating
- Informs on circumstances of the case
- Details points to prove for the FSP
- Agrees target dates for case management
- Early liaison with BFM/CPS essential

MG21

SUBMISSION OF WORK FOR SCIENTIFIC EXAMINATION

URN

1. Police Crime Reference Number:

....

3. FSP Reference Number:

2. Scientific Support Reference Number:

....

(FSP Use On

4. Contact Details

Submitting Force: ....

Officer in the case: ....

Division / Area: ....

Tel: ....

Police Station (incl. Postcode): ....

Mobile: ....

....

Facsimile: ....

Force / Station Code: ....

E-mail: ....

Specify an appropriate alternative point of contact e.g. Scientific Support / Crime Scene Manager, DNA Liaison Officer.

Contact other than the OIC: Name: .... Rank / Job Title: ....

Tel: ....

Mobile: ....

Fax: ....

E-mail: ....

CPS Prosecutor Contact details: Name: .... Office / Area: ....

Tel: ....

Mobile: ....

Fax: ....

E-mail: ....

5. Supervisory authority for submission:

Name: ....

Rank / Job Title: ....

Signature: ....

6. Budgetary authority for submission:

....

Authorised by: ....

Rank / Job Title: ....

Aspects of submission required URGENTLY Refer to Section 10

Date / Authorisation Stamp

If for any reason the circumstances in this case change or the case is discontinued and the forensic evidence no longer required then the FSP should be immediately informed by facsimile or E-mail.

2006/07 (1)

URN

7. Circumstances of Incident(s)

Date:...Time: ....

Specific offence(s) being investigated: ....

☐ Suspect(s) identified   ☐ No suspect(s) identified

a) Give details of surrounding circumstances and MO of offence, include address, location, or vehicle reg. where appropriate:

....
....
....
....
....
.... *Continue on separate sheet if necessary*

b) What account (if any) has been given by the **suspect(s)**, [specify who] include admission, denials, defences etc?

....
....
....
....
.... *Continue on separate sheet if necessary*

c) Add any other relevant information eg an account provided by the **subject(s)** [specify who], other aggra-vating factors or whether there is a child victim, vulnerable / intimidated witness involved.

....
....
....
....
.... *Continue on separate sheet if necessary*

8. What are the points to prove?

What are the **reasonable lines of enquiry and / or the evidential points to prove** (e.g. whether or not sexual intercourse occurred between the suspect and complainant, whether or not the suspect is the person who broke the window). These issues should reflect the advice, the case strategy and the decisions that have been agreed between the investigator, prosecutor and, where appropriate, the forensic scientist. Specify the aspects of the examination necessary to support a charging decision.

....
....
....
....
.... *Continue on separate sheet if necessary*

If for any reason the circumstances in this case change or the case is discontinued and the forensic evidence is no longer required then the FSP should be immediately informed by facsimile or E-mail:

URN

9. Additional information attached to this form

Please indicate what this is by either ticking the relevant box(es) below or by describing the nature and relevance of the material:

Sexual Offences Form	☐	Scene Examiner's Report ☐
NFFID Form	☐	Photographs / Visual records ☐
Firearms Safety Form	☐	Plans ☐
Toxicology Form	☐	Witness / Victim's Statements ☐
DNA Match Report	☐	Critical Success Factor Forms ☐

Other (please specify): ....

....

10. Contact with FSP

It is advisable to contact the FSP **before** submission where there is **NO SUSPECT** and / or where there is an **URGENT** aspect to the work:

Are aspects of the submission required urgently?   Y / N

If YES to whom does the urgent aspect relate?

Deceased / Victim / Witness number
(1, 2 and / or 3 etc, if applicable)   (Refer to Section 11)

Suspect number (1, 2 and / or 3 etc, if applicable)   (Refer to Section 12)

Has the work been discussed with any representative of the FSP?   Y / N

If YES – provide the time, date and name of the FSP representative:

Specify any related Police or FSP reference numbers:

Provide FSP reference numbers of any **previous submissions** (e.g. related DNA crime stain submission):

....

Provide details of what was discussed and agreed with the FSP prior to submission: ....

.... *Continue on separate sheet if necessary*

11. Details of Deceased / Victim / Witness (For SUSPECTS go to section 12):

1. Surname:.. Forename(s): .... M / F

  D.O.B.: ..../........./.......... Deceased / Victim / Witness / Subject for Elimination (delete as applicable)

Occupation: .... *Ethnicity code: .... PNC Warning Signs ....

2. Surname:. .... Forename(s):. .... M / F

  D.O.B.: ..../........./.......... Deceased / Victim / Witness / Subject for Elimination (delete as applicable)

Occupation: .... *Ethnicity code: .... PNC Warning Signs ....

3. Surname: .... Forename(s): .... M / F

  D.O.B.: ..../........./.......... Deceased / Victim / Witness / Subject for Elimination (delete as applicable)

Occupation: .... *Ethnicity code: .... PNC Warning Signs ....

*16 point +1

MG21

SP Ref. No:.. URN

12. SUSPECT KEY DATES – complete ONE per suspect

Suspect Number   of   Surname: .... Forename(s): ....

Date of Birth: .... PNC warning sign: ....

Occupation: .... Ethnicity code (16 point +1) ....

Date of arrest: .... Time of arrest: .... A / S Number: ....

DNA PACE sample barcode reference (beginning 96 or higher)

PPO ☐   YO ☐   PYO ☐

KNOWN SUSPECT – NOT YET ARRESTED

Date agreed for despatch of work after discussion with the FSP

PRE-CHARGE – ARRESTED (currently in police custody)

Date agreed for despatch of work after discussion with the FSP

PRE-CHARGE AND ON POLICE BAILED TO RETURN

Return Bail date

Items for examination to be received at the FSP Laboratory by

Date agreed with the FSP by which the necessary results to assist the charging decision will be despatched

CHARGED AND BAILED TO COURT

Date Charged

Date fixed for service of the prosecution case (if known)

Next key court date (e.g. Trial Date)

CHARGED AND REMANDED IN CUSTODY

Date charged

Date of next remand hearing

Agreed action date for full code test (if applicable)

Date fixed for service of the prosecution case (if known)

Items for examination to be received at the FSP Laboratory by

Date agreed with the FSP by which the necessary results will be despatched

POST PLEA REQUIREMENT

Date agreed between the Prosecutor and the FSP by which any additional examinations and / or evaluative reports will be despatched

If for any reason the circumstances in this case change or the case is discontinued and the forensic evidence is no longer required then the FSP should be immediately informed by facsimile or E-mail.

2006/07 (1)

MG21

ITEMS FOR SCIENTIFIC EXAMINATION (Complete in duplicate)

All items must be properly packaged and labelled to preserve the integrity of the evidence

(The exhibit number and description given below must correspond with the exhibit label. Include barcode reference number of all PACE and Volunteer samples)

FSP Reference Number: ....

URN ☐ ☐ ☐

Serial No.	Exhibit or Barcode (DNA) Ref.	Exhibit Bag Seal No.	Description of Item(s)	This item relates to: (Subject or location recovered from)	Date and time found / taken	Name of person seizing item

Any known health and safety risks e.g. Aids, Hepatitis, Scabies etc must be stated – the notification should be provided as SECTION of the description of the item to which it applies, fuller details being supplied on a separate sheet if appropriate. NB Sharp / hazardous items must be appropriately packaged and labelled. For advice on these matters contact any member of Scientific Support.

Method of delivery: By hand ☐ Couriers ☐ Registered / Recorded Post ☐

Seal numbers: ....

....

Name of person delivering (block letters): ....

Rank / Job Title: .... Signature: ....

(FSP use only)

Person receiving at FSP

Print name: ....

Signature: ....

Date: ....

FSP Date Stamp

Indicate here if the SIO / Exhibits Officer needs to be contacted prior to the return of any exhibits to the force ☐

If for any reason the circumstances in this case change or the case is discontinued and the forensic evidence is no longer required then the FSP should be immediately informed by facsimile or E-mail.

Page No. .... of ....

2006/07 (1)

SUBMISSION OF ADDITIONAL WORK FOR SCIENTIFIC EXAMINATION

URN

SECTION A – Police and FSP reference numbers

Police Crime Reference Number: ....

FSP Reference Number: ....

Officer in the Case: ....

FSP Scientist: ....

Section B – Additional laboratory examination / work required as a result of:

☐ Additional exhibits (see items for examination page) ☐ Further information the the case (specify in Section E)

☐ Additional deceased / victim / witness (specify in section D) ☐ Additional suspect(s) (see Key Dates page(s))

Other reason (*specify precisely what is required:*) ....

.... (*Continue on separate sheet if necessary*)

SECTION C – Priority and authorisation

No Suspect	Known Suspect – Not yet arrested	Pre-charge – arrested in police custody	Pre-charge and police bail to return	Charged and bailed to court	Charged and remanded in custody	Post plea requirement
☐	☐	☐	☐	☐	☐	☐

Supervisory authority for submission:

Name and Rank / Job Title: ....

Signature: ....

☐ **Aspects of submission required URGENTLY Contact FSP prior to submission**

Budgetary authority for submission:

Authorised by: ....

Rank / Job Title: ....

Date / authorisation Stamp

Section D – Details of further deceased / victim / witness

Subject number: .... (*consecutive numbering from previous submission*)

Surname: .... Forename(s): ....

D.O.B. .... Deceased / Victim / Witness / Subject for Elimination

Occupation: ....*Ethnicity code: .... PNC warning signs: ....

*16 point +1

Section E – New information relating to the circumstances of the case and additional points to prove

Details: ....

....

....

....

....

....

....

....

he second page of this form headed items for Scientific Examination is identical to the back page
f the MG21 at page 331.

Checklist—Manual of Guidance Forms

- Do not be a mug—know and use the MOG

- Every form has its place and purpose

- Provide detailed information

- MG forms help the CPS do their job

- Quality information leads to quality decision making

Disclosure of Unused Material

7.1 **Introduction**

Police officers and lawyers alike tend to shy away from disclosure: there are a vast array of rules and obligations which must be followed. This chapter endeavours to simplify and clarify duties throughout the whole process within the Criminal Procedure and Investigations Act 1996 (as amended). It includes the handling of both non-sensitive and sensitive 'unused' material and third party material. It provides guidance throughout on making the key decisions and emphasizes the importance of unused material and the disclosure principles from the beginning of an investigation.

In recent years, and in particular in serious crime cases, disclosure has proved to be a very fruitful area for the defence and a minefield for the police and the CPS. Poor police and CPS performance in disclosure has jeopardized and lost murder cases. The principles of disclosure are exactly the same for all criminals, from the most common shoplifter, burglar, or car thief, to a rapist, murderer, or terrorist. Good practice learned at an early stage will pay dividends later in serious cases when police officers' decisions and actions will be most closely examined. If the handling of disclosure material can be improved then prosecution cases will become stronger. Getting disclosure right is key to the prosecution team playing its part in the delivery of justice:

> Disclosure is one of the most important issues in the criminal justice system . . . the application of proper and fair disclosure is a vital component of a fair criminal justice system. The 'golden rule' is that fairness requires full disclosure should be made of all material held by the prosecution that weakens its case or strengthens that of the defence.
>
> Foreword to Disclosure Manual, Lord Goldsmith, HM Attorney General

7.1.1 **A criminal investigation**

A criminal investigation amounts to an information-gathering exercise, for example, in a reactive investigation, finding out what has happened or, in a proactive investigation, what is going to happen. At its conclusion they may be seen first in terms of how the investigation has been carried out, or what the investigator has done: what lines of enquiry have been followed; what resources have been used; how witnesses have been traced and dealt with; what exhibits have been found, etc. Secondly, what has been discovered or what evidence the investigation has yielded; what the witnesses, who have made statements, have said; what the forensic findings are; what the CCTV footage shows, etc. In other words an investigation may be described as being an **investigative methodology** with a resulting **evidential product**.

7.1.2 **Unused evidence**

In a prosecution the evidential product will be used selectively to prove the Crown's case. That simply means that not all of the evidential product will assist the prosecutor. For example, some witnesses who can give evidence of being at a scene may not be able to describe what happened or what an offender looked like. A computer, mobile phone, or documents seized during a search because it was thought that they might produce evidence after examination may not contain anything of use at trial. So only some of the evidential product will be used, the rest will be unused.

7.1.3 **Unused investigative material**

As well as the unused evidential product there will be other material generated during the investigation—information, documents, and objects—detailing the enquiries made, in particular showing how the evidence has been collected. These would include such things as: notes made during the interviewing of a witness in preparation for writing their statement; the initial crime report; a note of a telephone conversation; or the record of messages reporting the incident in the first place.

7.1.4 **'Disclosure'**

The unused material in a case therefore amounts to all the unused evidence together with all the other background material generated by the investigation. The word 'disclosure' is properly used to describe this material and how it is dealt with by the investigators, prosecutors, and others within the CJS. However, the word is frequently misused in other contexts and this leads to confusion.

The word disclosure is often misleadingly used by the police to refer to the information provided to a legal representative before conducting an interview of a suspect before the suspect has been charged. Also CPS lawyers confusingly use the term 'advance disclosure' when talking about the evidence—or an outline of it—that they provide to the defence early in a prosecution with a view to encouraging a guilty plea. This should properly be called 'advance information'.

So, given that disclosure is about unused material, it is not unreasonable to ask how can such material have any significance in the trial process? To appreciate fully the answer to this question it is necessary to understand how the law on disclosure has developed over the last 25 years or so.

7.2 **Background**

7.2.1 **Common law developments**

Prior to 1982 the only obligations regarding unused material related to witnesses. If the prosecution decided not to call a witness to give evidence—that is to say that the witness became unused—there was a duty to provide the defence with the details of that witness. In addition, where a used witness had convictions, these too had to be disclosed to the defence.

Of course these obligations still exist today and are very important; issues with witnesses are fundamental to the disclosure process, whether they have convictions or any other matter that goes to their credibility must be spelled out to the CPS at the earliest opportunity.

Since that time a number of important cases have been before the Court of Appeal due to the non-disclosure of unused prosecution material. The Court has frequently concluded that among the undisclosed material lay evidence and/or information that arguably contradicted part of the prosecution case, or that at least threw doubt upon its accuracy or its truthfulness, and as a result convictions were overturned as being unreliable. The question generally was: what would a jury have made of this information had they heard about it during the trial? The Court of Appeal only needs to conclude that it might have made a difference for the conviction to be unsafe.

Such cases, which appeared throughout the 1980s and 1990s, led to progressively greater access by the defence both to the methodology of the investigation and to all of the material that it generated, subject to some restrictions with regard to sensitive information. This, however, led to new problems and in some serious cases the defence became focused as much on the unused material as on the evidence against the defendant.

The defence exploited this to the full. They tried to think of ways to make the sensitive material central to their defence and demanding access to it, not because their case relied on it, but in the hope that the prosecution would be discontinued if the court ordered such disclosure. Additionally, they employed ambush defences at court based upon information disclosed as unused.

The cost and logistics of providing the defence with access to and copies of unused material proved huge, particularly as the volume of unused material frequently dwarfed the volume of evidence.

7.2.2 **A statutory disclosure system**

In 1993, a Royal Commission concluded that the law had become imbalanced and that disclosure needed to be put on a statutory footing. The judges needed a system that remained focused on the issues in the trial; the defence needed access to unused material that supported their case—or went against the prosecution case—and the police needed a system that protected sensitive material. The result was the disclosure regime laid out in the Criminal Procedure and Investigations Act 1996 and the supplementary Code of Practice.

Triggers for statutory disclosure

The duty to disclose unused material comes into force in the event of a not guilty plea at a magistrates' court trial, or when a case is committed or sent for trial to the Crown Court.

7.3 The Criminal Procedure and Investigations Act (CPIA) Regime

7.3.1 Current law and sources

> **POINT TO NOTE—THE CURRENT LAW**
>
> The current law is set down in:
>
> - the Criminal Procedure and Investigations Act 1996 as amended (by the Criminal Justice Act 2003)
> - the updated Code of Practice, issued under section 23 of the Act
> - the Attorney General's guidelines on disclosure (2005)

In 2005, a Disclosure Manual was produced by a joint CPS and police team taking account of the changes brought about by the Criminal Justice Act 2003. This is a user-friendly document which emphasizes the partnership approach to disclosure and provides guidance in a variety of scenarios. In addition the Attorney General has formulated valuable new guidelines, and a new Code of Practice for police has been produced reflecting important changes. At relevant points throughout the chapter there will be cross-references to the Disclosure Manual (DM), the Attorney General's Guidelines (AGG) and the Codes of Practice (CoP). Familiarity with each of these documents is essential for the disclosure officer.

7.3.2 A partnership approach

This is an area in which the partnership approach is not only vital; it is enshrined in the law. The disclosure officer is required to make a series of important decisions including what material is relevant to that investigation and later what material s/he believes should be disclosed to the defence. It is the CPS lawyer, however, who has legal responsibility for the process. Indeed the final decision about what should be disclosed is for the CPS; the disclosure officer should not disclosure directly to the defence without the express authority of the reviewing lawyer.

7.3.3 **The regime itself**

The disclosure regime as laid out within the CPIA is summarized in Figure 7.1.

Figure 7.1 Disclosure regime within the CPIA

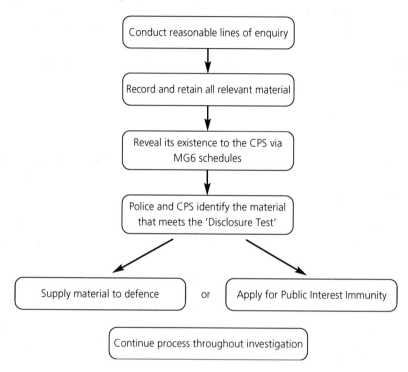

Behind this comparatively simple model, however, lie a number of potentially difficult decisions that need to be made. What constitutes a reasonable line of enquiry? What is relevant material? How is the existence of material revealed to the CPS? What is the disclosure test and how is it applied? Who makes the final decisions?

Effective disclosure calls for teamwork between the disclosure officer and the CPS reviewing lawyer, even though each will play a more significant role than the other at different stages of the process.

In this simplified model the requirement to conduct reasonable lines of enquiry is for the investigating officer, although the CPS may well have an input. Recording and retaining material are a matter for police officers and police staff in general, while revealing the existence of relevant material is a matter for the disclosure officer. Identifying material that meets the disclosure test is a matter for both the CPS and the disclosure officer. However, the final decision about what to supply to the defence rests with the CPS; equally so with Public Interest

Immunity. The material is commonly identified by the police but the decision to make an application to the court is one for the CPS.

If investigators can focus on disclosure from the outset of their enquiries the task becomes easier. The temptation for an investigator will always be to leave dealing with disclosure until such time as it is seems likely that a prosecution will result, because otherwise it is wasted work. While this is perfectly understandable it will always be more difficult to backdate disclosure especially where some time has elapsed between the start of the investigation and charges being brought. Unused material is now required at a much earlier stage than before and where there are any doubts the advice of the CPS should be sought.

7.3.4 When does it apply?

The obligations in relation to unused material and its disclosure are determined by the date the investigation begins and the disclosure officer must make this clear to the prosecutor. Major changes to the CPIA came into force as a result of the Criminal Justice Act 2003 and they apply to all investigations which started after 4 April 2005. This is important because, if an investigation started before that date, a different set of rules exist for how the unused material must be dealt with. **Please note that this chapter deals with a case where the investigation started after 4 April 2005.**

A reactive investigation will always begin when the crime first comes to the notice of the police but this will not necessarily be the time the crime was committed. For example, a murder investigation will generally start when the body is discovered, although in some cases where someone has been reported missing the investigation may start before they are found dead. In other cases, especially a proactive investigation, the investigation will generally begin once a decision is made to target the individual, or the proposed criminal objective. If there is any doubt about the start of the investigation—especially if it may be before 4 April 2005—advice should be sought from the CPS.

7.3.5 The disclosure officer

The officer in charge of the investigation will also carry out the role of the disclosure officer in most cases. In serious cases and where there are a sufficient number of people involved in the investigation someone from the team should be appointed as disclosure officer from the outset of the investigation. That person must be trained and competent to perform the job, and if there is any conflict of interests, for example if the officer is the victim of an offence being investigated, another person should be appointed as disclosure officer. It is preferable if that person has no other role in that case.

In some cases it may that there will be more than one disclosure officer, although there should always be a 'lead' disclosure officer appointed. This would happen, for example, in cases where there is source unit material involving a

Covert Human Intelligence Source (CHIS) and the lead disclosure officer cannot be allowed access to the material. A secondary disclosure officer would need to be appointed from within the source unit to deal with such material and liaise with the CPS reviewing lawyer directly.

7.4 Reasonable Lines of Enquiry

7.4.1 An objective investigation

A criminal investigation must be an objective process. It is the evidence and information collected by the impartial investigator which should lead towards the offender. There are clear dangers in becoming too focused on an individual suspect and so generating only those enquiries which confirm existing suspicions. This can become a particular problem in assessing the strength of witnesses or information for an investigator, leading to a tendency to confirmatory bias where material which does not support the hypothesis is disregarded or explained away while being unquestioning about that which does. In extreme cases this can lead to suppressing material which does not support a case in the mistaken belief that it is wrong.

7.4.2 Witnesses

This is especially significant in relation to witnesses. Witnesses are of huge significance to a criminal trial and those witnesses who do not support the prosecution case or decline to assist in circumstances where they might reasonably be expected to have witnessed something evidential must not simply be disregarded, but dealt with as important unused material. If someone is believed to be a witness but you do not know what they are able or willing to say it must be assumed that they might undermine the prosecution case and since there is no property in a witness, that is to say neither side 'owns' the witness, they must be made available to the defence. Close liaison with the CPS is vital here.

7.4.3 Suspects

The CPIA makes it an explicit duty to pursue all reasonable lines of enquiry whether they lead towards or away from a preferred suspect. What is reasonable will depend on the investigation and will be subject to time and resources, however it is important to be able to record decisions about lines of enquiry considered but not undertaken. The CPS may request further enquiries and it is quite likely that either before or after charge the defence may also request some, especially directed at identifying alternative suspects. These defence requests cannot be simply ignored. They will need to be considered on their merits and if reasonable it is the responsibility of the officer in the case to ensure the enquiries are properly completed.

> **KEY CONSIDERATION**
>
> Could I justify as reasonable those enquiries that I have made and those enquiries I have not made to the trial judge?

References: DM 4.2; CoP 3.5

7.5 **Record and Retain**

All police officers are required by the Act to record and retain relevant material generated by them during a criminal investigation. Disclosure has often resulted in a critical examination of the investigation itself at criminal trials, and lack of records has not helped officers to counter such criticism. Accordingly police record keeping has improved dramatically over recent years in particular in relation to decision making at scenes and during investigations. The requirement to conduct impartial investigations would be clearly undone if there were no duty to record and retain, allowing the possibility of discarding that which did not support the prosecution case.

Material must be retained in a form that is durable and retrievable but at this early stage it will be difficult to make decisions about whether material will ultimately be used or unused at trial. So the requirement is to consider relevance, and although the relevance test is applicable at the time of considering retention, it becomes even more significant when the disclosure officer has to decide what material s/he must reveal to the CPS through the unused material schedules. In practice this will be when the decisions are made about relevance.

> **KEY CONSIDERATION**
>
> Are there any missing records of my investigation?

References: DM 5.1; AGG 28; CoP 4, 5

7.6 **Relevance**

7.6.1 **A crucial decision**

In practice this may be the first step in the disclosure process. A disclosure officer must know this definition and understand how to apply it. In major investigations the gathering of relevant material is generally done for the disclosure officer by the enquiry officers bringing material into the incident room where it will be stored and recorded on a computerized database. However, most cases do not enjoy that luxury and if you are both the investigator and the disclosure officer the responsibility for identifying relevant material is yours alone.

It requires you to think about what there is in your office, in your police station, in other police stations, within other investigative organizations, or with any third parties, that meets the test for relevance. This test dictates what material needs to be identified and revealed to the prosecutor through the MG6 schedules. How a disclosure officer interprets this test in the context of their enquiry is vitally important. For example, the fact that the investigation revealed that a number of people were present at a particular place but did not see the crime that occurred, may be negative information but is still relevant.

Oversights here, or a too rigid interpretation of the meaning of relevance, can lead to material not being revealed to the CPS, and therefore not being considered for disclosure to the defence.

7.6.2 The relevancy test

POINT TO NOTE—THE RELEVANCY TEST

Material may be relevant if it appears to have some bearing on:

- any offence under investigation;
- any person being investigated; or
- the surrounding circumstances,

unless it is incapable of having any impact on the case.

CoP 2.1

It is a very wide test. It is difficult to think of anything that you would do, and any material that would be generated, during a criminal investigation that would not have at least some bearing on the offence, the person being investigated, or the surrounding circumstances. However, the test also contains the caveat 'unless it is incapable of having any impact'. It is worth thinking about what this says and importantly what it does **not** say.

7.6.3 Understanding 'incapable of having any impact'

Many police officers, when considering relevance, are confused about this part of the test. Assuming a piece of material satisfies one of the three limbs above—'it appears to have some bearing on . . .'—it is tempting to think about the next part of the test by asking yourself: 'Yes, OK it has a bearing on, but how could it have any impact on the case?'. This leads to considering what sort of material could have an impact on the case. Which in turn leads to the consideration that the only way material could have an impact on the case is if it was disclosed to the defence and the only material the defence are entitled to see is material which might undermine the prosecution case or assist the defence.

The result of this misreading of the test is that we turn the relevancy test into the disclosure test. Because we ask the wrong question—'How could this have any impact?'—we end up thinking about what should be disclosed and not the much lower threshold of what is relevant. The test does not say that material is only relevant if it **is** capable of having any impact. The safest position is that any material that has been collected and has some bearing is best considered as being relevant and should only be disregarded if the disclosure officer is convinced that it cannot have any impact.

7.6.4 Discarding material gathered as non-relevant

In the Attorney General's Guidelines it states that an investigator should err on the side of caution in concluding that material generated during an investigation is not relevant and should take advice from the CPS. In the Disclosure Manual some examples are given of material generated during a major investigation but which would not be considered as relevant. These include an application from an officer for annual leave and a message stating that exhibits are ready for collection from the laboratory. If in any doubt, treat the material as relevant.

7.6.5 The relevant unused material behind your evidence

This is a very important part of the disclosure regime and requires the disclosure officer to think widely about what material exists that meets the test of relevance. It might be useful to think about what lies behind your evidence. For example, you may have a signed witness statement which will be used at the trial. But what about how the witness was identified: was it through house-to-house or local enquiries; who else was seen; was it as a result of publicity; if so, what publicity; what contact has the witness had with police during the investigation; who took the statement; are there notes made in preparation; has the witness been offered a reward?

Equally, with a piece of forensic evidence, what is behind the evidence from the laboratory? How was the item identified, how was it dealt with, who packaged it, where and when, what else was found and submitted, what was requested of the laboratory? Of course it may well be that there is unused material that comes from lines of enquiry that proved not to lead to any evidence. It is relevant of itself that you have conducted lines of enquiry that were reasonable even though they proved not to be fruitful.

The Disclosure Manual—at annex D—provides examples of relevant unused material that is commonly generated during an investigation, however it is not conclusive. Some of the items might not exist in a particular case, and equally there will be other items that are not on the list. It is only a guide and must not be used as a checklist.

Examples of unused material that may be created or used during an investigation

- 999 voice tape
- Exhibits not referred to in statements
- Post-arrest photographs
- Details of other suspects arrested and interviewed but not charged
- Audio/videotapes of witnesses
- Potential witnesses' details where there has been no statement taken
- CCTV or other videos
- Media releases
- Fingerprint forms
- ID procedure forms
- Crime reports
- Log of messages (CAD)
- Officers' pocket books
- Custody records
- First descriptions
- Plans or photographs of a crime scene
- Unused forensic findings
- Preparatory notes for witness statements
- CHIS reports
- Offender profiles
- Ports warnings
- Wanted/missing circulations
- Intelligence material
- Police misconduct material
- Vulnerable victim/witness material
- Records of property from crime scenes
- Lay visitors reports
- Family liaison logs
- Witness contact logs
- Scene logs
- Decision logs
- Incident management logs

- Interview plans
- Notes of pre-interview briefing for legal advisers
- Medical examiners' reports
- House-to-house enquiry forms
- Operational briefing sheets
- RIPA authorities
- Observation/surveillance logs
- SOCO/HIDO work records
- Forensic examination forms
- Exhibit movement forms/books

References: DM 5.2, 5.3, 5.8; CoP 2.1

7.7 Third Parties

7.7.1 What is a Third Party?

A third party is anyone or any organization that has no responsibilities under the CPIA to record and retain material. Generally, investigative organizations such as any police service, HM Revenue and Customs or the Immigration Service have duties under the Act and are therefore not third parties, even though they are not the organization conducting a specific investigation. The primary danger with disclosure and third parties is that because they do not have the same duty as police to keep records, relevant material may be lost if the disclosure officer does not act promptly to inform the third party of the need to keep material and to make arrangements to obtain access to it.

7.7.2 Third party material

In many investigations third parties are involved. Common examples are:

- owners of CCTV material;
- social services departments;
- forensic experts;
- police surgeons; and
- GPs and hospital authorities.

Often evidence will be forthcoming from these sources, but in addition to the evidence that you will wish to use there will be other material relevant to your investigation. For example, CCTV footage that shows your defendant near to the scene of the offence will be evidential, however CCTV footage close to the scene that does not show your defendant may prove to be significant at a trial depending upon the defence case. Failure to secure CCTV footage may lead to allegations by the defence that reasonable lines of enquiry were not undertaken that would have exonerated the defendant.

Any third party involved in a case or—even if not involved—who may be in possession of material relevant to the case, should be informed of the investigation and alerted to the need to retain material. The Disclosure Manual contains sample letters that should be sent to the third party to this effect (see annexes B1 and B2). The disclosure officer should also inform the CPS and together they should consider the need to obtain access to the material, if necessary through a witness summons or court order. Third party material may be highly relevant to a case. In cases of domestic abuse local social services are very likely to be in possession of material relevant to any prosecution and are likely to have protocols in place for dealing with it because it so often becomes an issue.

In *R v Alibhai* [2004] EWCA Crim 681, a case involving disclosure of material from abroad, the Court of Appeal held that before taking steps to obtain such material the prosecutor should be of the opinion that the material satisfied the disclosure test. This now means that a disclosure officer need only obtain third party material if s/he believes, in consultation with the CPS, that it might undermine the prosecution case or assist the defence (the Disclosure Test—see 7.11).

KEY CONSIDERATION

Have I identified all third parties who may be in possession of relevant material in this case and informed the CPS?

References: DM 4.1, 4.11, 4.17; CoP 3.6

7.8 Revelation

7.8.1 Revealing relevant unused material to the CPS

Having considered relevance, and identified the pile of material, the disclosure officer is now required to reveal its existence to the CPS. Revelation is the term used to describe this process, not disclosure; which means providing material to the defence. The CPIA uses terms in a technical sense and these need to be properly understood in order to prevent confusion arising. Counsel in particular when considering unused material may well use the expression 'not relevant' when considering whether material falls to be supplied to the defence, when the proper term should be 'not disclosable'.

There are a number of ways in which material is revealed to the prosecutor through the various MG6 schedules (as seen in Chapter 6).

MG1	Front of case papers
MG6B	Officer's disciplinary records
MG6C	Non-sensitive schedule
MG6D	Sensitive schedule
MG6D	Highly sensitive material
MG6D	CHIS material
MG6E	Material which undermines or assists
Code 7.3	Material which must be copied to the CPS

7.8.2 The MG1

The first of these is referred to in the signed declaration found at the foot of the MG1. This states:

> I certify that, to the best of my knowledge and belief, I have not withheld any information which could assist the defence in the early preparation of their case, including the making of a bail application.

The declaration must be signed in every case and the officer who signs it must understand what it means. It refers to disclosure under common law and comes about as a result of the case *R v DPP ex parte Lee* [1999] 2 All ER 737. So despite the statutory regime of the CPIA we still have a preserved duty of disclosure under common law. This is intended to deal with disclosure of material which might assist the defence in the making of an application prior to CPIA disclosure being triggered. For example, if a defendant is remanded in custody and the defence wish to make an application for bail, is there material which would assist them in making that application, such as the victims or witnesses previous convictions, missing relevant CCTV, whether the victim wishes to make a withdrawal statement? This requires early liaison between the police and the CPS and such material is best recorded on the MG6.

> **KEY CONSIDERATION**
>
> Is there any material that I need to discuss with the CPS to ensure early disclosure to the defence?

A further issue of early revelation concerns the crime report and the log of messages (CAD). As an aid to case review the CPS must routinely be provided with copies of these documents and maybe other documents where local arrangements are in force. These should be edited for sensitive material before being supplied and this may well be carried out by a support unit unbeknown to the officer in the case. This material should not be routinely supplied to the defence, however, in practice, this has happened and officers should ensure that these documents are properly edited to prevent unwanted disclosure of sensitive information.

KEY CONSIDERATION

Have I checked the editing of the copies of the crime report and message log?

7.8.3 **The MG6B**

The MG6B deals with police officers' disciplinary records and the responsibility for supplying an MG6B lies with the individual officer. As a disclosure officer you would not be allowed access to a colleague's disciplinary record so the onus is on them rather than you. Your duties as the disclosure officer are satisfied providing you have brought it to the attention of each police officer involved that an MG6B is required from them if appropriate (see 6.14).

KEY CONSIDERATION

Have I reminded the police officers involved of their duty to supply me with an MG6B if necessary?

7.8.4 **The MG6C**

The MG6C will contain descriptions of all the relevant material in the case—**unless** that material is sensitive. It is the default schedule. If an otherwise non-sensitive piece of material contains sensitive personal details—such as names and addresses or telephone numbers—it should be scheduled on the MG6C with those details omitted but with a note made to the effect that it has been edited for personal details. This document will be copied by the CPS to the defence (see 6.15).

7.8.5 **The MG6D**

This is the sensitive material schedule and should only contain material judged to be sensitive in accordance with the test for sensitivity—dealt with in detail at 7.9. This will not be supplied to the defence (see 6.16).

7.8.6 **The MG6D—Highly sensitive/CHIS material**

These allow for particularly sensitive material to be dealt with and are new documents. MG6D highly sensitive schedules will be rarely needed, however the process for dealing with CHIS material may well vary from police service to police service. It is a matter for local practices whether CHIS material is dealt with as highly sensitive or not.

7.8.7 **The MG6E**

The MG6E is not a schedule of unused material. Entries on the MG6E should refer to material already scheduled on either the MG6C or MG6D, but which in the view of the disclosure officer fall to be disclosed because it either undermines the prosecution case or assists the defence. A reference to the relevant schedule entry—for example an item number—should be accompanied by an explanation of how the material undermines or assists. It must also be signed by the disclosure officer certifying that they have complied with their duties. It is a confidential document and will not be disclosed to the defence. It is vitally important that no disclosure to the defence takes place before this is fully discussed with the CPS and the reviewing lawyer has authorized it (see 6.17).

7.8.8 **Code 7.3**

This section of the Code of Practice deals with material which as well as being made the subject of a schedule entry, must be copied to—or shown to—the CPS. In short this is any material that the disclosure officer believes undermines the prosecution case or assists the defence—that is everything mentioned on the MG6E. It should include anything that casts doubt on the reliability of a confession or the reliability of a witness and also anything which has been provided by the accused and amounts to an explanation for the offence (although it is likely that this will be evidential and therefore not amount to unused material).

References: DM 2.5, 18.8, 9.4, 7.1, 8.1

7.9 **Sensitive and Non-sensitive Material**

7.9.1 **Non-sensitive material**

The practical decision to be made here by the disclosure officer is whether material is sensitive or not, because non-sensitive is the default position. Unless the disclosure officer can show that a piece of material is sensitive it shall be dealt with as non-sensitive. All cases are likely to have both non-sensitive and sensitive material and so it is important to understand the principles behind the label sensitive material. As has been said, the defence will be provided with a copy of the non-sensitive schedule and so it is especially important therefore that sensitive material is carefully identified in order that it may be protected.

It is sometimes useful here to think about material and not documents. The schedules list pieces of material not documents; one document may consist of both sensitive and non-sensitive material. A lengthy document, such as a liaison log with a family or a witness, or an investigator's decision log, may be dealt with as a series of pieces of material some of which may be non-sensitive and others sensitive, with each getting a separate schedule entry.

7.9.2 **Sensitive material**

Sensitive material is that which it is not in the public interest to disclose and the test for sensitivity comes from a Court of Appeal case: *R v C and R v H* [2004] UKHL 3. The disclosure officer must be able to show that disclosure of this material would give rise to:

A real risk of serious prejudice to an important public interest.

Each item needs to be considered and justified on its own merits and only where it can be done in accordance with this test, can the material be treated as sensitive. The Disclosure Manual 8.4 provides a list of public interests that are likely to impact upon these. These are three of those most significant for police officers:

- the ability of law enforcement agencies to fight crime by the use of CHIS, undercover operations, covert surveillance, etc;
- the protection of secret methods of detecting and fighting crime; and
- the willingness of citizens, agencies, commercial institutions, communications service providers, etc to give information to the authorities in circumstances where there may be some legitimate expectation of confidentiality (eg Crimestoppers).

Suppose you have material which details the location and occupants of a surveillance observation point (OP) in a private house. Look at the list of public interests above. What would be the effect on that public interest if the details of the location of the OP were to be disclosed? How would it affect our future ability to obtain OPs if the occupants knew that their details would be provided to the defence in any future trial? Clearly disclosure would have a strong adverse effect on our ability to obtain OPs in the future and what the test for sensitivity seeks to do is protect material which would jeopardize these important public interests.

The second public interest lays out how it is important to protect police investigative methods from disclosure if that disclosure would impact upon its effectiveness in the future. For example, in a case involving undercover officers or test purchase officers, any material which goes to the process of deployment or the tactics used would be sensitive. Indeed, anything beyond the bare evidential product is likely to be justifiably sensitive.

The third public interest acknowledges that people supply non-evidential information to the police in the expectation that it will not be disclosed. If it were routinely disclosed the supply of such information would dry up and this would have an adverse effect on the police's ability to combat criminality.

There are other public interests mentioned in the Manual but even that list is not intended to be exhaustive. The key is to ensure that each item is considered on its own merits. The CPS reviewing lawyer will be looking to ensure that material is justifiably put on the sensitive schedule and if they are not so persuaded you will be asked to move it to the non-sensitive schedule and so the description at least will go to the defence.

7.9.3 Highly sensitive and CHIS material

Highly sensitive material and CHIS material are effectively particular types of sensitive material. Highly sensitive material is defined as that which, should it be compromised, would lead directly to loss of life or threaten national security. This is not material which one would expect to come across in the course of general police investigations, however subject to local instructions all CHIS material should be dealt with as being highly sensitive. CHIS involvement in an investigation often creates difficulties for the disclosure officer because you may not have access to all the relevant material that relates to the CHIS or their deployment. Perhaps you will have only some form of sanitized intelligence from a CHIS or other source but have no idea what lies behind that material.

In these circumstances someone from the CHIS Handling Unit will be required to consider the material to which you do not have access. You will need to supply them with an outline of your case and any defence material and inform the CPS that a secondary disclosure officer from the CHIS Handling Unit will be in contact to arrange a senior CPS lawyer to have access to their material. This secondary disclosure officer will then complete an MG6D (CHIS) schedule and an MG6E relating to that material and arrange for the CPS to examine the contents of that schedule, usually at the CHIS Handling Unit. The CPS lawyer will endorse the schedule but will not compromise the material by removing a copy of the schedule or any of the material.

This is the system for dealing with highly sensitive material, but CHIS material is not always dealt with as highly sensitive and is subject to local arrangements. It is, however, a system that ensures the integrity of the CHIS handling system and best protects the police with regard to our duty of care to those people who provide us with information. Any cases involving CHIS material must involve close liaison with the reviewing CPS lawyer. There may well be a conference concerning the MG6D material and CHIS material in particular and it will be important to ensure that the right people attend including, if necessary, the handler and the controller.

References: DM 8.2, 8.4, 8.5, 9

7.10 **Scheduling**

7.10.1 **General**

In many cases the MG6C and MG6D schedules will be the first indication to the CPS reviewing lawyer as to the quality of your disclosure. Poor schedules will ring alarm bells about your competence throughout the process, for the ultimate responsibility for proper disclosure rests with the lawyer. Poor schedules will suggest doubts about your identification of relevant material and your ability to identify material that falls to be disclosed to the defence. The lawyer is likely to engage in a safety first attitude towards the process and this is why historically, in many cases, CPS lawyers have been complicit in allowing the defence access to all or much of the unused material regardless of whether it undermined the prosecution or assisted the defence. However, blanket disclosure is now in the past and dealing with disclosure in compliance with the CPIA is now a CPS priority.

7.10.2 **The non-sensitive schedule**

The most common problem with the MG6C is lack of detail in the description. What is needed is sufficient detail for the reviewing lawyer to not need to see the original in order to be able to make an informed decision about whether the material falls to be disclosed or not. If the description is not in such detail the lawyer will request to see the original or a copy. The time taken to ferry material, back and forth for inspection by the lawyer will be saved by investing a greater effort in the writing of more detailed descriptions in the first place.

Referring to form numbers is very common but often means little to the lawyer. Although the Disclosure Manual says that such schedule entries should be returned for correction, in practice shortage of time will often make this impractical. This may lead to the defence being allowed widespread access to material regardless of whether it undermines the prosecution case or assists the defence.

If a document is non-sensitive with the exception of some personal details those details may be left from the description and the material shown on the non-sensitive schedule as 'edited for personal material'. If a document contains both non-sensitive and sensitive material it may usefully be dealt with as two entries; one MG6C entry and one MG6D entry. Think about material instead of documents or pieces of paper. If there was some local intelligence that started a case, say about a local drug dealer, it would be viewed as sensitive because it was provided to the police in confidence. If there was another document that simply amounted to an authorization from senior management for a proactive operation in the case—but did not mention the information itself or the source—it would be non-sensitive.

Now assume that in fact there is just one document which contains both the intelligence and the authority. In terms of material although there is only one document, there are actually two pieces of material, and each can have its own entry. This is not duplicating the same material on MG6C and the MG6D, it is focusing on the material, not on how many documents there are. Remember that actual copies of material will only be supplied to the defence where that material undermines the prosecution case or assists the defence.

KEY CONSIDERATION

Have I completed my MG6C schedule clearly, accurately, and in sufficient detail so the prosecutor can make an informed decision?

7.10.3 **The sensitive schedule**

The requirement for the description on MG6D entries is slightly different. The description needs to be in sufficient detail to enable the lawyer to decide whether or not the material should be viewed. Clearly the greater the detail the less likelihood it is that the CPS lawyer will feel the need to inspect the material itself. So the effort put into providing a good description may well save time in reducing or eliminating the need to collect all the material together and show it to the lawyer personally.

The main difficulty with the MG6D has traditionally been a poor understanding of the test for sensitivity and failing to justify why it is not on the MG6C. Careful consideration of the test for sensitivity and the appropriate public interest in the case of each individual item should ensure that all of your MG6D entries are fully justifiable.

KEY CONSIDERATION

Have I completed my MG6D schedule clearly, accurately, and in sufficient detail to enable the CPS reviewing lawyer to decide whether or not to view the material?

7.10.4 **Scheduling CHIS and highly sensitive material**

The material on these schedules must be examined by the reviewing lawyer in accordance with the system described above—subject to local policy. So there is no need for detail in the descriptions; a list of the material will be sufficient. These schedules will be retained by the disclosure officer and not sent to the CPS; inspection of the material and the schedule will be dealt with by arrangement with the reviewing lawyer.

7.10.5 **Scheduling in conclusion**

It cannot be denied that the scheduling process is an onerous job and if it is to be completed in accordance with instructions then some MG6C entries might be virtually word-for-word reproductions of the original material. However, time invested at this point will pay dividends later. Police knowledge and understanding of the case and material will be enhanced; the CPS lawyer will have confidence in the disclosure officer's decision making; the necessary ongoing review will be much more straightforward; there will be no need to keep referring to the originals; and the defence will have difficulty justifying why they should have access to material on the MG6C.

References: DM 6, 7.3, 8.7, 9.7; AGG 29; CoP 6.3, 6.4

7.11 **The Disclosure Test**

7.11.1 **What material are the defence entitled to?**

Although the defence will be provided by the CPS with a copy of the MG6C, and you will have completed it in the detail required, this does not count as disclosure of its contents. Having completed the schedules your next task—and probably the most significant in the whole disclosure process—is to assess the material for anything which falls to be disclosed to the defence. At this stage we are not concerned with sensitivity or whether material may be subject to Public Interest Immunity. Both the sensitive schedule and the non-sensitive schedule need to be considered for material that falls to be disclosed and then identified to the CPS on the MG6E.

The final decision on what to disclose rests with the CPS reviewing lawyer. However, it is the disclosure officer who in the first instance will identify such material. Failure to disclose to the defence material to which they are entitled lies at the heart of all of the stated cases which lead to the CPIA, and has been a recurrent issue during the time the disclosure regime has been subject to fairly regular judicial review.

The test was amended in 2005 by the Criminal Justice Act 2003, when primary disclosure—which dealt with material undermining the prosecution case—was conjoined with secondary disclosure—dealing with material assisting the defence—creating the single disclosure test which we now use. All of the material on each schedule needs to be assessed in the light of this test and anything which meets the test must be identified and made the subject of an MG6E entry explaining why it meets the test and therefore falls to be disclosed to the defence.

Definition—The Disclosure Test 2005

. . . any prosecution material which has not previously been disclosed to the accused and which might reasonably be considered capable of undermining the case for the prosecution against the accused or of assisting the case for the accused

Section 3 CPIA (as amended)

7.11.2 How to apply the test

The difficulty for the disclosure officer is how to apply this test to the unused material and a particular difficulty is being critical and objective about one's own case, its strengths, and its weaknesses. Only by bringing a defence attitude to the assessment of the material will the desired result be achieved. Police officers will often argue that they are not experienced or qualified to understand what they have that might assist an accused, echoing the sentiments of many defence lawyers. However, this really is a matter of attitude and knowledge; knowing the guidance available and approaching the task with an unbiased attitude will ensure a thorough, objective, and fair job.

7.11.3 Examples

The Attorney General's Guidelines indicate some examples of material which would fall to be disclosed because it undermines the prosecution case or assists the defence:

- Any material casting doubt upon the accuracy of any prosecution evidence
- Any material which may point to another person, whether charged or not having involvement in the commission of the offence
- Any material which may cast doubt upon the reliability of a confession
- Any material which might go to the credibility of a prosecution witness
- Any material that might support a defence that is either raised by the defence or apparent from the prosecution papers
- Any material which may have a bearing on the admissibility of any prosecution evidence

Consider reference numbers on the various forms relating to the movement of property through a police station and to a laboratory. Suppose errors were discovered relating to an important piece of physical evidence. Might the defence wish to challenge the integrity of any forensic findings in relation to this exhibit and if they do would these errors assist them to do so?

How many suspects were there in the case? Was there any kind of elimination criteria? Was there any material which pointed to someone else other than the defendant? If so, regardless of whether they were eliminated, that material falls to be disclosed.

Has this suspect made false confessions in the past? Are there parts of his/her account which could not be true? Does the suspect have a medical history suggesting their admissions could be unreliable? Is there any kind of motive evident for making a false confession? Does the confession contain only information in the public domain or supplied to the suspect during interview?

Has a witness been truthful throughout? Has their account been consistent? Do they have criminal convictions? Have they been offered or requested a reward?

357

Is there evidence to suggest their account has been contaminated by police or another witness?

Think about any material that might support a defence that is either raised by the defence or apparent from the prosecution papers. What the Attorney General is expecting here is not only anything that would help the defence they are running, but much further; to assess the unused material for anything which would support **any** defence. Again this requires a careful defence-minded assessment of the case, as well as a good knowledge of the appropriate defences to the offence charged.

For example, suppose the charge relates to a GBH outside a pub following an argument in the bar and the defence is one of alibi; he is saying he was not there. If there is information from someone who did not wish to make a statement suggesting that the victim started the argument, this would be material which might suggest self-defence and so would fall to be disclosed.

The Attorney General also observed that material might undermine the prosecution case 'by the use to be made of it in cross-examination'.

Suppose you find an error made by an arresting officer in their notebook or that a search record has not been signed as being supervised. If that officer were to be called as a witness might the defence wish to use these mistakes in cross-examination? Might the defence argue that supervision of records is an issue of integrity, and such a failure by an officer goes to their standing as a witness of truth? These are unpalatable truths for police officers and are examples of how it is necessary to be critical and unbiased in the assessment of the material in order to fulfil the duties of disclosure.

Success in identifying disclosable material is utterly reliant upon the objectivity of the disclosure officer and their ability to look at the unused material from a critical defence perspective. It requires a commitment to transparency in the investigation and a sure knowledge of the case. But be assured that engaging in this process will produce tangible gains for the investigation and prosecution. Knowledge of the case will be more extensive; there will be the opportunity to mitigate difficulties that are discovered in advance of trial and new fruitful lines of enquiry might be identified.

The Disclosure Manual includes a very appropriate quote from the philosopher John Stuart Mill: 'He who knows only his side of the case knows precious little of that.'

KEY CONSIDERATION

Have I identified all the material on the schedules that undermines the prosecution case or assists the defence?

7.11.4 **Completing the MG6E**

Having successfully completed the examination of the material in the light of the disclosure test, the MG6E will now contain references to material that is non-sensitive (from the MG6C) and sensitive (from the MG6D). The MG6E will explain how the disclosure officer believes it undermines the prosecution case or assists the defence and should—in their opinion—therefore be disclosed to the defence. The MG6E must be endorsed to the effect that all the material that is—or may be—relevant has been inspected, viewed, or listened to. Further, that all relevant material has been revealed to the prosecutor in accordance with the provisions of the CPIA. (This covers the identification of any material which meets the test for disclosure.)

KEY CONSIDERATION

Have I completed the MG6E either explaining why material falls to be disclosed or certifying that there is no disclosable material?

If there is no material identified that meets the disclosure test the second declaration at the foot of the MG6E must be signed to that effect. Should a defence statement be supplied the material will need to be re-considered in that light and a further MG6E endorsed. Copies of any material listed on the MG6E will be supplied to the CPS or made available for inspection. The MG6E itself does not go to the defence; they will have to work out for themselves how the material that they are served falls to undermine or assist!

Once the CPS lawyer has considered the case, copies of the non-sensitive material that meet the disclosure test will then be supplied to the defence or arrangements will be made for them to have access to it. However, the disclosable material that comes from the sensitive schedule will need to be carefully considered, because it will have already been demonstrated that disclosure of it would give rise to a real risk of serious prejudice to an important public interest.

KEY CONSIDERATION

Have I provided copies of all MG6E material to the CPS reviewing lawyer?

References: DM 7.7, 8.13, 10, 12; AGG 8, 10, 12; CoP 7.2, 7.3

7.12 **Public Interest Immunity (PII)**

7.12.1 **Conflicting public interests**

What we have here now is a situation where two different public interests conflict. You might well have been able to show that disclosure of a particular piece of material would seriously impact upon the willingness of members of the public to give confidential assistance to the police, however, because the material undermines the prosecution or assists the defence, it falls to be disclosed **in the interests of a fair trial**—which of itself is an important public interest.

Public Interest Immunity, in this context, is the principle that in certain circumstances it is in the greater public interest that material which is required to be disclosed in law, is nonetheless not disclosed to the defence. So even though the defence are entitled to the material, if a judge is persuaded that the greater public interest lies in not disclosing it, s/he can make such an order. A PII application is made by the CPS in these circumstances inviting a judge to make such an order.

7.12.2 Is a PII application needed?

It is very important to understand that just because we have sensitive material in a case, it does not mean that a PII application is required. It is a common misconception that in any case in which there is sensitive material a PII application needs to be made in order to protect that material. Considering PII is a three-stage process.

POINT TO NOTE—PII

The key decisions

Stage 1—Is there a legal duty to disclose the material?
Stage 2—Does PII arise?
Stage 3—Where does the overall balance of the public interest lie?

There is only a legal duty to disclose material which undermines the prosecution case or assists the defence. If it does not fall to be disclosed there is no legal duty to disclose it and no need for a court application. If it does fall to be disclosed, is it nonetheless in the public interest not to disclose it? This is the conflict of public interests which in a PII application the judge will resolve.

It is only therefore when there is sensitive material which also falls to be disclosed and a way cannot be found to satisfy both public interests, will there be a need to consider making a PII application. The decision to do this will be taken at a conference between a senior CPS lawyer—normally a Branch Crown Prosecutor—and according to the Disclosure Manual—a Detective Chief Inspector or a designated Detective Inspector. Although there are regional variations on this policy.

7.12.3 Satisfying both public interests

Every effort must be made to find a way to satisfy the defence right to have access to material which meets the disclosure test while still protecting the public interest, An example of a sensitive document would be an OP authority in accordance with *R v Johnson*. This is where the stated case calls for a sergeant to attend the premises in advance of its use as an OP. The authority would contain details of a certificate written by the sergeant and its location. Suppose that it was not a sergeant but a constable who certificated the document in breach of the stated case: this would indicate that we have not complied with case law in securing the OP and so would fall to be disclosed. However, there is sensitivity with regard to the location and occupants.

In this case we would not need a PII application because by editing the document we could supply the defence with the certification but not the location or occupants. This would satisfy our duty to supply the defence with material that falls to be disclosed while still protecting the location and the occupants of the OP.

If you do discover sensitive material on your MG6D that falls to be disclosed, close cooperation with the CPS reviewing lawyer is vital, and it must be brought to their attention at the earliest opportunity.

KEY CONSIDERATION

Have I drawn the attention of the CPS to disclosable sensitive material?

References: DM 8.22, 8.23, 13; AGG 20, 22

7.13 **Defence Case Statements**

7.13.1 **Legal requirements**

In this section, and in keeping with the terminology used in the Crown Court Disclosure Protocol (see 7.14), the term '**defence case statement**' will be used to describe a statement provided by the defence in accordance with section 5 (Crown Court cases) or section 6 (magistrates' court cases) of the Act. A major intention of the CPIA was to forge a regime that focused the court on the issues in the case. To that end the defence case statement is fundamental to the management of the case at trial. Under the amended CPIA a defence case statement should:

- set out the nature of the defence, including any particular defences on which the accused intends to rely;
- indicate the matters of fact on which the accused takes issue with the prosecution;
- set out, in the case of each such matter, why the accused takes issue with the prosecution;
- indicate any point of law (including any point as to the admissibility of evidence or an abuse of process) which the accused wishes to take, and any authority on which s/he intends to rely for that purpose.

There is also room for the Home Secretary to add to this list of requirements in the future. Also, in a case where the defence is one of alibi, the defence case statement should include details of the alibi witnesses and any other information which would assist the police in tracing them.

7.13.2 Disclosure officer's actions

A defence case statement should be sent in the first instance to the CPS and then be forwarded to the disclosure officer to address any issues arising from it. This may take the form of further enquiries, which if reasonable, must be carried out. It is likely that the defence will refer to material on the MG6C schedule asking for copies. If they can show how it undermines the prosecution case, or assists their defence case they are entitled to that material, but not otherwise. It is fundamental to the disclosure regime that the defence are only entitled to access to material which undermines the prosecution case or assists the defence, and demands for access to material which is not referable to an issue raised in the defence case statement should be resisted.

KEY CONSIDERATION

Have I identified any further reasonable lines of enquiry from the defence case statement?

It is a simple fact that the defence's failures to comply with their duties as laid out in the act is widespread. A defence case statement made in accordance with the act generally commits the defendant to a particular line of defence and in many cases it is preferable for the defence to avoid doing this particularly at an early stage. If the defence commit themselves early and without access to all the unused material they run two risks. First that the prosecution may have something among that material with which to disprove or undermine that defence and secondly that it allows the police/prosecution time to fully investigate that defence to the same purpose. It is often tactically preferable therefore either to provide a very vague defence case statement or provide none at all and just accept the sanction of comment to the jury by the judge.

Any defence case statement—no matter how inadequate it is regarding the requirements laid out in the CPIA—must be considered by both the CPS reviewing lawyer and the disclosure officer. It should be endorsed by the CPS reviewing lawyer indicating any particular issues that emerge from it, before being passed to the disclosure officer. It will require a reconsideration of the unused material by the disclosure officer who will then need to produce a further MG6E under their continuing disclosure duties. The defence will be informed by the CPS whether or not their case statement has generated any further disclosable material. Inadequate defence case statements will also be returned to the defence by the CPS.

> **KEY CONSIDERATION**
>
> Have I re-examined all my unused material in the light of the defence case state-ment and completed a further MG6E?

7.13.3 Defence applications for disclosure

Under section 8 of CPIA the defence may make an application to the court for an order that the prosecution disclose unused material where they can show that it falls to be disclosed because it might undermine or assists. Such an application should not be made until the defence have provided a defence statement, how-ever, in practice, judges have often allowed applications where there has been no defence statement and, worse still, ordered disclosure of material outside the CPIA.

This is a problem which can only be resolved by the judiciary itself when they recognize that departing from the CPIA regime in this way absolves the defence from properly engaging in the process. This should be remedied by the introduc-tion of the Disclosure Protocol and tighter case management by the judiciary in the Crown Court.

References: DM 15, 16; AGG 15, 36, 38, 40; CoP 8.3

7.14 The Disclosure Protocol

7.14.1 Judicial failure to enforce the CPIA regime

It has been a common complaint of police officers involved in disclosure issues that none of the parties involved in the judicial process appear to have any true desire to see the regime operating in strict accordance with the provisions of the CPIA. For a variety of reasons each of the parties involved in the criminal justice process have historically been complicit in the CPIA's failure to operate as it was intended. Most influential has been the attitude of judges to enforcement of the regime. In many cases judges have ordered widespread disclosure of material to the defence to which they had no entitlement under the Act. Judges have allowed applications for disclosure of material that are not referable to issues laid out in defence case statements and worse where there have been no meaningful defence case statements at all. Conversely, judges have been reluctant to bring pressure to bear on the defence to comply with their duties under the Act. In case management terms this has meant missing opportunities to identify the real issues in a case and so prevent the judicial process becoming sidetracked into ancillary issues.

7.14.2 A Protocol for judicial oversight of the disclosure process

This Crown Court Protocol has been in force since February 2006 and reiterates that disclosure of unused prosecution material must be dealt with in strict accordance with the provisions of the amended CPIA regime. It was produced by a judicial working group and has been endorsed by the President of the Queen's Bench Division, the Attorney General, the Lord Chancellor, the Director of Public Prosecutions, and the Chairman of the Bar Council:

> Disclosure is one of the most important—as well as one of the most abused—of the procedures relating to criminal trials. There needs to be a sea-change in the approach of both judges and the parties to all aspects of the handling of the material which the prosecution do not intend to use in support of their case. For too long, a wide range of serious misunderstandings has existed, both as to the exact ambit of the unused material to which the defence is entitled, and the role to be played by the judge in ensuring that the law is properly applied.
>
> All too frequently applications by the parties and decisions by the judges in this area have been made based either on misconceptions as to the true nature of the law or a general laxity of approach (however well-intentioned). This failure properly to apply the binding provisions as regards disclosure has proved extremely and unnecessarily costly and has obstructed justice.

Opening paragraph (part) of the Disclosure Protocol drawn up by Mr Justice Fulford and Mr Justice Openshaw (February 2006)

According to the DPP the Protocol:

> . . . rightly emphasises that investigators, disclosure officers and prosecutors need to be scrupulous in the discharge of their responsibilities, and its call for a complete culture change in the approach taken to defence statements by the courts and by the defence is very welcome.

The Protocol covers all aspects of the CPIA regime, but the conscientious disclosure officer has nothing to fear from it, quite the contrary. It is good news for the police/prosecution team; reinforcing their duties under the Act while at the same time ensuring that the judges take a far firmer stand with the defence in order to identify the trial issues at the earliest opportunity.

Further reading—Excerpts from the Crown Court Protocol

. . . it is also essential that the trial process is not overburdened or diverted by erroneous and inappropriate disclosure of unused prosecution material, or by misconceived applications in relation to such material.

Para 3

The overarching principle is therefore that unused prosecution material will fall to be disclosed if, and only if, it satisfies the test for disclosure applicable to the proceedings in question, subject to any overriding public interest considerations.

Para 4

Judges should not allow the prosecution to abdicate their statutory responsibility for reviewing the unused material by the expedient of allowing the defence to inspect (or providing the defence with copies of) everything on the schedules of non-sensitive unused prosecution material, irrespective of whether that material, or all of that material, satisfies the relevant test for disclosure.

Para 30

In the past, the prosecution and the court have too often been faced with a defence case statement that is little more than an assertion that the Defendant is not guilty . . . such a reiteration of the defendant's plea is not the purpose of a defence statement.

Para 34

There must be a complete change in the culture. The defence must serve the defence case statement by the due date. Judges should then examine the defence case statement with care to ensure that it complies with the formalities required by the CPIA.

Para 37

If no defence case statement—or no sufficient case statement—has been served by the PCMH, the judge should make a full investigation of the reasons for this failure to comply with the mandatory obligation of the accused.

Para 38

The consideration of detailed defence requests for specific disclosure (so-called 'shopping lists') otherwise than in accordance with (the rules) is wholly improper. Likewise, defence requests for specific disclosure of unused prosecution material in purported pursuance of section 8 of the CPIA and (the rules), which are not referable to any issue in the case identified by the defence case statement, should be rejected.

Para 45

The key point is that the Protocol reinforces the CPIA regime and the duties of all the parties involved. In particular it attacks the widespread defence non-compliance and judicial disregard for the system. This can only be to the benefit of the CJS. A similar Protocol has been proposed to address disclosure in magistrates' court cases.

7.15 Continuing Duties

It is very important finally to recognize that disclosure is a process that continues throughout the investigation: prior to charge, up to trial, and possibly beyond. At the pre-trial advice stage the CPS reviewing lawyer may well need to examine unused material as well as the evidence amassed. As the case progresses there may be developments that require further work to be carried out that will generate more unused material or require a reconsideration of the material that has already been generated. After charge the defence may provide a case statement or instigate further enquiries that will again generate more material or lead to a reassessment of unused material. These duties continue until the end of the judicial process, which may be the Court of Appeal or even beyond.

KEY CONSIDERATION

Am I carrying out my continuing duty to review the disclosure process throughout the life of the case?

References: DM 14; AGG 17, 44; CoP 8.2

7.16 **Conclusion**

The CPIA regime as endorsed by the Judicial Protocol is good news for the police and the CPS. It recognizes the potential importance of unused prosecution material to a trial in terms of what might undermine the prosecution case or assist the defence and provides a system for identifying and dealing with that material that serves the right of the defendant to fair disclosure. At the same time, through the PII rules, it provides a way of protecting sensitive investigative material even if it falls to be disclosed to the defence. Further, it requires the defence to participate in the process by providing a defence case statement that identifies the issues in a case at the earliest opportunity. All this good, however, will be undone if the disclosure officer and the CPS reviewing lawyer in partnership fail to fulfil their respective duties thoroughly, and as we have seen failures here can be as fatal to the prosecution as any difficulties with evidence or witnesses.

KEY CONSIDERATIONS

- Could I justify as reasonable those enquiries that I have made and those enquiries I have not made to the trial judge?
- Are there any missing records of my investigation?
- Have I identified all the relevant material in this case ?
- Have I identified all third parties who may be in possession of relevant material in this case and informed the CPS?
- Is there any material that I need to discuss with the CPS to ensure early disclosure to the defence?
- Have I checked the editing of the copies of the crime report and message log?

- Have I reminded the police officers involved of their duty to supply me with an MG6B if necessary?
- Have I completed my MG6C schedule clearly, accurately, and in sufficient detail so the prosecutor can make an informed decision?
- Have I completed my MG6D schedule clearly, accurately, and in sufficient detail to enable the CPS reviewing lawyer to decide whether or not to view the material?
- Have I identified all the material on the schedules that undermines the prosecution case or assists the defence?
- Have I completed the MG6E either explaining why material falls to be disclosed or certifying that there is no disclosable material?
- Have I provided copies of all MG6E material to the CPS reviewing lawyer?
- Have I drawn the attention of the CPS to disclosable sensitive material?
- Can I show that the entries on my sensitive schedule meet the test of risking serious prejudice to an important public interest?
- Is there any CHIS material in this case to which I do not have access and that requires making special arrangements with the CPS?
- Have I identified any further reasonable lines of enquiry from the defence case statement?
- Have I re-examined all my unused material in the light of the defence case statement and completed a further MG6E?
- Am I carrying out my continuing duty to review the disclosure process throughout the life of the case?

Further Reading

- The Disclosure Manual 2005
- The Attorney General's Guidelines on Disclosure 2005
- The CPIA Codes of Practice 2005
- 'Disclosure—A Protocol for the control and management of unused material in the Crown Court'

8

Giving Evidence in Court

8.1 **Introduction**

Police officers, just like advocates, can be assisted by training so that they give more effective evidence in court. The advice in this chapter will enable the officer to be better prepared and have a deeper understanding of the whole court process and the techniques used by advocates. The importance of preparation prior to going into court and the actual appearance and attitude of the officer in court is considered. Then the game plan of the advocate in court in relation to both examination in chief and cross-examination is explained, with key tips for survival and suggested coping strategies. By a deeper understanding of the court processes, and the techniques used by advocates, police officers should be better able to present their evidence more confidently and effectively in court.

It is absolutely vital that all police officers can perform effectively in the courtroom. This is the 'acid' test for any police officer, since they obviously have a major part to play in any case. The effective presentation of the case in court in a confident, impartial, and efficient manner may well determine the outcome. Everything read or done so far will count for nothing if the performance in the courtroom fails.

Unfortunately, it is a reality that many police officers have far less exposure to court work now than they used to. Gone are the days of police officers presenting their own cases with the inception of the CPS. There is certainly no substitute for experience but this chapter should give officers a more in-depth understanding and appreciation of what is going on in the courtroom from the advocate's mindset. How, for example, they can get both the best and worst out of a witness in examination in chief and cross-examination.

8.1.1 **Thinking trial**

We have already considered the prosecutor's mindset in Chapter 2, thinking 'trial' from the outset, applying a forensic detailed eye to the case from the beginning and building up a case to ensure the maximum prospect of success at trial. By frontloading and focusing on the trial from the outset prosecutors and police officers alike will hold the same mindset, with the giving of evidence in court merely the last stage of that continuing process.

8.1.2 **Witness familiarization not coaching**

There are presently a number of courses throughout the country for police officers whereby a lawyer (usually) trains them in court skills. This is commonly called 'witness familiarization'. In the Metropolitan area, the CPS has had a major part to play in these courses in conjunction with BPP Professional Education who believe that they will make a significant contribution to the quality of evidence in the case.

This phrase 'witness familiarization' is employed because both case law and guidance issued prohibits the actual coaching of a witness when giving evidence. Indeed, no one is allowed to influence or rehearse a witness in respect of their evidence for any specific forthcoming matter in court—they cannot put words into their mouths. That process is unlawful and can lead to major problems, as in the case of *Momadou and Limani* [2005] EWCA Crim 177. Here a number of security staff were witnesses against asylum seekers accused of violent disorder in 2002 at Yarl's Wood Detention Centre. They were given specific coaching in court techniques by a witness training company. The Court of Appeal was highly critical of this training calling it 'inappropriate' and 'improper' because they had used a mock trial example which heavily reflected a number of specific issues in the case and bore a close resemblance to the evidence which the security guards were subsequently giving.

However, what is allowed is to give potential witnesses greater familiarity with the court process and put them at ease by explaining the sequence of events and the different responsibilities of the participants. This in turn will provide greater confidence when giving oral evidence and ensure that evidence is presented to best effect. It is all about giving any witness, civilian, or police officer more confidence and support—it is not about telling anyone what to say in the witness-box.

The Court placed the CPS in a key role of being both informed in advance of such training programmes and then giving them effectively a seal of approval where appropriate.

8.1.3 The court as live theatre

Giving evidence is not an easy task and it is quite stressful, therefore we want to try to level the playing field between police witnesses and highly trained advocates in court. We want to ensure that when police officers give evidence in court they are properly familiarized with both the procedures and the physical environment of court. Remember the courtroom is effectively live theatre and the police officer must be aware that an audience is watching them throughout. Research studies have demonstrated that juries hold misconceptions and stereotypes of witnesses with much more of their perceptions based on how the witness looks and sounds, rather than what they actually say. The bottom line, therefore, is that police officers may not come across to the fact-finders in court (magistrates or judiciary) as well as, or in the manner in which, they think they do.

Scratch below the surface and think of the type of skills that are required to ensure that the jury will see a person as a reliable and trustworthy witness. What is it that they see in others, from their life experience, that makes them believe what is said? Is it their confidence, body language, knowledge, simplicity of expression, etc or is it something else? Think about it—do not be complacent. Giving evidence can be quite intimidating even for a police officer.

8.2 **Preparation and Anticipation**

Comprehensive preparation for your role is key here. An unprepared witness will come across as an unconvincing one. If you, as a police officer, follow this basic guidance and understand the role of the other participants in court it will assist you in anticipating the type of questions you will be asked so that you are not taken by surprise and can present yourself as an effective witness.

8.2.1 **Prior to court**

Mental preparation

Whenever a police officer receives a warning for court, as a witness they should mentally prepare and bear in mind the following:

- Ensure that you have read all relevant statements and documents in the case so that you have a detailed knowledge of what you are going to tell the court.
- You will need to be prepared to explain your specific job description without reference to police jargon which laymen may not understand. You must assume that the defence have researched all this and you need to know it to the same level. If you are the officer in the case you will be required to display knowledge of a greater range of operational matters and reasons for decisions than if you are merely the interviewing officer. Moreover, you may also have more onerous responsibilities by ensuring the relevant police file is brought to court together with the exhibits and that sufficient copies of transcripts of interview, diagrams, photos, etc are also available for all parties at court.
- You will need to possess a detailed knowledge of your own police powers to be able to demonstrate that you have acted lawfully when arresting, searching, detaining, cautioning, etc. You should have been focused from the outset on ensuring that everything you do can be justified in court further down the line.
- Your own prosecution advocate may ask you questions relating to job description, police powers and procedures as a means of laying a foundation for the factual evidence to follow on. This can insulate you from such a line of questioning at a later stage by the defence.

Establishing your credibility

- How long have you been a detective?
- What sort of training did you receive?
- What are the responsibilities for a detective investigating crime?
- How did you personally assist the investigation?
- What were your priorities in relation to this specific case?

- How do you record the details of the actions you take?
- How does this assist the investigation, etc?

Knowledge testing

- What does PACE allow you do with regard to questioning a suspect when not at a police station?
- Legally what allowed you to carry out the search on these premises?
- What powers allowed you to seize and retain property during that search?

- As a professional witness you have a set of professional standards, shortly to be embodied in a statutory code (National Professional Standards Code of Conduct 2008). It consists of a number of headline principles such as: police officers not abusing their powers; not acting in a discriminatory way; only using reasonable force and being honest and responsible in carrying out their duties; observing and respecting the rights of all including the arrested person. Such a code provides a benchmark by which you will be judged retrospectively in court so you will be familiar with it and adhere to it in practice.

- Never forget why you have been called to give evidence in the first place. As a police officer your job is to collect and collate evidence in the investigation of the crime then subsequently present that evidence to the court in an impartial fashion. You are not batting for the prosecution. Your evidence will relate to the facts you yourself have witnessed (seen or heard). It will be the court's task, it is hoped, to do justice according to the facts of each case. You as a witness, police officer, or otherwise will have no role whatsoever in deciding guilt or innocence (save in your effective presentation of facts to the court). For this reason you should treat both prosecution and defence counsel with the same demeanour and attitude throughout.

- The emphasis in your evidence is on facts because the court is only interested in the facts of the case not in any assumptions, conclusions or opinions derived from those facts by the witnesses (refer to fact analysis in Chapter 2).

POINT TO NOTE—KEEP TO THE FACTS

You have arrested a suspect for a public order offence because in your opinion he was being drunk, disorderly, and aggressive towards members of the public. Your notes should reflect what facts in terms of his demeanour and behaviour led you to arrest him. That's what the court will be interested in—what he will be looking like, saying or doing, not your conclusion or opinion that you decided he was a drunken lout, as it were. Police officers often fall into the trap of ignoring the facts and jumping direct to the conclusion. Any good advocate will be able to use this against you in the witness-box. You are far more persuasive if you always stick to the facts of the case

---

Physical preparation

Your mental preparation is hopefully completed but you will still need physically to get yourself to court in plenty of time before your case is called on and familiarize yourself with the court surroundings.

At this stage, it is helpful to consider the following:

- As soon as you arrive, you should notify the usher of your presence, ensure other witnesses are also there (if you are officer in the case), and then introduce yourself to the prosecutor to see if any issues need clarifying, or there are any further instructions for you.
- Check that the officer responsible for bringing the case papers to court is also in possession of relevant exhibits and unused material.
- You will need to ensure that all witnesses have had the opportunity to read their statements prior to court. This should be done individually so that the witnesses do not discuss their evidence together, which may prejudice the case. Any vulnerable witnesses may have special needs in accordance with the Victim Code or may just need some reassurance and a friendly face. The Witness Service will assist here and you should be liaising with them.
- It is better if you do not speak to the defendant or his representative, even if they approach you, without reference back to the CPS first. Remember you are also a witness in the case and you should be mindful of doing anything that could prejudice the trial.
- At all times try to be proactive at court rather than just sitting in the police room waiting for your name to be called. Whenever you get the opportunity, go into court and watch another case, utilizing the time to become familiar with the court scenario. Identify who you think is a good witness. What is it about them that makes them good?

8.2.2 **Going into court**

You only have one chance to create a good first impression. The audience in court will be looking at you the moment that you walk though the door of the court so this is your starting point.

Taking the oath

As you get into the witness-box the usher will ask you whether you wish to take the oath or affirm. Decide in advance which you are going to do and even if you have learnt them by heart read from the card provided. Do not however, switch onto auto-pilot when reading it out. Remember it is your promise to tell the truth so pay attention to it. It is advisable that you show that you recognize the solemnity of the occasion through paying attention to it because it is your opportunity to convince the magistrate or the jury that you mean what you say.

POINT TO NOTE

Oath

I swear by almighty God that the evidence I shall give shall be the truth the whole truth and nothing but the truth.

Affirmation

I do solemnly, sincerely and truly declare and affirm that the evidence I shall give shall be the truth, the whole truth and nothing but the truth.

Which do you choose?

The oath/affirmation will give you the opportunity to settle yourself and become familiar with the positioning of all the court personnel. At this stage you need to breathe slowly and calmly, relax and be yourself. As a professional it is important you appear as a confident witness even if you are not. Remembering the following motto may assist you to control those nerves:

Always behave like a duck. Keep calm and unruffled on the surface but paddle like heck underneath

Ask yourself: 'How do I look to the fact-finders?'.

The golden triangle

The court scenario is not easy to handle because you are essentially faced with the strange situation of being asked questions by one person—the advocate for the prosecution or the defence—and then addressing your answers to a completely different set of people—the magistrates or jury positioned somewhere else in the court. In ordinary day-to-day situations if someone asked you a question and you turned your back on them to answer it they would think you were rude. Not so in the court scenario, which is commonly called the '**golden triangle of communication**'. In fact you need to position yourself in the witness-box so that you can face the fact-finders (the magistrates or jury) remembering to look and listen to your questioner (the advocate) and address your answers to someone else (the fact-finders)—quite an uncomfortable setting. In the Crown Court you also have to be very aware of the judge, who effectively controls the court. Figure 8.1 may help you approach this situation.

Figure 8.1 The 'Golden Triangle'

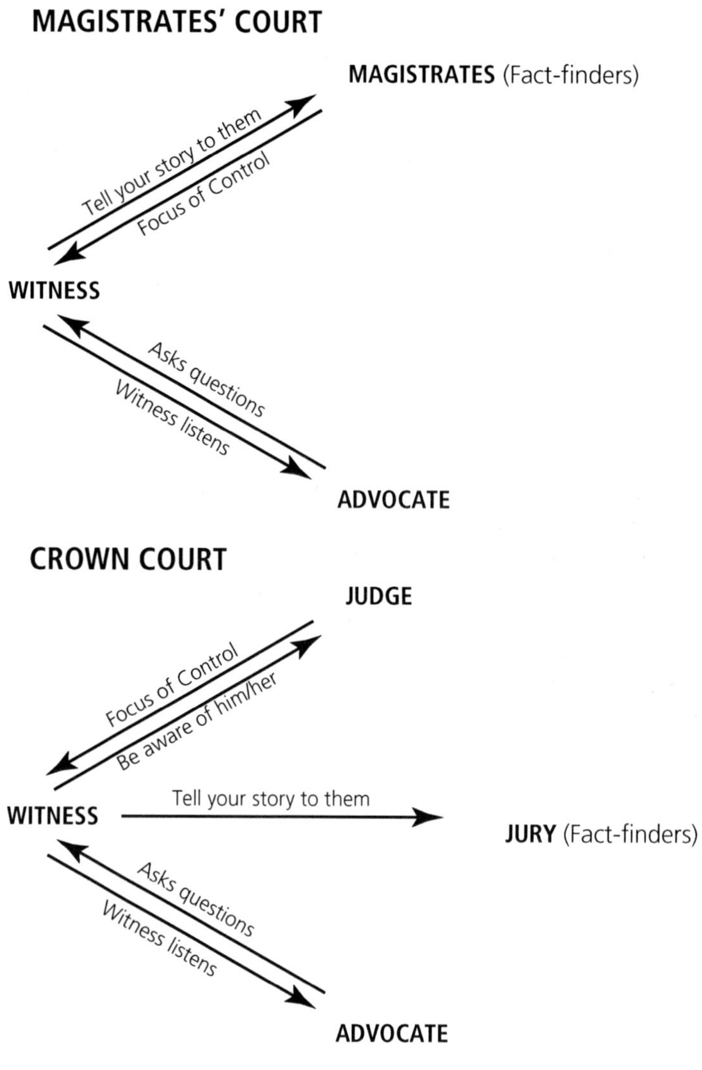

MAGISTRATES' COURT

MAGISTRATES (Fact-finders)

Tell your story to them
Focus of Control

WITNESS

Asks questions
Witness listens

ADVOCATE

CROWN COURT

JUDGE

Focus of Control
Be aware of him/her

WITNESS ——— Tell your story to them ———▶

JURY (Fact-finders)

Asks questions
Witness listens

ADVOCATE

8.2.3 **Giving evidence in court**

The basics

There are some very basic rules to remember when you give evidence in any court in respect of any type of case:

- The acoustics in many courts are poor so you need to project your voice to make sure everyone can hear you.
- You need to slow down your usual voice pace so that important points are not missed. Moreover, the clerk to the magistrates or the judge in the Crown Court will usually be making notes of everything you say. You have to watch their pens. If they are scribbling they cannot be listening!
- Whenever you are required to refer, for example, to the transcript of interview as interviewing officer, try to watch your voice intonation. If you read it in a monotone voice it will sound dull and boring.
- Remember to maintain eye contact with the fact-finder and to engage your audience (when reading a transcript as well).
- Know how to address the court correctly but try not to overuse the titles—magistrates' court: sir or madam (to the Chair of the lay bench or the District Judge) and Crown Court: Your Honour (to the Judge).
- Listen to the question you are asked at all times and make sure you are answering it properly. If you do not know any answer or you do not understand or want the questioner to repeat it, say so.
- Think before you speak on every occasion. Never just say the first thing that comes into your head.
- Always remember: keep it short and simple (KISS). Do not volunteer unnecessary information. Remember no one in court has any idea about the story you are going to tell them. They need to grasp it first time around; there are no second chances. You must try and see the case from the eyes of your audience who are not police officers but civilians (or lawyers).
- Be frank and candid at all times—honesty is the only policy. It is your straightforwardness and your integrity which will make you a credible witness in the eyes of the fact-finders. Whenever you slightly misquote the facts of a case or put a slight spin on the evidence it will open the door to a good defence advocate to cast a doubt in the fact-finder's mind on your veracity. You will be caught short.

POINT TO NOTE—KEEP TO THE FACTS

Where a victim of a robbery says s/he felt something sharp on the back of her neck—do not fall into the trap of embellishing the evidence into a description of the incident as a 'knife point robbery' unless you have clear alternative evidence that such a knife and indeed robbery occurred. It is easily done when telling your story to the fact-finders. In real life a little bit of exaggeration or embellishment keeps everyone interested. This has absolutely no place in court; there it is essential to stick to the facts.

An honest witness who is inaccurate is of no greater value than an accurate one who is dishonest.

R Bartle, *The Police Witness: A Guide to Presenting Evidence in Court* (New Police Bookshop, 2002)

Memory refreshing

Since 5 April 2004, section 139 of the Criminal Justice Act 2003 permits a person giving oral evidence in criminal proceedings to refresh his/her memory at any stage from any document made by him at an earlier time if: (i) he states in his evidence that the document records his/her recollection of the matter at that earlier time; and (ii) his/her recollection of the matter is likely to have been significantly better at that time than it is at the time of his/her oral evidence. What this means is that the old test of 'contemporaneous notes' has gone. By virtue of this section, any witness, civilian, or police officer, is allowed to refresh his/her memory in respect of any details of the case from any document (officer's pocket books, original statements, even a cigarette packet).

The test is whether at the time the original note was made one's memory was 'significantly better' than it is in court. Be alert therefore to this phrase from the prosecution advocate. Not all police officers seem to appreciate this and a common fault is routinely to produce one's notebook straightaway. Wait for the prosecution advocate to ask you what is often a series of questions (including when the notes were written), to lay the foundation for the admissibility of your original notes which will give greater weight and credibility to them when they are admitted.

POINT TO NOTE—LAYING THE FOUNDATIONS

- Do you recall an incident?
- Did you make notes about the incident?
- How long after that incident did you make those notes?
- Was that the first opportunity you had?
- Had you dealt with any other incidents in the meantime?
- Do your notes record your recollection of the incident at that time?
- Was your recollection of the incident better at that time than it is now?
- Did you make the notes on your own or in conjunction with other officers?

So you can, in nearly every case, refer to your original notes for the detail but remember what has been said about the importance of eye contact with your audience. You should only be using them to refresh your memory; it is not a signal to start reading from them like a script verbatim. It may be useful to point out to the court that what in fact you are doing is refreshing your memory with regard to specific details (eg verbatim comments, descriptions, registration numbers) if in fact this is the case and you do actually remember most of the incident from memory. Your original notes do act as a safety blanket but do not allow them to detract from giving your personal evidence.

To sum up

All this guidance comes under the umbrella of preparation and anticipation (see Figure 8.2). By effectively front loading and maintaining a 'think trial' mindset from the outset of the case and carrying it forward to the witness-box, you will have mentally prepared yourself for the ordeal ahead.

You should have a finite understanding of your role, the case details, and your police powers, so that you will be able to tell the court exactly what you have done, when you have done it, and precisely how you fit into the case in a concise, chronological, and, most importantly, simple fashion. You never want to be in the position of thinking about all this and verbalizing it for the first time ever as you get into the witness-box.

Figure 8.2 Preparation and anticipation

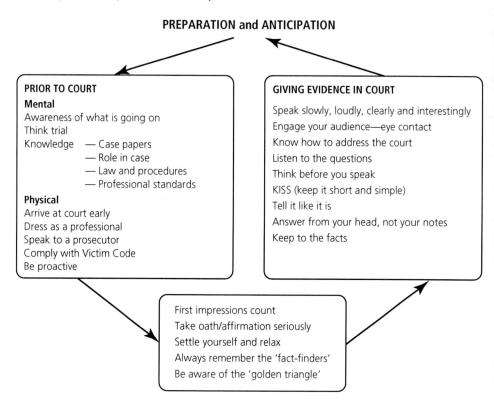

8.3 Looking into the Advocate's Mindset

What actually occurs in examination in chief by the prosecution advocate, and cross-examination by the defence? It will assist you when giving evidence to be more comfortable, feel more confident and come across to the audience more cogently if you understand some of the intricacies of advocacy.

8.3.1 Examination in chief

Purpose of examination in chief

Many officers are more wary of cross-examination (ie of being given a hard time by the defence), and assume that when they are giving their own evidence in chief in front of their prosecution advocate it is relatively easy. This could not, in fact, be further from the truth.

Examination in chief is all about telling your story to an audience (magistrates or jury). It is more difficult because the spotlight is on you, the police officer, throughout. A good prosecution advocate will, in effect, be working in the wings, taking second place, and merely facilitating the telling of your story in a clear, concise, chronological, comprehensive, and convincing manner.

Consider also why you have been called to give evidence—why are you there? Is all your evidence in dispute? Are you a crucial witness? Clarify in your own mind the key issues. It may be, for example, that the prosecution advocate only wants to concentrate in detail on particular key areas.

Questioning techniques—the advocate's toolkit

In this court scenario the good advocate will have his own toolkit to obtain the best evidence from you. Basically he will use non-leading questions (very similar to those used by police officers in interview) to elicit your story. Such questions generally begin with the words: who, what, where, when, why, how, describe, explain. They have the effect, by beginning with an interrogative word, of ensuring the questioner is only covering one point at a time.

POINT TO NOTE—NON-LEADING QUESTIONS

- Officer, I want to ask you some questions about a search that took place on . . . ?
- How did you arrive at the premises?
- Who were you with?
- Who answered the door?
- Please describe that person?
- How did you enter the premises?

The prosecution advocate can only ask you a leading question (ie a question that suggests a particular answer) in relation to matters that are not in dispute between the parties. Such leading questions are usually only found in cross-examination and may begin, for example, with words like 'did', 'would', and 'should'.

POINT TO NOTE—WHAT IS A LEADING AND NON-LEADING QUESTION?

What colour was the car? (non-leading)
Was the car black? (leading—not acceptable)
What did you see? (non-leading)
Did you see the knife in his hand? (leading)

A lawyer is not allowed to assume a fact that has not already been established by the evidence. So the advocate has to actually think of the answer they want to avoid putting in the question.

> **POINT TO NOTE—TYPES OF QUESTIONS**
>
> Answer wanted: The car was a black Chevrolet (where the colour and make of the car are in dispute)
>
> Questions: What colour was the car?
>
> What make was it?
>
> **NOT** was the car a black Chevrolet?
>
> It may even be necessary for the lawyer to lay a foundation by first asking 'how did the person get there?' to establish the fact it was by car in the first place.

It may also be necessary for the advocate to lay a foundation by a series of questions, where you are the exhibiting officer for real evidence, eg a gun. In this situation it is also vital to remember the importance of demonstrating the continuity of the exhibit from the time it leaves the crime scene and goes to the forensic laboratory, is examined, and is then returned.

This non-leading type of questioning by the advocate effectively allows him/her to control the way that you tell your story so that it comes out in bite-sized chunks rather than in one long narrative, which could leave your audience behind. He wants you to give your evidence in a chronological, logical, precise, and structured fashion without digression or embellishment.

Some advocates do not assist the witness by giving them little sense of direction. They may continually use the same open-ended question, for example, 'What happened next?' or 'And then?'. In this situation you as a professional witness will have to deliver your evidence slowly and in bite size chronological chunks, thereby painting a clear picture to your audience.

The poor advocate may also confuse you by rolling up a number of questions into one. This is called 'multiple questioning'. The word 'and' should alert you to this—for example, 'Where did you search and what did you find and what did the occupant of the house say?'. You will need to clarify exactly which question you are answering and deal with them individually. Otherwise, you will be tempted to forget to answer part of the question, or at the very least, in an attempt to answer all of it in one go, confuse the audience.

Occasionally, the good advocate may want you to explain to the court, for example, why you took a particular course of action. The advocate will therefore enable the police officer to paint a picture to the bench. Police officers sometimes seem to have difficulty in delivering the sort of detail which actually puts 'flesh on the bones' of the incident they are recounting. It is often just one of many incidents which they encounter. Similarly, they very rarely volunteer explanations for their actions or their own feelings. The advocate may therefore ask a more open question in order to get the officer to expand on his answer to the court.

POINT TO NOTE—RING OF TRUTH

- Why did you carry out a search?
- What happened after the arrest?
- How did you feel when the suspect did that?
- Why did you shout to your colleague?

Here the advocate is deliberately loosening his/her control in order to give you, as the witness, more opportunity to relate in your own words your explanation.

A 'wider' answer from you in this instance may have the effect of being more persuasive and credible to that audience than a series of non-leading questions. Eventually you will be able to work out what the advocate is trying to achieve and respond accordingly.

Active listening

You will always need to take particular care when listening to the question you are being asked. It may seem obvious but 'active listening', as it is called, is an art form. Under pressure in the witness-box it is not always easy to say that you did not understand the question and ask for clarification or ask him/her to repeat it or ask for time out perhaps to locate an answer in your papers.

Finally, never forget your purpose as a police officer, as the presenter of facts that are within your own knowledge to the court. Tell it like it is and let the court decide.

POINT TO NOTE—EXAMINATION IN CHIEF

- Good preparation and anticipation
- The spotlight is on the police officer
- Take responsibility for your evidence
- Actively listen to all the questions
- Tell it like it is

8.3.2 Cross-examination

Purpose of cross-examination

The myths that abound cross-examination are in abundance. They are mostly instigated by television where witnesses are totally discredited, defendants break down and admit their guilt in the witness-box, and the advocate wins the day. This rarely happens in real life.

Reality sees cross-examination for the good defence advocate as a constructive functional exercise. S/he wants to find evidence, to support his/her client's case and wants to challenge the case against his/her client. This latter function may involve him/her in either demonstrating that the witnesses themselves are unreliable or confused or have a poor recollection of events, or they are at worst biased and/or dishonest.

Yet again it is the importance of good investigation, preparation, knowledge of one's case, and anticipation of what questions the defence advocate might ask (eg from sight of the defence statement) which are the keys to survival under cross-examination.

Remember that the defence advocate often has nothing personal against the police officer. However, s/he will attempt, by his line of questioning: to bring out the worst in you; to make a meal of any inaccuracies or mistakes; to drag you into areas about which you know nothing; to concentrate on some minor red herring to which you may become evasive or defensive so that s/he can make a mountain out of a molehill; to get you to engage with him/her directly thereby making you lose eye contact with the audience so that they are alienated or disinterested.

You, as a professional witness, must keep your wits about you and not rise to his/her bait. Stick to your story, remaining focused on the facts within your knowledge. Never fight the advocate. Present your evidence in a calm, confident, credible manner at all times, always avoiding the temptation to prevaricate, digress, or be defensive. Admit your mistakes and give straightforward answers to all the questions.

Questioning techniques—boiling the frog

You can see that in cross-examination the spotlight shifts totally from the police officer telling his story onto the defence advocate. The latter will have prepared a series of carefully thought-out leading questions, which are all designed to lead through the facts to a conclusion. S/he will attempt this by telling you (not asking) what his/her client's version of the events is. By means of such direct questioning the advocate gains control closing down the options available in response from the witness.

This whole process may be described as 'boiling the frog'. It is a useful term to remember to remind you where the advocate is trying to lead you. What does it mean? Well, if you put a frog into boiling water it will jump straight out again. If the advocate aggressively goes for your jugular and calls you mistaken, confused, or even a liar, you will undoubtedly dispute it. However, if you put a frog into cold water and gradually turn up the temperature it never really notices until it is too late. Similarly, by a gradual, controlled questioning technique the defence advocate may put you in the latter position of the frog. He will basically deconstruct a factual scenario picking out the facts and putting them back together again with a slightly different spin so that it ultimately casts doubt on your veracity. Even if you finally still say 'no' and disagree that you were mistaken or confused that will be irrelevant. The advocate merely wishes to create doubt about the witness and thereby the case.

POINT TO NOTE—ADVOKATE

Remember the mnemonic ADVOKATE, used as an aide-memoire by all police officers—the defence certainly will:

A   Amount of time under observation

D   Distance between suspect and witness

V   Visibility at time

O   Observations

K   Known suspect

A   Any reason to remember

T   Time lapse since witness saw suspect

E   Error or material discrepancy

Imagine the scenario of an eyewitness standing by a window of the third floor of a building looking down onto the street and seeing a man rob a woman of her handbag. A parked car, in fact, partially shielded the woman. The man runs off down the street with the bag. The witness positively picks out the robber at an identification parade. If the defence case is that the witness was mistaken the advocate will concentrate on the available facts (eg distance, angle of view (looking down), duration of incident, visibility partially obscured, robber moving at all times, etc) in order to achieve this objective.

Instead of just one question ('Isn't it possible you were mistaken about identifying my client'?—Answer, 'No'), the questioning may go something like this:

You were working on the third floor of a building weren't you?	Yes
Above the location of the incident?	Yes
About 100 yards away from the scene of the robbery?	Yes
You weren't expecting to see a robbery, were you?	No
There was a parked car in the street, wasn't there?	Yes
It obscured part of the pavement didn't it?	Yes
And you had a 'bird's-eye view' looking down didn't you?	Yes
You saw the man approach the woman?	Yes
You saw him take her handbag ?	Yes
You saw him run away, didn't you?	Yes
At that point you were looking at the back of the youth?	Yes
It's fair to say the youth was always in motion?	Yes
In fact he never stood still and you never made eye contact with him?	No
As he was always in motion the incident took a few	

seconds didn't it?	Yes
So you had a fleeting glance at best?	Yes
Then isn't it possible in these circumstances you are mistaken in identifying my client?	No

Does his answer matter? The advocate has surely created a doubt in the minds of the audience as to whether or not the witness can positively identify the robber—sufficient doubt for a jury to acquit.

What can you do to prevent yourself being that boiled frog?

It is back to basics again of 'thinking trial' from the onset, being as prepared as you possibly can to start with and anticipating and being aware of what is actually going on in this courtroom scenario, pinpointing the factual issues which the defence may use in their cross-examination.

Handling the defence

Discussion of some further techniques used by the defence advocate may assist you in understanding their method of questioning and enable you to cope better when in the witness—box:

- A non-leading open question by the defence advocate may put you on the alert that s/he is actually trying to give you a rope to hang yourself—think carefully before answering such a question and keep to the facts. Where you have no clear recollection of the events say so.
- The defence advocate may often try to unsettle the inexperienced officer by implying that s/he has no independent recollection of events because s/he has written up notes with colleagues. This is a perfectly correct procedure, which does not imply collusion, so you do not need to be defensive in your response. However, always ensure that your notes reflect only what you have witnessed not something imported from your colleagues.
- Remember always to keep to the facts within your knowledge. You cannot give evidence on matters which are not in your statement and which are another's responsibility or experience. Similarly do not get dragged into expressing opinions, speculation or making assumptions or irrelevant comments. You are witnesses of fact not opinion, especially if you are asked, for example, how another witness was feeling; you simply cannot answer that.
- Never try to score points over the advocate or argue with him/her. Behave like the duck at all times with no additional non-verbal communications thrown in like hunched shoulders or particular facial expressions. Such behaviour will not impress your audience.

- Try not to get flustered so that where you need time, ask for it admitting any mistakes from the onset and never trying to bluff your way out of the question.
- At all times keep your focus on the audience—do not allow yourself to be pulled into a two-way conversation with the defence advocate leaving the audience out in the cold.

Checklist—Cross-examination

- Good preparation and anticipation

- Beware of the myths

- The spotlight is on the defence advocate

- S/he is telling, not asking, and 'boiling the frog' via leading questions

- Stick to the facts as you know them

  (ie no opinions, speculation, assumptions, irrelevant comments)

- Keep your composure—it is nothing personal

- Do not be defensive, admit your mistakes

- Do not forget it is your audience that is all-important

8.4 **Conclusion**

The insight into the advocate's mind and some of the coping strategies we have suggested in this chapter may enable you to produce a more effective presentation of your evidence to the court. As a professional witness you will have the opportunity also, when handling other lay witnesses, to familiarize them with the court processes so that they too may feel more confident when entering the witness-box.

9

Conclusion—The Future?

9.1 **Introduction**

Statutory charging is now embedded throughout England and Wales. Police officers and CPS prosecutors are beginning to work together as one prosecution team proactively investigating and prosecuting on the front foot—so what is next?

9.2 **Simple Speedy Summary Justice (CJSSS)**

In July 2006, the government published *Delivering Simple Speedy Summary Justice* aimed at improving the speed and effectiveness of the 95% of cases heard in the magistrates' courts. This report followed cross agency reviews of the Crown Court and magistrates' court which found that some criminal cases were taking too long with too many hearings before a conclusion was reached. Very seldom was a plea taken on first appearance. The prosecution or the defence was not ready, there was a lack of advance information, or the court itself was insufficiently robust in dealing with unmeritorious applications.

The principal aim therefore was to reduce the number of hearings in the magistrates' courts to one in the case of a guilty plea and two for contested matters (ie with a plea on first appearance and then straight to trial). The aim was also to reduce the period from offence to disposal to 6 weeks, thereby ensuring a robust, speedy summary court process for adult offenders initially in the more minor cases. In order for this initiative to be effective, cultures again had to change, with all court users working together to support the suggested new development.

Criminal Procedure Rules 2005

Introduced in April 2005, these rules consolidated all previous ones and were the beacon for the new way ahead. They confirmed that it was the courts' duty to actively manage all criminal cases at an early stage, by giving directions to both prosecution and defence. Furthermore, they also placed, on both the prosecution and uniquely the defence, obligations actively to assist the court in that duty. The overriding objective was to ensure that all cases were dealt with justly.

9.2.2 **Implications**

All players within the CJS are therefore affected by the proposals coming from this government report. They required the collaboration of all to make justice faster, fairer, more effective, and more efficient.

CJSSS was piloted in 2006 originally in four magistrates' court centres, with impressive results at the tail end of the CJS, for example:

- a faster judicial process;
- fewer court appearances (ie less adjournments/mentions);
- more guilty pleas at first hearing; and
- more effective and efficient use of court time.

This was achieved by better preparation prior to and after charge, improved prosecution readiness and defence readiness for first hearings, and robust case management throughout by the magistrates and the judiciary.

These pilots originally covered only adult offenders and only those cases where a not guilty plea was anticipated in the magistrates' court. CJSSS has now been rolled out in all youth courts and CJSSS for adult offenders has now been implemented nationally in every magistrates' court. This effectively cut out most police charge cases since they were only charging themselves in relation to anticipated guilty pleas.

Cases considered suitable for trial and sentencing in the magistrates' courts are as follows:

- where the loss or damage to be charged is under £5000; or
- where the overall circumstances of the offence are not so serious that the magistrates' courts are likely to decide that the defendant deserves more than 6 months' imprisonment (the present statutory limit) therefore they will not send the case to the Crown Court; or
- where the offence is not committed at a time when the defendant is subject to a Crown Court order in force such that s/he has to be dealt with by that court.

Front loading

Potential not guilty pleas (to be heard in the magistrates' courts) therefore require a great deal of work from the police prior to charge. Essentially, 'evidential files' are necessary prior to the duty prosecutor taking a final decision to charge and put the case before the court. In some cases the police attend a first appointment with the CPS early on and the latter then provides a detailed action plan to assist their investigation and case building.

The final result should be a prosecution file in bail cases effectively only a few days after charge which will have all the relevant information for the prosecutor in order for a plea to be taken and a trial date to be set, taking availability of witnesses into account where it is a 'not guilty'. At that first stage, if it is a not guilty plea, all trial issues will be settled including special measures, bad character, hearsay and also witness warnings or formal admissions by parties.

Again the CPS and the police are required to work closely together to identify and resolve issues prior to that first hearing.

Advance information

Both the defence and the court receive advance information prior to the court hearing. Either the District Judge or the magistrates' court legal adviser where there is a lay bench as well as the defence, will hopefully have read the papers prior to coming into court. This pre-court briefing for the court enables the magistrates to challenge and probe both prosecution and defence seeking to avoid an adjournment and make progress. All key evidential issues in the case will also be identified. Such a development therefore better enables them to comply with the Criminal Procedure Rules and actively manage the case.

The defence have been given short shrift if they are unprepared or not ready to plead. This attitude has been backed by recent case law in the higher courts, indicating that delays in criminal proceedings are scandalous and bring the law into disrepute

Magistrates must ensure that the case is being dealt with expeditiously by all parties, and any application for an adjournment should be carefully scrutinized before being allowed. Everyone therefore is required to adhere to the CJSS timetable.

Defence criticism

The original pilots did not receive universal support and were subject to some criticism especially from the defence. They were not used to putting their cards on the table from the outset but more used to ambushing the prosecution at trial, or taking a last minute technical point in order to obtain an acquittal of their client. They were also concerned that matters could move too quickly and against the defendant's interests. On the 13 November 2007, Stephen Smith in *The Times Law Supplement* referred to this initiative as 'Falconer's Folly' comparing speedy justice to having a baby: 'It takes nine months, you can deliver it early but it increases the chances of it coming out wrong.'

Hopefully, by working together, front loading and placing the courts in a far more active case management role, the prosecution team have prevented this from happening. The duty of the court will be to see that justice is done (ie acquittal of the innocent and conviction of the guilty). New commercial arrangements for defence solicitors in terms of how they get paid for work done have also encouraged improved efficiency, in ensuring that key decisions in cases are made at that first hearing.

Crown Court

Similarly, in the Crown Court, dealing with the more serious and complex cases, delays, aborted hearings and cases listed for mention were often the norm. The Criminal Procedure Rules apply equally to these higher courts so that by ensuring proactive case management, the judiciary may deal more effectively with early guilty pleas; ensuring operational oversight at preliminary hearings of complex indictable offences and eliminating some of those unnecessary pre-trial hearings (approximately 200,000 'mention hearings' a year!).

Checklist—Key Principles

- Getting it right first time, with all the relevant papers at the outset in relation to a potential not guilty plea, is the motto in case building

    This involves managing and utilizing the time when most suspects are on bail to investigate the case to the full pursuing all reasonable lines of enquiry, focusing on quality investigation, and ensuring that all case papers are complete for the prosecutor. Given speed is of the essence this approach must be seen as the norm and not the exception

- Improved defence readiness is required at the first hearing. The defence are to be provided with advance disclosure prior to that hearing and are then expected to enter a plea there and then

- Active case management by the court is required. They themselves will receive advance information in the case ahead of the first court hearing and are expected to take a firm line. They must ensure a plea is taken and where it is a contested case, potential issues are identified from the outset

- A commitment from all sides is required to ensure that contested cases are progressed out of court between the first hearing and a short trial date rather than numerous interim hearings and adjournments

9.3 **Proportionality—The Streamlined Process (SP)**

As has been seen, given that the police are required to do a considerable amount of additional work prior to a first court appearance in a not guilty plea case in the magistrates' court, a further initiative called the 'streamlined process' is also being piloted to redress the balance. Basically the police could not cope with the level of file building required for CJSSS and this process aims to reduce unnecessary file preparation. This will deliver a more proportionate streamlined prosecution file for both anticipated guilty and not guilty plea cases suitable for sentencing in the magistrates' court. SP also provides for a staged and proportionate approach in the preparation of cases which must be referred to a prosecutor for a charging decision. This more proportionate approach to case file build therefore now supports and builds on CJSSS enabling the court to make effective case management decisions, and ensuring more focused preparation of cases.

The Director of Public Prosecutions has issued guidance to police officers and Crown Prosecutors outlining minimum standards of file content which underpin and support the new processes (*Director's Guidance on the Streamlined Process* (October 2008)). This means police will save time and reduce paperwork by proportionate file preparation depending on the type of charge and anticipated plea and consequent decisions required by the court.

This may have the effect of changing some of the file content and procedures previously outlined in Chapter 3 and 6 where the SP is operational, however, it will not affect basic principles and guidance on quality file content and submission.

9.3.1 **The police report**

Central to the scheme is the new MG5 **police report** using a much simplified file build procedure for the first hearing. This form is to be completed in all police charged cases. The police report together with other documentary and evidential requirements (as set out in the Guidance) will also be submitted in cases where CPS has authorised charge following referral.

The emphasis will be on good quality accurate summaries in a revised and improved MG5 format. Early front end proactive police supervision will be crucial to the success of SP.

POINT TO NOTE:

The Streamlined Process relies on focused quality investigations to maximise the potential efficiencies available to all agencies. It does not however, imply that the investigation should be curtailed. The Criminal Procedure and Investigations Act 1996 places a duty on investigators to pursue all reasonable lines of enquiry and to record and retain all relevant material.

Director's Guidance on the Streamlined Process (October 2008, para 4.1)

For a guilty plea the prosecutor will be able to provide the defence with the police report as advanced information to enable the defendant to understand the case against him or her. The prosecutor will then be able to inform the court of the nature of the case and assist in the sentencing process.

A further key feature of SP is the **reduction in taking of witness statements by the police.** Witness statements from non-police witnesses should be concise covering only the essential points to prove and may be recorded on pro forma documents for ease of processing. Corroborative statements or continuity evidence will not be required to be submitted at this stage.

Thus in anticipated not guilty cases or where the CPS has authorised a charge following referral, the police report will be accompanied by key evidence or key witness statements or other relevant documentation sufficient for the needs of the particular case and the stage it has reached as set out in the guidance. This will allow the court to take a plea at the first hearing, identify major issues for trial and which witnesses will be required to testify. **A court case management report** has been devised for use by the prosecution, defence and court for this purpose.

After the first hearing it will be the responsibility of the CPS to inform the police of issues identified for trial and provide the police with information on all court directions, further evidence required for trial, witnesses to be warned or served section 9, within 3 days.

POINT TO NOTE: DEFINITION OF KEY EVIDENCE

That evidence which either alone (ie the evidence of 1 witness) or taken together with other evidence (eg a number of witnesses, each of whom provide some key evidence and any key exhibits) establishes every element of the offence to be proved and that the person charged committed the offence with the necessary criminal intent.

DPP's Guidance on the Streamlined Process October 2008, para 18.4

9.3.2 Contents of police report

The report that follows is taken from the Director's Guidance on the Streamlined Process at Annex B. There are notes of guidance contained on the form itself.

POLICE REPORT   URN

Name (hit return for additional defendants)		Anticipated Plea	
Name (hit return for additional defendants)		Anticipated Plea	

---

1. KEY EVIDENCE. 'key evidence' is that evidence which either alone (i.e. the evidence of one witness) or taken together (e.g. a number of witnesses each of whom provide some key evidence and any key exhibits) establishes every element of the offence to be proved and that the person charged committed the offence with the necessary criminal intent. The summary should be set out in chronological order so that it tells the story of the offence (not the investigation) and covers each of the **'points to prove'**. It should be made clear which witness (provide name, age, occupation & status: e.g. key eye witness, victim) can provide the evidence summarised. The Summary should be **balanced & fair,** setting out the facts in a narrative style. Witnesses who give the same evidence or deal with procedure (charge, interview etc) should be listed in Section 3 below. *State value of property stolen or damaged and what recovered.* Address and contact details of the civilian witnesses to be entered on form MG9 (their leave dates on MG10) and provided to the prosecutor.

Key witness list

facts of offence

---

2. DEFENDANT INTERVIEW. *Identify the interviewing officer, defence solicitor, appropriate adult and other person present.* Set out any explanation the defendant gave as to **how/why** offence happened; include any mitigation and remorse put forward. If **CCTV** is **'key'**, record the defendant's response/reaction if it was shown in interview, and attach a copy.
Summarise the explanation of the defendant aloud at the conclusion of the interview and note that here. State if no comment made in interview or prepared statement handed over and obtain a copy. Note any special warnings given.

Date ../../20.. Time ..:.. Location   Interviewing officer   Persons present

Summary

CCTV   shown and response

---

3. NON-KEY EVIDENCE. List the witnesses not summarised in section 1 and state what they contribute eg. additional eye witness, arresting officer, present at arrest but dealing with passenger/member of public, charging officer, officer seized CCTV. Address and contact details of the civilian witnesses to be entered on form MG9, leave dates on MG10 and provided to the prosecutor.

---

4. VISUALLY RECORDED EVIDENCE. CCTV, photos, photocopies if any. State if '**Key**' and give a brief summary of what it shows, attach a copy (identifying the play back format for discs). If no visual evidence or not key, give reasons.

---

5. INJURIES. A medical statement is not needed unless required to interpret x-rays, or otherwise described injuries not visible to the naked eye. A victim/eye-witness/police officer should describe visible injuries, photographs should be taken and attached (if none state why).

6. FINGERPRINT/FORENSIC/DRUGS EVIDENCE. Weight of drugs, number of wraps etc. is essential sentencing information as is the street value and purity if known. State if drugs field tested and by whom. State timescales for a full statement if required.

7. DIP TESTING

Defendant NAME Tested	Trigger offence	Result	Drug
Defendant NAME Tested	Trigger offence	Result	Drug

8. ORDERS ON CONVICTION. State how much compensation is sought (if an estimate say so). An address for compensation must be provided to the prosecutor on form MG6. Consider forfeiture and destruction of drugs/weapons or forfeiture of motor vehicle on driving offences. State if ASBO/SOPO/Football banning/restraint/non-molestation order required and attach the appropriate MG forms with copies for court and defence..

Compensation   detail and additonal orders

MG18	Attached ☐	Pre-cons/ cautions Must be attached for each defendant even if none recorded	Attached ☐	MG6 MG17	Attached ☐ Attached ☐

OFFICER'S CERTIFICATION – I certify that to the best of my knowledge and belief I have not withheld any information that could assist the defence in early preparation of their case, including the making of a bail application.

Name of Officer:		Number:	
Signature:		Date:	
email: Single point of contact			

SUPERVISOR'S CERTIFICATION – The information in parts 1 to 7 is an accurate summary of the available evidence in this case and complies with all parts of Paragraph 11 of the DPP's Guidance for a Streamlined Process. The file has been built to the required standard. If not complete, please use form MG6 to indicate why and when missing information/evidence will be available.

Name of Supervisor:		Number:	
Signature:		Date:	

Confidential Information not to be disclosed

Not Suitable for conditional caution because

OR

Suitable for conditional caution because
custody officer is satisfied:

☐ There is sufficient evidence to charge the offence and offender has fully admitted the offence in PACE interview; and

☐ The public interest is better served by offering a conditional caution, and

☐ Both the circumstances of the offence and the offender make it appropriate to offer a conditional caution, and

☐ Column A offence (DPP's Guidance).

INFORMATION WHERE A CONDITIONAL CAUTION IS PROPOSED

OFFENDER'S FINANCIAL CIRCUMSTANCES

Compensation is a punishment and is meant to take priority over all but necessary living expenses. Bearing this in mind, where compensation is proposed, provide brief details of the offender's financial circumstances including any major commitments for necessaries. State if in receipt of state benefit and indicate family commitments if any. Express outgoings either as weekly or monthly commitments.

Income		Outgoings	
Wages: (take home pay):		Rent / mortgage:	
Benefits:		Other essential living expenses:	
Other:			

Checklist—Contents of proposed MG5

1   Key evidence—story of the offence and points to prove, aggravating and mitigating factors to be mentioned. Indicate which witness provides the summarised evidence. Attach VPS if appropriate. Note circumstances in no comment cases for provision of non-police statements

2   Defendant's interview with admissions, explanations, mitigation, and remorse to be included.

3   Non-key evidence—list of witnesses not summarized in 1 and what they contributed to the case. Note paragraph 8.4 of Guidance clarifying which statements need not be taken.

4   Visual evidence—summary stating what it shows and whether it is key. If there is none or not key give reasons. CCTV to be provided in every case where it is of evidential value.

5   Injuries—victim/OIC/eye witness description of injuries and photos. Medical statement not required, save as in circumstances described on form

6   Fingerprint/forensic/drugs evidence—quantity/purity, field test, etc. Time it will take to obtain a full statement

7   DIP Testing—Is it a trigger offence?—What is the result? And what is the drug?

8   Orders on conviction—compensation sought, ASBOs, forfeiture, destruction, etc. Attach appropriate forms

9   TIC and previous convictions—tick appropriate box and attach relevant documentation

10 Officer's Certification—assurance that no undermining or assisting information which fulfils the disclosure test has been withheld

11 Supervisor's certification—assurance of accuracy

12 Suitable/not suitable for conditional cautioning—complete giving reasons where appropriate

It is to be noted that further additional MG Forms should also be submitted if appropriate: MG4, MG4A or MG7, MG6, MG10, MG18, phoenix printout of previous convinctions, VPS. In anticipated not guilty pleas or CPS statutory charged cases other forms may also be required: MG2, MG3, MG11 (key witness statements/EABs and copy of any other key evidence), MG16, MG19.

9.4 **Implications**

Such initiatives currently taking place throughout the country may have major implications for the police way of working. They will see the defendant sentenced only a few days after charging in the vast majority of cases in the magistrates' courts in guilty plea cases. Short trial dates in not guilty pleas should increase witness satisfaction, with fewer adjournments and less delays.

In particular, reducing some of the unnecessary bureaucracy in straightforward low level cases should ensure proportionate file building in line with the recommendations of the Flanagan Report. Together with the implementation of a single case file system within the framework of Integrated Prosecution Teams in some areas, it should go some way to allay police concerns about red tape and form-filling.

9.5 **Conclusion**

There is no going back—only forward to a first class prosecution service comprising a joint partnership between the police and the CPS. The joint professionalism of both and increased confidence and understanding in each other's way of working will ensure well-investigated cases, correct charges, more informed decision making, and well-prepared and presented cases in court.

We hope that this book plays some part in enabling the police and the CPS to move forward together in a shared understanding of how joint partnership works and the respective roles, responsibilities, and mindsets of each.

Index